Eco-Critical Literature: Regreening African Landscapes

Edited by
Ogaga Okuyade

AFRICAN HERITAGE PRESS
New York • Lagos • London
2013

AFRICAN HERITAGE PRESS

NEW YORK
PO BOX 1433
NEW ROCHELLE, NY 10802
USA

LAGOS
PO BOX 14452
IKEJA, LAGOS
NIGERIA

TEL: (Toll Free) 855-247-7737; 914-481-8488
FAX: 914-481-8489
ahp@africanheritagepress.com
www.africanheritagepress.com

First Edition, African Heritage Press, 2013

Copyright © African Heritage Press, 2013

All rights reserved. No part of this publication may be reproduced or transmitted in any form or by any means, electronic or mechanical, without permission in writing from the publisher.

Library of Congress catalog number: 2013932982

Okuyade, Ogaga

Cover Design: Dapo Ojoade

Distributors: African Books Collective, www.africanbookscollective.com

ISBN: 978-0-9790858-8-8

Contents

Foreword v
Tanure Ojaide, The University of North Carolina at Charlotte

Introduction: African Cultural Art Forms, Eco-activism, and (Eco)-logical Consciousness ix
Ogaga Okuyade, Niger Delta University, Wilberforce Island, Bayelsa State

1: Representations of the Effects of Colonial Land Policies in Two Zimbabwean Novels 1
Maurice Taonezvi Vambe, University of South Africa

2: Landscaping as a Plot and Character Development Medium in Ngugi wa Thiong'o's *Wizard of the Crow* 15
Ifeyinwa Okolo, University of Ibadan

3: Eco-activism in Contemporary African Literature: Zakes Mda's *Heart of Redness* and Tanure Ojaide's *The Activist* 31
Enajite Ojaruega, Delta State University, Abraka

4: Isidore Okpewho's *Tides* and Ken Saro-Wiwa's *A Month and A Day*: A Kinesis of Eco-activism From Theory To Praxis 47
Charles Cliff Feghabo, Niger Delta University, Wilberforce Island

5: Nature and Environment in Chinua Achebe's *Things Fall Apart* and *Arrow of God* 75
Gloria Ernest-Samuel, Imo State University

6: Degraded Environment and Destabilized Women in Kaine Agary's *Yellow-Yellow* 95
Sunny Awhefeada, Delta State University, Abraka

7: The Niger Delta, Environment, Women and the Politics of Survival in Kaine Agary's *Yellow-Yellow* 109
Ngozi Chuma-Udeh, Department of English, Anambra State University, Nigeria

8: Women as Victims, Environmentalists and Eco-activists in Vincent Egbuson's *Love My Planet* 123
Ovwoke Dorcas Owhofasa, University of Ibadan

9: Can the Earth Be Belted? Rethinking Eco-literacy and Ecological Justice in Wangari Maathai's *Unbowed: A Memoir* 139
Ogaga Okuyade, Niger Delta University, Wilberforce Island

**10: Nature and Social Responsibility in Rachel Carson's
Silent Spring and Tanure Ojaide's *The Tale of the Harmattan*:
Cross-Border Studies in Social Responsibility**   161
Roselyne M. Jua, Department of English, University of Buea, Cameroon

**11: Poetic Rites, Minority Rights, and the Politics of Otherness
in Tanure Ojaide's *Delta Blues and Home Songs***   175
James Tsaaior, Pan-African University, Lagos

**12: Transcending the Discontents of Global Capitalism: Toward
the Dialectics of De-commodified Environment in Tanure Ojaide's
Daydream of Ants and Niyi Osundare *The Eye of the Earth***   191
Uzoechi Nwagbara, Greenwich School of Management, London, UK

**13: Poetics of Environmental Agitation: A Stylistic Reading of
Hope Eghagha's *Rhythms of the Last Testament* and *The Governor's
Lodge and Other Poems***   215
Macaulay Mowarin, Delta State University, Abraka

**14: Niger Delta Dystopia and Environmental Despoliation
in Tanure Ojaide's Poetry**   239
Obari Gomba, University of Port Harcourt

15: Eco-survival in the Poetry of G. 'Ebinyo Ogbowei   259
Bernard Stephen, Niger Delta University, Wilberforce Island

16: Poetics of Environmental Degradation in Tanure Ojaide's *Delta Blues*   273
Olusegun Adekoya, Obafemi Awolowo University, Ile-Ife

**17: For Common Corn: Eco-ing Bole Butake's Concerns in *Lake God,
The Survivors*, and *And Palm-Wine Will Flow***   303
Joyce Ashuntantang

**18: Destabilizing the Images of the African Forest as a Conceptual Space
for Renegotiating African Identities during the Zimbabwean Armed
Liberation Struggle in the Film *Flame* (1996)**   319
Urther Rwafa, Midlands State University, Zimbabwe

Notes on Editor and Contributors   337

Index   343

Foreword

Tanure Ojaide, The University of North Carolina at Charlotte

Eco-critical Literature: Regreening African Landscapes is perhaps the first major book project to date on eco-criticism written or edited by an African literary scholar. I congratulate the intellectually indefatigable Dr. Ogaga Okuyade for his foresight, intellectual acumen, industry, and determination to pioneer this field of study in contemporary African literature and other fields in a purposeful way. While there are articles here and there on the relationship between African literature and environment, one hardly finds a book-length project dealing with different authors covering all the genres of literature and other cultural art forms. (Under)Graduate students in Africa and elsewhere working on different authors and books with eco-critical topics will find this book fascinating because it brings together eco-critical approaches to the entire African literature in one volume. A coordinated approach to African literature focusing on the environment has been long overdue.

In this work, the editor and contributors take African literature and criticism to their functional role of addressing important issues of the society to draw attention to them so as to generate ideas and actions toward the solution of problems. This book thus carries African scholarship further than mere analyses of themes and style to ethical and activist roles of literature having an impact on readers and the public. It is a scholarship geared toward rectifying ecological imbalance that is prevalent in many parts of the continent that form the setting, context, and thematic discourse of the works or authors studied in this book. This work hopes to sensitize the African readership to the need for the restoration of harmony between man and the environment.

What is eco-criticism? It has to do with ecologically sensitive creative writing and criticism, which, according to Michael Branch, is meant to promote "ecological literacy" (viii). As I wrote elsewhere:

It is meant to make readers not only aware of the global environmental crisis but also for literature to "suggest[s] means by which we might read literary texts with a new appreciation for what they reveal about the complex of relationships that mediate interactions between humans and their environments" (xiii). It is a call for a change in culture towards a more "biocentric worldview, an extension of ethics, a broadening of human conception of global community to include nonhuman life forms and the physical environment" (xiii). With awareness of ecocriticism, what Cheryll Burgess Glotfelty calls "the relationship between human culture and the environment," literature will lead towards "an ecologically sustainable human society" (qtd. in Branch 29).

The environment has always played a significant role in African life and society. As Ali Mazrui says in the first part of his series of documentaries "The Africans," there existed in traditional society a partnership between humans and nature. Some animals were domesticated while others roamed the wild. Humans relied on animals and plants for sustenance—food in crops and fruits, fish and animals, firewood for cooking, timber for building, and more. Man held aspects of nature sacred—mountains, rocks, rivers, trees. The forest was the home of ancestors. In the religions of Africans, nature became an integral aspect of their spirituality in the form of groves, thus giving the environment a spiritual dimension. But with the coming of Christianity and Islam to Africa, the natural world became a servant of man rather than a partner because of an aloof God, leaving man to control and exploit nature. The result of the Western and Islamic intrusion into Africa and the superstitious and other practices of Africans led to the massive environmental degradation of the continent.

A specific case in point that has attracted creative writing and criticism is the Niger Delta area of Nigeria where multinational oil corporations have done massive environmental damage through oil spills, blowouts, gas flares, and other forms of ecological despoliation. While oil exploration and exploitation are meant to bring wealth to the region, this has not happened in the Niger Delta, which remains not just one of the poorest parts of Nigeria but also of the entire world. As the multinational oil companies have done in other parts of the world (as in Ecuador), little of the oil wealth filters to the local communities whose traditional occupations of farming and fishing are destroyed. The health hazards are enormous and go unchecked, such as the methane and other chemicals that poison the people from the air they breathe, the land they farm, and the water they drink. Even chemicals used by the oil companies to service their equipment percolate from wells and bore holes, while the rivers are clogged with crude oil in unchecked spills and blowouts. This is one of the contexts in which eco-criticism is set in Africa.

What happens to the environment intersects with a multiplicity of issues. Again, as I once wrote, "The study of the environment inevitably leads to issues of land, culture, agriculture, politics, and economy, among others. These issues are related to ownership of land, oppression, and exploitation. These issues and the environment call for an "ecology of justice" or human rights that will bring harmony to the relationship between humans and their environment for their respective wellbeing in the interconnected cycles of life" (Ojaide 66). In recent times, the actions of multinational oil companies out for profit for Western shareholders at the expense of local communities have drawn attention to the relationship between the North and South as far as globalization is concerned. In the Niger Delta, this has given rise to what Al Gedicks calls "resource resources" in youths of local communities fighting the multinational oil companies and the Nigerian Government for resource control (qtd. In Ojaide 77). The African environment and its resources have engaged sensitive writers and scholars in multiple and interdisciplinary discourses.

Before concluding the Foreword, I want to draw attention to Emmanuel Obiechina's seminal book, *Culture, Tradition and Society in the West African Novel*, published in 1975. There has been some form of eco-criticism in African scholarship long before it became vogue in the Western academy. Also, traditional African literature has always been sensitive to nature and the environment in many ways. Obiechina should be applauded for his eco-critical concern far back at a time when most critics had no awareness of the environment. He writes in his book:

> The traditional world view has an important bearing on attitudes to nature and this in turn is reflected in the novels. It implies a mystical yet utilitarian outlook on nature instead of an externalized appreciation of it in forms like fine landscapes, beautiful flowers, cascading waters or the colours of the rainbow. In this tradition the beauty of the particular tree comes to be inseparable from its "vital" property, demonstrable in pharmaceutical or magical efficacy or the shade it provides from the heat of the sun. The uniqueness of a particular stream or wooded landscape resides in some supernatural manifestation, either as the abode of a communal deity or a local spirit identifiable with the destiny of the community. The rainbow is apprehended first and foremost as an externalization of an internal force portending good or ill for an entire community.

> **Nature is not "other" as in the industrialized and urbanized West, but is apprehended by the traditional West African as an integral part of his world order** [emphasis mine]. (Obiechina 42)

I end this Foreword by emphasizing the importance and sense of urgency of this work in the form of the creative works and the critical discussion engendered by them. The book adds to the effort to fight the global environmental crisis. The contributors of these essays, as the authors studied, all promote what Michael Branch describes as the "ethics of caution and reciprocity" (xix) in the interactions of humans with nonhuman nature. *Eco-critical Literature: Regreening African Landscapes* is a groundbreaking contribution to African literary scholarship, and I applaud the editor and the many contributors to this book project.

Works Cited

Branch, Michael, Rochelle Johnson, Daniel Patterson, and Scott Slovic. *Reading the Earth: New Directions in the Study of Literature and the Environment.* Moscow: U of Idaho P, 1998. Print.

Gedicks, Al. *Resource Rebels: Native Challenges to Mining and Oil Corporations.* Cambridge: South End, 2001. Print.

Obiechina, Emmanuel. *Culture, Tradition and Society in the West African Novel.* Cambridge: Cambridge UP, 1975. Print.

Ojaide, Tanure. *Contemporary African Literature: New Approaches.* Durham: Carolina Academic, 2012. Print.

Introduction: African Cultural Art Forms, Eco-activism, and (Eco)-logical Consciousness
Ogaga Okuyade, Niger Delta University, Wilberforce Island, Bayelsa State

One of the most problematic issues the world continues to contend with even beyond the close of the twentieth century is the unimaginable disappearance of the nonhuman world. Mankind continues to make concerted efforts to ensure that the other worlds are kept alive since the human world solely depends on them for sustenance and existence. Interestingly therefore, the nonhuman world appears to be more important than the human since it provides the material support base for the latter. Summits of different kinds with the environment forming the basis for such ensembles are organized across the world in order to draw man's attention to his inordinate exploitation of natural resources, which in turn continues to make human existence precarious. However, as world leaders continue to advocate the need for an eco-friendly universe, there appears to be a basic problem with fashioning pragmatic policies that will ensure the preservation and sustenance of the environment. This may be viewed as a moot point, but the absence of a pragmatic and proactive eco-policy and its strict implementation essentialize the need to protect these worlds that cannot fight for themselves, but can only draw attention to the debilitating and devastating blows (un)consciously and constantly thrown at them by man's sense of capitalist industrialism and consumerism through their visible disappearance.

Africa appears to be the only continent that hardly participates in any form of mercantile-based revolution that powers the economy of the world. Africa was visibly absent during the industrial revolution, even if it actually oiled the process. The technological and scientific revolution which most Western countries launched in the twentieth century seems to be too complex for the African peoples, and as such, they appear to be mere observers and consumers of whatever projects or products emanating from this ever present and evolving revolution. If there is any one thing Africa has in abundance, it is, without doubt, natural resources. Invariably, nature-cum-environment becomes the base of the new revolution. As noted above, Africa is heavily endowed with natural resources, but the inability to translate these natural endowments into socioeconomic bliss for the empowerment of the African peoples, which will in turn power their economy, lamentably positions Africa once again at the margins of this revolution. This inability to purposively utilize natural endowments to empower the African people is usually attributed to the governmental misrule and bureaucratic inefficiency of Africa's political systems, which are usually predicated on the dialectic of belly and the individualization of the commonwealth. Thus, it has become commonplace to remark that the "disruption of the landscape is tied to political corruption" (Slaymaker, "Natural Connections" 131). However, the environmental crisis in Africa today spans beyond the moral depravity of government and the bureaucratic inefficiency with which the business of governance is run or conducted. The crisis is complex, if we consider Rob Nixon's idea of "slow violence" (2), the kind which encompasses all brands of chaos that occur steadily and out of sight. A kind of violence that is monumental but its consequences are strategically delayed. For example, one will wonder how a gas flare or incessant oil spill can deprive a child from attending school three years after the flare or spill, when the school is many kilometers away from the site of the flare and spill. Nixon's idea of slow violence expresses violence without blood. This kind of violence is neither spectacular nor instantaneous, but "incremental and accretive" (2).

Eco-criticism as a theoretical approach to the study of cultural art forms offers an appropriate middle ground, thereby making emphatic a vibrant relationship between the humanities and other disciplines. As an interdisciplinary field it enables us to reassess African writings in different frameworks within a single forum. The most fundamental feature of eco-criticism is basically to theorize the unending environmental crisis mankind continues to create and invoke different strategies (which are usually interdisciplinary) as means of bridging the frightening gap between humans and the environment. Hence Richard Kerridge and Neil Sammells remark that the dominant tradition of eco-criticism is to "evaluate texts and ideas in terms of their coherence and usefulness as responses to the environmental crisis" (5). Cheryll Glotfelty's formulation of cardinal aspects of eco-criticism has become perhaps the most quoted definition in the field. Her definition of the term is somewhat simple when she remarks that eco-criticism is "the study of the relationship between literature and the physical environment." The definition above accentuates an "earth-centered approach to literary studies" (Glotfelty xviii). This relationship between humans and the environment is not that simple if one considers the fact that humans continue to consistently reduce the environment to a mere object or item that can be exploited for their sustenance or corporate greed. Eco-criticism, I think, is more of an attempt to counter an (un)conscious violence orchestrated by humans on the environment. This approach, therefore, becomes an alternative means of advancing the recovery and preservation of the nonhuman worlds.

The twenty-first-century person negotiates existence under chaotic environmental conditions. Beyond drawing attention to the interface between environment, literature, and other cultural art forms, eco-criticism reminds us that we are in an age of global environmental and biological catastrophes and the need for exigent remedies for our ever-vanishing worlds. Raj Kumar Mishra puts it explicitly when he remarks that:

> Today we live in a world of tropical warmth, chronic drought, desertification, deforestation, acidifying of oceans, frequent coastal inundation, tsunami, cyclones, increasing food and shelter shortage, accidents at nuclear power stations, oxytocin applied vegetables, industrial pollution, and many more lethal activities. It is most pressing need to keep our environment safe so that we can live and let other beings live and survive too. Environment affects and even largely determines all things ranging from food, fashion, technology to race, class, gender, sexuality, mentality, nationality, law, religion, economics etc. Eco-imbalance is not specific (one nation, one place, or one city) problem. It is a global phenomenon. Hence whole world unanimously whether partially or fully affected, should come forward and launch a global campaign with honesty for the service of environment and the restoration of healthy environment. (1)

In view of the persistent disappearance or, simply put, extinction of different species from the nonhuman world, the knowledge-based industries continue to evolve or inaugurate concepts and theories that are geared toward drawing or attracting attention to these dangerous ecological situations mankind has created, and foreground the fact that s/he is duty-bound or has the ethical responsibility to protect and preserve the physical environment. Invariably, raping—the materialist wastage of the environment for the advancement of society—is problematic by all standards. This is so because such capitalistic acts cannot help sustain human development, but rather endanger mankind's existence because as the natural resources continue to be depleted without conscious efforts for their replenishment, the life expectancy of man will definitely be reduced.

The advocacy for the respect and the proper usage of natural resources is therefore not negotiable. Rather, it is a task.

Like Ify Okolo suggests in her essay "Landscaping as a Plot and Character Development Medium in Ngugi wa Thiong'o's *Wizard of the Crow*," critics like William Slaymaker argue that African literature has not contributed much to eco-criticism or environmental literature because writers see eco-criticism as Western and in conflict with African concerns. Slaymaker's argument is contentious if one considers the fact that environment as Tanure Ojaide suggests is a necessary aspect of African experience that informs the literature (*Contemporary African Literature* 65). African literature is therefore socially conditioned, especially considering the utilitarian function of art in the continent. The socioeconomic conditions of the African people are without doubt a primary propeller when the African writer creates. African literature from the very beginning continues to pay attention to environmental issues if one considers how Achebe's canonical text *Things Fall Apart* gives life to the environment. Although the novel gives expression to the colonial incursion into Africa and how that incursion sent Africa crashing from its vital balance, the narrative equally demonstrates how rural people use environment, thereby bringing to the fore the symbiotic relationship between man and his environment. It is therefore pertinent to note here that within the tradition of African creativity, the environment is arguably part of what I call the cultural construction of the text. The representation of the environment in African literature has taken a new dimension, considering the spate of crises emanating from resource wars, which range from the asymmetrical distribution of resources to the outlandish strategies governments deploy to silence the civil society when the state society is engaged diplomatically through the resources of the public sphere on pressing ecological issues. African literature on the environment continues to be engagingly combative, in order to re-order the lopsided ecological geometry of the continent.

The publication of this book is geared toward assessing Africa's contributions to the environmental crises of our age and how artists deploy cultural art forms to arrest the reader/audience with different rhetorical strategies, thereby making them come to terms with the fact that we are not only in an age of global environmental catastrophe, but the twenty-first-century person is in a perpetual state of crisis. A situation created by mankind's uncanny translation of the functions of the environment to meet his ever insatiate greed for satisfying his unquenching taste for resources. From this dimension, the earth becomes a mere product that is to be constantly consumed. The environmental crises that man continues to try to surmount are not visceral, but human made. However, the most amazing feature of eco-critical studies remains the fact that regardless of the fact that mankind has created a kind of apocalyptic state as Lawrence Buell puts it in his book *The Environmental Imagination* (1995), the idea of the apocalypse has become "the single most powerful master metaphor that the contemporary environmental imagination has at its disposal" (285), which has awakened in many concerned persons the awareness of the need for corrective action to halt the pillage of our planet.

African literature on the environment invokes environment, and challenges capitalist industrialism through transnational engagements and the visionless government policies that are not people-oriented. Interestingly therefore, like other literatures, there appears to be a conscious relationship between environmental and human rights in African cultural art forms. The advocacy for environmental rights will be inconsequential if the advocator is unable to assess the varied instruments and facilities which bequeath him/her regarding the nomenclature of freedom. No human rights, no environmental rights. With the enthronement of democracy in Africa (even if it is nominal), the time to question the relationship between the African and the nonhuman world need not be postponed to when democracy becomes enduringly functional.

This book aims to further familiarize scholars and students working in African literature with the theoretical concerns of eco-criticism within a postcolonial African space. Moreover, it particularly reflects new developments in African eco-critical studies with regard to texts studied as well as the approaches that the contributors have taken. Like Sule Egya observes, "The question of environmentalism is arguably most radically manifest in *African* poetry written in recent times [emphasis mine]" (1). Although not a response to Egya's charge on the over-concentration on poetry when issues bordering on environment are explored in African literature, the essays in this book pay attention to other genres, especially prose narrative, and other cultural art forms. It is equally imperative to note here that Tanure Ojaide's writings attracted the attention of most of the contributors—a point that indicates he is arguably Africa's most prolific writer today and his writings deal mostly with the environmentalism of his homeland, Nigeria's Niger Delta. Ojaide's writings equally articulate how the environmentalism of minority spaces across the world have become the theater where the lopsided distribution of resources and the blatant exploitation and destruction of the resources of nature are vibrantly played out. All the articles in this book address topical issues bordering on the environment, ranging from poetry, fiction, autobiography, drama, and rhetoric to film. All the texts that form the basis for analysis in this book make one glaring point: the ambivalence of the contemporary situation in which the environment is idolized, idealized, or lamented about; vanishing or on the verge of being permanently lost.

Using Mungoshi's *Waiting for the Rain* (1975) and Chinodya's *Dew in the Morning* (2001), Maurice Vambe in the first chapter of the book explores how fiction uses locale and geography to manifest conflicting attitudes toward the land, and social identities. He further articulates how in Zimbabwe the link between the environment and fiction is not at all surprising because the idea of "race" as a marker for identity construction based on skin difference between blacks and whites was a direct result of forces of colonial capitalistic attempt to control African land and make black people become sources of cheap labor. Ify Okolo's essay on *Wizard of the Crow* redefines the borders and limitations of characterization as technique in the African novel. Using the landscape and environment to develop characters in the novel, Okolo argues that it is easy to discern that characters are zoned into two in Ngugi's narrative: those for and those against ecological advancement. All the characters who have some positivity in them and in one way or another contribute to the sustenance of their environment are on one side, while the ones whose activities deplete the environment either by commission, omission, or ignorance are on the other. The essay pays attention to how characterization helps to propagate eco-literacy and the plot of the novel.

Enajite Ojaruega's essay examines how Ojaide and Mda affirm that a society could be modern and developed while at the same time having an environment that is healthy and eco-friendly. In the two works, the writers also send a message to their people that it is possible to have a clean, sustainable environment. Feghabo's reading of Isidore Okpewho's and Saro-Wiwa's narratives reveal a symbiotic relationship between the people of the Niger Delta and their environment. The narratives disclose that ethnic and environmental politics promoted by imperialist oil companies supported by indigenous military leaders result in "eco-cide" in the region. Gloria Ernest-Samuel's "Nature and Environment in Chinua Achebe's *Things Fall Apart* and *Arrow of God*" examines Achebe's use of nature and environment in achieving and expressing the Igbo experience in the pre- and postcolonial era. Sunny Awhefeada's essay attempts a reading of Kaine Agary's *Yellow-Yellow*, probably the first novel written by a female about

Nigeria's Niger Delta situation. Awhefeada argues that in this remarkable debut novel, Agary brings a significantly fresh perspective that has been hitherto ignored to the front burner. Agary reframes the Niger Delta story into a metaphoric novel that can be read along two narrative leads. He suggests that the novel parallels the woman's body with the environment and leaves a visible signature of the easily identifiable product of the union between Western men who come to Africa for different forms of mercantile engagements and African women who are incapacitated by the inability to access the environment for legitimate means of sustenance, which are usually subsistence agricultural practices. Like *Yellow-Yellow*, the scars and the potholes created from the bombardment and rape of the environment remain eloquent pictures of man's exploitative tendencies.

Ovoke Dorcas Owhofasa explores eco-feminism as the ideological grid with which she reads a male author who uses his narrative to demonstrate the parasitic relationship between mankind and the environment. From this perspective, Owhofasa examines this phenomenon in Vincent Egbuson's *Love my Planet*. Specifically, this chapter not only refamiliarize mankind with the fact that if the environmental conditions of our world are subjected to dialectics and substantiated with the facts of history, one will observe that our world is fading very fast, but also equally attempts to reevaluate the contributions made in Africa by women to save and preserve the environment from complete obliteration. Okuyade's essay deals with the strategies Maathai employs in her memoir *Unbo: A Memoir* to afforest the Kenyan environment that is visibly balding from human exploitation of natural resources. The essay re-theorizes the idea of eco-literacy and environmental justice and foregrounds how African governments, the Moi administration in particular, compounds Africa's environmental problems and the impunity with which it deforested the Kenyan environment.

Like Awhefeada's essay, Ngozi Chuma-Udeh's "The Niger Delta, Environment, Women and the Politics of Survival in Kaine Agary's *Yellow-Yellow*" appraises the consequences of ecological disasters brought upon the Niger Delta people and their natural world, especially those caused by the exploration and exploitation of oil. The chapter closely examines Kaine Agary's *Yellow-Yellow*, with emphasis on how she artistically explores environmental issues and the effect of these ecological problems on marginal groups like women and the girl-child in her debut novel. The chapter further examines *Yellow-Yellow* as an attempt to give a nuanced view of women entrapped in the Niger Delta turmoil with a more chronological accuracy. Chuma-Udeh achieves her set objectives by analytically demonstrating that the sociopolitical conditions in the Niger Delta compel women and girl-children to daily confrontations with forces militating against their existential survival and that these women and girl-children lack substantive protection at the immediate domestic environment, and as such, are the real victims of the oil exploitation.

Roselyne Jua's essay is very insightful as it examines how Rachel Carson, a white American scientist, and Tanure Ojaide, an African poet, raise awareness against all forms of ecological desecration in their works. She insists that a contrapuntal reading of Carson's *Silent Spring* and Ojaide's *The Tale of the Harmattan* reveals that these intellectuals are aware of the hazardous use of nature by man, and through their different texts (Carson's being a series of scientific essays on the environment, and Ojaide's a collection of poems) raise awareness for man to redeem nature. James Tsaaior, Obari Gomba, and Olusegun Adekoya's papers demonstrate how Tanure Ojaide uses his poetry to negotiate the fabrics of environmental degradation, minority rights, and the politics of otherness practiced by the counter-discourse strategies against marginal and peripheral categories like the minorities that populate the Niger Delta, employing *Delta Blues and Home Songs* as a paradigm. Most of their essays submit that Ojaide's oeuvre is angst-ridden and his poetic afflatus and sensibility evince a corrective and rehabilitative vision that hope to reverse the calculus of political and economic power to privilege the minority who are, in fact, the majority.

Uzoechi Nwagbara's essay is predicated on the commodification of the natural world as well as human relationships through global capitalist practice, thereby foregrounding how eco-poetry is steeped in negating this condition. The paper argues further that unequal levels of development between core and periphery nations are associated with the rhetoric of globalization, which comes in deferent hues. He engages this argument through a comparatist reading of Ojaide's and Osundare's poetry.

Stephen Bernard's essay explores what makes the poetry of Ogbowei relevant within what Nigerian scholars now label Niger Delta literature from an eco-critical perspective. Although Ogbowei's poetry has attracted a handful of scholarly attention, most of them are disturbingly skewed in favor of political concerns. Invariably, critics are yet to fully come to terms with this poet's environmental sensibility. Therefore, the essay attempts to dissect Ogbowei's eco-friendly poems in order to bring to the fore how they give expression to the transformations that have occurred in the Niger Delta biosphere as a result of human activities. Thus, Stephen's reading of select poems from Ogbowei's published collections is premised on his eco-poetics.

Macaulay Mowarin's paper addresses the theme of environmental and ecological disaster in Nigeria's Niger Delta from a stylistic perspective. It focuses on how Eghagha employs the rhetorical strategies of imagery, metaphor, personification, syntactic repetition, and pronominalization in the two collections of poems titled *Rhythms of the Last Testament* and *The Governor's Lodge and Other Poems* to foreground the theme of environmental degradation in the region.

Joyce Ashuntantang's essay attempts an eco-critical reading of Butake's plays, which critics celebrate as works that articulate the recent political changes taking place in Cameroon. She pushes the debate beyond the socio-economic underpinnings, which some critics observe as topical in Butake's dramaturgy, in order to engage how the plays explore environmental issues. She concludes that the three plays reveal that Butake is also concerned here with the relationship between people and their environment. In fact, at the center of these plays, the playwright seems to make the argument that unless community leaders take environmental issues seriously, the consequences of man's constant exploitation of environmental resources without making room for their replenishment may spell doom for mankind.

Urther Rwafa's essay examines how the film *Flame* deploys the image of the African forest to discuss normative approaches to issues of environmental conservation. The aim is specifically to show that in African imaginative compositions, themes related to the African environment are imbued with symbolical meaning so that they take on board more than one explanation or meaning. Interestingly therefore, in reexamining *Flame* the essay articulates the images of the African forests and how they are associated in the psyche of an African audience as conceptual spaces for rethinking African identities.

It is clear that though these critics whose articles make this book may not have had formal learning on environmental studies, they have fundamentally raised and engaged very topical ecological issues from different dimensions. Their analyses are apt and thought-provoking. Though they may not have answered numerous questions bordering on the issues raised in this book, they certainly have inaugurated and launched critical questions and challenges that may not demand immediate response. If we respond constructively as inhabitants of the earth to the challenges raised in the book, we may yet manage to save ourselves from the rapid disappearance of our world.

Works Cited

Buell, Lawrence. *The Environmental Imagination*. Cambridge: Belknap, 1995. Print.

Chinodya, Shimmer. *Dew in the Morning*. London, Heinemann, 2001. Print.

Egya, Sule E. "Eco-human Engagement in Recent Nigerian Poetry in English." *Journal of Postcolonial Writing* 49.1 (2012): 60–70. Web. 13th April 2012. <http://www.tandfonline.com/loi/rjpw20>.

Glotfelty, Cheryll, and Harold Fromm, eds. *The Ecocriticism Reader: Landmarks in Literary Ecology*. Athens: U of Georgia P, 1996. Print.

Kerridge, Richard, and Neil Sammells (eds). *Writing the Environment: Ecocriticism and Literature*. London: Zed Books, 1998. Print.

Mishra, Raj K. "The Village by the Sea: An Ecocritical Reading." *The Criterion: An International Journal in English* 2.3 (2011): 1–5. Print.

Mungoshi, Charles. *Waiting for the Rain*. Heinemann, 1975. Print.

Nixon, Rob. *Slow Violence and the Environmentalism of the Poor*. Cambridge: Harvard UP, 2011. Print.

Ojaide, Tanure. *Contemporary African Literature: New Approaches*. Durham: Carolina Academic Press, 2012. Print.

Slaymaker, William. "Natural Connections; Unnatural Identities: Ecocriticism in the Black Atlantic." *Journal of the African Literature Association* 1.2 (2007): 129–39. Print.

_____. "Ecoing the Other(s): The Call of Global Green and Black African Responses." *African Literature: An Anthology of Criticism and Theory*. Ed. Tejumola Olaniyan and Ato Quayson. Malden: Blackwell, 2007. 683–697. Print.

1

Representations of the Effects of Colonial Land Policies in two Zimbabwean Novels

Maurice Taonezvi Vambe, University of South Africa

Introduction: Eco-criticism and Zimbabwean Literature

In Africa as a whole, and Zimbabwe in particular, published works on criticism of the representations of the environment in fiction are scarce. One of the possible reasons for this lack is that criticism of African literature has tended to explore themes related to the liberation struggle, betrayal of independence, and despair fomented by bad governance in post independence Africa. These thematic foci—though important—tended to push analyses of representations of the environment in African novels, poetry, and drama to the margins of critical discourse. Julia Martin provides another reason for the paucity of critical literature on African environment. She suggests that in South Africa under apartheid, the environment and its people were depicted as opposites, and not entities that allowed each other to survive. For her, "under the Nationalist apartheid government, 'environment' meant nature conservation—wildlife, rhinos and game reserves, a white man's preserve from which the majority of South Africans were excluded" (Martin 10). Furthermore, in African fiction, the loss of African freedom was figured through the rape of the land. In this depiction, land ceased to be a theme that could be explored in its own right outside the metaphors of nationalism. Maggie Ann Bowers notes that outside African fiction, environmental critics have tended to view or comment on the African environment as a "generic commodity [as well as] space intrinsic to cultural and personal memory" (268). Where the environment is viewed as a "generic commodity," it is depicted as an exploitable commodity for profit, many times with little or without reclamation, and consequently leading to environmental degradation. On the other hand, viewing land as space for cultural and personal memory has in other cases led to romanticizing the environment and prevented from creatively using it in innovative ways that balance the ecosystem in order to benefit the communities involved.

However, the paucity of works on eco-criticism in Africa does not mean that creative writers have not used the environment in their works. In Zimbabwe, for example, the novels *Waiting for the Rain* (1975) and *Dew in the Morning* (2001) link the "geographical context of the novel[s] clearly to the marginalized nature of [their] characters" (Bowers 270). Fiction uses locale and geography to manifest conflicting attitudes toward the land and social identities. In Zimbabwe, the link between the environment and fiction is not at all surprising because the idea of "race" as an identity construction based on skin difference between blacks and whites was a direct result of the forces of colonial capital's attempt to control African land and render black people sources of cheap labor. In his book *Land and Racial Domination in Rhodesia* (1977), Robin Palmer noted that the processes of African land alienation carried out under the aegis of the notorious Land Apportionment Act of 1931 divided the population of Rhodesia into two noncompeting racial groups. Between 1926 and 1936, African cattle increased while European cattle decreased. The ecological crises created by these historical processes are given literary form in *Waiting for the Rain* and *Dew in the Morning*.

The Ecological Crisis and its Effects in *Waiting for the Rain*

In Mungoshi's *Waiting for the Rain*, the environment—particularly the land—is depicted as both metonymic and metaphorical. Land is physical; its characteristics vary depending on the location and place where it exists in Zimbabwe. For example, the reader is made aware of the discriminatory practices of colonial governments through the different distribution of land patterns and usage between blacks and whites. In the novel, there is no ambiguity about who controls good land and who farms on infertile land. Land controlled by white people comprises "rolling ranches of Hampshire Estates," which has tall dry grass and fertile soils (Mungoshi 39). This is contrasted with land reserved for black people, which is "scorched," unfertile "white lands," indicating that it is sandy and from it there is nothing that grows in an "empty field" (Mungoshi 39). The narrator marks out the differences of land ownership patterns when it is observed that:

> The sudden transition from the rolling ranches of Hampshire Estates, with their tall dry grass and the fertile soil under that grass, into the scorched

nothing-between-here-and-the horizon white lands of Manyene Tribal Trust Land, with the inevitable tattered scarecrow waving a silent dirge in an empty field, makes a funereal intrusion into the bus. (Mungoshi 39)

In *Waiting for the Rain* there are other symbols used to depict land as barren and degraded. In his dream, found in the first chapter of the novel, the Old Man equates Manyene where black people live with "dust-storms in desert wastes" (Mungoshi 2) with "rivers which don't seem to flow any more" (Mungoshi 2). Lucifer, one of the central characters, describes the rural reserves, its physical landscapes and environment as a desert with heaps of "dust and rubble" (Mungoshi 52). Overcrowding among black communities caused by colonial segregationist policies has rendered communal land "useless, too tired to support any form of life except the hard, thick-leafed charurwi. Charurwi and acacia, the curse of the dry lands" (Mungoshi 162). *Waiting for the Rain* ascribes the degraded African land to the violent intrusion by colonialism in a very clear sense, so that the environmental or ecological crisis within black communities is depicted as the result of racialized division of land. In the novel, the Old Man remembers when the African people were defeated by colonial agents in the 1890s, the environment responded, and in particular rain did not fall; lack of rain meant that African families could not adequately sustain themselves in terms of food production. He says: "That year there was no rain. The Earth was angry with so much spilling of blood" (Mungoshi 115). Although colonial agents created the conditions of an ecological crisis in Rhodesia, Africans also worsened the situation. We read from the novel that the

people have cut down most of the trees for firewood and building material. They have been warned several times about soil erosion. Some were even arrested for cutting down the trees, but do they hear? They think it is more of the white man's lies. Like his cutting down the number of livestock each person ought to have. Like this family-planning thing now. More of the white man's tricks to keep the black man down. (Mungoshi 162)

In its mode of depicting the physical environment, *Waiting for the Rain* goes beyond metonymic representation and embraces the metaphorical portrayal of land degradation as representing something more than general physical abuse of land. The degradation of land is linked to particular attitudes to land of different people, whether these are black or white. For example, the image of the archetypal drought occasioned by environment mismanagement extends to the sexual and spiritual existence of the black people's lived experiences. It is said in the novel that the land or plain (Mungoshi 2) assumes a human character whose attitude toward the environment is manifested in how Africans respond to the effects of colonialism.

Old Man and Garabha

In *Waiting for the Rain*, the Old Man claims that he fought colonialism in order to reverse its negative impact on African land. For him, black people were "defeated but ours was a clean fight" (Mungoshi 115). Mungoshi is more concerned with revealing the psychological effects of colonialism through characterization. The Old Man retains his pride and embraces the philosophy of the Drum culture, which he uses as a form of cultural nationalist ideology to mobilize Africans to think of conducting another fight with the colonial agents. The Old Man's response to colonialism is summarized by the critic Zimunya who says of him that in his community, the Old Man had become synonymous with the Drum culture, itself transformed into a "collective hieroglyph" (Mungoshi 69) or mythology of African culture struggling against the "mine, mine, mine" (Mungoshi 114) individualistic philosophy espoused by colonialism. The irony of Old Man's depiction in the novel is that he is also contributing in degrading the environment. He cuts down trees, makes drums, and now has so many unfinished figurines, all suggesting that he is destroying the forest in the communal areas. This act of felling trees for cultural purposes without making room for replenishment is one of the primary causes of soil erosion, and by extension, desertification.

The metonyms of drought, dust, and potential desertification of the rural African lands find their metaphorical expression in the spiritual aridity experienced by some African characters. For example, in the novel, Garabha's art of drumming enables the reader to access and retrieve the history of the Samambwa. It is revealed through this drumming that Africans owned since time immemorial the land that the white people claim for themselves. The Old Man's advice to Garabha that the colonial values can "touch you on the outside, but they can't touch your heart" (Mungoshi 117) is anti-colonialist. But Garabha is also presented in *Waiting for the Rain* as someone who has been deeply affected negatively by colonialism because he cannot leave home to go and work in the new capitalist context. He spends most of his time following after home-brewed beer, a fact that undermines his desire to ensure the cohesion of his family and their lands.

Kuruku

In *Waiting for the Rain*, the peasants are not depicted as a homogeneous class in the ways they imagine solutions to the ecological crisis brought by colonialism. Uncle Kuruku envisions a political solution. He wears his *ngundu* in defiance of the colonial government's instruction to "arrest anyone seen wearing it" (Mungoshi 93). Kuruku purports to work for the collective good of the African people, and yet in reality, he behaves individualistically. Malaba captures this individualism as he observes that

> Kuruku refuses to be saddled with the burdens of the extended family and endeavours to concentrate on uplifting his nuclear family. Ironically, rabid individualism precipitates the disintegration of that branch of the family: Oblique hints that Kuruku and his son John are sellouts abound (in the novel pages 66, 69 and 94): we learn that John fell out with his brother, Paul, and then took the latter's wife; and five of Kuruku's children are in self-imposed exile in Zambia. (Mungoshi 121)

Lucifer

In many ways, the African people's responses to the ecological crises in Zimbabwe as depicted in *Waiting for the Rain* is encapsulated in Lucifer's response. He observes that the land Africans call home has been denuded and reduced to rubble and dust. He further describes home as a "failure's junk" (Mungoshi 52) to which he will not return. He is justified in expressing revulsion against his environment that has been destroyed by the imperative of colonial capitalism to a point where the communal lands have become "scrub, in this arid flatness, in this sun-bleached dust" (Mungoshi 162). There is no reason why Lucifer should love home, especially in its present condition of being a scrubland. As portrayed in *Waiting for the Rain*, Manyene is a colonial creation, a result of discriminatory economic policies that saw Africans being pushed to areas where the soil is sandy and unproductive, and where rainfall is erratic. From a political angle, the revulsion that Lucifer has over the tribal Trust Lands because they are now rendered barren is well placed. However, the same Lucifer betrays this denuded environment because his goal is that when he leaves Manyene, his home, he will never come back to it again. This resolve can be taken as misplaced because, in the first place, the environment he now rejects ironically needs the likes of him to rehabilitate it.

Running away can only let the colonialists continue to squeeze Africans until the ecosystem further undermines the survival of its inhabitants. As the Old Man points out, it is more the reason why Lucifer should come back to reclaim the land and its people, instead of deciding to go away from home for good as he misplaces his regrets for having been born black and in Rhodesia when he says

> I am Lucifer Mandengu. I was born here against my will. I should have been born elsewhere—of some other parents. I have never liked it here, and I never shall and if ever I leave this place, I am not going to come back. (Mungoshi 162)

This self-defeating decision never to come back to work to transform the poverty of home and country actually supports the continued domination of his people by the settler system. In other words, the physical destruction of the land by colonialism occasions in Lucifer some forms of alienation. These forms of spiritual emasculation from the land induce in the native a nervous condition causing him not to fight and reclaim his land from white settlers and rehabilitate it.

If this analysis of Lucifer's response to the ecological disaster brought by colonialism in Zimbabwe is correct, then his mode of response reveals the psychic wounds that colonialism inflicts on Africans so that one can argue that the psychological neurosis and damage on black minds can be taken as the inside of the outside physical degradation of land in the novel. In short, in *Waiting for the Rain*, Mungoshi depicts a gallery of African people responding to the ecological and environmental disaster visited on African land by colonialism. The strengths of these depictions is that they exhibit forms of diversity: while some characters respond by way of attempting to take up arms in order to redress the land issue, others like Lucifer have had their confidence in their capacity to reclaim the land severely subverted by colonialism to a point where the marker of individual alienation from communal hopes of regaining the lost land manifests in Lucifer insisting on abandoning the ruined home (Zimbabwe) forever. Both solutions to the ecological crises depicted in *Waiting for the Rain* need to be worked on to reconcile their seeming contradictions.

Environmental Degradation under Colonialism in *Dew in the Morning*

Like in *Waiting for the Rain*, Chinodya's *Dew in the Morning* vibrantly articulates how colonialism alienated African land. In the novel, we read that the Africans live in overcrowded rural areas where land is no longer productive. Africans are also removed from ancestral land and carted to areas infested with tsetse flies. For example, in the novel, "families came in convoys of closely packed government lorries, taking two or three days to complete the journey, so the passengers frequently camped out for the night" (Chinodya 30). The sheer brutality that is exercised in forcibly removing the black people is captured by Godi who says that people were "rumbled (and shunted) into the remote forests" (Chinodya 30). *Dew in the Morning* is set somewhere in the Midlands during the mid-1950s when land alienation had intensified.

In the novel, the rural landscape in the south of the country is no longer able to sustain the volume of ever-increasing black rural small farmers. In the Chivi district area where some of the people are being removed from, "the pressure on land there is three times what it is here. No one owns more than six acres" (Chinodya 148). This ecological disaster is a product of Rhodesian land policies based on racial segregation and founded on separatist policies geared toward permanent marginalization of Africans. The irony in *Dew in the Morning* is that this ecological disaster is blamed on the perceived poor farming methods by Africans. Consequently, a plan is hatched to move some Africans from the crowded reserves. The removed populations are dumped into areas such as Gokwe, and Sanyati in the midlands. In 1948, the director of native agriculture, Mr. Alvord, remarked that it was "unwise" to give land to Africans, although there is a "cry for more land"[1] from Africans. In *Dew in the Morning*,

> For seven successive years the weather had been harsh in the region. The government had observed the area with a wary eye, resenting the erosion, land wastage and the diminished contribution to the economy. At last it was decided that more people should go into the remote virgin land in the north to give the denuded region a chance to become green again. At first there was opposition to this plan by the villagers but eventually, after much persuasion, they agreed to destroy their homes, leave their deceased king's graves and their fatherland and move into the new land. (Chinodya 29)

Anthony Chennells (viii) argues that in such a context, "persuasion and agreement are mere euphemisms for coercion." Chennells argues further that "colonialism is always a system of unequal power relations and power resides with the wary, alert government" (viii).

Land Reclamation and Dynamic Farming in Black Communities in *Dew in the Morning*

However, despite the use of force to remove Africans from productive land, Shimmer Chinodya is more concerned in depicting and celebrating the spiritual resilience and the sheer vigor with which the newcomers embrace the forced peasants' options, tame nature, and produce for both their families and for European markets. In this alternative narrative, Africans have not experienced harsh colonial policies in similar ways. For instance, Godi registers the enthusiasm of his family and those of the other *Deruka* people who are the new farmers, at being given as much as 30 acres by Jairos, the headman. One of the consequences of colonial policies was to produce strata of successful peasants. It is the vitality and rhythm of turning over rich soil, dropping seed that sprouts into green tendrils that Chinodya evokes with relish. In one of the most celebrated passages, elements of the pastoral are counterpoised to the logic of the capitalistic in a memorable manner, which will for a long time remain unsurpassed in revealing the spirit of rural entrepreneurship. We read that instead of mourning at the loss of some characters in *Waiting for the Rain*, those characters in *Dew in the Morning* actually embrace some opportunities made available by colonialism. The ecological crisis depicted in *Dew in the Morning* is managed by enterprising African farmers in the short term via the production of subsistence goods. The narrator in the novel is aware of the damage to land by colonialism, but still celebrates the human spirit that insists on triumphing over man-made adversity:

> As soon as Jairos found us a small plot of land we started planting our crops. Matudu, the man who built our huts, came to plough our fields with his fine pair of oxen. We followed behind the plough, dropping seeds into neat brown furrows and savouring the smell of oxen and newly turned earth. The seedlings soon germinated, small and tender in the dew. We rose early in the blue-grey dawn to the shouts of the ploughboys and the bustle of yoking up the oxen. We walked across the glistening green, dew-laden grass to the fields. While the sun ascended in the sky, we sweated in the fields. Our backs ached, hot sand burnt our feet, and the hoe-handles drew blisters. We drank maheu, worked again, then went home for a late breakfast at noon, when we usually met the herd boys bringing the cows home to be milked. Usually we returned to the fields late in the afternoon, when it was cool, to put in a few more hours of work. Then after supper we read for an hour or two in the lamplight before going to bed. The nights were short it seemed. Dawn came soon with mother, hoe in hand, rapping on our door. (Chinodya 6–7)

The novel foregrounds the "small acts of courage, moments of defeat and fear" (Kahari, 55) in competing with Europeans on the produce and labor markets. Although Africans in *Dew in the Morning* also suffer from forced removals from their land, the novel is keen to depict how the Africans pushed to the margins of Zimbabwean land have reclaimed that land, making it productive in ways that colonialism had not anticipated. The Wamambos own more than thirty acres, which is a feat in a colonial context where discriminatory policies worked to undermine African entrepreneurs. In *Dew in the Morning*, Godi's father is "too busy working for our education to participate in its pleasures and fruition" (Chinodya 140) and a mother who "spent the day weeding, and pacing the fields in her tattered gumboots, defending her precious crops from cattle and goats" (Chinodya 141). Reclamation of land is not done through an organized resistance that is politically or militarily visible in order to try to understand human motivations, attitudes, perceptions, and cultural values. Mugova is portrayed as an illustrious agricultural demonstrator. "He was a very wealthy man. He owned two ploughs, two barrows and a tractor. He grew groundnuts, cotton and sunflowers in two huge fields" (Chinodya 101). Mugova has successfully appropriated for himself the discourse of commercial farming, which is a consequence of colonial modernity. He owns ploughs, barrows, and a tractor, all of which are the technical machinery that colonialism has made available to African communities. With these instruments, the African can produce for domestic consumption and also for the colonial produce market. The peasants can also compete and challenge colonial agriculture by an ironical act of producing for the market in order to ward off the possibility of being absorbed into the unequal matrices as providers of cheap labor. Pius Nyambara wrote that

> [i]n 1952, peasant cotton production averaged (3) three million pounds with an output of 1.1 million lbs. Native Commissioners, Land Development Officers and Agricultural Instructors complained about the large number of peasants who wanted to grow cotton but were not registered cotton growers. ... [Else in colonial Rhodesia,] in 1948, the growers of Mhondoro reserve and Msengezi Purchase Area both in the Hartley District were paid a total of 5200 pounds, and an average of 7.1 0s per household. (106)

In *Dew in the Morning*, Mugova is shown as adaptable and bound to survive in the new dispensation. However, he too has begun to acquire the negative aspects of colonial modernity that can destroy the land. For example,

> he kept his soil drugged with manure and fertilizers, so that even in bad years his mealies grew tall, and his acres went white with cotton balls. He was one of those derukas who enslaved the soil, overworked and under paid their servants. (Chinodya 101)

The vocabulary of "drugged," "enslaved," "overworked" and "underpaid" belongs to the political economy and the development of a "staggered" but also crude capitalist modernity in Rhodesia. The fact that this vocabulary has infiltrated the daily language and modes of organizing the popular imagination and creation of wealthy persons among African communities complicates the notion of blackness as a putative signifier of who is oppressed and who is not, especially in a colonial context where African lives are undergoing rapid change from the exterior. In fact, in *Dew in the Morning*, the unsavory aspects of the rugged capitalist sensibility manifesting among the derukas is revealed in the ways they employ locals whom they pay meager wages.

However, and on balance, the depiction of new black farmers gives expression to their sense of innovativeness in a context where land was scarce or denuded if it was available to Africans. We read, for example, that the derukas "brought with them a distinct deruka life-style based on shrewd hard work" (Chinodya 31). Elsewhere in the novel, it is indicated that the derukas or newcomers are

> generally great farmers. They cleared huge fields and grew maize and groundnuts. A few started to grow sunflower and cotton to sell to the Grain Marketing Board. They kept many cattle, grew vegetables, dug fishponds by the river and raised chickens. Some of them sold vegetables, milk and eggs. In contrast, the local people seemed to live from one day to the next, eating sadza, drinking beer and raising children. They built their huts with grass and poles, seldom bothering to plaster the walls with mud firelight peeped through the gaps between the poles. (Chinodya 31)

The sense of budding individualism that colonialism brings is also symbolized by the fences that the new deruka farmers erect against goats, and against uninvited guests and neighbors (Chinodya 102) such as the local people who are depicted as backward because they still "wore pieces of cloth between their legs and girls went around bare-breasted" (Chinodya

30). Godi's father puts the processes of the conflation of rural nationalism based on land with urban African nationalism which is itself dependent on educational entitlements when he reminds his children that

> [i]t doesn't matter if you are all going to be graduates and live in the nice big houses. Then you can buy a tractor and have someone plough your fields for you. You will be able to use fertilizers and manure and plough five acres. You will grow hundreds of bags this way. You can never make a final break from the country. (Chinodya 144)

For Godi's father, land reclaimed for producing food crops feeds the towns. In exchange, the towns introduced into the rural areas, the "village pump" (Chinodya 1), "zinc tiles" (Chinodya 15), and fertilizer. Godi's father is aware of the intensifying struggle to control land between blacks and whites and ultimately among blacks. Godi's father knows that land is a critical productive force. For him, the land has been denuded; it now needs "fertilizer" (Chinodya 144) and manure. Important for him is that though degraded, Africans cannot make a "final break from the country" (Chinodya 144) symbolized in the novel by the rural land, its rugged environment and chores.

Another entrepreneurial African depicted in the novel is Masiziva's father who was distinguished for his work in the family plots and fields. He grew potatoes and kept cows. He also traded to buy his potatoes and his rich milk. He was also a farmer – growing peanuts and raising chickens (Chinodya 80). It is from her parents that Masiziva—Godi's mother—learned how to produce food for her family as well as food that she sold in order to raise school fees for her children attending school in town. While Godi's father was in the urban areas saving for the family's education (Chinodya 140), the mother—Masiziva—was "a hundred miles away, in the fields in the early morning dew ... she was the human fence to our fields" (Chinodya 140–141). In the novel, she is depicted as a workaholic who "spends the day weeding, and pacing the field in her tattered gumboots, defending her precious crops from cattle and goats. In the blazing sunshine or drenching rain she was the human fence to our fields" (Chinodya 141). Black women doubled-up their functions as up-bringers of children and producers of domestic consumption while subsidizing European markets. Women's labor on land was enterprising, but was also a drudgery. As Elizabeth Schmidt notes, the opening of new markets and the imposition of taxes

> following European occupation served as an impetus to increased peasantization and the burden of augmented agricultural labour fell heavily on women's shoulder. Resisting state attempts to enforce male proletarianization, peasant households, with female produces at the fore, devised new strategies for meeting urgent cash needs. (43)

In *Dew in the Morning*, early morning dew is linked to rural women's sexuality and manual labor, and the dew becomes a metaphorical narrative of African female nationalism in which women took over the control of rural space and its rhythms of production. The political space inhabited by the colonized women in relation to their physical environment is dynamic, for as Bayart notes, in Africa, under colonialism, there was nevertheless no obvious contradiction between the promotion of the personal interests of a class of African entrepreneurs and the desire for progress in the community which they claimed to represent. To found a transport business or a school, buy some land, increase one's maize harvest, or send a child to mission school—all had the side effect of undermining the colonial myth of the "backwardness of the natives" (Bayart 73).

Dew in the Morning represents the colonial space as an ambiguous one; on one hand, the productive land belonging to Africans was expropriated by white settlers who then confined black people to marginal and infertile soils. On the other hand, the Africans worked these poor soils and fed their families, often at the cost of further worsening the degradation of the rural environment. However, the novel celebrates the spirit of adaptation among Africans and refuses to minimize the creative minds of Africans who made colonialism work to their advantage.

Conclusion

As already noted in the introductory part of the essay, there is paucity of works on eco-criticism in Zimbabwean literary scholarship. The paper advanced some reasons for this lack, including the fact that critics of fiction have tended to preoccupy themselves with political themes associated with the liberation struggle and its betrayal in the postcolonial period. However, this does not indicate in any away that writers from Zimbabwe do not explore environmental issues in their works. It becomes imperative that critics should beam their search light toward environmental issues, as they are becoming very fundamental in the progress of mankind. In *Waiting for the Rain*, Charles Mungoshi depicted how colonial segregationist policies resulted in overcrowding of Africans and the subsequent degradation of that land. The characters in *Waiting for the Rain* responded to the ecological crisis in various ways. The Old Man, Uncle Kuruku, and to some extent, Garabha have been depicted as Africans who favor a political solution to the ecological crisis depicted. In different tones, each of these characters intimated on the possibility of armed nationalist struggle as the panacea to arrest the continued environmental degradation in Manyene Tribal Trust Lands. Conversely, in *Waiting for the Rain*, Lucifer's responses to the ecological crisis reflected how he has also been spiritually denuded by the alienating effects of colonial policies to a point where he commits himself to abandoning the struggle to rehabilitate the land, whether through armed struggle or through any other form.

In *Dew in the Morning*, Shimmer Chinodya foregrounds the deleterious physical effects of colonial policies to the African environment. However, Chinodya is more concerned with depicting how Africans, confined to margins of land, managed to reclaim this land through displaying their farming skills. In the short term, the responses of Africans to the ecological crisis occasioned by colonialism in Rhodesia in *Dew in the Morning* revealed the entrepreneurship expertise of Africans. The novel celebrated this aspect in a way that suggested and made the reader feel that if Africans commanded political power, they could reclaim and rehabilitate their environment in ways beneficial to them.

The novel also embedded an irony in its narrative structure. This was expressed through the fact that the very enterprising spirit of farming in places with poor soils resulted, in the long run, in further overcrowding among Africans—a situation that, in turn, created conditions suitable to aggravating soil erosion, thereby further degrading an already exhausted land. In short, both *Waiting for the Rain* and *Dew in the Morning* suggested in their depictions of the ecological crises in Rhodesia and African people's responses to these crises that African peasants (men, women, rich, and poor) embraced offered opportunities they did not want to give up, and at the same time contested some forms of inhibitions they saw arising from environmental degradation produced by colonial policies. Therefore, what came out of the two novels is that in dealing with the ecological disaster on land occasioned by colonialism, the African peasants did not possess uniform skills to develop similar strategies of coping, or seizing niches within changing economics of multisided engagement with forces inside and outside the Rhodesian colonial system.

Note
1. *Bantu Mirror*, July 1948, p. 5.

Works Cited

Bowers, Maggie Ann. "Eco-Criticism in a (Post-)Colonial Context and Leslie Marmon Silko's Almanac of the Dead." *Towards a Trans-Cultural Future: Literature and Society in a 'Post'-Colonial World*. Ed. Peter H. Marsden and Geoffrey V. Davis. Amsterdam: Rodopi, 2004. 268–276. Print.

Chennells, Anthony. "Introduction." *Dew in the Morning*. London: Heinemann, 2001. v–xiv. Print.

Chinodya, Shimmer. *Dew in the Morning*. London: Heinemann, 2001. Print.

Kahari, George. "Black Zimbabwe Literature in English." *Post Colonialism: Culture and Identity in Africa*. Ed. D. Pal Ahluwalia and Paul Nurse-Bray. Commack: Nova Science, 1997. 49–58. Print.

Martin, Julia. "Long Live Fresh Air! Long Live! Teaching and Truth-telling about the Environment in South Africa, 1986–96." *Scrutiny 2: Issues in English Studies in Southern Africa* 2.2 (1997): 10–29. Print.

Mungoshi, Charles. *Waiting for the Rain*. Heinemann, 1975. Print.

Nyambara, Pius. "Colonial Policy and Peasant Cotton Production in Southern Rhodesia, 1904–1953." *The Journal of African Historical Studies* 33.1 (2000): 107–115. Print.

Palmer, Robin *Land and Racial Domination in Rhodesia*. London: Heinemann, 1977. Print.

Schmidt, Elizabeth. *Peasants, Traders and Wives: Shona Women in the History of Zimbabwe, 1870–1939*. Harare: Baobab Books, 1992. Print.

2

Landscaping as a Plot and Character Development Medium in Ngugi wa Thiong'o's *Wizard of the Crow*

Ifeyinwa Okolo, University of Ibadan

Introduction

The current urbanization trend in the twenty-first century has made the African writer who cannot be divorced from his/her environment to focus more on urban concerns and settings. Yet, underneath these concerns is his/her effort to restore some sort of balance/healing to the society in disharmony. In various cases, the African writer's choice has been to create (a) subsetting(s) of rural areas where s/he allows peace and calm to dominate and, in essence, point the cities back to their rural roots for correction. In keeping with these responsibilities, the African writer becomes an environmental advocate, thereby promoting the need to "regreen" the disappearing ecosystems.

Land, as part of the human world and the item needed for the sustainability of human life, has always been a subject of artistic re-creation of African cultural art forms. Thus, the African writer, through the medium of imaginative composition, continues to explore how it is possessed/acquired and tended/nurtured. The importance of land is seen in inheritance procedures: land is held on to as a sign of belonging to a particular community, a link to one's roots and source. For this reason, this link is regarded sacred and its sanctity is not only sustained, but it becomes a foundation through which most individuals connect the homeland from the outside during the periods of sojourning in foreign land. Consequently, African literature pays emphasis on the relationship between humans and the land through different cultural observances like festivals and other rituals are enacted from time to time in order to sustain such a link.

From this perspective, landscape takes on a personality, a character of its own that is identifiable and requiring close study of its growth and metamorphosis. Regreening African fiction is seen as preserving the rural environment, while much pollution and environmental hazards plague the cities. This is evident in the slums in the urban settlements, while serenity is enjoyed in the rural spaces. In some cases, as observed in the literatures on the Niger Delta areas of Nigeria, writers have to fall back on the serenity of their rural areas before the takeover of the oil companies, as there is actually no safety in the rural areas to be offered to the lost urban souls in need of healing.

For Ngugi wa Thiong'o, devotion to land is a theme that runs through all his novels. His landscaping in *Wizard of the Crow* forces his readers to recognize them as personalities that tell their own stories. By placing the slum and disease-ridden Santalucia on the outskirts of rich and beautiful Eldares, a sharp contrast is drawn on the reader's sensibilities that no amount of storytelling would have done as effectively as the landscapes. The rural subsetting comes into picture only twice throughout the novel, but in the little space given to it, the calamity in the urban sections of the novel is given a source of healing. Characters in the novel are seen reacting to their environment in amazing ways. New family bonds are formed as a result of the proximity in the slums that provides the close-knit family tie as experienced in the rural areas. While characters like Wariara, ruined by the city, go to the village to die in peace, others like Kamiti go there to be rejuvenated. Ngugi's success in this novel is achieved to a large extent by his dexterity in exploring the reactions of characters to their environments and using environment to control the development of his characters.

African Letters and the Politics of Greenness

Critics like William Slaymaker argue that African literature has not contributed much to eco-criticism or environmental literature because writers see eco-criticism as Western and in conflict with African concerns. Although the above assertion is contentious, especially because from the publication of Achebe's *Things Fall Apart* (a novel that occupies an inaugural and canonical position in the evolution of African literature), the African writer has always given expression to environmental issues albeit in trado-technological schemes, it is the criticism on African literature that appears not to have considered the need to promote an ecological dimension in the examination of African writings. The reason for this is understandable. African history has been very turbulent considering the politics of colonialism and the postcolonial experiences and how they continue to incapacitate the African identity from time to time. The African writer and the critic saw the need to engage these issues using literature as a potent medium for engagement, thus little wonder that African literature and criticism seem to be geared toward liberation politics and by extension the ordering and reconstruction of the African identity. Slaymaker's pegging their land and nature concerns to human political concerns and not to the preservation of the environment for the environment's sake is not enough to limit eco-criticism and environmental literature to the kind of definition he has in mind: the kind that Aderemi Bamikunle does not adhere to in classifying Niyi Osundare "as a nature poet interested in both Edenic and exploited West African landscapes" without going "so far as to use the words *ecology* and *environment* in any of their current incarnations in the developing lexicon of ecocrit and ecolit" (686). Furthermore, Slaymaker declares Ken Saro-Wiwa's literary works as dwelling on non-ecological and non-environmental themes, particularly with *A Forest of Flowers*, which he dubs "antipastoral" because the stories in the collection "do not celebrate rural life in Nigeria, but criticize its narrowness and superstitions" (Slaymaker 686), the conclusion one arrives at is that the celebration of the pastoral rural life qualifies a literature as eco-activist. It is partly on this understanding that this chapter attempts to redefine the idea of environmental literature and eco-critical studies.

Byron Caminero-Santangelo's descriptions of eco-critical and environmental studies are engaging and more encompassing. From Caminero-Santangelo's position, eco-critical or environmental examination of African literature could be appraised "in the light of issues raised by eco-criticism and African environmental history (and relationship between them) in order, on the one hand, to enable them contribute to developing discussions within eco-criticism and African environmental history" (699). Thus, where eco-criticism "aims to decenter humans, often by giving nature 'back' its subjectivity ... represent nature (speak for *and* about it) as a subject with rights by finding (listening to) nature's voice" (Caminero-Santangelo 699). Caminero-Santangelo also observes that "many eco-critics embrace the kind of vision offered by Ngugi, which assumes an alignment between the fight for environmental preservation and anti-colonial struggle, and which romanticizes pre-colonial (especially animist) societies as being in harmony with nature" (702). From the above position, one can therefore foreground the concept of landscaping as environmental discourse.

Currently, as noted earlier, urbanization trends in this century are taking a lot of the attention of the African writer who cannot be completely divorced from the environment that provides him/her with the subject of his/her artistic engagements. Invariably, s/he continues to focus more on urban concerns and settings in his/her writings. However, underneath these concerns are the agenda and efforts to restore some sort of balance to a society plagued by ecological crisis created by humans.

Ngugi wa Thiong'o has shown a remarkable attachment and devotion to land in most of his works. In *Weep Not Child,* Ngotho chooses to be a tenant on his own land in order to be there to tend and love it. In *The River Between,* Waiyaki's basic reason for embarking on formal education from the missionary is to acquire a tool that will enable him to lead the people in taking back their lands from the colonialists. *A Grain of Wheat* runs a fictional parallel to the Kenyan historical struggles for land and Uhuru via the Mau Mau. The villagers' long march from Ilmorog to the capital (seat of government) to present their impoverished plight as a result of drought stands out as eco-activism in *Petals of Blood.* Ngugi has, in different ways, captured numerous ecological concerns over time. His *Wizard of the Crow* is not an exception, thus it forms the basis for textual analysis in this chapter.

Characterization and Landscaping in *Wizard of the Crow*

The narrative in *Wizard of the Crow* is arguably satiric; this in turn places Ngugi's arguments and ideas about environment and landscape in the proper perspective. The dramatic introduction, which Ngugi gives the protagonist using the refuse dump site, is remarkable. Leaving his body at the foot of the mountain of garbage, Kamiti goes on astral travel from where he absorbs the entire landscape of Aburiria. His discoveries are instrumental to the development of the plot:

> He could still see his own body lying on the ground and the mountain of garbage, where children and dogs fought over signs of meat on white bones. . . . He decided to let his body lie there in the sun, and free of the body, he wandered Aburiria—why leave the exploration and enjoyment of our country to tourists? he said with a chuckle to himself—comparing the conditions in the different towns and regions of the country. . . . From his vantage point, he had the bird's-eye view of the northern, southern, eastern, western and central regions of Aburiria.
>
> The landscape ranged from the coastal plains to the region of the great lakes; to the arid bushlands in the east; to the central highlands and northern mountains. People differed as much in the languages they spoke as in the clothes they wore and how they eked out a living. Some

fished, others herded cattle and goats, and others worked on the land, but everywhere, particularly in towns, the contours of life were the same as those of Eldares. Everywhere people were hungry, thirsty, and in rags. In most towns, shelters made out of cardboard, scrap metal, old tires, and old plastic were home to hundreds of children and adults. He found it ironic that, as in Eldares, these shacks stood side by side with mansions of tile, stone, glass, and concrete. Similarly, in the environs of cities and towns huge plantations of coffee, tea, cocoa, cotton, sisal, and rubber shared borders with exhausted strips of land cultivated by peasants. Cows with udders full with milk grazed on lush lands as scrawny others ambled on thorny and stony grounds.

So I am not alone, he heard himself say to his bird self. Maybe he should abandon his human form and remain a bird, floating effortlessly in the sky, bathing in the fresh air of Skyland, but then he started sneezing as a whiff of gases from the factories below reached him. Is there no place on earth or in the sky where a person might escape this poison? (Ngugi, *Wizard* 38–39)

Ngugi's position is not mistaken in this excerpt. In a short space, he lays down his Marxist framework for the novel using landscaping: a glaring contrast in the living conditions of people living in the same geographical area who are zoned by economic conditions into the healthy and diseased surroundings.

The protagonist, Kamiti (the wizard of the crow), arrives the outskirts of Santalucia near Eldares in search of a job clothed in rags and faints at the foot of a mountain of garbage. His transmogrification into a bird form to survey the whole of Aburiria is symbolic. He represents the masses who are undergoing various kinds of suffering and who like him need to rise above their situation, which is clearly represented by the garbage mountain where children wrestle with dogs for bones. There are numerous resources to be explored in the country that could make life pleasant. However, it appears that only tourists and the wealthy citizens have access to these resources. In the brief time of his astral survey of the country, Kamiti rediscovers the country's wealth. It is not surprising that these objects of beauty are natural: the coastal plains, the great lakes, the arid bushlands, the highlands, and mountains. There is a comparison of people's lifestyle in the rural areas with those in the towns and cities. Rural areas concentrate on fishing, animal farming, and land cultivation, and the representation in the excerpt above does not use any language that is damaging whereas in representing the farming style in areas near the towns and cities, Ngugi employs a comparative language that presents the cities as having a malevolent influence on the activities of the rural areas:

> Similarly, in the environs of cities and towns huge plantations of coffee, tea, cocoa, cotton, sisal, and rubber shared borders with *exhausted* strips of land cultivated by peasants. Cows with udders full with milk grazed on lush lands as *scrawny* others ambled on *thorny* and *stony* grounds [emphasis mine]. (Ngugi, *Wizard* 39)

While peasants have control over their resources in the interior rural areas, they are robbed of their gains by the proximity of industrialization to their farming activities. The whiff of gases from the industries is enough to make a bird in flight sneeze. The bird (Kamiti) asks if there is "no place on earth or in the sky where a person might escape this poison?" (Ngugi, *Wizard* 39). This question is explanatory, as it provides the reason behind the deterioration in the agro production of the environs of the towns and cities.

The use of the description of Eldares as a yardstick for measuring cityscapes is striking:

> In most towns, shelters made out of cardboard, scrap metal, old tires, and old plastic were home to hundreds of children and adults. He found it ironic that, as in Eldares, these shacks stood side by side with mansions of tile, stone, glass, and concrete. (Ngugi, *Wizard* 39)

The divide between the rich and the poor is clear. The slums are constructed from the waste generated from the rich divide of the cities. The environmental description of the slums is a clear indication that Aburirian cities do not have good waste management schemes. The fact is supported by the actions of the garbage collectors. Waste is dumped on the already existing mountain of garbage, and when "corpses" are found in refuse dumps, the major interest of the garbage collectors is to steal from them and bury them under piles of refuse to evade the law (which doubtfully is only interested in what the collectors' fingerprints are doing on the corpses and not on the issue of wrongful disposal of corpses in refuse dumps). The poor management of waste is not limited to Eldares only because much of the waste spills over into Santalucia, a slum on the edge of Eldares, bordering the prairie. This disease-ridden area, which the novel sometimes calls a village, should be recognized as a carryover of the kinship rural attribute to a city that cannot handle and has not made provisions for such communal existence, and as such, condemns the area to a slum on its outskirts, hence the description:

> Santalucia was a sprawling village of tiny houses of every shape and material. Tiled roofs with walls of well-cut stone shared narrow streets with tin roofs and walls of red clay and cardboard. The sewage pipes were always clogged and there was a permanent stench in the air that was particularly nauseating on a hot day. But when the moon shone at night . . . the village looked peaceful and quite attractive. (Ngugi, *Wizard* 75)

This is the environment that gives shelter to the protagonist and his female counterpart, Nyawira, in the novel. Interestingly, Kamiti gets to stay with Nyawira through an incident: Nyawira, the leader of the Movement for the Voice of the People, had led her group in disguise as beggars to Paradise—one of the biggest hotels on the Ruler's Square—to draw the attention of the foreign delegates from the Global Bank to the suffering of the masses, while the Aburirian leaders waste the country's funds in senseless projects. Kamiti, on the other hand, had been driven by hunger and desperation to beg in front of Paradise. When the police attack the "beggars" for chanting slogans against the government, the two find themselves running in the same direction, weaving through Santalucia, the prairie surrounding Eldares, and back to Santalucia again where Kamiti puts up a notice about wizardry on the doorpost to scare the police away, but end up having a new role carved out for himself in the novel. It is remarkable that the prairie helps them to lose and confuse their assailants, with the wizard's signpost finishing the job.

The prairie is a significant part of Aburirian landscape in the novel. Kamiti's astral travel from the dumpsite is not the first time he goes out of his body. The remarkable thing is in the contrast between that which introduces him in the novel and what he does in the wilderness, away from the corruption, dirt, and noise of the city:

> This is not the first time that he had felt himself ease out of his own body; he had had this sensation at night in the wilderness. There, in the open, lying on his back, looking at the stars and the moon, he would see himself abandoning his body for the sky as if pulled by a force intent on impressing him on the grandeur and mystery of the universe with no beginning or end. He would think of the prophets of old, Confucius, Gautama Buddha, Moses, John the Baptist, Mugo wa Kibiru, who had all retreated into the wilderness to commune, in total silence, with the law

that held the universe together. Were their lives not enhanced by what they had picked up during their pilgrimage? He would roam free in the universe the whole night, endlessly fascinated by the being of things, and when he returned to his body in the morning he would feel his spirit imbued with fresh energy, ready to face another day of walking about the streets of Eldares, knocking at every door, hoping for something that would improve his life. Thus he retained hope and even looked forward to his free flights into the universe as relief from the wounds of fruitless quests. (Ngugi, *Wizard*, 47)

The wilderness becomes a place of retreat where reconnection with goodness and life's essence is made. This is a way of importing the rural pastoral setting into an urban setting. Even at that, it cannot afford to blend with the urban rowdiness; hence the prairie exists on the *outskirts* of Eldares. The situation of this zone of goodness on the peripheries is strategic. The city is malevolent, and whatever good that comes to it cannot mingle with the malevolence but has to be sought after by a remnant of the city that still has traces of goodness left in them. The use of the wilderness as the city's "refuge" is enforced in Kamiti's retreat to the prairie (wilderness) when living the life of the wizard becomes demanding and he needs to sort his life out. He tells Nyawira: "I just want to stay in the wilderness to find myself. I want to know what I really want from my life. . . . One must find oneself before one can try to help others" (Ngugi, 208). Nyawira's reply to this comment is relevant to environmental studies:

> We cannot run away and leave the affairs of the land to ogres and scorpions. The land is mine. This land is yours. This land is ours. Besides, in Aburiria, there is nowhere to run. As you've said, even the forests are threatened by the greed of those in power. (Ngugi, *Wizard*, 208–209)

Retreats are good provided they are not means of escaping from the reality. Environmental activism should not just end in philosophizing and spreading feelings of concern berthed in moments of seclusion in solitary places but should be backed up with action. This is what she takes up with her Movement for the Voice of the People. Going by her statement, the fight of the movement is that for their land, thus tying Ngugi's efforts in this novel once again to land issues as in his other novels. This is not out of place—land, since the inception of African literature, has been a point of interest to most African writers: its possession/acquisition, tending/ nurturing, and otherwise. The importance of land is seen in inheritance procedures: land is held on to as a sign of belonging to a particular community, a link to one's roots and source. For this reason, this link is cared for and tended as carefully as one cares for a loved one. From this angle, landscape takes on a personality, a character of its own that is identifiable and requiring close study of its growth, metamorphosis, lovers and destroyers.

Ngugi's extra effort in painting the prairie before and after the invasion of eco-depleting forces is noteworthy. From a place teeming with all kinds of beautiful and interesting wild animals—rhinos, elephants, hippos, ostriches, and so forth—the prairie has become "abandoned . . . leaving it to the emaciated cows and goats whose ribs protruded in times of drought when the grass completely dried up" (Ngugi, 201). Ngugi's employment of the wilderness here does not have the kind of effect that Rob Nixon points out as one of the fears of postcolonial critics, that which erases "the history of colonized peoples through the myth of the empty lands . . . burying the very histories that they themselves (environmentalists) have sought to unearth" (*Wizard*, 717). Rather, it reaffirms the existence of this history and its near extinction as a result of industrialization. The breathtaking landscapes surrounding Eldares are turned into personalities whose lives are endangered by the activities of many world powers, with the Aburirian government backing them up in the desecration of their land:

> The prairie ended abruptly at the foot of ridges [. . .] Each ridge was a series of hilltops, which against the light of the setting sun, looked like undulating silhouettes of cow humps. But there were a few times when the wind swept the mist away and the ridges, hills, and mountains would reveal their breathtaking beauty, sun rays dappling the forest trees with their lowing leaves of green, yellow, and orange . . . This forest was now threatened by charcoal, paper, and timber merchants who cut down trees hundreds of years old. When it came to any natural resource, the Aburirian State and big American, European, and Japanese companies, in alliance with the local African, Indian, and European rich, were all united by one slogan: *A loot-a continua*. They knew how to take but not how to give back to the soil. The unregulated clearing of forests affected the rhythm of the rains, and a semidesert was beginning to creep from the prairie to the hills. (Ngugi, *Wizard*, 201)

While this excerpt makes a statement about neocolonialism and postcolonial disillusionment about Africans who do not love their lands enough to preserve them, it also traces environmental degradation to the West, and in a way gives some credence to Slaymaker's claim that

> Black African critics and writers have traditionally embraced nature writing, land issues, and landscape themes that are pertinent to national and local cultural claims and that also function as pastoral reminiscences or even projections of a golden age when many of the environmental evils resulting from colonialism and the exploitation of indigenous resources have been remediated. (683)

African eco-criticism did not escape the infusion of colonialism or its aftermath, which is still strongly felt both in African politics and environment. This infusion will not make the African contributions irrelevant to global eco-discourses as Robert Spencer acknowledges, but would rather form the basis of differentiation from eco-criticism in the North, which Anthony Vital agitates for.

Even in the ravished state, the wilderness still rejuvenates and is used as the site for the birth of new beginnings in relationships. This is where Kamiti and Nyawira find love. Ngugi appears to indulge the lovers a bit by giving them a splash of the original beauty of the landscape:

> On the ground, in the cave, now wrapped in darkness, they found themselves airborne over hills and valleys, floating through blue clouds to the mountaintop of pure ecstacy, from where, suspended in space, they felt the world go round and round, before they descended, sliding down a rainbow, toward the earth, their earth, where the grass, plants, and animals seemed to be singing a lullaby of silence as Nyawira and Kamiti, now locked in each other's arms, slept the sleep of babies, the dawn of a new day awaiting. (Ngugi, 203)

Elsewhere in the novel, in Kiambugi village, the wilderness marks the end of an unfruitful relationship for Kamiti and Wariara. Fomin Edward Efuet's analysis in trying to articulate the "justification of the importance of nature and natural species to man" (2) only sees the bright side of this relationship: the lovers' rendezvous "under a tree on the hill overlooking Kiambugi village ... while the cocks of the village were crowing and the dogs barking" (67). He even wrongly labels Wariara, Kamiti's first wife. As much as the nature and natural species are used to set the romantic atmosphere in this case, it must be stated that this atmosphere observed by Efuet is a fool's paradise because the real importance of nature is realized in the parting of the lovers and not in their being together. The first time they made love on the hill at Wariara's insistence and much against their plans to wait until they are married, Kamiti

> felt cheated out of a dream, a hope, a promise, and more so when the act turned out not to be so great, as if it had been forced on them. He felt as if he had swallowed dregs where he was expecting cool water. (Ngugi, *Wizard*, 67)

When Wariara breaks up with him, "he sat there under the tree, the shade and morning dew of which they had shared, watching her go down the hill until he could no longer make out her form against the distant landscape" (Ngugi, *Wizard* 68). It is evident that nature is selective in bestowing its goodness to people—it identifies with the goodness it sees in them. In Kamiti's relationship with Wariara, it does not take sides with the latter, and makes a statement that could be taken as a warning on her demise. She is the one that leaves Kamiti, and in leaving, nature's protective wings over her are withdrawn. The expression "watching her *go down the hill* until he could *no longer make out her form against the distant landscape*" succinctly captures what becomes of Wariara in the novel. Having no patience to wait until she gets a decent job or for Kamiti to find a job and marry her, she goes into prostitution, contacts HIV in the city, and comes home to the village to die.

Nyawira fares better with her departure from the wilderness. Her departure was to go and fight for the land and hence can only be seen as physical and not spiritual. This, coupled with Kamiti's admonition not to burn her bridges to the wilderness and to leave markers that will enable him to find her if she ever returns, leaves her connection to nature firmly in place. So, rather than *go down the hill* on leaving, "Kamiti watched Nyawira *cross* the expanse of the land until she became indistinguishable from the acacia in the distance [emphasis mine]" (Ngugi, *Wizard* 213). As such, it is easy for her to cross over again in her time of need:

> Weeks later when Nyawira was on the most wanted list and the police, under the Ruler's orders to take her dead or alive, were looking for her all over the country, what most helped was her knowledge of the prairie, and Kamiti's admonishment not to burn bridges was very much on her mind as she *crossed* [italics mine] the plains in the dark alone with nothing more than the dress she had worn to work and a handbag. She recalled how firmly she had resolved not to return to these parts anytime soon and

was struck by Kamiti's prophetic insight. She felt fearful of the darkness but also grateful for the protection it offered against pursuers. The stars above were her best companions, and it was now that she most appreciated the talks she and Kamiti had had about the sun, the moon, and the stars. (Ngugi, *Wizard* 215)

Again in the wilderness, the lovers reunite. This becomes an opportunity for Kamiti to teach Nyawira what he has learnt in the wild in preparation for usefulness in the city civilization. He tells her:

> I want you to learn what nature and solitude can teach us. Simplicity and balance, the Way. Call it the Forest School of Medicine and Herbology . . . Nature is the source of all cures. But we have to be humble and willing to learn from it. (Ngugi, *Wizard* 266–267)

Here, the Way reminds one of Ayi Kwei Armah's chronicles of African precolonial history in *Two Thousand Seasons*. In essence, the wilderness leads back to the precolonial Edenic Africa. Having learned much from nature, Kamiti and Nyawira reenter the city as a unified liberation force to guide and lead the masses to take their lands back from the corrupt leaders. The couple also return to the forest again for Nyawira to take care of Kamiti after he has been hit by bullets in the course of his arrest, which he manages to escape.

Close on the heels of the wilderness on the outskirts of the Eldares, Kiambugi reinforces the development of both the plot and the character in the novel, especially Kamiti. The two-week break that the protagonist gives himself to see his parents in the village after three years of absence in the course of job searching reconnects him to his roots and establishes him in the discoveries nature has given him in the wilderness. He learns the truth about his ancestry: "We are descended in part from hunters who dwelled in the forest, mostly, and came to know it well. Nearly all were healers. There was not an illness against which nature did not provide the necessary juices of life" (Ngugi, *Wizard* 294). It is striking to note that Kamiti's ancestors were environmentalists. Being hunters, it might be argued that they contributed to the depletion of the fauna, but their understanding of nature, their forest environment, and their maintenance of a balance between man and his environment qualify them as true environmental activists; what else is eco-activism if not the establishment of harmonious ecological interdependence? T. J. Abraham's analyses of the paradoxes surrounding eco-criticism brings to the fore that "human beings cannot entirely do away with the "use" of nonhuman sphere, as cultural productions of all sorts necessitate the use, and even some exploitation, of nature" (128). Kamiti's grandfather "lived with fighters in the mountain, teaching them how to be at peace with one another. . . . He knew every path, every plant, every living thing. No one knew the ways of the forest better . . ." (Ngugi, *Wizard* 294). Given Ngugi's preoccupation with Mau Mau, it might be implied that the fighters in the mountain refer to them. If this is so, then there is every indication that Kamiti's ancestors have contributed their share in the fight to regain their lands, which "slave raids, colonial ventures, and world wars" have denied them in the process of scattering them "to the four corners of the wind" (Ngugi, *Wizard* 294). This knowledge of who he really is imbues him with a new vigor to face the challenges of fighting the cause of the dispossessed masses on his return to the city of Eldares, thus advancing both the character and plot of the story.

Conclusion

In using the landscape and environment to develop characters in the novel, it is noticed that characters are categorized into two: those for and those against ecological advancement. All the characters who have some positivity in them and in one way or another contribute to the sustenance of their environment are on the one side, while the ones whose activities deplete the environment either by commission or omission are on the other. On the positive side, Kamiti and his ancestors, and Nyawira and members of her Movement for the Voice of the People take the lead, with Vinjinia finding a little bit of space among them through her redemptive action of not being part of the husband's (Tajirika's) wicked schemes. Even with the husband's position in government, Vinjinia still keeps a garden behind her house. For her, it will be said that her connectedness to the land through farming redeems her. On the negative end, Nyawira's father, whose business empire and wealth depend on timber (deforestation), takes his place among others like the Ruler and all his ministers who mortgage the people's lands and future for foreign loans. Again, nature and environment are seen in the novel working for or against characters as in the case of Nyawira and Wariara, respectively.

Ngugi also makes the characters in this satirical epic stock/archetypical characters, so it might be argued by some critics and reviewers like Max Falkowitz that they do not really develop but go through the motions of the stock script. Falkowitz's reading of the novel, which sees the focus on characters as "weak" and "a half-done effort at archetypical characterization" (Falkowitz), may be attributed to his claim of being familiar with only one other African writer, Achebe—an indication of his judgment based on European archetypes. What Ngugi does is to infuse his characters with modern dimensions of what the traditional archetypes would have done and to lace these new archetypal creations with qualities that make them relevant to eco-critical studies. For example, the wizard is educated, and in the moments when he is not conducting his wizardry, is a man like any other who loves and needs to be loved; he has parents who love him dearly and would sacrifice anything for him to succeed as a normal person. Even the wizardry he practices is mostly herbal medicine with a twist of clinical/therapeutic psychoanalysis, so he is basically not the archetypal wizard with magic wands. In the creation of the archetype of the wicked ruler, Ngugi combines the lives of several African despots—Daniel Arap Moi of Kenya, Mobutu Sese Seko of Democratic Republic of Congo (even the crow on the book cover wears Mobutu's signature leopard-skin hat!), Idi Amin of Uganda, and others—in one entity called the Ruler, while his sycophantic ministers combine in several ways and in differing degrees the race of the new crop of African politicians. This blending makes Ngugi's archetypes unique.

Finally, Ngugi successfully drives home his arguments on environmental issues by strategically using them in honing his characters and charting a direction for the progression of the plot of the novel.

Works Cited

Abraham, T. J. "Ecocriticism, Ethics and the Vedic Thought." *STARS: International Journal of Humanities and Social Sciences* 1.2 (2007): 128–134. Print.

Armah, Ayi Kwei. *Two Thousand Seasons.* Nairobi: East African Publishing House, 1973. Print.

Bamikunle, Aderemi. "The Development of Niyi Osundare's Poetry: A Survey of Themes and Technique." *Research in African Literatures* 26.4 (1995): 121–37. Print.

Caminero-Santangelo, Byron. "Different Shades of Green: Ecocriticism and African Literature." *African Literature: An Anthology of Criticism and Theory.* Ed. Tejumola Olaniyan and Ato Quayson. Malden, Massachusetts: Blackwell Publishing, 2007. 698–706. Print.

Efuet, Fomin Edward. "Deconstructing Anthropocentrism in African Literature: An Ecocritical Study of Ngugi wa Thiong'o's *Wizard of the Crow.*" 2 June 2010. Web. 31 Aug. 2010. <http://votesizing.org/story/

Deconstructing-Anthropocentrism-in-African-Literature-An-Ecocritical-Study-of-Ngugi-Wa-Thiongo?page=2>.

Falkowitz, Max. "Book Review: Ngugi wa Thiong'o's *Wizard of the Crow*." Web. 31 August 2010.

Ngugi, wa Thiong'o. *A Grain of Wheat*. London: Heinemann, 1967. Print.

———. *The River Between*. London: Heinemann, 1965. Print.

———. *Weep Not Child*. London: Heinemann, 1964. Print.

———. *Wizard of the Crow*. Lagos: Farafina, 2007. Print.

Nixon, Rob. "Environmentalism and Postcolonialism." *African Literature: An Anthology of Criticism and Theory*. Ed. Tejumola Olaniyan and Ato Quayson. Malden: Blackwell Publishing, 2007. 715–723. Print.

Saro-Wiwa, Ken. *A Forest of Flowers*. Port Harcourt: Saros, 1986. Print.

Slaymaker, William. "Ecoing the Other(s): The Call of Global Green and Black African Responses." *African Literature: An Anthology of Criticism and Theory*. Ed. Tejumola Olaniyan and Ato Quayson. Malden: Blackwell Publishing, 2007. 683–697. Print.

Spencer, Robert. "Ecocriticism in the Colonial Present: The Politics of Dwelling in Raja Shehadeh's *Palestinian Walks: Notes on a Vanishing Landscape*." *Postcolonial Studies* 13.1 (2010): 33–54. Print.

Vital, Anthony. "Toward an African Ecocriticism: Postcolonialism, Ecology and Life and Times of Michael K." *Research in African Literatures* 39.1 (2008): 87. Web. 31 August 2010.

3

Eco-activism in Contemporary African Literature: Zakes Mda's *Heart of Redness* and Tanure Ojaide's *The Activist*

Enajite Ojaruega, Delta State University, Abraka

Introduction

A major topical issue occupying the attention of both developed and developing nations the world over is caring for the environment. There are warnings about the perils of global warming and the earth facing ecological crises. This condition is believed to have been triggered by the adverse effects of human actions that have become detrimental to the environment. One does not need to be a scientist to know that humans and their environments are connected. This idea is borne out of the obvious fact that the environment (and by this I mean the land, water, or air space) is primarily a means of sustenance for humans. It is a provider of means and as such is a hotbed of economic, social, and cultural activities in every society. Therefore, the condition of the environment at any point in time plays a very important role in the lives of the inhabitants. To a large extent, it enables them to remain self-reliant, hence the need to protect their fundamental human rights as well as environmental rights in instances where they perceive threats or negative encroachment.

Environmental pollution comes in the forms of blowouts, gas flares, and oil spills arising from oil exploration and exploitation activities. In addition, the nonpreservation of forest trees and wildlife as well as the natural seashores in the wake of modern architectural developments are also key factors responsible for the ongoing environmental despoliation being experienced in some parts of the world. But the danger goes beyond these, because what happens in one place could contribute to the general global warming that could adversely affect populations very far away. Thus, taking care of the earth involves local and global, individual and collective efforts because of the oneness of humanity as far as sharing one earth together is concerned.

Modern African literature from its onset has been (and still is) a literature of engagement as writers deploy their artistic resources toward addressing important issues concerning the individual and corporate existence of their various societies. There are copious works of fiction, poetry, and drama addressing the sociopolitical problems facing Africa. This utilitarian function is often directed toward any pressing problem that the writers want to enlighten the society about and toward its possible solution. Therefore, it is not surprising that African writers have also taken up environmental, ecological, and related issues as they attempt to sensitize the public about the deteriorating environment in the forms of decreasing biodiversity, environmental pollution, and other forms of degradation or acts of ecocide. These writers tend to see a use for literature in assisting to make the public more aware and sensitive to the environment and its restoration to a more pristine and healthier state than it is. In the light of the foregoing observation, writers appear involved in a "bioregional" concern, which has to do with using literature as advocacy for their different environments. Literary scholars thus use eco-criticism to interpret literary works with environmental and ecological preoccupations.

Eco-criticism deals with the study of works of literature with themes closely related to issues affecting the environment. According to Michael Branch, one of its purposes is to promote "ecological literacy" (xiii) or promote an awareness of the adverse effects of environmental degradation. Eco-criticism also aims to create in readers an awareness of the environmental crises while allowing for literature to suggest ways of conciliation between humans and their environments. Considering the works of eco-critics, Ojaide's scholarship and creative writing explore environmental issues to make readers not only aware of the global environmental crisis but also for literature to "suggest means by which we might read literary texts with a new appreciation for what they reveal about the complex of relationships that mediate interactions between humans and their environments" (*Contemporary African Literatre* xiii).

Ojaide also shares a similar view with Branch who further explains that eco-criticism as a branch of study is a call for a change in culture toward a more "biocentric worldview, an extension of ethics, a broadening of human conception of global community to include nonhuman life forms and the physical environment" (Branch xiii). Hence, Branch concludes that with the awareness of eco-criticism, which is what Cheryll Burgess Glotfelty calls "the relationship between human culture and the environment," literature will lead toward "an ecologically sustainable human society" (qtd. in Branch 29).

Eco-activism in Modern African Literature

Uzoechi Nwagbara sees this type of literature as a literary preoccupation that is environmentally conscious and ecologically sensitive to the plight of people and their environment (33). The need to protect and preserve Africa's rich biodiversity as well as proffer alternative solutions in achieving and sustaining a pristine environment is therefore one of the cardinal preoccupations of the two African writers, Zakes Mda of South Africa and Tanure Ojaide of Nigeria, whose respective novels *The Heart of Redness* and *The Activist* will be used to examine the concern for environmental and ecological awareness in contemporary African literature. Surprisingly, even though both novels were written by African writers residing/working abroad, their respective narratives focus on pertinent issues concerning the need to address environmental rights and justice from different perspectives. Their respective artistic visions for the preservation of a healthy environment give them free range to explore issues of economic exploitation, political marginalization of minority groups, as well as other sundry hazards the people contend with as a result of the negative impact of modern tourism and oil extraction activities. Clearly, these writers array themselves on the side of the poor and oppressed, and their brand of eco-activism is an intercession of many issues. Based on the above, this essay undertakes a comparative discussion of both novels from their areas of similarities and dissimilarities as espoused by the writers' critical engagement with issues of environmental activism.

It is significant to note that the issue of the environment fuses with other socioeconomic and political matters that African writers deal with. Nigeria's Ken Saro-Wiwa's activism on the Niger Delta environment is linked to political, economic, and cultural issues in propagating the marginalization of minority groups in a large Nigerian federation with numerous ethnicities. This also affects the people culturally, as their languages are neglected at the expense of the languages of the majority groups. In addition to the pollution of the environment, there is the destruction of the means of livelihood of the Niger Delta people as well as being cheated of the natural resources found in their area. Similarly, in

Kenya, the late Nobel laureate Wangari Maathai struggled to protect the Kenyan environment, not only by planting trees but also sensitizing the entire nation to the need to have a good environment. Her *Unbound: A Memoir* aptly captures the tale of her struggle and the passionate effort to keep humans and their environment in a healthy symbiotic relationship. Al Gedicks succinctly sums up the ongoing condition of the regions where natural resources are being exploited:

> The close connection between native peoples and their land has made them particularly vulnerable to change in their ecosystems. Because of their direct dependence on the earth for subsistence, they suffer more acutely than others when toxic materials pollute their lands. In the cases of oil extraction in the Niger-Delta of Nigeria, the Amazon rainforest of Ecuador and the Colombian cloud forest, there is an inseparable connection between the assault on the environment and the assault on human rights. In all of these cases, multinational oil companies have not only degraded the environment but colluded with the government of these countries to deny native people their basic political and civil rights to resist environmental damage that threatens their subsistence and their very survival. (41)

It is the symbiotic relationship between humans and their environment that this chapter explores the narratives of Ojaide and Mda. The persistent assault on the natural habitat of a people invariably implies a resultant effect on almost, if not all, aspects of their existence. Besides the advocacy for eco-logicality in the exploration and exploitation of natural resources within the African continent, this chapter essentializes the artistic cum pragmatic strategies the African writer deploys in the bid toward environmental and ecological sensitization of the public on resource utility and regeneration.

Zakes Mda's *The Heart of Redness* (first published in 2000 in South Africa by Oxford University Press) and Tanure Ojaide's *The Activist* (first published in Nigeria by Farafina in 2006) are novels that clearly situate their authors as artists who are very much concerned with the welfare of the earth. In their depiction of rivalry, greed, exploitation, marginalization, and other vices plaguing their postcolonial societies, both writers are unequivocal in their support for the preservation of the environment. Yet, both have different opinions on how best to go about their eco-activism. For instance, as part of efforts to safeguard the people's seashore land from modern incursion, Mda, through his major character, suggests a quaint method of preservation—one where the alternative lies in launching a campaign tagged "Let the Wild Coast Stay Wild." On the other hand, Ojaide appears to be in support of allowing external incursions with respect to drilling for mineral resources. However, he seems to advocate a situation where adequate preventive and palliative measures are put in place during the process of oil exploration to forestall the people and environment from suffering from the adverse fallouts of oil exploration and exploitation activities. As environmental activists, the respective protagonists of both *The Heart of Redness* (Camagu) and *The Activist* (the Activist) do not only stop at just drawing attention to the adverse effects of exploiting natural resources, but go a step further in providing alternative solutions in combating the menace of environmental degradation.

Zakes Mda's *The Heart of Redness* is set in South Africa. Camagu Cesane is the protagonist of the narrative. He is a South African who has lived in the United States of America for over thirty years and suddenly decides to return home in the wake of the country's independence. All his efforts to fit into his country's new sociopolitical system prove abortive, as he is treated like an outcast because he appears to be out of sync with the current situation of things at home. In frustration, he decides to go back to the United States, but changes his mind at the last minute and instead undertakes a journey to the hinterlands in search of NomaRussia, a young lady whom he became besotted with after a brief contact at a wake in the city. In between focusing on Camagu's quest for his elusive love, the narrative is spiced with the author's use of the flashback technique to reveal the age-old rivalry between the Believers and the Unbelievers. This conflict is still very much present in modern times as both factions, represented by Zim and Bhonco respectively, are enmeshed in a tug-of-war. This has to do with whether or not to allow new developments as planned by a big South African company to make Qolorha-by-Sea a gambling city and water-sports tourist haven by taking advantage of its seashore environment. While the Unbelievers support the idea mainly because it would help usher into the quiet village some of the benefits of modernization and thus help remove their uncivilized state or "redness," the Believers are of the opinion that this external interference would only succeed in desecrating the land and pristine environment and they therefore oppose the change.

Mda's story is full of descriptions of the unfettered and unspoiled sea and landscape of Qolorha-by-Sea. For example, its mountains and valleys are presented as lush with green vegetation and a breathtaking view of the sea (Mda 7). On his first entry into the village of Qolorha, Camagu cannot help but be captivated by the rustic environment which he describes as "... a canvas of blue and green" (Mda 53) and "the most beautiful place on earth" (Mda 63). Therefore, no sooner does he settle down, he gets embroiled in the fight for the preservation of this beautiful environment.

In Tanure Ojaide's *The Activist*, the protagonist who is simply referred to throughout the novel as the Activist is also a returnee from the United States who relocates to his Niger Delta region to take up a teaching appointment at the state-owned university. While abroad, he is quite active in protest marches against human and environmental injustices. He becomes an interested stakeholder when he returns to his native land and observes the devastating changes wrought on the environment by oil exploration and exploitation. On a boat ride through the creeks with Ebi, a female friend, the Activist is saddened by the fact that with the discovery and extraction of crude oil onshore and offshore, the people and region "... are in for disaster, if nothing is done to save our waters, land and air" (Ojaide *The Activist*, 86). He is appalled at the extent of pollution to the environment without any serious efforts to tackle the excesses of the oil companies who ironically enjoy the support of the nation's federal government. Hence, he is of the opinion that the people as owners of the polluted land need to do something themselves in forcing the change the environment needs to usher in positive developments for the region and people, and he is quite optimistic that the people can indeed effect the change (Ojaide *The Activist*, 96).

In the remaining part of the chapter, it shall foreground how the two narratives are used to address environmental rights and by so doing delineate the type of eco-activism that the writers recommend. By "environmental rights," it is meant the people's fundamental entitlement to a clean and healthy environment or surrounding. This involves water, landscape, and source of livelihood (farming, fishing, and others). The absence of these basic needs, when naturally available but abused through powerful companies and governments, denotes oppression, marginalization, exploitation, and hazardous living. It can therefore be assumed that environmental rights establish a connection between the impoverishment of human communities and environmental degradation.

Eco-activism, however, challenges the violation of environmental rights and creates awareness to sensitize the people to their plight. As mentioned earlier, the eco-activist ranges on the side of the oppressed, exploited, marginalized, and abused to attract attention to and support for victims of environmental degradation locally and globally. The environmental activist proffers an alternative vision and holds perpetrators accountable for the injustices. By siding with victims, the eco-critic or writer uses epistemology that uplifts rather than downgrades the victims. This is probably why Al Gedicks calls such agitators resource rebels, struggling for their resource control to retrieve or recover by force, if necessary, what rightfully belongs to them. The integration of the needs and concerns of local communities and peoples makes the eco-activist and those campaigned for partners and joint beneficiaries. It is in the light of writers as eco-activists seeking environmental justice that both Zakes Mda and Tanure Ojaide should be seen in their respective narratives.

Eco-activism in *The Heart of Redness*

Although Mda's narrative is largely preoccupied with the generational rivalry between the Believers and the Unbelievers over religious issues, the novelist nevertheless deftly projects the series of environmental challenges threatening to destroy the fragile peace existing between both groups who share a common ancestral lineage. Never before have the two warring parties come to an irreconcilable difference as in the matter of the proposed changes that will affect the physical landscape of their small rural village, Qolorha-by-Sea. In the opening chapter of the novel, the author presents this place to the reader as a rustic village with flowing rivers and rich pastures, situated along the seashore and possessing "a wistful beauty." Through Bhonco's hilltop view, Mda describes the environment:

> Down below, on his [Bhonco's] right, he can see the wild sea smashing gigantic waves against the rocks, creating mountains of snow-white surf. On his left his eyes feast on the green valleys and the patches of villages with beautiful houses painted pink, powder blue, yellow, and white. . . . Indeed, Qolorha-by-Sea is a place rich in wonders. The rivers do not cease flowing, even when the rest of the country knells a drought. The cattle are round and fat. (7)

The existence of this type of idyllic setting in a modern dispensation is what makes the idea of developing the village as a haven for tourism a welcome development. But the nature of tourism to be encouraged is what generates the bone of contention among the villagers. Characters like Dalton, the local storekeeper, Zim and his daughter Qukezwa, and other Believers are worried that the type of development via business tourism advocated by Bhonco, his daughter Xoliswa Ximiya, and other Unbelievers will only cause more harm than good to the environment. According to the former group, turning the village into a celebrity paradise by encouraging outsiders to build gambling and water-sports resorts will only be to the benefit of a few villagers. First is the obvious fact that these modern architectural facilities cannot be built without first cutting down the forests of indigenous trees, disturbing the bird life, and polluting the bodies of water, including Nongqawuse's pool, which happens to be a place of significant historical value to the people (Mda 119).

These series of activities amount to stripping the earth of its rich biodiversity as well as defacing the natural and pristine environment. Again, the village women and others who depend on harvesting the sea for their food and income will be prevented from having unrestricted access to the seashore as well as contend with other negative effects of this modern development when it becomes a water-sports resort. Apart from compromising their sources of livelihood, the Believers go on to argue that in return, the gambling and water sports centers will only provide employment for a negligible percentage of the working force population (many of whom would have lost their original means of sustenance by now) and even at that, only at a lowly paid status as car washers, cleaners, maids, and so forth. Already, by allowing them to erect small cottages along the seashore, he observes that these outsiders are violating some of the environmental laws that forbid building within one kilometer from the coastline. According to the Believers, who are regarded as conservatives by the opposition, the disadvantages of the plans for modernization and progress being offered far outweigh the advantages. Therefore, ensuring that they do not succeed in bringing in the developers becomes a task that must be done for the Believers.

The Unbelievers, however, led by Bhonco, seem to think otherwise; they are bent on allowing the external developers in. They strongly believe that "this is a lifetime opportunity for Qolorha to be like some of the holiday resorts in America" (Mda 67). They do not understand why then the conservatives are bent on retaining the "redness" or "bushness" of the land. As far as they are concerned, there is a need to get rid of the bush, which to them is a sign and a constant reminder of their uncivilized state. For them, development means attracting tourism with people coming in from all over the world, economic investments, employment generation, and other perks of modernization like electricity and foreign interests. But their opponents, the Believers, feel that they (the Believers) are agitating for development that will bring positive changes like health delivery services, clean and affordable water, as well as unbridled access to the sea and its bountiful harvests. They constantly harp on the importance of preserving the environment by conserving nature, forests, and rivers and still are able to attract tourists who are interested in the things of nature.

The Activist

Tanure Ojaide's *The Activist* presents an impressive perspective on oil exploitation and its attendant effects on the environment and people of Nigeria's Niger Delta region. The narrative highlights the incontestable reality that oil exploitation has been (and still is): a case of the strong taking by force the natural resources that rightfully belong to the weak; in this case, the multinational oil companies and the series of military governments represent the strong. This is reflected in the plight of the people and their region, since in spite of many decades of oil drilling in the area, there has been negligible economic benefit to show in terms of development. At the same time, the newly retuned Activist observes sadly that "the region now possesses a new and ugly face different from the once pristine visage" (Ojaide *The Activist*, 46). On a boat ride downstream with his female companion, he is appalled at the amount of damage done even to the bodies of water. Gone was the large population of fish in the water because of chemical pollution resulting from oil extraction. Once famous fishing markets in the area have now become depots for the imported varieties of frozen fish. Ocean supertankers that take the oil away discharge sluices, further contaminating the water. Naturally medicinal waters of the cove, famed for potency for men and fertility for women, have turned greasy and smelly.

During a forum organized by the women on the negative effects of oil exploration, cases are pointed out of rising infertility of women and impotence of men. Some members of the female gender experience early menstrual onset and later early menopause, with pregnant young women sometimes giving birth to malformed babies. There is also the devastation of the once-rich fauna and flora as well as the biodiversity of the area. Apparently, the careless and insensitive actions of the oil prospecting companies are a violation of what the organization Green Peace calls the law of mutual preservation, which prescribes a mutually beneficial relationship between man and his environment. As things stand now, these oil-rich communities are caught up in the quagmire of the proverbial man who lives by the bank of the river yet uses spittle in washing his hands. While the region produces so much oil wealth, the physical landscape is left greatly devastated and unattended to and the people greatly impoverished because of the present condition of their environment.

The region lacks basic social amenities, including electricity, good roads, potable water, and infrastructural and recreational facilities. Youths have been displaced, as the ecological disasters caused by oil exploration deprive them of access to their independent sources of livelihood. Generally, the region and its inhabitants are left in an unenviable condition by their present circumstances. By blatantly disregarding the environmental protection laws, the oil companies continue to deface the earth surfaces of this region as well as rid them of their valuable uses. Land, water, and air spaces acquired for the purposes of drilling oil and for gas flarings are no longer useful for any other form of human sustenance. Oil pipelines are haphazardly and shoddily laid across human, plant, and animal habitats, even within domestic settings such that they pose great danger to the well-being of the people, but the oil companies do not seem to care about the risks they expose the people to.

The greed to maximize profits drives them to increase drilling and production without putting in place commensurate measures to prevent or deal with accidents. Nor do they put in place measures to assist the locals whose sources and standards of living have been sorely compromised. As a result, the people are not only deprived of economic independence, but they contend with sundry health hazards. Some of these debilitating conditions are artistically represented in this novel through the interactions between some characters. The writer's observation is that external incursions into the region have had more negative than positive effects. For example, in recruiting workers for the oil firms, only the menial jobs are allocated to the locals. Women are employed as cleaners, while young female graduates are made to serve tea and sometimes the personal needs of oil workers after office hours. Indigenes of the region like Dennis Ishaka, who are highly qualified engineers, are employed only to be kept in the dark about the actual drilling activities, thus effectively blocking them from gaining the appropriate training needed to enable them participate in improving the condition of their environment. The marginalized position of the region does not get any better with the activities of some locals who for a small amount of financial gratification collude with the foreigners to betray their people.

In light of this dismal state of affairs, Ojaide's Activist refuses to be a passive observer of the environmental endangerment going on in his beloved region. He enlists the assistance of other characters like Pere Ighogboja, Omagbemi Junior, and Ebi, his wife, in mobilizing the people against the injustices being perpetuated against them. In his review of the novel under discussion, Sunny Ahwefeada (2007) likens the efforts of the Activist and his associates to that of a redemptive mission, which entails the constructive subversion of the state's economic apparatus for the common good of the people.

Alternative Vision/Eco-activism

Both Zakes Mda's *Heart of Redness* and Tanure Ojaide's *The Activist* no doubt share similarities, while also maintaining their uniqueness. In both novels, we find male protagonists who return home from the United States to their respective African countries after a long period of absence. Leaving their nations in the first place was informed by the unsavory conditions prevalent in their respective countries at particular points in their histories. Mda's Camagu's opportunity was during South Africa's apartheid era, while Ojaide's Activist's involvement was the sacking of his oil-rich community by soldiers on the orders of the federal military government. Their reverse trip home symbolically represents both writers' advocacy of a homecoming that will initiate and establish positive changes and transformation in the face of new realities in their communities and countries. Their aim is to assist in righting the wrongs prevalent at home, whether it is exploitation, oppression, marginalization, or nation-building. Similarly, both Camagu and the Activist are professionals in their respective fields, and they bring in their wealth of experience and intellectual knowledge to help the locals enthrone environmental rights.

One of the banes of infrastructural developments in the host communities where natural resources are harnessed for greater economic uses is lack of integration. Often, in establishing projects aimed at benefitting the indigenes, the community's input is rarely sought, and as a result, such laudable efforts at improving the lifestyle of the people easily fail or fall short of their expected usefulness. It is quite clear that both writers through their novels advocate the integration of indigenous communities and peoples, what is referred to as grassroots consultation, in establishing projects meant to benefit them. In *The Heart of Redness*, Camagu falls out with Dalton the storekeeper because of his penchant for planning things "for" instead of "with" the people (Mda 180). On his own part, Ojaide presents the Activist as being uncomfortable with the fact that owners of the land where oil exploration activities are carried out are usually not consulted on issues affecting their well-being. Specifically, Chief Ishaka's constant disagreements with members of the traditional council are usually over members' collusion with external agents of exploitation (oil companies) to rob the people of the benefits accruable to them from their oil wealth. Part of the Activist's redemptive mission is the desire to put in place concrete measures to help ameliorate the sufferings of the people as caused by oil exploitation.

It is significant too that in their fight for the enthronement of environmental justice for their respective regions, both writers indict local authorities who are here regarded as internal agents of oppression. This is because they connive with outsiders, the multinational oil companies, to short-change the people. These people divert public funds for their personal use, while remaining impervious to the negative and far-reaching implications of ecological atrocities the outsiders perpetuate. The local chiefs in Mda's novel are bribed with brandy in exchange for land to build cottages along the coastline, and they even go further to violate the laid-down environmental laws of the land. In *The Activist*, the council of chiefs as well as Professor Tobore Ede, the liaison officer for Bell Oil Company, can be regarded as the internal oppressors as they appropriate and share among themselves bribes from the oil companies. The fact that Chief Tobi Ishaka and the Activist do not cooperate with such persons attests to the writer's artistic vision of fighting corruption to stop the community's exploitation. Chief Ishaka is constantly on the warpath with his fellow chiefs and the traditional ruler of his community, while Professor Ede receives the "neck-lacing" treatment for provoking the youths with his insensitive utterances and high-handedness (Ojaide *The Activist*, 156–157).

The novelists seem to advocate the promotion of self-reliance for the rural people whereby they do things for themselves. Their suggestion is that projects should be owned and managed fully by them as part of the measures for caring for their own environment. In other words, the writers advocate resource control. In keeping with this, Camagu floats a cooperative society in partnership with some local women. Their business involves trade in indigenous materials (fresh seafood, traditional isiXhosa costumes and accessories) marketed in the city. The Delta Cartel business of The Activist and Pere Ighogboja become an avenue for gathering the resources with which they will later use to overthrow their oppressors and take charge of their collective destinies as a people and a region. This affords the parties involved a measure of economic independence and self-reliance and amelioration for their embattled environments.

Again, Zakes Mda's brand of eco-activism is such that prescribes the preservation of the environment as much as possible in its original state but which nevertheless encourages stimulating development. The Believers, Camagu and Dalton, are able to secure the land by the seashore and keep the external aggressors out by going as far as obtaining a court order restraining the latter from encroaching on the land in question. As an alternative, Camagu suggests working out a plan on how the community can benefit from the "things they wish to preserve" (Mda 119). He goes into partnership by floating a cooperative society with some village women where they sell seafood and isiXhosa costumes and accessories to the people in the city. Dalton comes up with the idea of cultivating a botanical garden as part of the "Let the Wild Coast Stay Wild" (Mda 148–149) campaign where rare indigenous plants, especially endangered species, will be grown. Finally, the land space, which the land developers from the city wanted to confiscate, is later used to build a backpackers' hostel with self-catering facilities for nature-loving tourists.

In his own way, Ojaide's Activist tries to create awareness of the deplorable condition existing in the region as caused by oil exploitation when he joins ranks with locals like Pere, Omagbemi, Dr. Biriye Otite, Chief Tobi Ishaka, Mrs. Timi Taylor, Ebi Emasheyi, and others. He encourages the idea of sending a delegation to the United Nations and attracting global attention in order to curtail the excesses of the oil companies in the Niger Delta region. The novelist writes:

> For months Pere, the Activist, and Omagbemi worked hard to assemble materials to make a case against the oil companies. The Activist knew the impact of pictures on Westerners and made sure that they hired an experienced professional photographer to have coloured photos of their exhibits to present at the court of world opinion. (Ojaide *The Activist*, 201)

Although their overseas trip was stopped at the airport by security agents who confiscated their pictures and other related documents, they nevertheless succeed in using *The Patriot* newspaper to create some level of fear in the management of the oil companies, which try to cover up their tracks. In the same vein and still toward the need to sensitize the international world to the inhuman conditions existing in the Niger Delta environment, the Activist starts a newspaper through which significant happenings, including the agitation for resource control, in the Niger Delta are published and so publicized. It recorded instant success as "the newspaper was patriotic, pro-people, and for justice and fairness" (Ojaide *The Activist*, 230).

All in the attempt to enthrone environmental rights and justice for his region, the Activist goes into politics, which he feels would be a veritable platform for reaching out to the people and affecting them and their land effectively. As Activist governor, his goal is to ensure enough measures are put in place to ameliorate the sufferings of the embattled region and its people. Some measures he hopes to undertake and implement as part of his plans to upgrade the condition of the Niger Delta environment include ensuring oil companies clean up their mess. He also hopes to establish indigenous oil companies to compete with foreign ones drilling for oil. Similarly, he intends to employ qualified youths from the region to manage key areas of the oil sector and ministry. The Activist creates a ministry of Environmental and Mineral Matters to help with the proper harnessing of the state's natural resources as well as help clean the polluted environment.

Conclusion

From the discussion so far, it is quite obvious that while both writers in their separate novels fight against the despoliation of their environment, they adopt or advocate different approaches toward solving the problem at hand. For Mda's protagonist and his group, preserving the environment in its natural state involves the total exclusion of modern architectural interference, and Ojaide's main character encourages the participation of local and external oil prospectors to be ecologically sensitive to the environment but also causes to be put in place adequate measures to take care of the negative consequences of environmental pollution when they occur.

Both Zakes Mda and Tanure Ojaide teach in the United States; the former at Ohio University at Athens and the latter at the University of North Carolina at Charlotte. It is interesting that the protagonists of their respective novels leave the United States for their respective African nations of South Africa and Nigeria. Both are treated as foreigners, but eventually, through chance or sheer patience, stay to make a difference in their societies. The writers in all likelihood have gained from their

American experience to contribute to the environmental debate in Africa. The writers, like their protagonists, seem to be paying back to their native homelands from their experience abroad by sensitizing the public on the ongoing environmental degradation in their respective home regions. While the writers could be writing out of nostalgia, their protagonists are able to make a difference in their respective societies. Camagu brings the Believers and Unbelievers together through eco-tourism that would allow the environment to be protected while at the same time allowing tourism that would bring money, development, employment, and openness to self and others. The Activist eventually establishes a system in which those who are sensitive to the environment, native-born folks who know the importance of the land and rivers as the occupations that sustain the local communities, are placed in charge of the oil exploration and exploitation.

The two writers have a middle way that balances taking care of the environment and at the same time allowing development. They affirm that a society could be modern and developed while at the same time having an environment which is healthy and eco-friendly. In the two works, the writers also send a message to their people that it is possible to have a clean, sustainable environment. That is, while oil can be explored and exploited, the local communities can still derive their sustenance from fishing and farming. Local communities could be healthy by avoiding the callous excesses of foreign exploiters. On the other hand, in South Africa, the environment is able to unite two historical foes toward maintaining a sustainable environment to the benefit of all. The two writers have given African environmental activists one way toward promoting development in the midst of sustaining a healthy environment.

Works Cited

Adamson, Joni. *American Indian Literature, Environmental Justice, and Ecocriticism: The Middle Place*. Arizona: U of Arizona P, 2001. Print.

Awhefeada, Sunny. "A Nameless Activist in the Service of the Fatherland." Lagos: *The Guardian*, January 22 (2007): 45. Print.

Branch, Michael. "Introduction." *Reading the Earth: New Directions in the Study of Literature and Environment*. Ed. Michael Branch, Rochelle Johnson, Daniel Patterson, and Scott Slovic. Idaho: U of Idaho P, 1998. Print.

Gedicks, Al. *Resource Rebels: Native Challenges to Mining and Oil Corporations*. Cambridge: South End Press, 2001. Print.

Mda, Zakes. *The Heart of Redness*. New York: Picador, 2000. Print.

Ojaide, Tanure. *The Activist.* Princeton: AMV Publishing, 2010. Print.
_____. *Contemporary African Literature: New Approaches.* Durham: Carolina Academic Press, 2012. Print.
Smith, Eric Todd. "Dropping the Subject: Reflections on the Motives for an Ecological Criticism." *Reading the Earth: New Directions in the Study of Literature and Environment.* Ed. Michael Branch, Rochelle Johnson, Daniel Patterson, and Scott Slovic. Idaho: U of Idaho P, 1998. 29–40. Print.

4

Isidore Okpewho's *Tides* and Ken Saro-Wiwa's *A Month and a Day*: A Kinesis of Eco-activism from Theory to Praxis

Feghabo Charles Cliff, Niger Delta University, Wilberforce Island

Introduction

Literary scholars interested in issues bordering on how to redeem the vanishing greenness of the earth continue to admonish humanity to cultivate eco-commitment to the preservationist cause. For such eco-critics, the writer should employ his/her imaginative prowess to salvage the environment from destruction by man and corporate bodies. For African literature, Niyi Osundare, with his *The Eye of the Earth*, appears to have inaugurated an eco-lit dimension in African letters. However, Tanure Ojaide appears to be the most consistent in the deployment of literature for ecological preservation. Other writers like Isidore Okpewho and Ken Saro-Wiwa have equally demonstrated this commitment in their imaginative composition. While Okpewho's novel fictionalizes the ecological challenges faced by the people of the Niger Delta, thereby espousing the politics of eco-activism in the region, Saro-Wiwa's autobiographical text actualizes Okpewho's prophecy. Thus, the two texts demonstrate a progression from fictionalization to actualization in eco-literature.

Literary scholars are hard put to delineating the borders between fiction and history, and fiction and facts. History and fiction, in spite of their superficial dissimilarities, have society as a common bond: society provides the threads with which factual or fictional stories are spun. Consequently, it inextricably strings the fringes of history or fact and fiction together. This inseparable interlacing makes some scholars describe them as strange bedfellows who cannot cohabit and cannot be divorced from each other. Even with the historian's attempt at disengaging his writing from fiction to ensure fidelity to truth, his writing however remains tainted by some doses of fiction. This results from his personal interpretations of seemingly or overtly silent areas about events. While for the creative writer, history about the different epochs of human socioeconomic and political evolution provides the raw material for his imaginative weaves, the historian deals specifically with exactitude of history. Interestingly therefore, the creative writer downplays the historicity, exalting instead his artistic finesse through the dislocation and reconstruction of history. Thus, he distinguishes his work from historical or sociological documents, and gives it the stamp of fictionality.

Autobiography, under which the literary genre called prison diaries or prison notes are subsumed, even as it is historical in nature is also considered a part of fiction. Its major qualification as a subgenre of prose, among other qualities, is its stain of unavoidable falsehood. Bernard Shaw's statement about autobiography validates its fictiveness when he avers that:

> [a]ll autobiographies are lies. I do not mean unconscious, unintentional lies: mean deliberate lies. No man is bad enough to tell the truth about himself during his lifetime, involving as it must, the truth about family and his friends and colleagues. No man is good enough to tell the truth to posterity in a document he suppresses until there is nobody left to contradict him. (qtd. in Oriaku 7)

The deliberate lies discernable in autobiographies legitimize the seal of fiction on autobiographies even as its historicity retains its unquestionable nature.

Given the peculiar sociopolitical experiences of Africans and African nations—experiences such as slave trade and colonialism that midwived the birth of African American and African literature—the written literature from inception consequently has been a blend of history and fiction that is sometimes autobiographical with fictional blemishes. The autobiographical tradition has enjoyed the deployment of some African writers from the early nationalist writers like Kenneth Kaunda in *Zambia Shall be Free*, to later writers such as Camara Laye in *The African Child*, Wole Soyinka in *The Man Died*, Ngugi wa Thiong'o in *Detained*. Even the works that can be arguably referred to as fiction draw profusely from the historical experiences of Africa at various epochs. Examples of such writing include Achebe's *Things Fall Apart, Arrow of God, Man of The People*, and *Anthills of the Savannah*; Ngugi wa Thiong'o's *The River Between, Weep not Child, A*

Grain of Wheat, Petals of Blood, and *Devil on the Cross;* Ayi Kwei Armah's *The Beautyful Ones Are Not Yet Born, Fragments,* and *Two Thousand Seasons;* and Wole Soyinka's *The Interpreters.* While this list of works consists of early African writings, the most recent works by a much younger generation of writers are not divorced from the tradition of borrowing from history. It is worthy of note that, by definition, history is not circumscribed to the past but is inclusive of all human experiences with social import. This inextricable relationship between history and literature is what Ernest Emenyonu gives expression to when he remarks that:

> [t]he writer needs to use the fact of history to dramatise for the people the realities of their common existence, as well as dramatise for them their predicaments so that they can make correct and appropriate choices in the future. (vi)

The engagement of the African writer with history stems from the fact that African history for over five hundred years has been that of struggle against forces that have threatened to obliterate the destiny of the people (Ogude 1). These forces against the people of Africa—forces that have existed from the period of slave trade, all through colonialism and decolonization, unto the present—have been from without and within.

From the close of the twentieth century until the twenty-first century, the socioeconomic and political stability of Nigeria has been menaced by insurgency in the Niger Delta. The insurrection was occasioned by the environmental degradation, neglect, and exploitation of the people of the region by the Nigerian state misruled preponderantly by succession of military juntas that often carried out apparently genocidal, repressive actions against the people of the area. The literature provoked by this ferment in the region is revolutionary, reflecting the activities in the region. This corpus of writing differentiates itself from the larger body of Nigerian literature by its eco-consciousness. The Western capitalists' adventure into Niger Delta and other parts of Nigeria through colonialism is often associated with the postcolonial traumas that include the degradation of the environment. The multinational oil companies operating in the Niger Delta are seen by the people of the region, especially writers, as an extension of the imperialists' enterprise beyond the colonial era. In the artistic creations that have emerged therefore, there are references to colonial and postcolonial Nigerian history in fictionalized or factualized forms. Thus, there is a convergence of history or facts and fiction about the revolutionary ferment in the region. This, consequently, validates our examination of Isidore Okpewho's fictional text *Tides* and Ken Saro-Wiwa's autobiographical work *A Month and a Day*.

Okpewho's *Tides* that dwells on the ecological and sociopolitical challenges of Niger Delta is one environment-conscious work that presages the Niger Delta ferment, which later peaked before the first decade of the twenty-first century. The neglect of the area by the Nigerian state long predates the emergence of Okpewho's novel. Through their advocacy of activism for the environment, Okpewho and Saro-Wiwa affirm their distinction from writers that merely capture nature in their writing. J. P. Clark in *The Wives Revolt* (1991) had earlier explored the oil-related unrest in the region without a call for eco-activism. In the early postindependence Nigeria under the military rule of General Yakubu Gowon, there was an insurrection in the Niger Delta led by late Major Isaac Adaka Boro. Okpewho's novel predicts hazily the recrudescence of revolutionary activities in the region. The title *Tides* is emblematic of the deltaic milieu of people even as it also symbolically envisages the resurgence of the insurgency in the area years after its publication. The novel, written about the time of the burgeoning of Saro-Wiwa's nonviolent protest against the despoliation of the Ogoni environment by Shell Petroleum Development Company, is a prophecy as well as a wakeup-call to eco-activism in the region. This prophecy is realized through Saro-Wiwa's environmental struggles that led to his arrest, trial, and hanging by the military government of late General Sani Abacha in 1995. The aggression of the youths of the region in the years after Saro-Wiwa's death is a response to Okpewho's challenge of commitment to the environment.

Ethnocentrism and Environmental Politics in Okpewho's *Tides*

Employing an epistolary style, Okpewho explores the plight of the people of the Niger Delta whose environment is depleted though oil and gas exploration activities by multinational concerns. Through the correspondences of two journalists, Piriye Dukumo and Tonwe Brisibe, who are both victims of the apparently immanent effusion of ethnic politics in Nigeria even into the workplace, Okpewho attributes the breath stifling environmental traumas faced by the people of the Niger Delta to ethnocentrism that characterizes the Nigerian existence. He argues that ethnicized politics works to the disfavor of the people of minority ethnic groups, particularly those of the oil-rich Niger Delta. Ethnic sentiments, therefore, serve as the basis of most of the actions and reactions of the principal and other lesser characters in the work. In the novel, among other sundry references to palpable distasteful Nigerian realities, Okpewho draws the readers' attention to such experiences and their negative implications on the Nigerian society. With regard to the oppression suffered by the people of the Niger Delta and the resultant upheaval, through one of the three major characters in the novel, Tonwe Brisibe, he warns that the crisis in the region will rob the nation of peace. Through another major character, Piriye Dukumo, Okpewho foresees the insensitivity to the appalling experience of the Beniotu minority group by the other ethnic nationalities forcing everyone to his own ethnic cocoon. Beniotu is an Ijo expression meaning riverine dwellers. Okpewho has chosen this expression aptly to designate the people of the Niger Delta living there.

Since independence, the people of the Nigerian nation have had to contend with negative effects of misrule by military and civilian leaders. Beyond the general maladies suffered by all, Okpewho discerns ethnocentrism as the basis of the marginalization and exploitation suffered by the ethnic minorities in the Niger Delta region represented in the novel by Beniotu people. He also associates ethnocentric politics with the environmental degradation of the region. He interprets this tribal politics promoted by the military government as injustice and repression against the people of the Niger Delta. These twin evils, with smothering effects on the people and their environment, in Okpewho's view are acts of alienation that could engender a revolution. This opinion is the central motif of his novel.

In the ecological woes of the people of the Niger Delta occasioned by tribalism, Okpewho implicates imperialists' politics. The imperialists' involvement is highlighted through their insensitivity to the environmentally hazardous activities of multinational oil companies operating in the region. The callousness of the oil companies and the military government toward the sufferings of the people of the Niger Delta—maladies engendered by pollutions from oil exploration activities—in Okpewho's reasoning are made possible by the flourishing of ethnocentrism. The imperialists' politics of the exploitation of the colonized territories, in the case of Nigeria, finds vibrant expression in ethnocentrism promoted by the military. The ethnicized nature of the military is obvious in the novel, especially in the story of the visit of a delegation of people of a host community to an oil company. In the novel, some noble men of the Ebrima fishing village are compelled by the noxious effects of oil exploration activities to visit an oil rig to complain to its operators—Atlantic Fuels, an oil company. The visit to the oil rig is prompted by the fact that:

> ... enormous search-lights which they train on the waters around their offshore rig were drawing the fish away. They wondered if there was anything the company could do to save them the trouble; their lives are dependent on fishing, and they faced certain disaster if the schools of fish were forced permanently out of their area of activity. The spillages from the rigs and pipelines have done enough harm to their trade, and the activity of this new rig would only snuff out their lives for good. (Okpewho 11)

While the mission is to seek a compromise with the oil company, the team of negotiators for peace gets the reverse. The engineer radios for a boat loaded with soldiers one of whom on arrival slaps Opene, the head of the delegation, across his face. This forces the members of the team to escape for their lives. Repressive action such as this experienced by the people of Ebrima is a regular feature in the lives of the people of the Niger Delta. Tonwe's visit to a naval base in Warri to speak for his uneducated people only unfurls the ethnocized military politics in Nigeria that encourages the exploitation of the minority people of the Niger Delta. His meeting with the commanding officer, Commander Bayo Adetunji, is a disappointment as the latter is rather unfriendly, taking sides with the oil company to which he grovels for pecuniary gains. Commander Adetunji is a non-Beniotu. This informs his attitude toward Tonwe and the suffering people of Ebrima. His approach, despite the obvious plight of the villagers, is expressive of a national problem, as Tonwe's earlier statement reveals "ethnicity has become a major tragedy in the Nigerian body politics, and has hindered many a fine relationship among Nigerians" (Okpewho 5).

Such ethnocized politics in the military helps to cement the collaboration between the imperialists and the military leadership. Such an alliance with a repressive and corrupt leadership, to the imperialistic multinational oil concerns, is a good one. This is so because it provides the enabling environment for the execution of their imperialistic politics of exploitation of the resources of the people. Ethnicism supported by avarice on the part of the military leadership is a weakness exploited by the multinationals for the fulfillment of the imperialistic agenda of their owners—the exploitation of the natural resources of the subjugated or alienated through an alliance with internal perfidious collaborators. The military became ally of the multinational oil companies. The veracity of this is established by the admission by Chevron (an oil company in the Niger Delta) of sending Nigerian forces to crush upheavals in Rivers State in Nigeria (Vitalis qtd. in Nixon 107). This is articulated in the novel through the question of a white engineer on the oil rig to which Ebrima villagers have gone on their innocuous protest against the activities of the oil companies. Tired of what he considers too frequent protests by illiterate fishermen, the white engineer reasons aloud, "What . . . did the inconvenience suffered by a few scruffy fishermen matter to the general prosperity which the oil has brought to Nigeria?" (Okpewho 12). To the multinational oil companies, they have no part in the blame for the environmental woes experienced by the villages because the white engineer further reasons that they have been given "the franchise to exploit oil here" (Okpewho 12)—after all, they are only "businessmen, and had no political interest or social welfare . . ." (Okpewho 12).

Okpewho, through the musings of the white engineer, discloses the profit-centeredness that obscures the sensitivity of the imperialists represented by the multinational oil companies. This profit-mindedness, even at the expense of the lives of the oppressed as evidenced in the above referenced statement of the white engineer, also reveals what informs their employment of the state apparatus—the security agents—as well as their deception. The treachery of the multinational oil companies' operators is made possible by the support they readily enjoy from their internal accomplices. This can be seen in the actions of the multinational oil companies during the visit of a task force constituted by the military government to investigate the oil pollution in the Niger Delta. The inaugural meeting of this task force, to which Tonwe is invited, also has in attendance, among others, military officers like Commander Adetunji and Major Haruna Ismaila, executives of oil companies, and local chiefs. While speaking on the cleaning of pollution from oil exploration activities, Mr. Segel, the exploration manager of Freland Oil Corporation, representing all companies, tries to hoodwink the aggrieved people of the oil producing communities and the government representatives. He contends that the oil companies are determined to clean up oil spills using what he deceptively describes as the most advanced detergent for oil spills. In this gathering, which has come to be as a result of repeated grievances of the people over the pollution of their environment, Tonwe, who is representing the people Beniotu, is a lone voice in the midst of the two allies. The loneliness of

Tonwe's voice is a metaphor for the marginality of the people of the Niger Delta in relation to the people of the major ethnic groups and their collaborators (the multinational oil companies). The consequences of this marginality are evident in Opene's experience with the soldiers on the oil rig. As noted earlier, Tonwe becomes frusted in his effort to ascertain the claims of Mr. Segel by a dishonest chief who claims to be a true representative of the people of Beniotu, and the government representatives. These actions of the internal traitors encourage the insensitivity of the multinational oil companies' operators toward the pains of the people of the Niger Delta.

Considering the streak of strategic-cum-diplomatic ignorance displayed on the part of multinational oil companies toward the oil producing communities, and the country's military leadership's capitalistic arrogance and depravity, the struggle to liberate the Niger Delta environment from ecological hazards brought about by oil exploration and exploitation become increasingly unattainable. Diplomatic ignorance in the latter influences the activities of the former vis-à-vis the unpleasant experience of the people of Niger Delta. This is validated by the respective actions of the oil companies and the government. In the novel, the callousness of the government is demonstrated in the construction of Kwarafa Dam by the government and the effects on the people of Beniotu. According to Piriye in his maiden correspondence to Tonwe, the construction of the dam is carried out without regard to its negative implications on the people of Beniotu who are mainly anglers. The construction of the dam has occasioned a reduction in "the volume of water flowing down the Niger Delta and so curtailed activity in the Delta and our people are nothing if not fishermen" (Okpewho 2).

Kwarafa Dam is the corruption of Kainji Dam in the northern part of Nigeria. In real life, the water level of this dam affects the agricultural activities in the Niger Delta. Okpewho has fictionalized this real-life experience to explore the provocative effects of the dam on the livelihood of the people of the Niger Delta. He sees the ethnocentric insensitivity of the government and the activities of the multinational oil companies as engendering a feeling of alienation in the people of the Niger Delta and contributing to the destruction of their ecology. The novelist believes that these effects felt by the people of the region will grow from harmless protests to a revolution in the future. The novel establishes these prophetic and historical qualities by capturing the graduation of the agitations of the people of the region from simple complaints to nonviolent protests, then to belligerent resistance. The stages of the struggle of the people of the Niger Delta parallel the historical realities of the growth of the struggles of the people. C. B. N. Ogbogbo validates this in his depictions of the various phases of the reactions of the people of the zone (1–324). He opines that the armed response had been preceded by complaints and writings by prominent educated sons and daughters of the Niger Delta to draw the attention of oil companies and government to their predicament. Okpewho depicts these futile historical attempts and the reactions of the people through the peaceful visit of the people of Ebrima to the oil platform of Atlantic Fuels.

Piriye's revolutionary fervor and eco-activism are stirred up by the callousness flaunted by the multinational oil companies. His wake-up call through his letter to his friend Tonwe is a challenge to the Niger Delta people; it is one that is propelled by their attempt to breathe by salvaging their environment and the future of the children. The effort of the villagers to invert their suffering through the Opene-led peaceful delegation is the first step of the fight of the people against their marginalization. The second phase consists of the efforts of Tonwe and Piriye to utilize their knowledge and professional skills to alter the plights of their people. Piriye and Tonwe had both lived and worked in Lagos as journalists with the *Chronicle* newspaper. Their lofty positions as editor-in-chief and editor, respectively, in the newspaper had drawn to them the envy of their colleagues from major ethnic nationalities that were not comfortable with their exalted positions. Inexplicably, both were hurled out of their jobs at the same time by the Chairman of the Board, Mr. Ajibade, whom Piriye thinks had ethnic resentment against them. Tonwe was compelled to return to his roots in the Niger Delta on losing his journalist job because of tribal politics. Tonwe discovers to his chagrin that, contrary to his expectation of peace at his Niger Delta village, he has the ubiquitous ethnic politics of Nigeria on his trail. His village, Seiama, which he returns to, and other neighboring villages in the Niger Delta articulate the socioeconomic burden and historical reality of the woes of the people of the area. In these villages, through oil exploration activities by multinational oil companies, the ecosystem on which the people depend for their daily sustenance is ravaged with impunity—an act that Rob Nixon aptly describes as "slow violence" (11). The devastation of the environment by the oil companies is enabled by the insensitivity of the Nigerian military leadership. This collaborative thoughtlessness of the two, in Piriye's opinion, is provocative of revolt from the people who are alienated from their ecosystem and the

Nigerian state. Thus, in his maiden letter, he attempts to arouse Tonwe to a revolutionary consciousness, configuring a picture of the degradation experienced by the people:

> First, there is the Kwaràfa Dam, which has severely reduced the volume of water flowing down the Niger and so curtailed the fishing activity in the Niger Delta—and our people are nothing but fishermen. Secondly, the spillage of crude petroleum from oil frigs down there—one of which is in fact located near your village has proved an absolute menace to agricultural life, for many farms are practically buried in the thick layers of crude oil, which kills off many fishes and other forms of life. (Okpewho 2)

It is worth mentioning that, in spite of the above terrific portrayal of the environment, Tonwe at this point is yet to be jolted to engage in eco-activism that his friend advocates. The reason for his nonchalant response is founded on his earlier distaste for ethnic politics, which to him, only polarizes the nation. He is, however, later compelled by his personal experience of the effect of the pollution and the brutal frustration of the Opene-championed protest to change his previous stand against tribalism. After the objectionable experience of Opene in the hands of the soldiers, he informs his friend Piriye that:

> [i]t may come as a surprise to you when I say I feel better disposed to your project now than I did at first. Something happened here recently which has shaken me from my complacency and inspired me with concern not much below the zeal that you require of me. I have indeed become a little sadder than when I came here. (Okpewho 11)

Tonwe's transformation from complacency to activism is provoked by the despoliation of ecosystem that also threatens the breath of the living and the unborn people of Beniotu. Through this change in Tonwe, Okpewho captures the compelling nature of the plight of the people of the Niger Delta. This interpretation of Okpewho finds expression in Nelson Fashina's argument on some distasteful experiences in Africa with revolutionary pressures. The events that are provocative of insurrection that Fashina identifies include election rigging, expropriation of national wealth by the ruling class, racism, ethnic discrimination, and hunger (5). In the novel, the plight of the people in the villages of Beniotu meets the inciting conditions pointed out by Fashina.

The blaze of activism to reverse the oppression of the people is manifest in Tonwe's subsequent moves. His visit to Commander Adetunji and his attendance of the inaugural meeting of the Task Force on Pollution (all of which had earlier been highlighted in this chapter) demonstrate his eco-activism intended to influence change in the lot of his fellow Niger Delta citizens. His craving for the amelioration of the woes of his people drives him to extend a call to other Niger Deltans or Beniotu. To him, this clarion call to other Benitu kindred is inevitable. He expresses this in his letter of concession to Piriye when he says, "I have come home to lead a peaceful life, but how can I honestly disown a cause which has everything to do with the peace that I crave" (Okpewho 14). This inexorable need for a peaceful existence that is guaranteed only by an environment free of pollution from oil exploratory activities informs Tonwe's later attempts to get the government to intervene in the despoliation of the environment by the multinational oil companies. This commitment to the rescue of the environment also makes him persuade the city-corrupted (consequently) insensitive Beniotu indigenes in the Diaspora who are represented by Commissioner Freeborn Batowei in Benin. He tries to persuade the elite to use their exalted positions to influence the government. While exchanging views with Batowei, he argues:

> I have been driven from Lagos. Now I am home, there is nowhere else for me to run to. Take your mansion in the village. I imagine you have built it so that when you finally retire, you will have a good place to go home to and spend the rest of your days in peace and comfort. Now, how would you like it if this whole oil palaver got out of control, and your own village, and with your beautiful house, bogged down by oil spillage? So, if you ask me what is in it for me, I say it comes down to that . . . But let us look at it from another angle. We talk about the civil war, and we should always remember that such things usually start from one small localised problem, which ends up engulfing the whole country because nobody is giving a chance to peaceful approach. So the fishermen get angry and blow up the oil installations, and the Federal Government brings down its might on our people, and another Isaac Boro rises up to try to fight the cause of the people, and the whole Niger Delta goes up in flame once again. Now, where does that leave you and me (sic) and all the beautiful homes we hope to retire to? (Okpewho 80–81)

The excerpt above is an apt prognosis by Okpewho on the recent restiveness in the Niger Delta championed by youths from the region. The nonviolent eco-activism led by Ken Saro-Wiwa in the 1990s and the later belligerent attempts of the youths of the region to save their ecology menaced daily by oil companies and the insensitivity of the Nigerian state, are the fulfillment of Okpewho's prediction. The agitations of Saro-Wiwa in the '90s and the insurgent activities of the youths of the region in the twenty-first century are responses to the wake-up call made by Okpewho through Tonwe.

In the novel, Tonwe's plea to his Beniotu kindred to resist the exploitative activities of the oil companies and the repressive actions of the Nigerian military government is a struggle to secure a space for his breath and that of his Niger Delta compatriots—born and unborn. It is the response to this urgent call to duty that commands Tonwe, Piriye, Bickerbug or Ebika Harrison, and the Lagos-based Beniotu elitist group, Committee of Concerned Citizens, to rise up to reverse the destiny of their people, employing their exposure to the city and Western knowledge differently— through peaceful protest to outright forceful activities. For Tonwe at the village in the Niger Delta, challenged by the repressive activities of the oil companies and their collaborators, it is time to use his position as an educated man and erstwhile Chief Editor of the *Chronicle* newspaper to lead his people out of the mire of oppression. His method of the liberation for his people is through peaceful mediations and motivation of privileged indigenes to get the government's attention to end the despoliation of the environment.

Piriye is the one who influences Tonwe into eco-activism. Employing his craft as a journalist, the former, on his part, becomes an offence to the military. He writes in national and international dailies to arrest the attention of the national and international community to the horrors of ecological injustice experienced by the people of Beniotu. He ferrets for information from Lati, a former female Yoruba colleague of his at the *Chronicle*. His writing and activities intended to unshackle his people, get him hurled into prison by the authorities. His subsequent conditional release from prison by security agents flings him into a quandary as to what approach is the best solution to the problem of his Beniotu—the violent revolution sought by Bickerbug or the nonviolent change desired by Tonwe.

Ebika Harrison, or Bickerbug on his part, employs militancy as the most diplomatic strategy in the resolution of the problem. It is noteworthy that through the divergent approaches of the various categories of the people, Okpewho examines the varied reactions of the people of the Niger

Delta to the environmental despoliation in the area. In doing this, he tries to detach the struggle of the people from any ideological strings, especially Marxism, as most advocates of the oppressed are wont to do. This is obvious even in Bickerbug, the major character with violent revolutionary traits. In spite of his resentment against the oppressors of his people, he is disconnected from any ideology. Bickerbug is a graduate of English. His aggressive reaction to the repression of his Beniotu people presages the final stage of the resistance of the people of the Niger Delta that Tonwe has adumbrated in his argument with Commissioner Freeborn Batowei. Bickerbug is the resurrected late Major Isaac Boro, who is the precursor and symbol of armed resistance by the youths of the Niger Delta against the Nigerian state. Boro, with some of his friends from the Niger Delta, in the early years of military rule in Nigeria, had staged a brief but inspiring revolt against the Nigerian state. Saro-Wiwa, whose environmental activism coincides with the time of Okpewho's novel, to some extent shares resemblance with Bickerbug. This is apparent in Piriye's description of Bickerbug:

> Not in the fashionable ideologue mould—he doesn't flog the names of Marx or Lenin or Fanon or any people. At least I haven't heard him do so and I haven't seen any of their books in his—well library, if you call his collection by that name. But he is a true guerrilla type, with a lot more time for planning action and executing it than for the more comfortable ways of doing things. He doesn't shave, wears nearly the same clothes all the time, gets what he wants as fast as he wants it. (Okpewho 38)

From Piriye's description of Bickerbug above, Okpewho envisages the emergence of a true revolutionary leader not distracted by materialistic pursuit, but genuinely committed to the liberation of his people. This picture of a non-materialistic and non-ideological activist truly devoted to the salvation of his people matches Saro-Wiwas' personality. Like Bickerbug, he was a graduate of English, not known for materialism or as a Marxist. Okpewho's belief in a non-covetous leader is founded on his reasoning that the economic prosperity of one or few individuals in the midst of millions will not translate to plural fiscal and political emancipation of the people of the Niger Delta. In Okpewho's opinion, therefore, financially successful Beniotu indigenes such as Batowei in Benin, Chief Zukumor in the village, and Tari Strongface are simply self-seeking opportunists who easily compromise the benefits of the collective struggle of the people.

This is manifest in the treacherous acts of the already mentioned perfidious elites. On different occasions in the novel, Commissioner Batowei and Chief Zukumor, who symbolize the compromising Niger Deltans, attempt to frustrate the agitations of their people for personal gains. Batowei, who through his personal struggles has become rich, refuses to be persuaded by Tonwe to lend his privileged financial weight behind the general struggle of his own people. In his egocentric thinking, he is rather surprised at Tonwe's selfless interest in the plight of the people. He therefore asks him, "That's why I asked you, how has the oil problem affected your life? I really meant to ask you what's in for you?" (Okpewho 79). Zukumor, on his part, exhibiting similar self-interest, frustrates Tonwe's attempt to interrogate the claims of the oil companies that they employ a detergent in the cleaning up of oil spills.

Ignoring perverse characters such as the above, therefore, Okpewho chooses Bickerbug, who is not an ideologue, to predict the resurgence of violent revolutionary activities in the Niger Delta region. Bickerbug is not an avaricious character, but a self-effacing simple activist who is sincerely committed to freeing his Beniotu people from the claws of oppression of the multinational oil companies and the Nigerian state. In his one-track-minded commitment to the salvation of his people and their ecosystem, he parts ways with the Lagos-based Beniotu people's Committee of Concerned Citizens (CCC). The committee, whose leadership is made up of opportunists seeking to exploit the sufferings of their people back in the Niger Delta for their selfish interest, as is typical of Nigerians. Consequently, he refuses to align with this group, which he sees as part of the forces bent on keeping his people under the yoke of oppression. Bickerbug, after his release from confinement (he had been arrested on grounds of being a threat to security), recruits young men from the dregs of society and blows up an oil rig in the Niger Delta and then goes ahead to blow up the Kwarafa Dam, thereby causing a deluge that disrupts the supply of electricity nationwide. Through this act, Okpewho's vision of the triumph of the oppressed people of the Niger Delta through a revolution becomes glaring. This visualization by Okpewho finds expression in the statement of Bickerbug at his arrest by the Nigerian police after he has blown up the Kwarafa Damp:

> Well, well, well, Piriye . . . we have won, haven't we? Our people have won.
> . . . The water is flowing again, full stream. The tides are here again. Soon there'll be plenty of fishes swimming again, eh? (Okpewho 188)

The above expression therefore, also serves as a caveat to the military leaders on the likelihood of the evolution of the crisis in the Niger Delta into a revolutionary level with nationwide negative consequences.

Okpewho's predictions of insurgency with far-reaching implications for the Nigerian state has since been validated by Saro-Wiwa's arrest and subsequent execution through hanging by the government of General Abacha, and the recent rebirth of restiveness in the Niger Delta. Okpewho's fiction draws its contents from the history of the immediate past before the time of his novel. It is a history of immediate recall. By the fictionalization of such not-too-distant history or the immediate past history of oil politics in Nigeria, he has used literature to mediate the real present.

The realization of Okpewho's prophecy through the Saro-Wiwa–led activism that was succeeded by insurrection in the region shows some form of transition in the writing on the Niger Delta eco-crisis—from theory to praxis just as it indicates a kinesis from fiction to facts.

Ken Saro-Wiwa's Eco-activism: From Shadow to Substance

Ken Saro-Wiwa's prison diary, *A Month and a Day*, posthumously published, marks a new beginning in African literature vis-à-vis the praxis of eco-activism in literature. The work does not inscribe its distinctiveness by its autobiographical contents, but by its practical concern for the environment. William Slaymaker also attests to the novelty of eco-consciousness (139) that is noticeable in Ken Saro-Wiwa's last work. The newness of the focus of Saro-Wiwa's last narrative agrees with Charles Nnolim's call for a universal canvas for African literature in the twenty-first century (Nnolim 4). Though autobiographical in content, the work is part of Saro-Wiwa's environmental conflict with Shell Petroleum Development Company and Nigeria's Federal military government that colluded to devastate the ecosystem and consequently impoverish the minority people of Ogoni in the Niger Delta. His agitation, which is foreshadowed in Okpewho's novel, is the realization of Okpewho's prophecy. Saro-Wiwa's struggle for the Ogoni's despoiled environment is a response to the call for activism made by Tonwe in Okpewho's *Tides*. Saro-Wiwa utilizes his craft as a writer in his eco-activism. We thus, see a link between the two works of art—Saro-Wiwa's environmental activities in textual form, being not only a fulfillment of Okpewho's prognosis but also a continuation of Okpewho's novel. Saro-Wiwa's physical contention against the forces within and without documented as diary can further be seen as eco-literature in praxis, while

Okpewho's novel is eco-literature theorized. As a realistic work, we find Okpewho's adumbrations expanded in Saro-Wiwa's narrative. The validity of our argument about Saro-Wiwa's prison notes or diary as a practical literary text on environmental struggle is obvious in a letter he had sent to his British writer friend, William Boyd. Part of the letter reads:

> I am in good spirits. ... There is no doubt that my idea will succeed in time, but I'll have to bear the pains of the moment ... the most important thing for me is that I have used my talent as a writer to enable the Ogoni people to confront their tormentors. I was not able to do this as a politician or as a businessman. My writing did it. (Saro-Wiwa 66)

Saro-Wiwa's eco-activism on behalf of his minority Ogoni is simply the practical reiteration of his belief that the writer should use his craft to prosecute the war against injustice perpetrated by the Nigerian military leaders. It is a credo he never fails to verbalize at different convocations of writers. He recapitulates this creed in his *A Month and a Day* thus:

> ... literature in crucial situation such as Nigeria must serve society by steeping in politics, by interventionist role, and the writer must not merely write to amuse or to take a bemused, critical look at society. They must play an interventionist role. (Saro-Wiwa 81)

Saro-Wiwa's advocacy for what he refers to as an interventionist role expected of the writer is informed, according to him, by his personal experience that:

> African governments can ignore writers, taking comfort in the fact that only few can read and write, and that those who read find little time for the luxury of literary consumption beyond the need to pass examinations based on set texts. Therefore, the writer must be *l'homme engage*: the intellectual man of action. He must take part in mass organizations. He must establish direct contact with the people and resort to the strength of African literature-oratory in the tongue. (81)

Saro-Wiwa's involvement in the direct mobilization of his Ogoni people for their emancipation from the shackles of neglect, exploitation and ecocide, to him is African literature in practice or the advocacy of literature made palpable. His practical engagement in eco-activism is in line with Lawrence Buell's call for commitment for the environment (qtd. in

Harman 47). His involvement of the intelligentsia and the ordinary people of the communities of Ogoni is a demand of many a writer, especially those with Marxist leaning. Tanure Ojaide in *The Activist* equally makes a similar call. Saro-Wiwa's activism, as chronicled in his novel, is therefore a kinesis of literature from abstract to reality. In contrast, works like Okpewho's *Tides* and Ojaide's *The Activist* are reality transcribed into fiction. Saro-Wiwa's vision, vis-à-vis the aggregation of the respective classes for social revolution, is harmonious with that of Ngugi's Marxian-influenced vision. He not only expresses his desire for social change through his creative writings, but also uses such, especially his dramatic works, to mobilize the people to engineer social change.

Considering the ideological position of Saro-Wiwa and Ngugi with regard to the employment of the creative art as an instrument of change, one can easily locate Femi Osofisan (2001) and Niyi Osundare (2007) within a similar artistic vision. For Osundare, the writer should not just be in the vanguard of revolutionary positive change, but should be at the forefront of such vanguard for social change. In the contest against the junta and the oil company for the reversal of the destiny of the people of Ogoni, Saro-Wiwa puts himself at the forefront of the vanguard of Ogoni people genuinely committed to the retrieval of their destiny violated by the Nigerian state and oil companies. Saro-Wiwa's undoing was unfortunately his involvement of all classes, especially the elites. The murder of some members of this class because of their perfidy eventually provided the last nail for his coffin.

In the epic struggle that later abridged his life, Saro-Wiwa's fundamental method of protest is nonviolent. His knowledge of the superiority of the pen to the gun comes alive when he realizes that the objectives of the struggle, which are environmental, economic, political, and cultural, can be best achieved in a military regime only through the drawing of the attention of the international bodies to which Nigeria belongs. Saro-Wiwa's novel is a factual or historical document of the experiences of the people of Ogoni, whose experience, vis-à-vis their environmental desecration and ethnically prejudiced position, is representative of the minorities in the Niger Delta. The work captures the daily experiences of Saro-Wiwa during the period of his arrest for campaigning against Shell Oil Company. His daily experiences in the environmental activism are the mirror through which the unappealing conditions of the people of the Niger Delta are reflected. *A Month and a Day*, a text based on his experiential knowledge, expands on Okpewho's fictional story on the plight of the people of the Niger Delta.

Unlike Okpewho's imaginative work with only dots of history, Saro-Wiwa's narrative discloses the details about the history and the reason for the struggle of the people of the area. We shall examine in turn the contributions of the multinational oil companies and the Federal government of Nigeria to the smothering of the people of the Niger Delta, their environment with its flora and fauna, and the consequent restiveness.

The Historical Background to Saro-Wiwa's Environmentalism

Oil was first struck in the Niger Delta in commercial quantity in 1958. The nation has made much gain from the exploration of oil since then. On the contrary, fifty years afterward, the people of the oil-bearing communities have continued to live their lives in a manner that is antithetical to the wealth from the bowels of their land. This is as a result of the insensitivity of the oil companies and the Nigerian state. As at the time of the resurgence of agitations that Saro-Wiwa captures, it was thirty years of oil exploration in Ogoni land and other parts of the Niger Delta by Shell Petroleum Development Company and other oil companies. He estimates thirty billion dollars as the gains of Shell operating in Ogoni land at the time of the protest of the people. In spite of these huge proceeds, he reveals that there is a disproportionate attention to the people and the environment. The activities of Shell have rather impoverished the people as a result of the despoliation of their farmlands and aquatic lives by frequent oil spills. This injustice compels Saro-Wiwa to identify with other ethnic minorities at the international level suffering similar ecological degradation. A part of his address to an international assembly of such minorities under the umbrella of Unrepresented Nations and Peoples and Organization (UNPO) at Geneva in 1992 graphically captures the ecological woes faced by the people of Ogoni as a result of the activities of the multinational oil companies:

> Oil exploration has turned Ogoni into waste land: lands, streams, and creeks are totally and continually polluted; the atmosphere has been poisoned, charged as it is with hydrocarbon vapour, methane, carbon monoxide, carbon dioxide and soot emitted by gas which has been flared twenty fours a day for thirty-three years in very close proximity to human habitation. Acid rain, oil spillages and oil blowouts have devastated Ogoni territory. High pressure oil pipelines crisscross the surface of Ogoni farmlands and villages dangerously. (Saro-Wiwa 96)

The environmental havoc caused by the activities of Shell as depicted by Saro-Wiwa's text above is similar to the ecological effects suffered by the people of Beniotu from Atlantic Fuels in Okpewho's novel. In both texts, the oil companies are presented as the means of perpetuating capitalism in the erstwhile colonies. In Saro-Wiwa's narrative, the consequence of the environmental pollution by the activities of the multinational oil companies on his people and his psyche form the crux of Saro-Wiwa's struggle for environmental justice from the Federal Government of Nigeria and the international organizations.

Shell, Strategic Capitalism and the Exploitation of the Poor

The lack of social commitment on the part of the transnational oil companies—callousness symbolized by Shell's activities in Ogoni land—is informed by the capitalist cupidity for wealth that goes along with alienation. Shell's representative insensitivity, with regard to the relationship between the oil companies and their host communities, reveals the profit-mindedness of the multinationals that is privileged over humans. Such callousness associated with the exploration of oil done with frequent spills alienates the people from their environment. The victims of exploitation are often alienated by the exploiters from the proceeds that come from their oppression. Alienation is associated with capitalism. In the Ogoni's agony—an experience that is a consequence of alienation by the multinational oil companies and the Nigerian state—Saro-Wiwa sees the perpetuation of colonialism by the British through her transnational oil company, Shell. He remarks, "British imperialism imposed on them oil exploitation and the Nigerian nation-state with powerful and dangerous forces which together spelt omnicide in Ogoni" (Saro-Wiwa 190).

As part of its imperialistic stratagem to sustain its exploitation of the people, armed with surplus profits from oil exploration in the Niger Delta, Shell employs the media—local and international—to have its image immaculately laundered. By such image laundering, its terrorism against the environment, especially in the erstwhile colonies of the empire, is obscured. Through the media, for instance, Shell publishes a few of its social projects that are not proportional to its huge proceeds it rakes from the environment. This subterfuge is intended to arrest international bodies' attention, thus veneering its insalubrious activities in the Niger Delta region. These deceitful acts are what Okpewho fictionalizes in his novel.

Shell sees his activities, therefore, as affront, especially when such activities are coming from a black man or a black community when its environmentally friendly activities are eulogized in Europe and America. It is thus a conflict to whittle away Saro-Wiwa's influence on the international community that it engages in when it comes out with a publication, among other things, discrediting Saro-Wiwa as one merely seeking to increase the international profile of his people. This action of Shell against Saro-Wiwa is an apt demonstration of the imperialistic hegemony on the colonized that Saro-Wiwa captures in the narrative.

Military Politics and the Dynamics of Internal Colonization

Shell is able to perpetrate this act of suppression and estrangement of the people of the host communities in the Niger Delta with impunity because of the minority status of the people and the prevalence of ethnic politics in the country that also works against ethnic minorities vis-à-vis the control of political and economic power. The silence of the military leadership that is constituted of the people from the major ethnic groups on the ecological terrorism bears testimony to Saro-Wiwa's cry of marginalization of his people. Ethnocized politics, hence, plays a major role in the underdevelopment of the country—politically as well as socially. This is a reality Okpewho fictionalizes in his artistic creation and Saro-Wiwa actualizes in his work. Saro-Wiwa sees tribalized politics manifest in the binary relationship between the ruling major ethnic groups and the ruled or exploited minor ethnic nationalities. He explains this as the consequence of the age-long struggle for the emancipation among subjugated minority ethnic groups in the country.

This ethnicized politics overtly influences Saro-Wiwa's interpretation of the actions of people from the dominant ruling ethnic group. For instance, he attributes his arrest in Port Harcourt to ethnic politics, which, in his opinion, also informs the insensitivity of the military leaders to the environmental degradation suffered by the people. He discloses that it is based on ethnic prejudice that he is related to by the exploiters and he relates with his oppressors. He graphically captures this through his experience at the state office of security agents. At the said office in Port Harcourt where he is being detained, he encounters an unsociable superior officer from the North who is rather terse in his intercourse with Saro-Wiwa. The security officer appears to be concerned only with the biddings of his overlords who are his compatriots from the North as well. The affable attitude of an Izon (Ijo) female security officer and her husband contrasts with the unfriendliness of the Northerner:

> The young lady returned and smilingly engaged me in conversation. We spoke about Nigeria, about the suffering of the people of Rivers State, of oil and the sorrows it had brought those on whose land it is found, of the social inequalities in the country, of oppression and all such. She was an Izon, neighbours of the Ogoni and the fourth largest ethnic group; they lived in the main oil producing area of the country. She fully understood all the arguments I had been making and certainly sympathized with them and with me for the travails I had suffered in recent months. (Saro-Wiwa 5)

The friendliness shown him by the Ijo officer evinces camaraderie between a people suffering the same fate of internal colonization—an experience where the Northern officer and his people are lords over the minority Southerners. This indicates the existence of a Self and Other relationship that is symptomatic of the colonial dispensation. This binary relation, in the case of the Nigerian state, facilitates the repression of the postcolonial Other that the minorities are.

This internal hegemony is obvious in the dichotomized official positions occupied by the people of major and minor ethnic groups in Nigeria: the people of the major ethnic nationalities are favored with topmost positions, while the lowest levels, which Saro-Wiwa refers to as slavish positions, are reserved for the oppressed minorities. He notices this at the State Security office in Port Harcourt, where:

> [d]ownstairs, you would meet men and women from the slave areas of the modern slave-state called Nigeria. Upstairs were the indigenous colonizers. They were not necessarily well spoken or well educated either. But they had power at their fingertips and knew it (Saro-Wiwa 7)

The "upstairs" and "downstairs" "indigenous colonizers" and "slaves" (Saro-Wiwa 7) are metaphoric configurations of the oppressors and oppressed binary relationship. He thus sees the people from the major ethnic nationalities as the oppressive overlords, while those from the minor ethnic nationalities are the oppressed. These metaphors, which run through the whole of Saro-Wiwa's prison notes, form the basis of the actions of the multinational oil companies backed by the military leaders from the major ethnic groups as well as his interpretations. The metaphor "indigenous colonizers" (Saro-Wiwa 7) explains his views about the majority ethnic groups as neo-colonialists that have succeeded the British in Nigeria. It is the metaphors of oppressors and oppressed that he attempts to justify when he posits that the military government, through the imposition of a unitary system on the country in the '70s, inaugurated the internal subjugation of the people of the Niger Delta. According to him, this politics, initiated by the military, enables them to transfer the resources of the minorities to the center for the exclusive advancement of the ruling major ethnic nationalities, while the former remain backward in terms of infrastructure. He therefore argues that it is the oppressors and the oppressed duality that is the cause of the neglect of the region by the federal military government. The effort to reverse this duality pits Saro-Wiwa against the military government and their collaborators—the multinational oil companies. He gives an instance that provokes his inexorable commitment to the social change. When he is being transported as a suspected insurrectionist from Port Harcourt to Lagos along the East/West Road, he feels his ethnic sensibilities assaulted by the deplorable state of the road. The East/West Road is the only road that links the Niger Delta with the west and north of Nigeria. The sorry state of the road, in spite of the wealth from the region, propels him to express his pledge to combat this injustice even with his life:

> The state of the road irked me. It was one of my overriding concerns. Not the road itself, but the fact that in this rich, oil- bearing area, the roads should be so rickety, while in the north of Nigeria, in that arid part of the country, there were expressways constructed at great cost with petroldollars which the delta belched forth. The injustice cried to the heavens. The fact that the victims of this injustice were too timid or ignorant to cry out against it was painful in the extreme. It was unacceptable. It had to be corrected at no matter what cost. To die fighting to right the wrong would be the greatest gift to life! (Saro-Wiwa 19)

Saro-Wiwa is not only vexed by the infrastructural neglect of the region, he is peeved also by what he explains as a calculated attempt by the military government of Ibrahim Babangida to subdue the people of the Niger Delta area for the prosperity of the major ethnic nationalities. For these major ethnic groups, more states and local governments are created to be funded by the resources from the oil-bearing minorities of the deltaic region. He describes actions such as this as a violent robbery on the people of the region. This marginalization is but another burden added to the frustrating environmental degradation suffered by the people. Consequently, an angry Saro-Wiwa becomes the voice for all the muffled voices of the repressed people of Ogoni and, by extension, the people of the Niger Delta whom he conscientizes to reverse their situation, even at the cost of their lives. In his own words, the injustice from both foes of the people of Ogoni "was unacceptable. It had to be corrected at no matter what cost. To die fighting to right the wrong would be the greatest gift of life! Yes, the gift of life" (Saro-Wiwa 19). This revolutionary stand of Saro-Wiwa, which later became the resolve of the youths of the Niger Delta years after Saro-Wiwa's death, is what Bickerbug in Okpewho's novel envisions.

It is not only the exploitative tendencies of Shell that the Ogoni have had to contend with, they also have government at the state and central levels that attempt to frustrate their struggle as their foes. At the level of state government, Saro-Wiwa and his compatriots had to fight against a state governor who is working in league with the repressive military government at the center. On its part, the central military government attempts to scuttle the struggle of the people by engineering a division among the people of Ogoni. There are some prominent leaders of Ogoni holding key positions in government that become easy tools of division in the hands of government against the collective concern of their people. These treacherous elements try to discredit the patriotic acts of Saro-Wiwa and his cohorts through publications and advertisements in a state-owned media to discredit the Saro-Wiwa–led Movement for the Survival of Ogoni People (MOSOP). These activities from some indigenes of Ogoni have their fictional parallel in the opportunistic drive that conditions the warped activism of the Concerned Citizens Committee (CCC) in Okpewho's novel. Some of the compromised members of the executive of CCC aided by government at the center also place an advert that is intended to dissociate the people of Beniotu from the struggle for emancipation, thus dishonoring Bickerbug and others with revolutionary intentions. The similarity in the two cases, though characteristic of all human liberation struggles, establishes the veracity of the relationship between fiction and fact. It also validates the link between the two novels: one being the substance of the shadowy picture in the other.

Not only through such divisive action that the government attempts to frustrate the realization of the dream of freedom of the Ogoni people, but also through the use of state security apparatus. Through threats, intimidations, and arrest, they attempt to sustain the exploitation of the people. Saro-Wiwa discloses that from the federal military government, for instance, comes a decree with death penalty for illegal gathering. The decree is promulgated to stop his eco-activism that the military leaders consider an international embarrassment.

Unfortunately, the activities of such repressive government and their elitist compromisers within, in both texts, only hone the resolution of the people to remain committed to wresting their destiny and ecosystem free from the hands of their destroyers. Such immutable resolve of Saro-Wiwa and his people is not strange because of the bond between the people and their environment. Saro-Wiwa sees environmental right as man's first right. This view may have informed his resolve that later becomes the creed of the generality of Ogoni through his effort at sensitizing them. The environmental struggle of Saro-Wiwa and his people, consequently, is prompted by the need to secure their human and environmental rights from the violent violators of such fundamental rights. Saro-Wiwa establishes this through a story about unarmed men and women of Ogoni land who have been aroused to eco-consciousness through his activism. It is this attempt at protecting their primary right to their environment that is demonstrated by the people in the story about the confrontation between armed soldiers and unarmed villagers. The simple unarmed people file out to confront armed soldiers brought in by Shell Petroleum Development Company to aid the laying of oil pipes. Members of the community had earlier protested against such action and were brutalized by soldiers, yet remain undaunted; they march out for the second time against their oppressors. Through this story, Saro-Wiwa not only reveals the repressive attitude of Shell that is symptomatic of the oil companies in the Niger Delta, but he also captures the irreversible resolution of the people to protect their first right. Shrouded in the reaction of this unarmed people is the psychology of the oppressed. Saro-Wiwa makes the point that protracted exploitation propels the victim of oppression to turn against his tormentor, especially when such exploitation impinges on the breath of the oppressed.

The reaction of the people, who had been docile until Saro-Wiwa's arousal of their consciousness, manifests a dose of Fanonnian advocacy. Christian Opukiri and Ambili Etekpe (2008) see Saro-Wiwa's mobilization of the distinct classes of people for the alteration of their subjugated position as an application of pluralistic approach—an approach they associate with Fanon's "human ecology psycho-social factors" (137). These scholars explain that Fanon in this approach advocates the aggregation of the youths, men, women, and others for violent or civil disobedience in order to destroy the institutions of exploitation.

The direct confrontation of the oppressor by the erstwhile docile people as recorded foregrounded in the narrative is reminiscent of the black South African's graduation from docility to consciousness in the days of Apartheid. The Ogoni here have been conscientized by Saro-Wiwa to confront their tormentors. Their reaction to protracted injustice, exploitation, ecoterrorism, and alienation is a demonstration of the psychological state of the oppressed whose response, according to psychologists, may be violent or aberrant. The fierce reaction of the people of the Niger Delta is a reality chronicled by Saro-Wiwa and fictionalized by Okpewho and other writers.

Conclusion

Our reading of the narratives by Okpewho and Saro-Wiwa reveals a symbiotic relationship between the people of the Niger Delta and their environment. The texts disclose that ethnic and environmental politics promoted by imperialist oil companies supported by indigenous military leaders result in ecocide in the region. The success of the collaboration between the multinational oil companies the Nigerian military leadership is due largely to the flourish of ethnicized politics promoted by the military leadership and drawn mostly from the major ethnic nationalities. The existence of ethnocized politics provides the binary relationship between the multinational oil concerns assisted by the military and the oil-bearing communities—oppressors and the oppressed, exploiters and the exploited. The major ethnic groups and the multinational oil companies are the oppressors, while the minorities of the Niger Delta are the oppressed who struggle to retrieve their right to the environment. These metaphors of majority and minorities, and indigenous colonizers resonate in both works of Okpewho and Saro-Wiwa. Through such metaphors, they capture the unwholesome experience of the people of the Niger Delta as the oppressed. While Okpewho fictionalizes the experiences of the people of the region, calling for environmental activism to alter their experience, his violent revolutionary character, Bickerbug, however, falls short of the makings of a revolutionary hero. He acts alone and, consequently, fails to mobilize the masses for a revolutionary change. Therefore, he does not serve as the symbol of Okpewho's advocacy for change. Okpewho's vision on the need for intellectuals' involvement is instead obvious in the eco-conscious efforts of the transformed Tonwe. Saro-Wiwa's eco-activism documented in his autobiographical text provides a practical response to Okpewho's call for eco-activism to be championed by the elites from the Niger Delta. Saro-Wiwa's mobilization of his Ogoni brethren is the substance of what Okpewho adumbrates through Tonwe. Thus, one finds a progression from a prophecy to its realistic fulfillment. In addition, we found the fruitfulness of Saro-Wiwa's efforts at conscientizing his people, evident in the actions of the youths, as an indication of the possibility of change engineered by the intellectual elites—a thing foreshadowed in Okpewho's work and actualized by Saro-Wiwa's eco-activism.

Works Cited

Egbuson, Vincent. *Love My Planet*. Ibadan: Kraft Books, 2008. Print.

Emenyonu, Ernest. "Introduction" African Literature and African Historical Experiences. Ed. Chidi Ikonne, Emelia Oko, and Peter Onwudinjo. *Calabar Studies in African Literature*. Ibadan: Heinemann, 1991. Print.

Fanon, Frantz. *The Wretched of the Earth*. Middlesex: Penguin, 1967. Print.

Hartman, Steven. "The Rise of American Ecoliterature." 2007. Web. 8 March 2010. <http://uu.diva-portal.org/smash/get/diva2:212772/FULLTEXT01>.

Nelson, Fashina. "Alienation and Revolutionary Vision in Post-Colonial East African Dramatic Literature." *Ufahamu: A Journal of African Studies* 35.2 (2009). Print.

Nixon, Rob. *Slow Violence and the Environmentalism of the Poor*. Cambridge: Harvard UP, 2011. Print.

Nnolim, Charles. "African Literature in the 21st Century, Challenges for Writers and Critics." *African Literature Today* 25 (2006). Print.

Ogbogbo, C. B. N. "Niger Delta and the Resource Control Conflict: 1960–1995." PhD Thesis. U of Ibadan, 2004. Print.

Ogude, Steve. "African Literature and the Burden of History." Ed. Chidi Ikonne, Emelia Oko, and Peter Onwudinjo. *Calabar Studies in African Literature: African Literature and African Historical Experiences*. Ibadan: Heinemann, 1991. Print.

Ojaide, Tanure. *The Activist*. Lagos: Farafina, 2006. Print.

Okpewho, Isidore. *Tides*. Longman: London, 2003.

Opukiri, Christian, and Ambily Etepke, eds. "Conflict Management and Strategy for Peace Building in the Niger Delta." *International Conference on the Nigerian State, Oil Industry and the Niger Delta*. 11–13 March 2008. Niger Delta U, 2008. Print.

Oriaku, Remy. *Autobiography as Literature*. Ibadan: Humanities Research Centre, 1998. Print.

Osofisan, Femi. *Insidious Treason: Drama in a Postcolonial State.* Ibadan: Opon Ifa Publishers, 2001. Print.
Osundare, Niyi. *The Writer as a Righter.* Ibadan: Hope Publications, 2001. Print.
Otite, Atare. *Ethnic Pluralism and Ethnic Conflicts in Nigeria.* Ibadan: Shaneson C. I., 2000. Print.
Saro-Wiwa, Ken. *A Month and a Day.* Ibadan: Spectrum Books, 1995. Print.
Slaymaker, William. "Ecoing the Other(s): The Call of Global Green and Black African Responses." African Literature: An Anthology of Criticvism and Theory, Ed. Tejumola Olaniyan and Ato Quayson. Malden Blackwell

5

Nature and Environment in Chinua Achebe's *Things Fall Apart* and *Arrow of God*

Gloria Ernest-Samuel, Imo State University

Introduction

Chinua Achebe's rural novels are arguably the most popular and most studied African literary works globally. From 1958 when he wrote his first novel, *Things Fall Apart*, until 2007 when he won the prestigious Man Booker International Prize, several scholars have written books and academic articles on his works. This trend may continue for a long time to come, specifically because his debut novel recreates the African life before the colonial incursion and what that historical contact between Europe and Africa did to the African identity. Most of the study on Achebe's rural narratives concentrates on how the writer, through the resources of art, opens a window into the understanding, preservation, and reflection on the Igbo culture, and by extension, the African culture and worldview during the pre- and postcolonial era around the turn of the nineteenth century. One of the finest issues Achebe aptly deals with in both narratives (*Things Fall Apart* and *Arrow of God*) is the travails of a society in transition.

With more than ten million copies of Achebe's *Things Fall Apart* sold worldwide in about fifty translated languages (Msiska i), no other African literary text has achieved a similar feat, or can compete with the work; hence, the continuous academic interest and attention the book continues to attract become understandable. *Things Fall Apart* remains a classical dramatization of a historical tragedy involving a respected titled Igbo man whose tragic flaw was his phobia for failure. In a similar vein, in *Arrow of God*, Achebe, true to his skilled narrative style, captures Ezeulu as another protagonist who suffers a personal loss, due largely to his arrogance or his nonconformist stance in a dynamic Igbo cultural setting.

Many scholars have tried to draw strength from the documented historical archives of Igbo worldview in their critical appraisal and analysis of Achebe's works; this chapter will toe the path of Michael Brauch's crusade of promoting "ecological literacy" by X-raying the nature and environment of Umuofia and Umuaro—the two clans that represent the Igbo nations in Achebe's *Things Fall Apart* and *Arrow of God*. This is important because as Ojaide (2010) observes, "Literature in Africa continues to be deployed toward the environment whether as geography, nature, culture or other aspects" (6). As in canonical texts in the evolution of African literature, Achebe's narratives carry the signatures of African oral tradition, and so are replete with the flora, fauna, and landscapes with symbolic meanings.

This chapter will therefore examine Achebe's use of nature and environment in achieving and expressing the Igbo experience in the pre- and postcolonial era. To achieve this, the chapter will be divided into three parts. The first part will discuss the background of *Things Fall Apart*, before highlighting and discussing key environmental elements in the novel. It will further make textual references to how they are employed and their utility in the narratives, as well as in everyday experience of the Igbo. The second part will examine the social, cultural, and religious background of Umuaro—the setting of *Arrow of God*—and further discuss the key flora and fauna utilized in the narrative for wider understanding of the Igbo worldview. Finally, in the third part, which will serve as the concluding part of the essay, the two narratives will be compared and used to assess the present Igbo environment, and thus justify this study by throwing more light on deeper understanding and appreciation of not just Achebe's narratives, but the African experience.

Things Fall Apart and the Socio-ecology of Umuofia

Things Fall Apart is set in a remote clan of nine villages (Umuofia). The remoteness of Umuofia, the major setting of the narrative, makes it possible for Achebe to explore the rural and natural attributes or features of the society. For instance, as a community in transition, not yet exposed to the vagaries of colonial development and intercourse, the village is what may be referred to as a "bush village"; hence, densely taken over by bush, or what may better be called forests made up of trees, plants, and other wild features that characterize a rustic space, otherwise known as flora. In the same vein, certain animals or fauna have social and religious symbolisms among the indigenes due to the people's deep religious root; hence, are seen as sacred or taken as totems of worship. Some are symbols of wealth, while others possess some cultural underpinning. The remoteness of Umuofia equally determines the vocation of the inhabitants—they are predominantly farmers who are conscious of their weather, with keen interest on the weather condition, which regulates the environment.

Therefore, the indigenes are interested in the day, time, weather, or the general mood of the earth where they conduct their affairs. The nature of the environment, to a large extent, determines the actions, decisions, and possibly the people's trend of thoughts in connection to their lives as Africans, farmers, and family members. Therefore, the rainy and dry seasons determine the people's way of life, just like daylight and darkness. In *Things Fall Apart*, Achebe discusses two types of night; namely, a dark night and the moonlit night. Achebe describes the dark night thus:

> The night was very quiet.... Darkness held a vague terror for this people, even the bravest among them. Children were warned not to whistle at night for fear of evil spirits. Dangerous animals became even sinister and uncanny in the dark. A snake was never called by its name because it would hear.... (*Things Fall Apart*, 8)

The moonlit night is quite different, as Achebe reveals, when compared to a dark night because "the happy voices of children playing in the open fields would be heard" (*Things Fall Apart*, 8). Chielo, the priestess of Agbala, the Oracle of the Hills and Caves, comes to carry Ezinma to the cave on one of such dark nights, whereas Nwoye, his siblings and other children in the village listen to their mothers' folktales on such moonlit nights. Rains, air, or breeze, and moonlight also affect the mood of the night as well as the action of the entire people, not just the African children, as revealed in the narrative. Each of the conditions has its unique attributes and features. Men of Umuofia rely on the beginning of the rain to know when to start planting their yam and other farm seedlings every planting season. It is believed that the earth is ready for tilling and planting; hence, good farmers commence farming when the first seasonal rain starts. However, when there is a change in this normal ecological system, it portends danger for the people, as one will notice in the year Okonkwo borrowed some eight hundred yam seedlings from Nwakibie:

> The first rains were late and when they came, lasted for only a brief moment. This blazing sun returned, more fierce than it had ever been known, and scorched all the green that had appeared with the rains. The earth burned like hot coals and roasted all the yam that had been sown. (Achebe *Things Fall Apart*, 18)

During that "mad" planting season, Okonkwo lost the initial four hundred tubers of yams he had planted. This was because when the rain commenced, instead of coming and going like they have always observed, "rain fell as it had never fallen before. For days and nights together it poured down in torrents, and washed away the yam heaps. Trees were uprooted and deep gorges appeared everywhere" (Achebe *Things Fall Apart*, 19).

Generally, African traditional literature highlights natural and environmental elements and issues that hinge on African culture. This may not be divorced from the fact that as Ojaide observes, African traditional literature is barely arts for art's sake like most arts, but is generally "functional, didactic and very utilitarian" (5).

In this narrative, set in an era when there are no motorable roads, but footpaths, environment is deployed from different aspects, including geography and nature, involving plants and animals, culture, and others. We shall, therefore, examine some of the key elements of nature and the environment (of Umuofia) as portrayed in the novels.

The Forest

The forest is a cluster of huge overgrown trees, plants, and climbers that serve ecological functions. Besides the ecological functions the habitat performs, it equally functions as a security wall for the clan. Interestingly, therefore, the eco-habitat serves as boundary that separates the villages, thus bonding the people from separate villages into a clan. Hence, indigenes have to create footpaths within the forest to access other neighboring villages. While reminiscing about his sojourn at Umuofia, Ikemefuna observes that he was brought "a long, long way from home, through lonely forest paths" (Achebe *Things Fall Apart*, 12). However, when the people of Umuofia eventually decide to perform the ritual of cleansing with Ikemefuna, apparently unaware that he is the major item for the ritual, Ikemefuna is assured completely that he is on his way to visit his home and family. The narrator observes that:

> The footway had now become a narrow line in the Heart of the forest. The short trees and sparse undergrowth which surrounded the men's village began to give way to giant trees and climbers which perhaps had stood from the beginning of things, untouched by the axe and the bush fire. (Achebe *Things Fall Apart*, 47)

Given the importance of this vegetation, the forest serves several purposes. It is used to cover and protect certain sacred and deeply spiritual and mysterious things in the society. Bushes are cleared to make new farms. "The cut bush was left to dry and fire was set to it. As the smoke rose to the sky, kites appeared from different directions and hovered over the burning field in silent valediction" (Achebe *Things Fall Apart*, 26).

The men of Umuofia, farmers by occupation, also rely on the luxuriant shed of leaves from the trees in the forests to fertilize the earth, as they serve as manure necessary for good agricultural harvest. Furthermore, the forest also serves as a protection for the spiritual abode of the community deities. The oracle of the Hills and Caves, abode of Agbala, was positioned at the heart of the forest in a cave. When Ekwefi followed Chielo, the priestess of Agbala, who took Ezinma to the Oracle of the Hills and Caves, they walked through a damp footpath, "hedged on either side by branches and damp leaves, as well as outcropped roots" (Achebe *Things Fall Apart*, 82). The leaves from the trees and plants in the forest are used for medicinal purposes. Okonkwo gathers some leaves, roots, and barks of medicinal trees and shrubs in the forest to prepare medicinal concoctions for Ezinma (Achebe *Things Fall Apart*, 68) when she falls sick with *iba*. The women also fetch firewood from the dead and dry trees in the forests.

It is imperative to note that although the element in discourse here is the forest, the majority of the purposes listed here are accessed in a normal forest, not the evil forest as mentioned before now. The evil forest has a special purpose:

> In it were buried all those who died of real evil diseases, like leprosy and smallpox. It was also the dumping ground for the potent fetishes of great medicine men when they died. An 'evil forest' was, alive with sinister forces and powers of darkness. (Achebe *Things Fall Apart*, 119)

In the precolonial era, twins were also thrown into the evil forest to die because it was believed that twin birth was an abomination. Thus, the evil forest, the abode of evil spirits, is not open to free citizens to wander in.

Yam

This is one of the most important crops in the narrative, as well as in Igbo land. Among the Igbo, of which Okonkwo is a part, yam is held in high esteem because it is a masculine crop and known as the king of crops. The cultivation of yam is an exclusive preserve of the men, especially as it involves intensive labor. Also, it is a key determinant of a man's acceptance into the enclave of wealth. As such, a man's yam barn or field says a lot about his wealth and work ethics. Ownership of a large barn, therefore, portrays the man as a wealthy man who is capable of providing for his family. It equally makes such men marry many wives and produce many children who will help in the seasonal farming.

Thus, the resultant wealth empowers them to take titles as respectable men in the clan. Nwakibie, the man in Okonkwo's village who lent him eight hundred seedling of yam, was described as a wealthy man "who had three huge yam barns, nine wives and thirty children" (Achebe *Things Fall Apart*, 15). Odibo (2004) observes that not only is yam held in high esteem because it is a man's crop, "in some part of Igboland like Afikpo and other places, women may plant or harvest any other crop but not yam . . . even the mounds of yam are specially made by men" (43). Owing to the cultural esteem of yam, the Igbos celebrate the yam, hence the New Yam festival, culturally known as *Ikeji*. Good harvest earns the successful farmer titles such as *Ezeji* and *Diji*. The feast of the New Yam festival in Umuofia was, therefore, a festival to celebrate yam and give "thanks to Ani, the Earth goddess and source of all fertility" (Achebe *Things Fall Apart*, 29). The New Yam festival takes place during the harvesting period, whereas the Week of Peace is celebrated before the planting season, to appeal to Ifejioku (or Ahiajoku), the god of yam, Ani, the Earth goddess, and the ancestors to bless their crops that they may produce a bountiful harvest. The point I try to make here is to reestablish the need for ecological consciousness. Yam as a crop is derived from nature, the soil. This crop in *Things Fall Apart* as well as in the real world determines so many things about how some African societies celebrate life and evaluate power. Consequently, a society that fails to understand how crops derivable from the soil (the soil being a very important ecological marker) can articulate the relationship between man and his environment stands the chance of losing the most fundamental aspect of his base—the environment.

Earth (Ani or Ala in some parts of Igbo Land)

Earth or Ani is the spiritual abode of Agbala, the owner of the land. Ani is the mother of good harvest. People make supplications and appease Mother Earth in order to get answers to their prayers. This is why the elders pour libations, throw out pieces of kola nuts, and make sacrifices to

Mother Earth in times of need. The Agbala priest is the mediator between *Ani* and the people; hence, if one offends *Ani* by committing *nso-ani*, the Igbos say that the person *meruru ani*; in other words, he has committed an abomination or taboo (*aru*). A ritual or appeasement presided over by the priest is required to cleanse the Earth. This is called *ikwuala*. It is particularly necessary when someone is believed to have committed an abomination against the Earth, or does what is prohibited in the society. The Earth, therefore, needs to be cleansed and wiped clean of the pollutions and taboos. Such abomination may include incest, stealing, and murder, to mention a few. In Igbo culture, the major requirements used for such cleansing include goat, kola nut, cow, cock, palm wine, or money. The nature of an abomination determines what is required for the appeasement. When a villager commits an abomination, he is compelled to appease the Earth or the repercussion will fall on all the villagers. This is because the Igbos believe that when a finger is soiled by palm oil, it smears or pollutes the other fingers. Moreover, an action seen as an abomination before human beings is also abomination before the gods. Thus, the punishment is acceptable to men, spirits, and the dead ancestors. Okonkwo's exile to his maternal home, and some of the rituals Ezeulu performs at the festival, were all part of a ritual to appease the land for the taboos committed by Okonkwo and Oduche. The above demonstrate that the fictional world of Achebe's narratives are organized around nature and the environment.

Weather/Climate

Like in a normal environment, the climate addresses the nature of the ecological weather. It is therefore dynamic, sometimes changing for good and sometimes being violent and bad. In the novel, when the climate is good, it is breezy, benevolent, and bright. When it is bad, it could be violent, thunderous, rainy, or moody; or harsh and sunny. The climatic condition of the farming season, during which Okonkwo lost his four hundred seedlings of yam, was violent. The narrator establishes that the year had "gone mad" (Achebe *Things Fall Apart*, 19), hence

> rain fell as it had never fallen before. For the days and nights together, it poured down in violent torrents, and washed away the yam heaps. Trees were uprooted and deep gorges appeared everywhere ... the spell of sunshine which always came in the middle of the wet season did not appear. (Achebe *Things Fall Apart*, 19)

That season was therefore remembered as a "tragic year" (Achebe *Things Fall Apart*, 19). At other times: "the rain fell in thin slanting showers through sunshine and quiet breeze. Children no longer stayed indoors but run about singing" (28). During the ominous days, "the world was silent except for shrill cry of insects" as seen on the dark night Chielo took Ezinma to the Oracle's cave (76). Similarly, in the farming season, Okonkwo took his family to his maternal home for refuge after he mistakenly killed Ezeudu's son, and "the climate sang a new song . . . there was claps of thunder" (104).

Most festive days are cheerful. Hence, even the beating of drums at the village square throb "in the air, in the sunshine and even in the trees, and filled the village with excitement" (Achebe *Things Fall Apart*, 35). This implies that the climatic nature of the environment influences, as well as affects, the lives and culture of the people.

Ilo

This is the Igbo name for an open natural clearing in a form of a main road used as playground (Achebe *Things Fall Apart*, 34). It is a village square where the villagers meet for social, political, and religious interactions. Among the Igbo, some people call it *ama* or *mbara*, suggesting it is a clearing for communal meeting. Often, the *ilo* has no physical structure to shelter people, but may have one or two trees under which people take cover or refuge, to shield themselves from the intensity of the sun and torrential downpour or light showers. The feast of the New Yam festival in Umuofia took place at the *ilo* (Achebe *Things Fall Apart*, 34). It is an arena setting; hence, the center is reserved for the performers like dancers or wrestlers to perform in, while the audience watches at a close circle. The *ilo* also serves as a venue for judicial ruling; hence, the egwugwu deliberated on the Uzowulu case (Achebe *Things Fall Apart*, 70) at the *ilo*. The situation of the egwugwu house close to the *ilo* gave the *ilo* a certain sense of power, as it equally stands as a potent spiritual ground for oath taking, ritual cleansing, and other cultural observances.

Environmental Issues in *Arrow of God*

Achebe's *Arrow of God* is set during the colonial era, unlike *Things Fall Apart*, which captures a society in an idyllic state during the incursion of Europe—a phenomenon that sent most rural societies crashing from their vital balance. *Arrow of God*, therefore, captures the travails of a society in transition. The background of the setting highlights certain features bordering on both the traditional occurrence and unfolding new order, which followed the interaction between the people and the colonial masters. As a result, there were fragments of modernity in the social and religious lives of the Umuaro people. For instance, the people of Umuaro and Okperi lived in mud and thatched houses in the rural area, while the colonial masters lived in bungalows, around the Government Hill of Okperi, the Administrative headquarters, which is established at a reserved area.

The presence of the Europeans, who were already residing within the environment, enabled them to control and administer the affairs of the people according to the dictates of the ruling imperialists in Britain, although the deity priests play their religious roles to the people. The residence of the colonial masters within the neighborhood instructed the intervention of the colonial administration on the war between the people of Umuaro and Okperi. In like manner, their supervisory role at the road construction site for Umuaro people enabled Mr. Wright to be present to witness Obika's misbehavior, which led to Mr. Wright flogging Obika when the Otakagu age group to which Obika belonged was assigned the job of working at the road construction site. The novel showed how the white men came and asked for a piece of land to build on, and the community willingly gave them the Evil forest. However, *Arrow of God* shows that the colonial masters were already comfortably settled and had built churches in the neighboring communities as the plot of the narrative develops; hence, they have many converts amongst the rural people.

Umuaro people are not so blind to social realities and development, as some of their young men had left the traditional and rural lifestyle in search of greener pastures under the tutelage of the Europeans. Nwaka's five wives usually dress in mainly anklets and colored velvet, an evidence of apparent commercial interactions between the rural Umuaro people and foreign traders. Several key environmental elements are quite pronounced in *Arrow of God*. I shall now discuss the relevance of some of them.

Yam

The social and physical setting of *Arrow of God* is not too different from that of *Things Fall Apart*, except for the position of the colonial masters in both narratives. Yam holds as much regards in Umuaro as it holds in Umuofia because the yam, like in Igbo culture, is the king food crop of the people;

hence, it is celebrated and seen as a symbol of masculinity and status. In Umuaro, the yam is a religious icon, too. The twelve yams representing the twelve moons in a year must be eaten by the priest before the annual harvest of yam would take place in the community. Out of vindictiveness and stubbornness, Ezeulu refuses to eat the remaining three yams he missed while in the white man's detention. This dramatically resulted in mass suffering by all and sundry in the clan, and the abandonment of Ulu.

Palm Tree

Umuaro village is projected as a rural village dependent on several agricultural products to eke out a living. One of these important products is the palm tree. The palm tree is appreciated for its palm wine, which is vital for social and religious use. It is used as a drink for entertainment in social gatherings, and for pouring libation to the gods and deities. Also through the palm tree the women access tissues and fibers used to make bush palm oil lamp, a common lighter in the rural areas. The night Aniegboka, the medicine man, performed rituals for the newly married Okuata—Obika's wife and the team used a palm oil lamp to find their way in late that night (Achebe *Arrow of God*, 117).

The palm trees also provide the men with smoked raffia, which is used as a deity priest's costume during ritual festivals, such as the festival of the Pumpkin Leaves and the New Yam festivals, just as it was used during masquerade performances (Achebe *Arrow of God*, 70). Also, families in Umuaro rely on the palm tree to produce brooms for sweeping clean their compounds and homes (125). The palm tree, therefore, is an essential environmental element that is necessary for the optimal existence of the people and some of their animals.

New Moon

Although to the outside world the moon remains what it is—the moon—and is naturally created by nature to light the face of the earth at night, to the people of Umuaro, the moon is a symbol of hope, future, and new life. Hence, it is often welcomed with joy and optimism as demonstrated by Achebe: "'Moon,' said Matefi, 'may your face meeting mine bring good fortune'" (*Arrow of God*, 2). The expectation of the new moon makes the people to monitor it for signs to find out if it is a good moon or a bad moon. This is why Ugoye asks her co-wife:

But how is it sitting? I don't like its posture. "Why?" asked Matefi. "I think it sits cowardly like an evil moon." "No," said Matefi, "A bad moon does not leave anyone in doubt. Like the one under which Okuata died. Its legs were up in the air." (Achebe *Arrow of God*, 2)

The new moon is also a religious symbol and determines certain aspects of religious and social life and culture of Umuaro people. Hence, Ezeulu's insistence on the refusal to eat the new yam after the appearance of the new moon dealt harshly on the people, as well as it dealt on Ezeulu's position as the priest of Ulu.

Python

The python may physically be a large snake to some people, but among the people of Umuaro and many other parts of Igbo land, it is sacred and so remains a religious icon. As a consequence of this, it is not killed by human beings but is seen as a deity and thus a superior being. When one kills it, the person is punished by giving it a decent burial like a human being. In *Arrow of God*, the python symbolizes the traditional African god; hence, Oduche's attempt at killing it was like the symbolic religious doctrine of a son rising up against his father, showing the conflict between the old and the new religions in Umuaro.

Ezeulu's rescue of the royal python shows the Ulu priest as living up to his spiritual role, while the weak, meandering slip of the python into the bush suggests that the old gods and religion were gradually losing their ground in their erstwhile domain.

Ulu

This is the head god of Umuaro. It is the most superior of all the deities in Umuaro. It guides and guards the six villages of Umuaro. Through the Ulu priest called Ezeulu, the deity directs, guides, and protects the affairs of the Umuaro people. Incidentally, the superior role of Ulu and its priest did not augur well with the lesser deities and their priests, particularly the Idemili priest. This resulted in some of the challenges and obstacles that amounted to the failure and demise of the Ulu deity in Umuaro.

Water/River (Mmili)

Water is of immense importance to humanity, not just to the Igbos. In Igbo land, however, it possesses spiritual reverence as abode of the gods and the deities. Thus, people go to the river to make rituals and supplications to the gods. In *Arrow of God*, Ezeulu's young children go to the river to fetch water for the family use. Odibo (2004) observes that the Igbo do not live close to the water. According to him, "our forefathers did not believe in having their homes near water, because they regard rivers and stream as the home of gods and spirits" (Odibo 17). Most rivers have priests and priestesses because they are believed to be demigods. In *Arrow of God*, the priest of Idemili (meaning Pillar of Water) is a priest attached to Idemili, a water god that was seen as a superior god. At death, priests are beheaded, and their heads are hung in the shrine to show their importance. Incidentally, the repositioning of the Ulu into a god of the clan placed Idemili in a subordinate position compared to Ulu. This caused a lot of bickering among the Idemili faithful.

Climate/Weather

These are parts of the universal natural resources or elements within which human beings and wildlife revolve in. Located in the tropics, Umuaro is blessed with forest vegetation, although the people are conversant with that. Incidentally, to the European colonists, the tropical hot weather was not palatable. As the narrator states:

> Captain Winterbottom stood at the veranda of his bungalow on Government Hill to watch the riot of the year's first rain. For the past month or two the heat had been building up to an unbearable pitch. . . . (Achebe *Arrow of God*, 29)

The weather provided temporary relief at sundown when a cool wind blew. The discomfort had cost the stranger, Captain Winterbottom, sleep since the December dry and cool harmattan ceased. As a result, this affected his physical outlook. He developed white gums, and imprisoned himself in a mosquito net all night just to chase out the suckers, thus preventing himself from enjoying fresh air. This made him sweat and stay awake most nights.

The aftermath of the first rainy day did not help matters. It worsened the atmosphere and humidity of the air. As the narrator states:

> Throughout the day, the sun had breathed fire as usual and the world had lain prostrate with shock. The birds which sang in the morning were

silenced. The air stood in one spot, vibrating with the heat; the trees hung limp. (Achebe *Arrow of God*, 30)

As the air comes into the atmosphere in anticipation of another rain, the atmosphere changes:

> A great wind arose and the sky darkened. Dust and flying leaves filled the air. Palm trees and coconuts swayed from their waist; their tops gave them the looks of giants fleeing against the winds.... (Achebe *Arrow of God*, 30)

Winterbottom, as a foreigner, does not find the weather enjoyable given that it scatters the papers and photograph in his room. Yet, as the sharp and dry barks of thunder broke into the tumult, blowing dust into his eyes, he cannot help but envy the poor rural children running around naked and singing to the coming rain. The rain is heralded by "restless black cloud and long streaks of lighting" (Achebe *Arrow of God*,) and after a short while, the rain fell like large pebbles. Ironically, regardless of Captain Winterbottom's discomforting experience and feelings after the rain, the trees feel the impact differently. They "were washed green and their leaves fluttered happily" (Achebe *Arrow of God*,). This is a clear testimony of the vast divergent appreciation of the environment or the climatic weather among two classes of human beings (the rural people of Umuaro and the Europeans) on one side, and plants on the other.

Dogs

In most homes in the rural Umuaro village, the dog is one of the most helpful of domestic animals. It performs security functions, especially as a watch animal that alerts the family of the approach of visitors as well as unwanted guests. At nights, they become watchdogs and so may harm intruders or strangers coming into the family compound. Incidentally, unlike other domestic animals that feed on plants, dogs rely on human excrement for survival, and so help to rid the environment of waste which stands to pollute it. The narrator in *Arrow of God* gives a graphic account of Nwanku's approach to Amoge's (Edogo's wife) baby's feces in the novel:

> Her crying child sits on the angle of her two feet which she had brought together to touch at the heels. After a while she lifted her feet and child together on to another spot leaving behind on the floor a round patch

of watery, green excrement. ... Then, she called: Nwanku! Nwanku! Nwanku! A wiry, black dog rushed in from outside and made straight for the excrement which disappeared with four, or five noisy flicks of its tongue.... (Achebe *Arrow of God*, 90)

Goats/Cocks

These are domestic animals used in assessing the wealth of the owner, for providing meat for the family, for ritual purposes, and for being given away as gifts to friends and others. Obika presented his mother-in-law with a goat just to show appreciation that she gave him a reserved woman as wife. The cock has a special use, as it remains the traditional timekeeper for the rural people.

Reading Achebe's Deployment of Nature and Environment in his Rural Novels

The social and physical settings of the two literary works were exposed in the narrative discourse of the nineteenth-century villages. The social setting provided a window for Achebe's readers to imagine and picturize the changes encountered by people of Igbo culture and society, before and during the colonial administration. For instance, they clearly distinguished between the traditional judicial system in Igbo land and the judicial system presided over by the European imperialist. Whereas the traditional judicial system was jointly assessed and publicly settled without sentiments, the European system smirks of favoritism, corruption, and partiality. This is very obvious in chapter ten of *Things Fall Apart*. There, the nine masked egwugwu, representing the nine villages in Umuofia, presided over the case between Uzowulu, his wife, and in-laws. As Orabueze notes, Achebe highlights the wisdom and sense of natural justice of the traditional or precolonial judges in dispute resolution, through the words of the Evil Forest—the leader of the egwugwu: "We have heard from both sides of the case," said the Evil Forest. "Our duty is not to blame this man or to praise that, but to settle the dispute" (Achebe *Things Fall Apart*, 74). This is quite different from the British system where one person is accused and fined for an alleged offence. The physical setting shows that Umuofia and Umuaro have solidly elaborate religious system based on their natural environment. This is because the villages are typically African in nature, and as Obiechina observes, in Africa, "nature is not 'other' as in the industrialized and urbanized West, but is apprehended by the traditional West African as an integral part of his world order" (42). We therefore see two rural communities that are surrounded by dense, dark woods and forests, which are feared and respected as a chief God—Evil Forest. Even the Earth (*ani*) upon which the people walk, work, and live is worshipped as a god on its own. The yam, cassava, palm tree, medicinal leaves, and so forth are all produce of the Earth; hence, as farmers, the people rely specifically on them to survive. While the people require such reverence to sustain their religious faith and balance, the wildlife, being the flora or the fauna, need such reverence to guarantee their survival. Hence, the people of Umuofia and Umuaro are equally as dependent on nature and environment as much as the nature and environment depend on the people to thrive. Ewah puts this more succinctly when he remarks that "man and nature depend on each other for ecological balance and optimum survival" (293).

However, the traditional Igbo concept of nature reflects the justification of material things based on the purpose it serves. This informs the idea of trees and animals being regarded not based on their beauty, but on their usefulness and worth. As Umezuruike observes, *Ndigbo* do not regard the attractiveness of the tree, for instance, if the tree does not provide shelter or food for animals or human beings. He insists that:

> the society is primarily concerned with formulation and reformulation of the basis of life in regard to food, shelter, health, security and procreation, and thus emphasizes the empirical, practical, and intellectual activities that can satisfy its needs. (Umezuruike 23)

Ndigbo dismiss any person, plant, or animal without any serious worth in these words: *O nweghi isi*, meaning "he/it is useless"; and *O nweghi ihe o di mma ya*, meaning "he/it is good for nothing." Thus, the things that are found worthy and useful must be appreciated, sustained, and preserved. Africans therefore appreciate these gifts of nature from the Earth goddess and the other deities. This informs why people are compelled to please, appease, and appeal to the Earth goddess for good weather/climatic conditions, productivity, and good fortune in order to ensure bountiful harvest and wealth. Achebe portrays some flora and fauna in his works as not just some piece of nature, but ones with deep spiritual and awesome respect among the people. One may therefore state that, being also an Igbo man with a good cultural orientation and imagination, Achebe seems to be "acutely aware how closely human life is integrated with physical nature" (Obiechina, 43), just like his people.

Given that the rural environment involving man, forest, and wildlife is shown as a world or social system with unified sets of elements that remain unapologetically interdependent, it becomes imperative that any act that may be inimical to human survival is punished, since it is believed that man's abusive activities may jeopardize wildlife and other elements, and thus, adversely affect man, nature, and environment. This justifies why one sees Okonkwo beating his second wife for cutting some leaves off a banana stalk in *Things Fall Apart* (30). Similarly, in *Arrow of God*, we also see Ezeulu with a matchete, waiting for Oduche's return, just to punish Oduche for attempting to harm the sacred and royal python. Such misadventures stand as taboo that must be appeased because the people share Al Gedicks' belief that human actions that desecrate sacred lands or destroy an entire ecosystem upset the delicate balance in the universe, which otherwise should be maintained by reverence toward the natural world.

Nature as environment, which Achebe explores, in a way reflects the environment that Chris Nwamuo captures in his play *The Wisdom of the King*. As Ekong (2010) observes, the play captures the religious and superstitious belief system of the Africans, particularly of the Igbo extraction, highlights the democratic and consultative style of governance among the people, and projects reasons why the people adopt such a system in resolving social or personal problems. With a plethora of sacred flora and fauna, and cultural norms and values, the African society is projected as a very complex one, with its people's way cohesive enough not to require the intrusion of the colonial imperialists who are acclaimed to have brought civilization, new religion, and modernism to Africans. This informs why Obierika, in his ferocious outburst to the District Commissioner at the concluding part of *Things Fall Apart*, laments Okonkwo's demise in these words: "That man was one of the greatest men in Umuofia. You drove him to kill himself; and now he will be buried like a dog . . ." (Achebe *Things Fall Apart*, 165). In this era of eco-criticism, one begins to reflect on Achebe's conclusion to appraise his work, to ascertain his stand on the import of nature and environment in his imaginative composition.

One cannot help but submit that Achebe may have done so much to promote the African nature and environment in his works; hence, in a way contributing to Brauch's concept of *ecological literacy*. This writer believes he, however, failed to indulge in "conscious" ecological advocacy. The typical postcolonial and precolonial life of the normal and traditional Igbo man revolves around nature and environment, or the ecosystem. This implies that any committed writer who embarks on a sincere task of capturing the reality of the Igbo man's life and traditional background may truly be unconsciously contributing to ecological literacy. Eco-advocacy is an elaborate part of ecological literacy that articulates the writer's conscious and conscientious efforts to illustrate and embark on a campaign that borders on the importance of ecology to our environment. Below is a good example of ecological advocacy from Movement Two of Chris Nwamuo's play *The Wisdom of the King*:

> COUNCILLOR: *(Still holding the man firmly)*. My lord. The villagers caught this idiot burning some bushes near Amata river. He had already cut down a palm tree which had blocked the road. They were angry and wanted to kill him but I intervened. When I asked him who gave him permission to do all that, he lied. *(Pause)*. He said it was you. *(The Chiefs look at one another)*. I know you couldn't have given him such orders. So, I gave him a serious beating and dragged him to your presence.
>
> KING: *(Completely weakened)*. Well done, faithful one. *(Pause)*. Good. *(Silence)*. Why do you think I could not have sent him?
>
> COUNCILLOR: *(Cautiously)*. Because as a wise king, you know that bushes and natural environment provide us with most of what we need for survival. The environment is like a mother to us. To destroy the bushes and forests, is to threaten our existence. *(Pause)*. You could not have sent him.
>
> KING: What do you mean threaten our existence, you smart fool?
>
> COUNCILLOR: *(Still holding his captive)*. That palm tree he cut down gives us oil, kernel, fibre and palm fronds. Its trunk is used for building culverts.
>
> KING: *(Looking in a different direction)*. Yes!
>
> COUNCILLOR: We sell most of the things we get from the forests to buy our other needs.
>
> KING: Things like?
>
> COUNCILLOR: Things like plantain, banana, cocoa, pear, coconut, and of course wild animals.
>
> KING: Yes! *(Silence)*. Go on, learned councillor.

COUNCILLOR: *(Trembling and cautious)*. We use trees to beautify our roads, homes, and important places. Certain trees around our homes help to drive away evil spirits.

KING: *(Slowly)*. Yes!

COUNCILLOR: My lord, the list is endless. Bush burning pollutes the air we breathe and so constitute a health hazard.

KING: *(Turning to him)* So?

COUNCILLOR: We should not destroy our environment or burn bushes. (22-23)

After this scene, at Movement Three in the play, the King made the following submission to his people:

KING: From today, no citizen shall cut down a tree, kill an animal, burn bushes or destroy wild life in our environment without our permission. *(Pause)* the punishment for deforestation of our natural environment will be seizure of farmlands from any offender. *(Pause)*. We must be grateful to nature for providing us all we need for existence.... (Nwamuo 35)

There is a *conscious* effort by the author of the above play to campaign for the sustenance of the ecosystem. Colonial intervention in African states actually ushered in deforestation and other ecological catastrophes; Achebe appears to be a little silent on that, perhaps because he did not see it as a serious problem. For example, in some parts of Southern Nigeria, it is a taboo to commit suicide. When a person commits suicide on a tree, it is believed that the tree has been defiled; hence, it is cut down. If Achebe was alert on the need to consciously create awareness on ecological literacy, Okonkwo's suicide on a tree would have provided an opportunity for him to oppose the annihilation of a tree because someone committed suicide on it.

Conclusion

Today, many young Nigerian writers are all toeing Achebe's path in representing the now dimming image of the pre- and postcolonial Igbo traditional environment. *Things Fall Apart* will remain a classic of all times: it captures the Igbo environment that most of our generation can only identify, a childhood imagination, particularly from the bushy and dark forests that are presently absent in most rural villages today to the fearsome masquerades and masquerade displays at the village squares. No single piece of African literature has captured as many environmental elements and nature as Achebe's *Things Fall Apart* and *Arrow of God*. Based on this assertion, such criticisms as those above may be referred to as the proverbial case of telling a pretty girl to go and take her bath just for the sake of telling her something, as it will not change the obvious. Also, the classics have long been concluded decades ago; hence, Achebe is not expected to start rewriting works he concluded more than half a century ago. However, the global image of Achebe at this juncture calls for his conscientious interest on issues bordering on the welfare and future of humanity, irrespective of race, class, and so forth.

Achebe is an icon that may be referred to as a goldfish in the African literary pond. He has no hiding place. Having acquired a lot of exposure over time on the politics of writing, one expects him to lead the way in identifying viable aspects of literary discourse that need attention in the under-studying of our traditional life and culture. This will help encourage, motivate, and influence younger writers into campaigning for such cause. It is therefore imperative that as critics and scholars, who are watchdogs in the literary circle, we need to highlight some of these bleak areas in order to draw the attention of our creative talents on the need to channel interests in such areas.

Achebe, therefore, owes his people—the Igbo—another classic that will specifically focus on not just ecological advocacy, but on other intricate human right issues faced by the people. That he is a world-acclaimed literary colossus is not in contention. As the Igbo traditional proverb has it, *nku no na mba na eghere mba nri*, which means that the firewood in a community cooks for the community. He has proven himself a pace-setter; therefore, there is every need for him to show the way, so that the teeming younger and upcoming Nigerian writers will follow.

Works Cited

Achebe, Chinua. *Things Fall Apart*. London: Heinemann, 2008. Print.

———. *Arrow of God*. London: Heinemann, 1986. Print.

Branch, Michael, Rochelle Johnson, Daniel Patterson, and Scott Slovic. *Reading the Earth: New Directions in the Study of Literature and the Environment*. Moscow: U of Idaho P, 1998. Print.

Echeruo, M.J.C. "A Matter of Identity." (Ahiajoku Lecture Series) Owerri, 1979. Print.

Ekong, Monique. "Environmental Protection and Chris Nwamuo's The Wisdom of the King." *The Dramaturgy of Liberation and Survival: Festschrift Essays on Chris Nwamuo's Scholarship*. Ed. Andrew H. Esekong and Babson Ajibade. Calabar: U of Calabar P, 2010. 295–310. Print.

Ewah, James O. "Ecodrama and Conservation Philosophy: A Review of Nwamuo's The Wisdom of the King." *The Dramaturgy of Liberation and Survival: Festschrift on Chris Nwamuo's Scholarship*. Ed. Andrew H. Esekong and Babson. U of Calabar P, 2010. 290–295. Print.

Gedicks, Al. *Resource Rebels: Native Challenges to Mining and Oil Corporation*. Cambridge: South End Press, 2001. Print.

Obiechina, Emmanuel. *Culture, Tradition and Society in the West African Novels*. Cambridge: Cambridge UP, 1975. Print.

Odibo, Uche C. *The Igbo World Yesterday, Today and Tomorrow*. Lagos: Network Design, 2004. Print.

Ojaide, Tanure. "Deploying African Literature Towards the Environment and Human Right." MS.

Orabueze, F.O. "Achebe's Image of Colonialism in His Literary Works: The Triumph of Materialism in Igboland." *Journal of Igbo Studies* 1 (2006). Print.

Umezuruike, G,M. "Amamihe na Ako-na-Uche: The Hub of Igbo Cultural Renaissance in the Scientific Age." (Ahiajoku Lecture Series) Owerri, 1992.

6

Degraded Environment and Destabilized Women in Kaine Agary's *Yellow-Yellow*

Sunny Awhefeada, Delta State University, Abraka

The outburst of ecologically conscious writing in Nigeria since the 1990s is by no means fortuitous. The phenomena can be described as a programmed response to the danger posed by the large-scale ecological disaster occasioned by oil exploration and industrialization. This new literary gusto, according to Byron Caminero-Santangelo,

> points not only to the ways that Africans have mobilized against environmental degradation, but also to the grave environmental problems faced by Africa which have become, especially in conjunction with social problems, a significant threat to its present and future well-being. (698)

Though, the point must be made that Nigerian writing, which thematizes the environment, predates the 1990s. J.P. Clark's "Streamside Exchange," Gabriel Okara's "Piano and Drums," and Wole Soyinka's "Idanre," among others, make profound philosophical and metaphysical statements regarding their milieu. These works fit into what Kwaku Asante-Darko describes as "embody[ing] a pedagogy of ecological awareness" (6). However, it is in Niyi Osundare's *The Eye of the Earth* and Tanure Ojaide's *Labyrinths of the Delta*, both published in 1986, that one encounters a programmed and well articulated apprehension of the danger to which the environment is subjected. While Osundare bemoans the destruction of the pristine forest due to capitalist encroachment, Ojaide laments the devastation of his Niger Delta ecology by oil exploration. Both works, though considered as eco-lit, respond to different vistas of environmental degradation. Osundare views this phenomenon from the prism of deforestation and other eco-hostile activities of man, while Ojaide apprehends it from the trepidation of being a witness to a frazzled environment arising from the dire consequences of oil exploration. What can be said of Osundare's and Ojaide's nature writing is articulated in William Slaymaker's view as follows:

> Black African critics and writers have traditionally embraced nature writing, land issues and landscape themes that are pertinent to national and local cultural claims and that also function as pastoral reminiscences or even projections of a golden age when many of the environmental evils resulting from colonialism and the exploitation of indigenous resources have been remediated. (684)

These two poets who have remained Nigeria's most significant poets since the 1980s can be regarded as pathfinders for the genre of eco-conscious literature that is fast evolving in Nigeria, especially among writers from the country's Niger Delta region. This is so because as has been noted again by Slaymaker, "Ecocriticism and the object of its study—environmental literature—are more recent developments in the course of literary history" (129).

The predominance or concentration of eco-lit in the Niger Delta region derives from the reality that the region remains one of the most ecologically devastated in the world. The region's experience of the oil boom easily translated into doom as the oil multinationals as well as the nation's successive governments, whether military or civilian, connive to put the region's ecology under severe and inhuman pressure. While the oil multinationals indulge in environmentally unfriendly practices, the government looks the other way, provides security for them, and brutally represses any dissenting groups affected by the horrendous deeds of the foreign oil firms. Therefore, while the government remains rich alongside its foreign collaborators (the oil firms), the indigenes of the oil-producing Niger Delta continue to recede into the abyss of impoverishment.

Over the years, oil exploration and exploitation in the Niger Delta have assumed different frightening representations. It has become the harbinger of poverty, disease, death, pollution, extinction of biodiversity, loss of means of livelihood, agitation, restiveness, militancy, criminality, and varying degrees of ecocide pointing in the direction of Armageddon. The Nigerian writer Tanure Ojaide puts it quite succinctly, "[B]ut the major problem had to do with the discovery of oil in the Delta. The oil boom became doom for the inhabitants of the region" (*Poetic Imagination*, 122). This reality, frightening as it is, is the lived condition in the region today. It has generated different responses in the form of intellectual engagement and civil disobedience (as represented by Ken Saro-Wiwa, the late writer and environmental rights activist), armed struggle against the Nigerian nation by different militant groups, and, quite significantly, literary works—be they poetry, prose or drama. G.G. Darah avers that "[T]he contradiction and fury generated by the injustice perpetuated by the Nigerian ruling class are what animates the literary and artistic output of the Niger Delta . . ." (114).

There is at the moment a haul of literature dealing with the Niger Delta environment; its people, flora and fauna, as well as the rivers. The poet and critic Joe Ushie sums up this trend quite memorably when he says "[T]he Niger Delta literary landscape has continued to flourish even as its physical environment is wilting" (22–33). The multiplicity of the literary works that delineate the region's gory experience is a reflection of not only just how traumatic it is, but also the sense of immediacy and compelling urgency needed to remedy the situation. It is a realization of this that informs why Onokome Okome asserts that "tales coming out of the Niger Delta are not evidence of dead dreams. Rather, they are examples of dreams which the suffering people are trying to make into reality" (15). What is more, the titles of these works are as telling as they are evocative of the danger confronting the region. The title of Nnimmo Bassey's collection is a shocking testament: *We Thought it Was Oil But it Was Blood.* Ibiwari Ikiriko bemoans *The Oily Tears of the Delta*; Ebi Yeibo paints a sad picture of *The Forbidden Tongue.* Ogaga Ifowodo tells of the havoc wrought by *The Oil Lamp,* while Ahmed Yerima felt an imperative to stage the Niger Delta drama on *Hard Ground.*

The relevance of works dealing with the Niger Delta predicament in contemporary reckoning has also earned them some of the nation's biggest literary prizes. Yerima's *Hard Ground* and Kaine Agary's *Yellow-Yellow,* drama and prose, respectively, in quick succession won the LNG prize for Nigerian literature. Both works, which engage the disintegrating fabric of the Niger Delta, tackle the grim reality of the region from various perspectives that are quite refreshing. Their publication also coincided with the unprecedented surge in militant activities in the region, which threatened the nation's economic base. The hostilities escalating in the Niger Delta also caught world attention and have since become a buzzing preoccupation.

This chapter is a reading of Kaine Agary's *Yellow-Yellow,* probably the first novel written by a female about the Niger Delta situation. In this remarkable debut novel, Agary brings a significantly fresh perspective that has been hitherto ignored to the front burner. Agary reframes the Niger

Delta story into a metaphoric novel that can be read along two narrative leads. First, the region in all its pristine endowment and Edenic bliss was devastated and disrupted by the exploitation and exploration of oil by foreigners aided by local conquistadors. The second narrative thread depicts the violation of women in the region by foreign oil workers, and also by the indigenous bourgeoisie. What comes to the fore is the violation and debasement of both land and woman. Thus, while the land writhes in despoliation, the violation of women, which often results in unwanted pregnancy, amputates their ambitions, aborts their dreams, and confines them to the abyss of impoverishment. This synopsis is amply adumbrated in the novel's cover, which depicts the wasteland that the Niger Delta's natural landscape has become. Alongside the charred trees are oil rigs, which cause the degradation of the land, while below is a woman (Yellow-Yellow) lying supine owing to the devastation.

It is important to note that before *Yellow-Yellow*, no other work has so depicted the unsavory condition of women in the Niger Delta. Agary's attempt corroborates Juliana Makuchi Nfah-Abbenyi's opinion that:

> [T]hese writers show that African women's roles ... which are often linked to the land have seen drastic changes following the movement from colonialism, through independence, to the post colonial era that have (re)shaped African societies, histories and culture. They contend that women's lives have been most afflicted by these local and global shifts. (705)

The novel's plot mutates between environmental violation and women ruination. It is instructive to engage the novel's doleful, but remarkable opening as narrated by Zilayefa, the narrator cum protagonist:

> During my second to last year in secondary school, one of the crude oil pipes that ran through my village broke and spilled oil over several hectares of land, my mother's farm included. I was at home that day when she returned shortly after leaving for the farm. When she got to the house, she knocked on the door and said very coolly, "Zilayefa, bring me my bathing soap and sponge." As I was wondering why she needed them, I saw that her legs were stained black. "What happened?" I asked "And bring my towel too," she said ignoring my questions. "What happened?" There was more urgency in my voice as I touched her and looked over every part of her body. My heart was pounding against my chest as I tried to imagine what could have happened that left her void of words. (Agary 3)

The opening montage is betokening of the novel's twin preoccupation: the environment and women. Inherent in this inauspicious beginning is the hazard that the burst crude oil pipe poses to the environment, the loss of farmland, which also meant the loss of the means of livelihood for the villagers, especially for women like Zilayefa's mother. The gravitas of this ruinous occurrence can be located in the mother's dumbfounded shock, which robbed her of words. The new condition of dispossession and imminent impoverishment arising from the loss of farmland to the oil spill robs her of the agency of speech, as the narrator puts it, "void of words" (Agary 3). Thus, the silencing, marginalization, and suffering of women in *Yellow-Yellow* derive from the degradation of the environment.

The magnitude of the unfolding event is given grim representation in the narrative slant below:

> It was the first time I saw what crude oil looked like. I watched as the thick liquid spread out, covering more land and drowning small animals in its path . . . there was so much oil, and we could do nothing with it. . . . And so it was that, in a single day, my mother lost her main source of sustenance. However, I think she had lost that land a long time ago, because each season yielded less than the season before. Not unlike the way she and others in the village had gradually lost, year after year, the creatures of the river to oil spills, acid rains; gas flares, and who knows what else. . . . (Agary 9)

The pervasiveness of the destruction wrought by the oil spill is of ecocidal proportion. The doomsday scenario affects the entire village, thus leading to an environmental holocaust. The oil ought to have been a mascot of boom, but it has become an omen of doom. The loss of the "main source of sustenance" (Agary 9) should be taken to mean the starkest reality of deprivation. And, it inheres on all in the village. The narrator also hints at the gradual corrosion and attenuation of the land over the years, which reduce farm yields annually as the land loses its fertility due to oil exploration. It is not the land alone that is under eco-siege, the rivers are also polluted and their creatures are lost "to oil spill, acid rain, gas flares . . ." (Agary 9). The magnitude of the consequences of these eco-unfriendly practices constitutes a profound rupture in the lives of indigenes of the Niger Delta. That the narrator opens her story with the gory devastation is a pointer to the level of ecocatastrophe the novel limns on its canvas.

Having intimated the reader with the destabilization of the environment in the opening chapter, the narrator recounts the genesis of her mother's predicament, the circumstances of her degradation, in the second chapter. Again, quite doleful, the narrator observes:

> "Yellow-Yellow." That is what most people in my village, called me because of my complexion, the product of a Greek father and an Ijaw mother. My father was a sailor. . . . After months at sea, he was just happy to see a woman and would have told her anything to have her company. The woman he chose was my mother, a young and naïve eighteen years old who had just moved to Port Harcourt from her little village with visions of instant prosperity. . . . For the few weeks that he was in Port Harcourt, she was in heaven. She believed that she had found, her life partner. . . . Instead, he left Port Harcourt without saying good-bye. She went to the port to look for him one day, as had become her habit, and was told that his ship had left. There was no message; he was just gone, leaving behind his planted seed in my mother's *belle*. (Agary 7)

Encapsulated in the foregoing is the circumstance of the birth of the narrator called "Yellow-Yellow" because of her mixed parentage. Her mulatto status represents the hybridity resulting from a brief love tango between a Greek sailor and an Ijaw girl. The love affair, ephemerally euphoric, soon becomes the disruptive intrusion in the narrator's mother's life. The Sailor gets her pregnant and abandons her abruptly without notice. Thus, the mother, then a naïve teenager, had her dreams, aspirations, and hopes shattered. This new reality hobbles her ambition and casts a pall on her future.

Encoded in the quoted excerpt is the narrator's deliberate, but covert, attempt to weave the story of the environment and her mother's into one inseparable predicament. The oil exploration, which ravaged the environment, is largely a European invented affliction, just as the Greek sailor whose act put paid to her mother's aspirations by impregnating her. Hence, intertwined in the story is the deliberate undoing of the environment and the woman by unscrupulous foreign interests. This is consistent with the fate of Africa whose resources continue to be enticement to Europe who visits destruction on the continent.

The narrator's mother's predicament has a double edge. Apart from sounding the death knell of her socioeconomic empowerment, her pregnancy out of wedlock is a violation of cultural mores. However, being a strong woman she does not give up, but reconfigures her life by investing hope in her daughter Zilayefa, who recounts:

> Disillusioned, my mother went back to her village to face the shame of being an unwed mother with nothing but dreams about my future. She would make sure that I accomplished what she had not. She had inherited a small piece of land from her family, which she farmed, and sometimes she would go fishing. With the proceeds, she was able to feed us and pay my school fees . . . to make sure I got an education. (Agary 8)

The story's seeming redeeming glimpse is the accent on education for Zilayefa. Her mother sees her education as a countermeasure against the vagaries of oil exploration and male exploitation. In order to realize the new lease that Zilayefa represents, the mother takes to hard work. The land becomes the farm from which she ekes out a living with her daughter, in the same way the river provides her avenues for fishing. Through her obsession with hard work, she is able to pay Zilayefa's school fees "to make sure I got an education" (Agary 8).

The reader easily sympathizes with the narrator's mother's choice, her sense of purpose, and the equanimity with which she handles the situation. She did not bemoan her condition nor resign to fate, but she determinedly rethinks her situation and resolves to break away from it through hard work. This is perhaps a lesson in positive resolution—quite aggressive, but harmless, which oppressed and dispossessed women can imbibe as they seek liberation. Zilayefa's mother is bogged by the distortion of her life's spring, which has pinned her down to impoverishment, but she did not degenerate into disillusionment or self-pity as she bravely confronts the situation, and reinvests hopes and aspiration in her daughter. The narrator once more says:

> My mother used to tell me that I would do better than her, that, as long as I was educated, I would be able to take care of myself I did not question her. She said it with such conviction and made so many sacrifices to make sure that I went to school that I believed it to be true. It was almost as though she was obsessed, consumed by the idea that my education would save me from what I had yet to understand and what she could not explain to me. Perchance in saving me, she hoped to save herself. (Agary 9)

Mother and daughter thus become collaborating partners in the quest for redemptive independence. While the mother toils in order to achieve her vision of her daughter, the latter becomes the agent of their eventual socioeconomic emancipation. Embedded in this quest is an ennobling emphasis on independence—"able to take care of myself" (Agary 10)—not a grooming of the daughter for a man under whose authority she would cringe. In fact, throughout the novel is a negation of patriarchal presence. The predominance of enterprising and aspiring female characters in the novel bespeaks the novelist's deliberate showcasing of a world of women without men. The few male characters in the novel are treated as ciphers of male retardation.

Zilayefa's mother's courage and determination, which yield her hopeful stance, are uncommon. This is so because the social milieu as much as the environment has been assailed to the point of disorientation. The rupture occasioned by dehumanizing capitalism and monstrous industrialism finds a correlate in the total disintegration of the society, which the people did not envisage. The catastrophe which torpedoed the existence of the villagers is oil-induced. Zilayefa recalls:

> My ears still rang from maternal wails piercing the foggy days when mothers mourned a child lost to sickness or to the deceptively calm waters that lay hungry below the still latrines, waiting to swallow the children whose unsteady feet betrayed them before they had learnt to swim. How many move times could I bear the pain like a hundred razor blades slashing my private parts because the river water that washed it was the same water that received the waste, rejected by my body in its attempt to cleanse itself? The water that flowed with streaks of blue, purple and red, as drops of oil escaped from the pipelines that moved the wealth from beneath my land and into the pockets of the select few who ruled Nigeria was the same water I drank. (Agary 39)

What it entails is a cul-de-sac in every ramification of the villagers' fractured existence. Allied to the degradation of the environment are health hazards with untold harmful effects. Sickness, death, and associated human discomfitures are the order of the day. The vivid narrative slant of the story opens the reader's eyes to the squalor, extent of river pollution, and how wretched the villagers' lives are. Ironically, what causes the villagers' abject poverty is a source of wealth for the ruling class who continue to pillage the nation's resources.

Is it then possible for Zilayefa to realize her mother's lofty dreams and ambitious schemes for her while held down in the untoward ambience which the village represents? Zilayefa considers this question and also answers it as follows:

> I was open to all sorts of things. The only option I was unwilling to consider, that tormented my quiet moments the most, was to remain in my village. (Agary 39)

Thus, not wanting to suffer the same undesirable fate as women debased and humiliated by the assailing force they do not understand in the prohibitive recesses of the village, Zilayefa considers migration as the only viable option for her socioeconomic emancipation. Zilayefa's planned flight from the village is the only antidote against the fate suffered by her mother, and many other young girls driven by poverty into the arms of men who get them pregnant; an act which furthers rather than alleviates their predicament.

After completing her secondary school education, Zilayefa begins to envision the city of Port Harcourt as the *eldorado*. Her mother expresses resentment, initially thinking of her own fate and misadventure in Port Harcourt. But when she eventually gives in, Zilayefa goes to Port Harcourt where she joins two independent women, Sisi and Lolo, and then a sorority begins. A new world of learning, a transition from innocence to experience, begins for Zilayefa. Thus, the novel enters the domain of the bildungsroman. Zilayefa's escape from the web of socioeconomic inhibition is anticipated in the anxiety she records:

> ... when the day finally came, the reality of being on my own sat heavily on my chest ... I knew my life had changed. I was seventeen years old, and even though I had no idea what kind of life lay ahead of me, the feeling that things were not going to be the same again made my ears red and my nose tingle as tears glazed my eyes. (Agary 45)

What the narrator encounters and experiences in the city as expected is radically different from what life in the village offers. Salutary as her flight from the village to the city might be, her new experience is one of anxiety and disruption.

Overwhelmed by the glitz and glamour that the city of Port Harcourt offers, Zilayefa almost forgets her purpose of leaving the village and her mother's dreams for her. However, it is instructive to note that the older Sisi and younger Lolo represent the guardian angels Zilayefa needs to accomplish her ultimate mission in the city, which is to obtain University education. Nevertheless, the city holds temptations and distractions for a beautiful girl like Zilayefa. In a moment of clear-headedness when the narrator receives a letter from her mother she slips into introspection and reconnects with her mother psychologically. Her thought of the mother runs thence:

> I felt guilty; things were going so well for me that I had almost forgotten her face. I had been in Port Harcourt for almost two months when my mother's letter arrived; until then, I had not experienced the crushing loneliness I had felt the day I first arrived. My new life in Port Harcourt was progressing with more success than my fantasies had pictured. When I read my mother's letter, however, I remembered her voice, I pictured her sitting on a low kitchen stool, talking to me. (Agary 79)

Her mother's letter is all she needs to readjust her and get aligned with her mother's objective in Port Harcourt. Zilayefa's city sojourn seems like a roller coaster, but then when viewed in the collective sense of the experience of women in the environmentally destabilized rural settings of the Niger Delta, her luck would fizzle into nothingness.

The collective socioeconomic bondage of Niger Delta women continues to loom large in Zilayefa's reckoning. Her mother remains the prime victim. There are also other women with various forms of inhibiting experiences, deriving from the nexus of oil and malfunctioning government. Zilayefa at various intervals in the narrative gives hints of these experiences. They range from teenage pregnancy, unemployment, prostitution, crime, and other social ills ravaging the region. In all of these, the representation of women is that of unfortunate victims caught in the matrix of what they hardly understand. On the other hand, those assailing the humanity of women range from the oil firms, the national government, and then men, both foreign and indigenous. The social degradation is captured in the narrator's words:

> When I got to Port Harcourt, most of the young girls who were looking to escape their poverty were looking to white men to rescue them. Every night, girls trooped into the hotel lobby, looking for a chance to snatch up a white man. Hundred of girls left their villages to go to places like Warri or Bonny, to get their chance with a whitey. (Agary 186)

The irony of the foregoing inheres in the fact that the white men whom the vulnerable girls see as redemptive figures, represent the agents of their socioeconomic ordeal, the oil multinationals. However, poor education, ignorance, and more painfully, poverty, drive them to the expatriate oil workers who also exploit them.

More often than not, the dalliance results in unwanted pregnancies. Hence, in the region, as portrayed in the novel, are numerous children that are born out of wedlock. Some of these children, like the narrator, do not know their paternity. Zilayefa tells of this tendency thus:

> May be then I could understand better or with less anger why there were more and more of my kind—"African-profits," "born-troways," "ashawo-pickins," "father-unknowns," running around the slums of Port Harcourt. Maybe then I would not hide from the facts of my birth that my yellow skin and curly hair put on display. (Agary 171)

The words in quotation marks are derogatory terms used in describing children begotten from conjugal relationship out of wedlock. The narrator admits of her being one of such.

Also arising from the crisis of oil exploration is a series of ethnic and communal conflicts. A great deal of these conflicts, often bloody, are caused by insincerity of the oil companies, greed of community leaders, government's insensitivity, and a poor sharing formula of funds accruing to the communities. There are also instances where disputes arise over land ownership. The narrator says:

> Communities were fighting over who legitimately owned what land. . . .
> Due largely to the politics involved in the distribution of funds by the federal government and the oil companies in the Niger Delta, all parties believed wrongly or rightly, that whosoever, owned the land controlled . . . whatever funds it received. (Agary 109)

The foregoing opens another vista in the environmentally scorched region. The problems of inter-ethnic and inter-communal or even intra-communal hostilities arising from manipulations by government or oil companies abound in the region. In recent times, the act has snowballed into criminality such as militancy and kidnapping. The narrator says the perpetrators are youths "who dropped out" of school "to join the growing army who claimed they were fighting for justice in the Niger Delta" (Agary 34).

The narrator brings to bear a strong political presence on the story. She recalls the hanging of the writer and environmental rights activist Ken Saro-Wiwa and the consequences thereof:

> It was the year after the government hanged Ken Saro-Wiwa ... for inciting an insurrection. ... Every young boy had visions of dying valiantly for the cause, as Ken Saro-Wiwa just had, and as Isaac Adaka Boro had done nearly thirty years before him. The reports were that Ken Saro-Wiwa's last words on the day of his execution were "Lord, take my soul, but the struggle continues" So boys wandered about the village aimlessly dropping the phrase "Aluta Continua" at the slightest provocation. (Agary 34)

Saro-Wiwa's martyrdom and Boro's death remain reference points in the history of the Niger Delta struggle. Saro-Wiwa's environmental activism was aimed at protecting the Ogoni environment and saving his people from annihilation, while Boro's rebellion was intended to liberate the Niger Delta region and make it an independent polity.

As the title of Wole Soyinka's novel goes, it was *a season of anomy*. Nigeria was under military dictatorship, which brooked no opposition. Zilayefa recalls:

> All those who complained about the land's leader mysteriously disappeared [...] one after the other, people who spoke out against the government were jailed, attacked and killed ... or, invited to meetings where they were served poisoned tea. (Agary 99).

This scenario is the stark brutal reality that military rule offered Nigeria in the 1990s. The atmosphere of fear and uncertainty was quite pervasive.

The novel's suspense-filled climax is Zilayefa's discovery that she is pregnant. This is tantamount to repeating the mistake that held her mother down. Worse still, she is not certain about the paternity of the child she is carrying. One of two men could be responsible. There is the old Admiral who is her father-figure lover, and the expatriate Sergio with whom she is intimate. After a critical thinking session, she puts her finger to Sergio as the man responsible for the pregnancy. She concludes:

> I could not bring Sergio's child into the world. I could not allow him a place in my heart. That would have been foolish. He was a white man ..., his type left when they had to—and without looking back. My views on the matter have been tainted by my circumstances. ...
>
> My mother was brave to have chosen to give me life over the pursuit of her dreams. I was not that brave. I would not deal with all the uncertainties. (Agary 173)

Unlike her mother, Zilayefa decides to abort the unborn child to avoid the same trajectory undertaken by the former. Keeping the pregnancy would only abort her aspirations and relegate her to the periphery of socioeconomic reality. The fate she has so much struggled to avoid would have been her lot. In terminating the pregnancy, she ambles between life and death. In her agony she expresses the following optimism:

> However, if I lived, it was an opportunity for a personal rebirth with Nigeria. I promised God and myself that I would focus only on completing my education and making my mother, Sisi and Lolo proud of me ... the choices also that came with an education. (Agary 177)

The harrowing experience of having to terminate her pregnancy jolts Zilayefa into a reassessment of her purpose of coming to Port Harcourt, which is to be educated. She also realizes that her mother's hopes are invested in her just as she owes the sisterhood of Sisi and Lolo a goal she must achieve via education. The moment of Zilayefa's ordeal coincides with that of Nigeria's political turmoil. She is thus able to draw a correlate between both experiences. She equates her survival to a rebirth alongside Nigeria.

Kaine Agary's narrative is quite novel in its focus on the plight of women and the socioeconomic strictures woven around them in the ecologically devastated Niger Delta. The plot is straightforward and open-ended. The reader does not know what befalls the protagonist in the end. The characters are also quite true to life. However, the treatment of the male characters remains deliberately jaundiced. The novel's language is simple, and there are instances of portrayals of the Niger Delta's linguistic ecology, especially through the use of pidgin expressions and coinages. There is no doubt that the novel will occupy a significant spot in the body of environmental-cum-gender-conscious writing.

Works Cited

Agary, K. *Yellow-Yellow*. Lagos: Dtalkshop, 2006. Print.

Asante-Darko, K. "The Flora and Fauna of Negritude Poetry: A Re-reading." *Ecology, Ecocritic and Literature* 11 (1999). Web. 10 Jan 2007. <http://www.arts.uwa.edu.au/MP1199kad.html>.

Bassey, I. *We thought it Was Oil, But it Was Blood*. Ibadan: Kraft Books, 2002. Print.

Caminero-Santangelo, B. "Different Shades of Green: Ecocriticism and African Literature." *African Literature: An Anthology of Criticism and Theory*. Ed. T. Olaniyan and A. Quayson. Oxford: Blackwell, 2007. Print.

Darah, G. G. "Revolutionary Pressures in Niger Delta Literature." *Nigerian Literature Today* No. 1 (2010). Print.

Ifowodo, O. *The Oil Lamp.* Trenton: Africa World Press, 2005. Print.

Ikiriko, I. *Oily Tears of the Delta.* Ibadan: Kraft Books, 2000. Print.

Nfah-Abbenyi, J. M. "Ecological Postcolonialism in African Women's Literature." *African Literature: An Anthology of Criticism and Theory.* Ed. T. Olaniyan and A. Quayson. Oxford: Blackwell, 2007. Print.

Ojaide, T. *Poetic Imagination in Black Africa.* Durham: Carolina Academic Press, 1996. Print.

_____. *Labyrinths of the Delta.* New York: Greenfield Review Press, 1986. Print.

Osundare, N. *The Eye of the Earth.* Ibadan: Heinemann, 1986. Print.

Saro-Wiwa, Ken. *Before I Am Hanged: Literature and Dissent.* Ed. Onookome Okome. New Jersey: Africa World Press, 2004. Print.

Slaymaker, William. "Natural Connections: Ecocriticism in the Black Atlantic." *Journal of the African Literature Association* 1.2 Summer/Fall (2007). Print.

_____. "Ecoing the Other(s): The Call of Global Green and Black African Responses." *African Literature: An Anthology of Criticism and Theory.* Ed. Tejumola Olaniyan and Ato Quayson. Oxford: Blackwell, 2007. Print.

Ushie, J. "Challenges of the Creative Writer in the Niger Delta". *The Ker Review: A Journal of Nigerian Literature.* 2.1/2 Dec. (2006). Print.

Yeibo, E. *The Forbidden Tongue.* Ibadan: Kraft Books, 2007. Print.

Yerima, A. *Hard Ground.* Ibadan: Kraft Books, 2006. Print.

7

The Niger Delta, Environment, Women and the Politics of Survival in Kaine Agary's *Yellow-Yellow*

Ngozi Chuma-Udeh, Department of English, Anambra State University, Nigeria

Introduction

Since the discovery of economically viable petroleum in the Niger Delta of Nigeria in 1957, the natives have witnessed their ecological, social, and economic apparatus rapidly deteriorating. The damage from oil operations is unremitting and collective, and has acted synergistically with other sources of ecological strain to result in a severely damaged coastal ecosystem that has compromised the livelihoods and health of the region's impoverished residents. The indigenes in that region have continually cried out against the absolute hopelessness and subjugation by the oil companies and the insensitivity of the federal government to their plight.

They cry out against a system that has compelled them to abandon their land for oil explorations without consultation while offering negligible compensation. Their nightmare is further compounded by what Ukpevo decries as the 1979 lurid constitution, which afforded the federal government full ownership and rights to all Nigerian territory and also the decision that all compensation for land would "be based on the value of the crops on the land at the time of its acquisition, not on the value of the land itself" (17).

Since the exploration and exploitation of oil in the region have become a potential danger to the existence of the people who occupy this marginal space called the Niger Delta, confrontations of different kind have become the most pragmatic means of resisting the destruction of their ecosystems and their future. The youths of the region have taken it upon themselves to resist the mindless rape of the Niger Delta. As the conflict between youths and the oil companies escalates to a level of greater seriousness and intensity on both sides, as terror reigned in the once fertile swamps of the Niger Delta, certain muffled voices occasionally pierce the sounds of gun and mortar. Beneath the rampaging youths and the ravaging oil companies lie a group whose squeals and squeaks are almost drowned and submerged by the violence around them—the anguished voices of the women and girl-children.

This situation has pushed writers in that region and some other concerned voices in the Nigerian literary scene to decry the sordid state of affairs through literary ecocritical and humanistic view points. Lawrence Buell defines ecocritical perspectives in literature as "[a] study of the relationship between literature and the environment conducted in a spirit of commitment to environmentalist praxis" (430, n.20). At the same time, Worster holds that "[e]cology . . . seemed to be a science that dealt with harmony, a harmony found in nature, offering a model for a more organic, cooperative human community" (363). Judging from the ecological disasters brought upon the Niger Delta people and their natural world, especially those caused by the exploration and exploitation of oil, this chapter examines Kaine Agary's *Yellow-Yellow*, with emphasis on how she artistically explores environmental issues and the effect of these ecological problems on marginal groups like women and the girl-child in her debut novel. The chapter also also x-rays *Yellow-Yellow* as an attempt to give a nuanced view of women entrapped in the Niger Delta turmoil with a more chronological accuracy. The scholarship will aim at proving that the sociopolitical conditions in the Niger Delta compel women and girl-children to daily confrontations with forces militating against their existential survival and that these women and girl-children lack substantive protection at the immediate domestic environment and as such, are the real victims of the oil exploitation.

Yellow-Yellow a Sociopolitical and Ecological Suppurate

Literature delves into ecological issues when it crosses into the boundaries of human inchoate imagination where critical perceptions of human psychological individuality and political themes merge with the subject and object, body and environment, nature and culture. The writer delving into ecological issues aims at manifesting that articulated form of analytic modes of academic discourse channelled toward the experientially based forms of writing that Scott Slovic terms the "narrative scholarship" (12). This means that ecological literature is to be located within the delicate balance of the relationship between the human and the nonhuman world where it seeks to bridge the chasm between the human and contemporary environmental situations.

Consequently, this concept denotes the writer's ability to explore the fundamental environmental principles. It is born out of a strong responsiveness of the writer to his immediate environment. In recent years, appraising the relationship between man and his environment through the perspective of creative writing has become a leading canon of literature all over the world, and the Nigerian literary scene is not an exception to the tenets of ecocriticism and the rapid expansion of its methodical canon. Agary's *Yellow-Yellow* is an aesthetic ecocentric literature that concerns itself with a holistic understanding of the relationship between the average Niger Delta character and the chaotic environment of oil exploration. It is a painful portrayal of the acrid relationship between man and the ecology in the Niger Delta which has led to a deliberate destruction that has deprived humanity and nature of their basis for subsistence.

Agary's *Yellow-Yellow* examines the eco-biological, political, and psychological effects of the despoliation of Nigeria's Niger Delta through oil exploration and the attendant maltreatment of the region. It is an in-depth portrayal of the destruction of intrinsic life patterns, culture, and norms of the communities in the Niger Delta by the oil explorers. *Yellow-Yellow* portrays the aggression, desecration, and infringement on the life of the people and their environment, which has tended towards instability, disharmony, and ecological disaster. The narrative revolves around the ecological dilapidation and social devastation perpetrated by Western oil companies. It is the inner search of a group of people for direction and purpose in their devastated environment.

The inner turmoil and confusion of the major character in *Yellow-Yellow* denotes the chaotic state of the region as it affects the women and girl-children. Zileyefa, the heroine persona, earns herself the name Yellow-Yellow because her skin is fair owing to the fact that she is a cross-breed of a Nigerian woman and a Greek father. She grows up with the scornful prejudice of being discriminatingly called *Yellow*. She goes through life with the stigma of being labeled with so many derogatory pseudonyms: *African profit, born throw-ways, Ashawo pikin, oil boom, hit-and-run, father unknown*. The society she finds herself in sees her and her kinds as abominable. In a society where adultery is deemed a dishonour, these cross-breed children become clear-cut evidence of their mothers' infidelity and sexual escapades. They are branded from birth; they coexist all through life in a community that views them with disgust and repulsion. It becomes a serious indictment on the foreign oil workers who disregard established norms. They trample over traditions wilfully by luring these deprived women through dangling a few currencies in their faces. *Yellow-Yellow* exposes a different angle of the Niger Delta oil issues by representing the angst of forsaken mothers. The novel points insistently at the humiliation of women in this environment as well as the deprivation of their livelihoods, thereby making them vulnerable and unable to organize their lives.

She presents the anguish of the women as a three-dimensional phenomenon. In one angle, the women lose their means of livelihood to environmental issues. In another, they are forced by hunger and privation to go through degradations in the hands of the alien oil expatriates. Then, they are subjected to unnecessary societal injunctions by their patriarchal society that naturally prejudices, subdues, and relegates women to the background: Zileyefa avers:

> It did not matter what people thought of me because of my complexion. I had to accept that I could not change the attitude of every person who saw my colour and judged me before they knew anything about me. (Agary 75)

Zilayefa grows up with the twin evils of being distraught and insecure. She represents the average Niger Delta woman struggling to rise above the surf of the debilitating effect of oil explorations. Her life symbolizes the life of a typical Niger Delta girl facing the harsh realities of the untold hardship brought upon this region by the discovery of economically viable petroleum. The novel presents the innermost complexities and turmoil of women in the Niger Delta of Nigeria. Agary opens a sordid can of worms with this in-depth exploration of the intricacies of the abuse of the female sexuality in the contemporary Niger Delta society. It is an exposition on the travails of the women as they struggle to find existential fulfilment in the sociopolitically devastated lands of the Niger Delta.

From the perspective of the narrator, Kaine Agary avers that the people and their environment have been subjected to violent suppressions by the oil companies, and the inconsiderateness of the federal government has not helped matters. The forceful abandonment of their land to oil companies without due consultations and with thrifty compensations have reduced these communities of people to mere refugees in their own land. She portrays the angst of the natives as they witness the ecological declining of their environment through series of oil spills that leave the land arid and infertile. The author decries the devastation from oil operations, which she holds to be chronic and importunate. She relays the desolate life of a people watching helplessly as the oil explorations merged synergistically with other sources of ecological pressure to result in a severely damaged coastal ecosystem that compromised the livelihoods and health of the region.

Agary's *Yellow-Yellow* becomes the conception of a writer's grief for her suffering people and their dying ecological sphere. Her cry is that of disharmony steaming from a member of a deprived and injured human community and their ecosystem. It is a painful portrayal of displacement and dislocation of a people by aliens with the full support of their own government.

Interestingly, therefore, *Yellow-Yellow* becomes a cry against injustice from a cheated, desecrated, despoiled, and cruelly marginalized people. The Niger Delta has suffered for decades from oil spills, which occur both on land and offshore. Oil spills on land destroy crops and damage the quality and productivity of the soil that communities use for farming, thereby impoverishing residents. Oil spills on water damage aquatic life and contaminate the source of the water that indigenes use for drinking and other domestic purposes. Zilayefa's mother's farm has been ruined by oil flowing out from a vandalized pipeline running across hectares of land, leaving destruction in its ferocious trail. She woke up one morning to see her farm destroyed by an oil spill. The confused Zileyefa narrates her mother's ordeal:

> During my second to last year in secondary school, one crude oil pipe that ran through my village broke, spilled over several hectares of land, my mother's farm included ... and so it was that, in a single day, my mother lost her main source of sustenance. However, I think she had lost that land a long time ago, because each season yielded less than the season before. ... The day my mother's farmland was overrun by crude oil was the day her dream for me started to wither ... the black oil that spilled that day swallowed my mother's crops and unravelled the treads that held together her fantasies for me. (Agary 4)

The bewilderment that follows the massive destruction of the flora and fauna is monumental. Zilayefa's community is thrown into deep mourning and gnashing of teeth. The confused girl runs to her mother's farm to have a direct observation of the wanton destruction of her their farm. The heroine narrates the horrific experience of an oil spill:

> It was the first time I saw what crude oil looked like. I watched as the thick liquid spread out, covering more land and drowning small animals in its path. It just kept spreading and wondered if it would stop, when it would stop, how far it would spread. Then there was the smell. I can't describe it but it was strong—so strong it made my head hurt turned my stomach. I bent over, and retched so hard I became dizzy. It felt like everything had turned to black and was spinning around me. There was so much oil, and we could do nothing with it—viscous oil that would dry out, black oil that was knee-deep. I stayed there, in a daze, until someone shouted at, "You no go commot for there? You dey look like say na beta tin'! Come on, leave dat place!" (Agary 4)

The author paints the gory sight of the incessant oil spillages that wrecked the people's subsistent existence. This is because for the people of the Niger Delta, the ecological quality and its subsequent sustainability are basic to their general wellbeing and development. According to UNDP Niger Delta Human Development Report of 2006, more than 60 percent of the people in the region depend on the natural environment for their livelihood (28). This means that for these communities of people, the environmental resource base, which they use for agriculture, fishing, and the collection of forest products, is their principal or sole source of food. Contamination and ecological damage, therefore, pose significant risks to human existence in this region. She states:

> The water that flowed with streaks of blue, purple and red, as drops of oil escaped from the pipelines that moved the wealth from beneath my land and into the pockets of the select[ed] few who ruled Nigeria was the same water I drank.... (Agary 39)

Life in the Niger Delta is depicted as one long strife and struggle for survival, especially for the women. It is a stiff rat race of resistance and tussle for the continued existence of their species by man, animals, and plants. The entire flora and fauna of the Niger Delta are depicted as engaged in a struggled to keep their heads above the destructive quagmire of oil explorations. Zilayefa's mother, Ina Binaebi, starts the vicious fight for her continued existence at a tender age when as a "young and naive eighteen-year old" she has come to the city from the village "with visions of instant prosperity" (Agary 7). She ends up becoming a mother as a result of an affair with a Greek sailor.

The struggle continues in Zilayefa's own struggle for survival after her disgusting sojourn to the city. Ina Binaebi's struggles, however, reached its peak the day she loses her farm, which is her only means of livelihood, in an oil spill episode. The attendant impoverishment resulted in her daughter dropping out of school. Agary particularly articulates Zilayefa's mother struggles to guarantee a decent life for her daughter. She fully realizes the shortcomings of her life and fights to redirect her child from falling into such ill-fated course as hers. Her means of livelihood is incidentally destroyed by the same forces that rendered her life useless, abandoning her with a fatherless child.

The novel is an outcry against the nefarious activities of the oil workers who not only render the Niger Delta arid but also destroy the lives of women and the society in general. They trample over traditions wilfully by luring these deprived women through dangling a few currencies in their faces. This loss of the society's ecology, "which was their main source of sustenance" to the spilled oil heralded a new era of lack, scarcity and impoverishment (Agary 4). Zilayefa describes life afterwards in their community as "colourless existence" (21).

Though the oil spill is a contributory factor to her dropping out of school, the heroine already has her soul entrapped in the lure of the white man's money. The city, with its bright light, beckons her like a moth to the fire. While her mother nurses the ambition of sponsoring her through university, she feels like a caged animal looking for the nearest route to escape to the city. She secretly affirms, "I knew that I was not very keen on attending university" (Agary 25). She later confesses, "Love was not my desire—I simply wanted a way out of the village, and if love came with escape, it would be a bonus" (23). The deplorable conditions in the village push the girl into impious thoughts:

> I started to consider options that had never crossed my mind before, and from what I knew of my mother, those options would never get her approval. I could find my way to a place like Bonny, the base of expatriates working for the oil companies, and sell my body to a whitey. Some girls from my town did that in order to send money home to their families. (Agary 35)

The novel delves into the consequences of the sexual escapades of white expatriates in the oil-rich Niger Delta and its resulting effects on the Nigerian society in general. The seeming betrayal of women is synonymous with the betrayal of the desecrated land. Zilayefa loathes the betrayal of her mother by the white man who gets her pregnant and abandons her to her fate. The pain of growing up without a father is so deeply etched in her consciousness that it finally destroys her life, too. All through her teenage life, she is presented as plagued by her anxiety to place a definite feature of the man that gave her life. She could not be assuaged by her mother's deep love and affections, as she succinctly declares, "My mother's total devotion to me had succeeded only in suppressing, not erasing, my desire to know about my other half" (Agary 108).

This character spends her life unconsciously searching for a father that is oblivious of her existence, a father who would obviously feel ashamed to acknowledge her existence, even if the facts of her birth were brought to his notice. This is a father who took his relationship with her mother as a meaningless, passing fad. The Greek obviously did not attach any importance to the girl he bedded as he sojourned through Port Harcourt. Yet, the desire for paternal relationship being foremost in the existence of every human child tore Zilayefa's life to shreds such that the mere sight of a white man fueled the hunger to see her father:

> While I was talking, I noticed a man across the room. I don't know how I missed him before, because his complexion stood out just as mine did in that room. His skin was colour of ripe plantain peel. His hair was black and had the same big waves as my own. I had been staring at him for much longer than was comfortable, so he smiled at me and I smiled back. I wondered if he was Greek. The similarities in our physical attributes reminded me how different I was from everyone else in the village. I cannot say that I ever really longed for my father; in fact, I barely thought of him at all. My mother hardly spoke about him. I had learnt not to ask questions, because each time I did, she very tactfully dodged them, changed the subject, or she would ask . . . I did not care for him one way or another, but seeing this man brought me thoughts of my father. Where was he? Did he ever come back to Nigeria? Did he ever think of my mother? Would I know him if I saw him? I had no clue what my father looked like. My mother had no pictures of him, and it did not help that, aside from my complexion, I looked just like her, right down to the little birthmark below her left eye. (Agary 19–21)

Her yearning for the physical form of Plato Papadopoulos, her Greek father, has an awful effect on her psyche. It is this psychology of paternal absence and privation that push her into a near fatal relationship with Admiral. Her feeling on the first night she spent with Admiral relays this inner angst:

Admiral was a very handsome man, tall with no potbelly and a charming smile that made his eyes shine. He had permanent dimples and, when he smiled, the dug holes in his face. Whenever I saw him, he was dressed in traditional attire and had a little bounce when he walked. In my eyes he looks so dignified. If I had the luxury of creation a dream father, he would definitely have come out looking like Admiral. (Agary 120)

No matter how much she tried, Zilayefa could not come to terms with the misfortune that brings about the circumstances surrounding her birth. She is a bastard of a derogatorily special kind. The anger in her kindles against man and nature. She yearns above all things to rebel against all established norms. By so doing, she hopes to get even with the anomaly of her birth. As against the social norms, she opts for older men instead of young men of her age bracket. Her anger rouses against the state of affairs that produce so many ill-fated children like her:

Why there were more and more of my kind ... "African-profits," "born-troways," "ashawo-pickins," "father-unknowns". .... Maybe then I would not hide from the facts of my birth that my yellow skin and curly hair put on display. (Agary 171)

The author presents economically deprived characters, especially ladies, who "sell their bodies" to lecherous men to make money. The author posits that the growing up girl children naturally fall into the tradition of throwing away their innocence just for material gains from white men as well as highly-placed Nigerian men. At the tender age of less than 17, characters like Binaebi, Ebiere, Zilayefa, and their cohorts sell off their dignity to the white man in quest of money. In their innocence, they are most often caught in the web of unwanted pregnancies. The writer is of the opinion that this desperate bid to get financial leverage prod the young girls into "getting belle" and giving birth to "African-profits," "born-troways," "ashawo-pickins," "father-unknowns" (Agary 141); whom the white "sweeties" would see as embarrassment. This is amplified in the chronological portrayal of Binaebi, who gave birth to Zilayefa out of a brief romance with a Greek sailor she met at a disco party in Port Harcourt. She is naively carried away by the expectations that the Greek will marry her because she got pregnant for him, only to discover that the man has left the country without her knowledge. She returns to her people to face the shameful life as an unwed mother of a mixed breed.

Again, there is Emem, who like Zilayefa, is born of mixed blood. Her father is Spanish, while her mother is Nigerian. Then, there is Zilayefa herself, falling into the same spider web of lusty deceits. She goes to the city at the age of 18, just like her mother. There, she gets pregnant again and suffers summary rejection by the man who got her pregnant. It all looks like a vicious circle. The life of every female seems condemned from birth to strife, prostitution, and sorrow. The fate of the abandoned and disillusioned Niger Delta women, of which Zilafeya's mother is just one of the countless many, or an apt representation of this group of women, becomes also the main focus of the writer. Women, economically and traditionally downtrodden, are reduced to something less than rags, to be used and dumped without a backward glance by these ephemeral company workers who trample on Nigerian women like dust. They leave in their trails children they never hope to see again, and move on as if nothing happened. These women, already living in very economically harsh conditions, are saddled with children who are traditionally nearly outcasts. The children, in turn, suffer from two hydra-headed evils: being raised by a single mothers under absolute humiliation by the societal ethics, and facing the colour bar, which continually reminded them of the crude truth of their bastard status.

The novel decries the lasciviousness of the white men who leave trails of bastard babies that may never know their fathers and were born of a "crop of yellows . . . full of variety, coloured by the Filipinos, the Chinese, the British, and the Americans who worked in the oil sector" (Agary 74). Agary condemns in totality the awful situation that pushes these girls into the arms of these maniac white oil explorers. She also looks with pity at the black women, who goes to the extent of bleaching their skins so as to be acceptable to the licentious white men, all because they need money to survive. The heroine of the novel views these women with disgust and pity:

> Some of them came back with skin that looked like someone had touched wet coal and rubbed it over them tauntingly—some here, some there. Their faces, hands, legs, and feet were yellow, though some parts have big smudges of black. Their skin had an acrid smell, worse than the odour of festering wounds, which they try to bury under scented powders and perfumes. We were told that these were all the effects of the chemicals in the creams they used to bleach their skins. The funny thing was that they admired themselves in mirrors and spoke with pride about the city beauty creams that made their skin look "smooth," as if they could not see and smell what the rest of us could. Perhaps they forgot that some of us could

still remember that they had flawless, ebony-dark complexion before they left the village. Some of them would even compare their new complexions to mine, saying how they were almost as yellow as I was. I could not understand why anyone would want skin colour that betrays their innermost feelings, from embarrassment to excitement. (35–36)

Also indicted by the author as partners in crime in the wanton destruction of the ecology of the Niger Delta are the Ijaw youths, who in defiance to the subjugation of their communities by the oil companies, generate trouble by kidnapping the oil workers and breaking open pipelines to tap crude illegally for personal profits. Agary views the sabotage and vandalism of oil infrastructure and theft of oil as having serious consequences for the Niger Delta ecology. Sabotage ranges from vandalism by community members to theft of oil and deliberate attacks by criminal groups. Some of these people go to the extent of wilfully damaging the pipes in a bid to steal small quantities of oil for sale at local markets or for personal use. Others damage pipes and oil installations to extort compensation payments or to secure clean-up contracts from companies. The resultant oil spill wrought heavy contamination of land and underground water courses, sometimes more than 40 years after oil spilled. The author unequivocally denounces the activities of the Ijaw youths for making their communities drink water with dangerous concentrations of benzene and other pollutants among other evils of the oil spillage. Yet, she attributes the rampancy in community sabotage activities to a reflection of wider problems existing in the oil-affected areas of the Niger Delta. There is the general feeling of betrayal by all at different levels of consciousness, ranging from ignorance and suspicion to outright knowledge of the appalling circumstances they all find themselves. The disoriented youths have no alternative to life and they feel that causing an oil spill, and getting a clean-up contract or compensation is the only way they can access any benefit from the oil operations. There is evidence to support the fact that an increasing number of oil spills in recent years are caused by vandalism or sabotage. Kaine Agary opines that:

> The so called youth groups had become well oiled extortion machines all in the name of the struggle. They stole, blackmailed, and vandalized for the progress and development of the Ijaw Nation, the Niger Delta, some days I appreciate their efforts-bringing focus on the sufferings of the Niger Delta people- but I could not help but feel that they were holding ransom on one of their own. (158)

The author also pins Zilayefa's predicaments to the inherent destructive influence of the oil exploration in the Niger Delta. The experiences of her friends who share the same unpleasant incident with her, her admiration for her city friends, her concern about her lack of a father, her racial identity, and her affair with a powerful older man all take root from the evil manoeuvres of the oil explorers. As Zilayefa faces the consequences of her irrational escapades, the realization of her seeming frustration begins to dawn on her. She admits to her "indiscretion," which landed her into an unwanted pregnancy (Agary 177). The 60-year-old man who got her pregnant looked "cold and distant" when he is told of her pregnancy, and without looking up from the newspaper he is reading calmly handed her money and instructed her to go to Island Clinic for an abortion if she is really pregnant (160).

When the abortion pains wracked her she petitioned God for help. In paroxysm, she takes stock of her life in retrospect:

> My life was out of focus, and I wished for the days when my mother planned my life, but I could not go back to what I had rejected. I needed to refocus, and this time I would have to do it myself. Everything I had had in life up until that point had been handed to me on a platter, and I had taken it all for granted. I had forgotten the coarseness of my mother's hands, which worked tirelessly so that I could achieve more than she did.... That evening I remembered. I saw my mother's face, and though there was very little I had done in Port Harcourt that would have made her happy, she was smiling. I cried because through her smile I could hear her say that I had let her down. I cried but could not feel sorry for myself because I had made the choices that got me into trouble I had allowed myself, like an empty canoe, to drift along with the flow of the river.... I lay curled up in the foetal position on the cold tile floor until my sweat and the blood that gushed from between my legs drenched my clothes, and I began to shiver from the cold and the pain. I begged God for forgiveness and called on my mother's spirit for comfort. Even so, I had to bite down on a towel to keep from screaming as my body pushed out blood and clumps of tissue that had been forming a little person inside me for almost three months. ... I was enveloped in darkness and kept company only by the sounds of the night that lulled me to sleep. (177–178)

Agary's *Yellow-Yellow* is a compelling statement from a region bedeviled with ecological problems as well as other social ills, ranging from restive youths agitating for development of their area and the instability occasioned by inter-ethnic clashes and violence, to fatal pipelines vandalization by impoverished residents who risk their lives to siphon off fuel.

Conclusion

Given the steady and increasing urgency of the ecological disaster in the Niger Delta of Nigeria, Agary's *Yellow-Yellow* presents an in-depth engagement with the sociopolitical framing of the ecological issues in the Niger Delta. It has fundamentally and explicitly related the traumatic experiences of women in the host communities of the oil exploration. It has represented fully the stiff ecological privations facing women in this region. *Yellow-Yellow* portrays these women as being most adversely affected by the harmful impacts of industrial activities in the Niger Delta. Hungry and wretched, and living in an ecologically destroyed arid environment, these women look for the next option to sustain their ebbing life. The narrative views the communities in the Niger Delta and their women as victims of the explorations. The major problem faced by Zilayefa and her community is the elusive search for a stable, dependable sense of community and of a consistent relation to nature as a result of the constant occupational changes, the loss of fishing grounds, the disappearance of livelihoods, and land shortages.

Through her strong inferences, Agary has created powerful images in support of the ecological movement by propagating the idea of a holistic, self-regenerating ecosystem in the Niger Delta. She believes strongly that the ecological quandary is tantamount to social and economic deprivation, thereby further complicating the developmental situation in the region. These changes have, in turn, threatened cultures, traditional systems, and values, and the authority structure in the region.

In addition, poverty has become a way of life for the ecologically devastated communities due to economic stagnation and unemployment, poor quality of life as a result of shortage of essential goods and facilities, unhealthy environment, and government insensitivity. The novel, however, suggests that if women are given equal opportunities to develop alongside their male counterparts, they will contribute more positively to the growth and development of the area. Tangible instances are given with the lives of such female characters such as Sisi and Lolo, who through their resourcefulness and conscientious efforts, are able to acquire great wealth for themselves and live worthy lives despite their limited education. A sharp comparison is drawn between these women and Admiral, who uses his wealth to entice ladies, while Lolo and Sisi use theirs for human development. They accept, adopt, and cater for Zilayefa as if she was their blood relative. Through these women, so many girl-children are given empowerment; for example, Sisi employed Clara as a sales girl in her shop. Finally,

Agary's novel exposes and interrogates the trauma of women in the Niger Delta who are wantonly dishonoured by white men who use women as nothing but sexual machines and objects that money can buy. This novel sends out a fervent appeal that women in this region should therefore be given opportunity and educational empowerments that will enable them to contribute to the growth and development of the region.

For the writer, a community of people thrive on the existence of an unadulterated ecological system. The fully mature ecosystem comprises, in the views of Kaine Agary's *Yellow-Yellow*, of compact and safe flora and fauna ideally adapted to their environment. With such a standard in mind, the narrative advocates an improvement in the lives of the suffering women in the Niger Delta. The novel laments the fate of women like Ina Binaebi, whose only means of subsistence existence is destroyed by pollution from oil spills, thereby decimating the environment to the extent that farming and fishing, which have sustained generations in the region, are no longer possible, and the women row canoes farther and farther to find land to cultivate.

Works Cited

Agary, Kaine. *Yellow-Yellow*. Lagos, NGR: Dtalkshop, 2006. Print.

Barthes, Roland. *Criticism and Truth*. London: Continuum, 2004. Print.

Buell, Lawrence. *Writing for an Endangered World: Literature, Culture, and Environment in the U.S. and Beyond*. Cambridge and London: Belknap Press, 2001. Print.

Onukaogu, A. Abalogu and Ezechi Onyerionwu (eds). *21st Century Nigerian Literature: An Introductory Text*. Ibadan: Kraft, 2009. Print.

Slovic, Scott. *Seeking Awareness in American Nature Writing: Henry Thoreau, Annie Dillard, Edward Abbey, Wendell Berry, Barry Lopez*. Salt Lake City: U of Utah P, 1992. Print.

Sokari, Ekine. *Blood and Oil*. London: Centre for Democracy and Development, 2001. Print.

Ukpevo, G., et al. "Exploitation: The Agony of Ogoni": *Newswatch* 25 January 1993, Vol. 17 No. 4, 17. Print.

UNDP. *Niger Delta Development Report 28*: "An NDES (Niger Delta Environment Survey)." 2006. Print.

Worster, Donald. *Nature's Economy: A History of Ecological Ideas* 2nd ed. Cambridge: Cambridge UP, 1994. Print.

8

Women as Victims, Environmentalists and Eco-activists in Vincent Egbuson's *Love My Planet*

Ovuoke Dorcas Owhofasa

Introduction

Environmental degradation involves the abuse and misuse of the environment through various ways and means. For many years, the African environment has undergone different forms of exploitation and degradation, especially with the incursion of the whites into the continent. These range from destruction of trees, pollution of water, pollution of farmlands, loss of pastoral beauty, the destruction of water, and diverse health problems, which before now were alien to Africa. Consequently, various attempts have been made by Africans to save the environment. The moral depravity of African leaders and the debility of the masses have created a serious environmental crisis in Africa because of the corporate greed of multinational oil firms backed by Africa's emergent leaders. The response to this environmental crisis has led to the burgeoning of insurgent groups in the continent. Nigeria easily comes to mind here, when one considers the serious tensions in the Niger Delta. The women and children in Africa suffer more from environmental degradation because they are not only vulnerable, they are equally the most powerless of the population. The "woman" is most times metaphorically associated with the "earth." As society, through different phallocentric standards, regards the woman as an object to be explored, exploited, degraded and dumped when she becomes barren, sterile, and fagged out at old age, so has the earth been looked upon as a thing to be explored, exploited, degraded, and abandoned when it appears to be infertile and unproductive. There are also occasions when the woman is forcefully taken, sexually abused, and then left to suffer, just like the land, which has often been taken forcefully, used, and left to deteriorate. Consequently, in recent times, women have been involved in the struggle to rescue, preserve, and conserve the environment from being destroyed completely; and in a way, they are also in the struggle to rescue and preserve the women folk.

Eco-feminism is a term coined by Françoise d'Eaubonne in 1974 to give expression to the woman's concerted efforts or struggles to preserve the natural world, which is constantly bombarded by humans in their bid to sustain themselves no matter how this agenda for human sustainability is negotiated. Eco-feminism, according to Cheryll Glotfelty, is "a hybrid label to describe a theoretical discourse whose theme is the link between the oppression of women and the domination of nature" (xxiv). It is significant to note that this trend has gained the attention of some African writers who now represent environmental issues in their writings. It is against this background, therefore, that this chapter attempts to examine this phenomenon in Vincent Egbuson's *Love My Planet*. Specifically, this chapter aims at not only refamiliarizing mankind with the fact that if the environmental conditions of our world are subjected to dialectics and substantiated with the facts of history, one will observe that our world is fading very fast, but the chapter equally attempts to reevaluate the contributions made in Africa by women to save and preserve the environment from complete obliteration.

Egbuson's *Love My Planet*: An Allegory of the Niger Delta

Vincent Egbuson is a teacher and a fiction writer. He has written and published several prose narratives. *Moniseks Country* (2000) was his debut. It was followed by *A Poet Is a Man* (2001), *Love Is Not Dead* (2002), *Womandela* (2006), and *Love My Planet* (2008). He is a winner of the ANA/NDDC Ken Saro-Wiwa Prize for Prose, 2006—a prize that he won for his fourth novel, *Womandela* (2006). Most of Egbuson's novels dwell on the corrupt African society, environmental degradation, and women in politics. Egbuson always endeavored to distance himself from his works; this is probably the reason most of his novels are often set in a fictional African society. This fact enables him to blend facts and fiction comfortably, thereby allegorizing pressing postcolonial issues in his novels.

There are several environmental problems plaguing Nigeria today. These environmental problems very often tend to be the result of extreme poverty and the lack of economic and social development in Nigeria. For instance, the quality and quantity of water supply is low; the standard of housing in urban areas is unsatisfactory; sanitation and nutrition are poor; disease and natural disasters are very destructive. Moreover, the destruction of vital natural resources such as soils, vegetation cover, and wildlife as well as pollution through oil spills are alarmingly evident in different parts of the country, while the impact of a fast-growing population are with us both in the rural and urban centers (Eniola 77). These devastating environmental problems and their severe effects are becoming the recurrent themes in most recently published novels in Nigeria. Chinua Achebe, Sefi Attah, Kaine Agary, Million John, Chimamanda Adichie, Tanure Ojaide, and Vincent Egbuson are some writers of prose fiction who have at one time or another used their writings to reflect and decry environmental degradation and to suggest solutions for the extreme environmental degradation in the Nigerian society, especially in the Niger Delta region.

Vincent Egbuson in *Love My Planet* (2008) allegorically explores various environmental problems plaguing and dehumanizing the Nigerian society. While allegory construes environmental problems in Nigeria generally, it has specific implications for the Niger Delta predicament. This allusion becomes true as the reader discovers that Egbuson's use of Daglobe, Dabakar, Daglobe Delta, Port Lander, and Kozi State as settings of the story is symbolic and at the same time allegorical. A critical reading of the text suggests that the setting is Nigeria. This again is true in the sense that the story reflects the situation in most African countries and Nigeria in particular, specifically the predicament of the Niger Delta. Instances of the above presumption exist and abound in Egbuson's *Love My Planet*. As stated earlier, Egbuson explores various forms of environmental degradation—a cankerworm that has eaten deep into the African society, and Nigeria being an African society is not left out. In fact, it has eaten deep into the fiber and fabrics of the Nigerian society. The flora and fauna are the most affected and this, in turn, affects the lives of humans dwelling in the African society. Among humans, children and women suffer more. Women are the most affected because they are much closer to the earth. He also presents a woman, Toundi, who through love for planet Earth tries in her own little way to save the situation. The environmental problems explored range from bad roads, gas flaring, polluted water, flood, to oil spills. The resultant effects of these aforementioned problems are also explored in the novel. They include, but are not limited to, the people's chains of poverty, hunger, disease, malnutrition, contaminated environment, and lack of drinking water, bad roads, armed robbery, prostitution, and youth restiveness.

Poverty, Gas Flaring, and Oil Spillage

Poverty, gas flaring, and oil spillage informs the engaging tripod of environmental degradation in the oil rich Nigerian society. These three cannot be separated easily, as one is a derivative of the other two. The effects of this have resulted into poverty, hunger, disease, malnutrition, lack of good drinking water, and joblessness in the Niger Delta region; the last two being the mother of all the others. For instance, in Egbuson's *Love My Planet*, we are informed of a family stricken with poverty and sickness waiting for death to claim them. Egbuson puts it this way:

> In a dingy room a family of four was imprisoned in poverty, hunger and disease. The parents were on the bed while the two sons were on a mat on the floor. The father managed to sit up as Wenni greeted them ... the visitors noticed their swollen bodies and the pustules on their skin ... we were taking injection till money finished.... Eglee is my eldest son. I sent Eglee to my brother in Inoge State yesterday, he has not come back, and since then we have not eaten, because all the remaining money in the house he took to manage to take him to Inoge. If he does not see my brother or my brother does not have money I do not know how he will come back. (Egbuson 89)

The protagonist of the novel, Toundi had earlier on invited her father to "come and see a family in excessive poverty" (Egbuson *Love My Planet*, 88). On getting to the house they meet the above scene. Being a wealthy man, Mr. Wenni, Toundi's father, gives them some money before leaving to see his in-laws' apartment. On getting there, he sees another family wallowing in poverty:

> Maria's house was an 18 ft by 10 ft bed sit in one of the houses consisting of ten rooms, five on each side of the corridor. Each house also had an outhouse kitchen, an outhouse bathroom and latrine.... (Egbuson 90)

When Mr. Wenni asks to be taken to a place where he can urinate, he is led to a small wooden structure with gaps between some of the planks so that if anyone places their face on the wall they could see the inside. As Wenni is peeping through it, "the piece of wood covering the hole on the concrete floor was removed and a wave of heat and flies rising from their feast hit Wenni's face ..." (Egbuson, 90–91). This instance reflects another poor state of the people living in an oil rich city—even their so-called comfort room (toilet) is the most uncomfortable. Another case of poverty highlighted in the novel is when Toundi accompanies her father on a business trip. On the way, she notices a dilapidated school signpost with the name of the school: "EDOTA BOYS AND GIRLS SECONDARY SCHOOL." On looking closely at the school, she discovers that the students are holding their class under a tree because the school buildings are unusable (Egbuson 131). After the business trip, Toundi and one of the maids, Rareh, accompany Larami, Toundi's mother, to the village. On their arrival, Rareh is amazed to see excreta falling into the water as she says "Auntie Toundi, see, shit is falling from under that house into the river. See shit is falling again" (Egbuson, 141). The poignant implication of this scene is telling because the people drink from the same water. Despite the fact that Ogazza accommodates an oil company, they still lack good toilet facilities and potable water.

Other instances of poverty abound in the novel. These include a record of an *Aljazeera* reporter's filming of Yenge, Araba's home village. Araba is one of the major characters in the novel who drops out of the University to form an activist/militant group to fight the cause of the Daglobe Delta. Daglobe Delta is an allegorical representation of the Niger Delta. The *Aljazeera*'s report and filming of Yenge community reveals two elderly men and a nursing mother dying of cholera, while several others are scratching their private parts and complaining of severe itching after bathing in water obviously polluted through oil spillage; when asked why they used the water to bathe, they respond thus:

> "Na dis one clean pass. If you go dat place" he said pointing at an oil–stained wet track, "de water there black well well. We been think say we fit drink dis one . . ."
>
> "You also drank from it?"
>
> "We no know na," the man answered defensively. "Weyting we for drink?" (Egbuson, 228)

Even the *Aljazeera* reporter covering the story wept at the sight of the water (Egbuson 228). The effects of gas flaring on plants and seafood can also not be overemphasized, as the people living around gas flaring companies also suffer severely from its effect. Egbuson's narrative aptly explores the effect of gas flaring in the following excerpt:

> The *NTA* screen showed the people of the village: barefoot adults in ragged clothes; naked children, a lot of them with distended stomachs due to malnutrition; . . . a bare breasted middle-aged woman with a sore

running on her left shin busy with waving the flies from her sore with a rag . . . ; a close up of the slimly edge of watery dump for house hold rubbish and human excrement; all the houses were the same—sticks and thatch on stakes. (Egbuson 243)

This excerpt above is a live press conference report following the release of some hostages by a militant group; so when the reporter asks a group of villagers what they feel about the hostages:

A middle-aged man replied: "Dem say na de white people responsible for dat fire wey dey burn there." He pointed to the gas flare in the distance. "For plenty year now de fire dey burn. . . . Make dem quench de fire and go to dem own country."

"Why? Is the fire not good?"

The people murmured their displeasure. The middle-aged man answered. "Dat place, you no fit go near am oh—at all at all. Even dis place wey hot so, na because of dat fire, wey no dey quench. *Yams, cocoyam and vegetable no dey grow well for our area like places wey no dey near de fire. Many many village, because of weyting dem call oil pollution, the rivers no get fish again.*" (Egbuson *Love My Planet*, 243)

The above excerpt reveals the level of poverty that the people of the Daglobe Delta (Niger Delta) are experiencing and suffering. And as if poverty is not enough burden for the people, their health is also endangered and at the mercy of various forms of diseases as a result of the twin evil of oil spills and gas flaring, as reflected in the excerpt below:

How about de type of sickness wey our people dey sick? Sometimes for night, person no fit breathe well, or skin dey scratch arm. When Orolo go Local Government hospital before he die last month, de doctor say na because we dey live near dat fire, and de rain water wey we dey drink. The doctor say de cancer done fill all him body, no way for cure arm. . . . (Egbuson 244)

Other Nigerian writers have equally explored the environmental catastrophes ravaging the Niger Delta, especially the effects of gas flaring and oil spills on the Niger Delta environment. Tanure Ojaide asserts:

The magnitude of the desolation of water shocked them. Where were the flying fish that used to shoot out of the water into the air and then somersault back into water? That spectacle was now confined to memory. The water was no longer the herbal dark draugh.... It was light green, greasy, and smelly. The large fish population had been decimated by chemical from oil industries or migrated downstream into the ocean. (101)

The people now depend on iced fish "imported from Warri to the most interior villages by villagers by water" (Ojaide 101). When the women come together to discuss the effect of environmental degradation and how to tackle it, some of the effects they mention include various forms of illness, ranging from women's difficulty in conceiving, women delivering malformed babies, loss of manhood for the men, young girls of ten menstruating, women experience menopause before forty in the same area where women used to conceive even when over fifty, women past childbearing age now feel burning inside their bodies (hot flushes), something which did not happen in the past, new sicknesses without known cures (Ojaide 237–244). To emphasize the aforementioned, one of the women announces: "[W]here did those flushes hide before oil came into our lives? Imagine me roasting in the harmattan cold! The discomfort of being a woman has definitely increased with the discovery of oil in our backyard ..." (Ojaide 241). In expressing the effect of environmental degradation, the narrator observes that:

> One of the crude oil pipes that ran through my village broke and spilled over several hectares of land, my mother's farm included ... oil companies had destroyed our Niger Delta with impunity ... the Ijaws and other ethnic groups were suffering and even dying while the wealth of their soil fed others. (Agary 19)

The level of poverty in Nigeria, especially in the Niger Delta, is indeed very pathetic and alarming. The discovery of oil and natural gas, which is supposed to be a blessing to the people, is now like a curse to them. The worst aspect is that the elders, community chiefs, and politicians are making themselves rich from the situation, while the masses are getting poorer. They even make the people feel that poverty is good. Nevertheless, women all over the world are now making efforts to save the environment, since they appear to be the most affected by the situation.

Prostitution, Oil, and Natural Gas

Prostitution is a deadly evil, which has eaten deep into the fiber and fabrics of the Nigerian society. It is the performance of sexual acts solely for the purpose of material gain. People prostitute themselves when they grant sexual favors to others in exchange for money, gifts, food, or other payment, and in so doing, use their bodies as commodities. In the Niger Delta, the prevalence of prostitution runs concurrently with the discovery of oil and natural gas. The oil and gas company workers exploit and oppress the people in various communities where they are located with their money. Since most of the people living in communities where these companies are located are poor, the women involve in the act of prostitution for material gains. Various instances of prostitution as a resultant effect of the discovery of oil and gas in Nigeria in general, and in the Niger Delta in particular, are represented in some Nigerian narratives. Some of these include, but are not limited to, Egbuson's *Love My Planet* and Agary's *Yellow-Yellow*. In fact, prostitution and exploitation by oil companies are major themes, which feature in Agary's *Yellow-Yellow*. *Yellow-Yellow* (2006) is about a young girl—Zilayefa—who grows up in a village where some young girls go to Port Harcourt to prostitute themselves and come back to the village with large amounts of money. The protagonist in Agary's novel eventually decides to go to Port Harcourt where she is seduced by a man old enough to be her father. Zilayefa eventually succumbs and so begins prostituting the body—sexual exchange for gift, money, and other material benefits.

In Egbuson's *Love My Planet*, the reader's attention is first drawn to the issue of prostitution when Toundi, the protagonist, confronts her friend Yiba with the rumor of her sleeping with white men for money. Yiba confirms the rumor, lamenting that:

> "Toundi, I can't tell you the things those shameful oil company workers do to us. Because they have money. It's too shameful to tell anyone. Toundi, I don't enjoy it. It's for the money. Oh a woman's life!" . . . "I am a victim of poverty."
> "Those white men are evil. Russians, Filipinos and Chinese. They use the money from our oil to turn us into animals. Toundi, I can't tell you the things they do to us," . . . her mind on the very sadistic small-statured white-haired Chinese who was financially very generous to any girl who could manage to bear his perversions . . . "Men are evil,". . . . (Egbuson 62)

As the story proceeds, we are introduced to the oil city in the fictional Ogazza community. The city is where the oil company workers live. Toundi's maternal aunt in the village describes the oil city as "a place where our girls sell their bodies for money" (Egbuson 63). The narrator gives a brief description of the Ogazza oil city as follows:

... Oil city where most of Ogazza's simple girls and a few house wives were bedazzled by the oil workers' mint fresh money, well fed looks and intriguing bedroom perversions. Oil City, the city of light, where there was electricity 24/7, sprang up from where wet land was cleared and sand filled—oil city tickled the young women of Ogazza also with its paradisiacal grid of paved ways, a mini football pitch, a concrete court for lawn tennis, many comfortable Portakabins, one shinny prefabricated bungalow, a swimming pool and a borehole that supplied running water. The bulk of its residents were Filipinos, Britons and Chinese. There were a handful of Nigerians and a couple of Venezuelans and Daglobans, *no one from Ogazza, no one from the Daglobe Delta* [emphasis mine]. (Egbuson 160)

The above description of Oil City gives us an insight into the relationship between oil and prostitution in most of our African countries. The Oil City for Ereki (Toundi's cousin) is synonymous with sorrow as he avers that: "Instead of happiness it is sorrow Oil City is giving us . . ." (Egbuson 161). This reveals the plight of Africans whose oil-producing communities have been and still are suffering adversely as a result of the oil companies in their communities.

Toundi, who had accompanied her mother to the village, tours it with her cousin, Ereki. On one of such tours, they went to the river where they met Olivia Yenkie, whose real name is Ereintukpa, and her boyfriend, Gesibebe—a 200-level student in a Nigerian university. Olivia herself is a student at the Balazza Secondary School. On discovering this fact, Toundi pleads with Olivia to take her to Balazza. On getting to Balazza, Toundi discovers that it is more developed than Ogazza. When she asks why, she is informed by Olivia that Ogazza's underdevelopment is the result of money wastage and mismanagement (Egbuson 168). At Balazza, Toundi sees fatherless children, and as she makes enquiries, she discovers it is a result of the Oil City in Balazza. Olivia tells Toundi how the fathers of these children impregnate their mothers and eventually get transferred, so that the relationship comes to an abrupt end. In some cases, "most of the men are temporary staff. Some of them gave their girl friends fake names" (Egbuson 169).

Apart from the Ogazza and Balazza communities, other communities such as Akawai and Akowai, all within the Daglobe Delta, also suffer the same fate of prostitution, sexual abuse, and fatherless children as a result of oil in the land (Egbuson 244). Egbuson's representation of the evils of prostitution and the exploitation of oil companies in the fictional Daglobe is not far from the factual Nigerian society. The oil firms operating in the

Niger Delta deploy strategic schemes in pauperizing the host communities, which are very debilitating, thereby rendering them vulnerable. This stand is given further credence by the following excerpt from the report by a U.S. delegation on their visit to Nigeria in 1999, titled *Oil For Nothing*:

> Joi Yowika, an attorney who is currently representing several young prostitutes explained to the delegation that many girls and young women claim that they prostitute themselves as a way to pay for their education and to support their families. She explained that the sex industry in the Niger Delta is directly linked to the oil industry, since it is oil company employees and the employees of oil-related service companies that patronise the prostitutes. As a result, prostitution is rampant in oil producing communities and cities where oil workers reside. Stories of extremely degrading and inhuman treatment of prostitutes by expatriate oil workers are common. Children sired by expatriate oil workers are frequently abandoned. (Clark 10)

Hammering on the evils of prostitution and the exploitation of the oil company workers, Anup also says:

> The presence of multinational oil companies has had additional adverse effects on the local economy and society, including loss of property, price inflation, *prostitution, and irresponsible fathering by expatriate oil workers* [emphasis mine]. (1)

Furthermore, Adejumobi, a lecturer at the Lagos State University, in an article culled from the *Guardian* newspaper of October 10, 2004, states:

> The Delta is a wasteland, a site of griming poverty, disillusionment, despair, frustration, and hopelessness. The sin of Niger Delta people is that they have oil, and produce the petrodollar that our . . . leaders and the rest of us share and spend. Because the Delta people produce oil, their farmland becomes barren, their water contaminated, their trees dwarfed. They cannot farm, fish, graze cattle, cultivate trees, and inhale good oxygen, which the rest of the country does easily. They are completely demobilised, helpless and hopeless. . . .
>
> Prostitution is the only viable vocation for all categories in the delta—young, old or middle age. It is the only place . . . in the world where mothers deliberately encourage their daughters to go into prostitution in order to raise money for the family. . . .

The oil workers are the "local emperors" in the Delta region. They flaunt their wealth, cruise the local girls, and drive recklessly through the cities.

Considering these facts, it will not be out of place to say that the oil companies and multinational oil corporations have done more harm than good to womanhood and humanity in the Niger Delta of Nigeria.

Militancy, Kidnapping, and Armed Robbery

Armed robbery, hostage-taking, and militancy are evil triplets also rocking and gradually destroying Nigeria's economy as a result of the activities of multinational oil firms operating in the Niger Delta. Since most of the host communities are denied access to some of the basic necessities of life, they embrace alternative means to sort themselves out of their predicament. Unfortunately, the dissenting scheme they sometimes deploy to alter their situation ends up becoming chaotic, as innocent citizens end up as scapegoats in these schemes.

In Egbuson's *Love My Planet*, Araba, Toundi's ex-boyfriend, admirer, and half-brother drops out of the University to become an activist following a student's demonstration in the school where he is the Student Union Government president. As an activist, Araba is the president of Simple Justice, an activist organization calling for justice in Daglobe. The organization defines justice and gives the government one month to tell the people of Daglobe how it intends to tackle the numerous political and social problems in the country, one of which is the unjust formula for sharing the nation's oil revenue. The nonnegotiable demand of the people of the Daglobe Delta for at least fifty percent of the monthly oil revenue for them to develop their region themselves is paramount. The organization, among other things, also orders the federal government to substantially relieve the people of Ogazza of the present hardship, and fill the potholes on the East-West Road—the single road that connects the oil-producing states in the Daglobe Delta—within two weeks (Egbuson 225–226). The federal government, however, fails to respond to the calls of the people until the militant groups start kidnapping foreigners and other oil company workers. This prompts several foreign governments to fret at the immediate effect of the Daglobe situation on world oil prices and mount pressure on the federal government to look at the harmless demands of the militants and also dialogue with all militant organizations

(Egbuson 236–237). The federal government, however, neglected this plea until a British woman whose husband is kidnapped and later released wonders why the government of a wealthy country like Daglobe could not do a simple thing such as fill the potholes on a road that connected five oil-producing states whose oil produced ninety percent of the nation's revenue (Egbuson 237).

After the Briton's comment, the federal government starts the filling of the potholes the next day. In response to the government's action, the narrator remarks that:

> Perhaps because a foreigner had said what the Daglobans had been saying all along the filling of the potholes started on the East-West Road the next day. Travellers on the road prayed for God to bless Araba and all the members of SJ. (Egbuson 237)

The aforementioned situation is true today of Nigeria. Even now, the East-West Road, which connects five oil-producing states, is still not motorable. However, if not for the loss of focus of some on this insurgent groups in the Niger Delta, militancy would have been the most pragmatic response by the people to redress the decades of the violation of human and environmental rights in the region.

The Quintessential Eco-feminist in Nigeria

In Egbuson's *Love My Planet*, Toundi literally stands out as the quintessential eco-feminist of her era, a young lady who decides to set up a nongovernmental organization (NGO) after her university career, having lived in a country where the environment is deteriorating every day. Through this organization, she intends to support the government in environmental management and control as well as contend for the rights of women in the country. She also intends to train and educate young men and women morally and literarily, and on how to care for the environment.

Toundi's determination to set up the NGO spurs up naturally and as a result of her membership in Moral Daglobe—a peaceful activist group—and the experiences she had in her daily encounter with the land, which has often been raped and abused. On two different occasions, she narrowly escapes being sexually raped, so she endeavors to rescue and preserve the land as well as herself and other women from further rape by setting up the NGO. Prior to her setting up the NGO, she has at some occasion reacted to environmental issues as well as women's abuse through writing; even after, she continues writing whenever the need arises. An instance is when she writes to the editor of *The People's Word*, reacting to the embezzling of public funds by politicians (Egbuson 247). Another point of reference occurs when Toundi looks out of the window and feels her life would be a waste if she does not devote it to loving the planet Earth (261). Subsequently, Toundi's sense of activism is fired up after seeing the morally disgusting TV news report of the Vice President of Daglobe in the company of some foreign presidents and CEOs of multinationals, watching bare-breasted teenagers in an East African country (264). Depending on the Internet and previous sights and experiences in Daglobe, she writes an article on women abuse:

> discussing examples such as female genital mutilation, child marriages, harmful widowhood practices, the preference for male children, the bride price in Africa, the dowry system in India, women—degrading advertisements, catwalks and modelling exposing women's breasts and legs, the use of the female body as a tourist attraction, the use of scantily dressed female cheerleaders in sports, honour killing in India, Iran and Iraq, honour suicide in Turkey, the absence of female governors in Daglobe, and the androcentric use of language. . . . (Egbuson 265)

As a result of the aforementioned piece of writing, the Vice President becomes angry with Mr. Wenni, Toundi's father, who in turn vents his anger at Toundi. Despite the problems this article causes, Toundi does not give up writing against the ills of the society. After some time, she writes yet another article on the problem of properly educating and bringing up young people:

> It was published in *The People's Word* on Wednesday, and it generated several articles in the newspaper and views in a phone-in programme, OPEN ACCESS, on *Minaj Broadcast International* in which the host, Ndee Amaugo, praised Toundi for her wickedly truthful comments on Daglobe society. (Egbuson 296)

The aforementioned article, however, incurs the wrath and fury of Toundi's father again on herself and her mother. He warns that she will be responsible for whatever happens to his business, but Toundi's response to him is to do clean business and fear no evil (Egbuson 296). Toundi's response here reveals that she has no respect for persons when it comes to speaking against evil and perpetuators of evil in the society, no matter how big or small. Consequently, the State Security Service arrests Toundi and tries to force her to confess and consent to knowing Araba and to say if he is helping the cause of the Daglobe Delta. Toundi, however, denies having any knowledge of or contact with Araba, but staggers the Chief Interrogator with the question: "Sir, . . . is Araba a hundred percent villain of the story of the Daglobe Delta?" (Egbuson 298). This action forces the Chief Interrogator, a Daglobe Deltan, to drop his face for a moment and walk out of the room. This is because "in his over thirteen years as interrogator nobody being interrogated had asked him a question back . . . and the question" (Egbuson 298). Consequently, on hearing about Toundi's arrest, all the other activist and militant groups as well as the Student's Union Government in Toundi's school give an ultimatum to the federal government to release her or face their wrath. This incidence reveals Toundi's sense of activism and her role in rescuing and preserving her environment from complete deterioration. She indeed is an eco-feminist.

Eventually, Toundi sets up Clean Daglobe, an NGO, with financial aid from her father. The vision of Clean Daglobe emerges from Toundi's thought of Maureen, a cleaner cleaning the environment, and she infers that she is cleaning the fictional Daglobe. "Anyone who cleaned their own corner of the world was cleaning the globe," she thought (Egbuson 309). The inauguration of Clean Daglobe brought together various women activists such as Professor Dora Akunyili and Alaere Alaibe (both from Nigeria) and Umya Song, a presidential aspirant in the fictional Daglobe. These women have at one time or another endeavored to save their environment and society in various ways. While Professor Dora Akunyili at this point in time as the head of NAFDAC (National Agency for Food and Drug Administration and Control) is contending with the production of fake drugs, drug abuse, and indiscriminate production of sachet and non-sachet food and water, Alaere Alaibe, on the other hand, runs an NGO with the acronym FREE, which stands for Family Reorientation, Education and Empowerment. FREE is a simple project for transforming people who cannot access formal literacy, teaching simple villagers various skills so that they could be self-supporting, freeing the human spirit from ignorance, and freeing humans from dependence on their fellow humans (Egbuson 75–76).

Through Clean Daglobe, Toundi helps a family to raise D$5 million ransom for the release of the kidnapped younger sister of one of her students; and through dialogue, argues against a particular custom in Inoge village that believes a young woman cannot marry, she can only bear children from men for her father, especially male children, because that was the culture every first daughter had to obey (Egbuson, 318). However, after several meetings and dialogue, the elders of Inoge village and all the villagers eventually agree to change their age-old custom of women abuse. Toundi also writes another article on a girl who is burned alive because she is not a man (320).

Furthermore, Toundi writes the thirty-three ways humans can take care of their planet (Egbuson *Love My Planet*, 344). She eventually decides to collect data and publish a pamphlet on gas flaring in the fictional Daglobe Delta region. Collecting data from the oil companies is not easy; in fact, they bluntly refused to help her with the data she requested. However, she eventually gets data from her alma mater's institute of pollution studies.

In addition, Toundi also engages Clean Daglobe in tree planting in the northern part of the country. More importantly, considering Toundi's activism and activities, it will not be out of place to argue that she represents the activities of the quintessential eco-feminist in Nigeria, which Egbuson calls Daglobe. Other African women whose environmental activities may not be discussed here for the sake of limited space include Shobita Jain, Wangari Maathai of Kenya, and Diana Barikor-Wiwa (sister-in-law to the late Ken Saro-Wiwa), Bessie Orhorhe, Grace Ekanem, the late Alaere Alaibe, and Dora Akunyili, all of Nigeria, to mention a few.

The analysis of Egbuson's *Love My Planet* reflects the efforts of Nigerian and other African women to save and salvage the Nigerian society as well as the African community from the unbearable causes of air pollution in the oil-producing areas, a situation that has become worse by the continuous and unpardonable flaring of gas and environmental degradation for over four decades. It therefore will not be out of place to conclude in the words of Sadik:

> The extent to which women are free to make decisions affecting their lives (*and that of the environment too*) may be the key to the future not only of the poor countries but of the richer countries, too. As mothers, producers or suppliers of food, fuel and water, traders and manufacturers, political and community leaders, women are at the centre of the process of change [emphasis mine]. (7)

Therefore, women should be vanguards regarding the efforts to protect, safeguard, and preserve the environment.

Works Cited

Agary, K. *Yellow-Yellow*. Lagos: Dtalkshop, 2006. Print.

Adejumobi, S. "The Niger Delta: An Open Sore of a Shameless Country." 2004. Web. 9 April 2011. <http://www.dawodu.com/adejumobi1.htm>.

Clark, H., et al. "Oil For Nothing: Multinational Corporations, Environmental Destruction, Death and Impunity in the Niger-Delta." US Non-Governmental Delegation Report. 2004. Print.

Egbuson, V. *A Poet is Man*. Ibadan: Kraft Books, 2001. Print.

———. *Love Is not Dead*. Ibadan: Kraft Books, 2002. Print.

———. *Love My Planet*. Ibadan: Kraft Books, 2008. Print.

———. *Moniseks*. Ibadan: Kraft Books, 2000. Print.

———. *Womandela*. Ibadan: Kraft Books, 2006. Print.

Eniola, O. A. "Environmental Management and Development in Nigeria." *Development and the Environment—Proceedings of National Conference*. Ed. O. A Eniola and I. B. Bellow-Iman, Ibadan: Nigerian Institute of Social and Economic Research, 1986. Print.

Glotfelty, C. and Fromm, H., eds. *The Ecocriticism Reader: Landmarks in Literary Ecology*. Anthens: University of Georgia P, 1996. Print.

Ojaide, T. *The Activist*. Lagos: Farafina, 2006. Print.

Sadik, N. "Women: The Focus of the Nineties." *Populi* 16:2 (1989). Print.

Shah, Anup. "Nigeria and Oil." *Global Issues*. 2010. Web. 8 April 8 2011. <http://www.globalissues.org/article/86/nigeria-and-oil>.

9

Can the Earth Be Belted? Rethinking Eco-literacy and Ecological Justice in Wangari Maathai's *Unbowed: A Memoir*

Ogaga Okuyade, Niger Delta University, Wilberforce Island

> Today we are faced with a challenge that calls for a shift in our thinking so that humanity stops threatening its life support system. We are called to assist the earth to heal her wounds. And in the process, heal our own. . . . In the course of history there comes a time when humanity is called to shift to a new level of consciousness. To reach a higher moral ground. A time when we have to shed our fear and give hope to each other. That time is now. (Wangari Maathai's Nobel Peace Prize acceptance speech, 2004)
>
> Perhaps one might ask what tree planting has to do with liberation. Planting a tree is the first step toward liberation—reclaiming one's own. (qtd in Kushner 4)

The term autobiography is so protean in nature that it continues to defy a straitjacket definition even in the twenty-first century considering when it first made its way into the critical vocabulary of humanistic studies. However, scholars and critics have resolved that the term autobiography encompass "the many different accounts that authors make of their experiences" (Berryman 72). Invariably, some critics prefer to demarcate the term auto/biography, to accommodate the various accounts that can be assembled under the roof of self-writing. The subject of my essay does not border on the argumentations and contestations of the definition of the term autobiography and I do not intend to dabble in that debate, but I make some clarifications because the narrative that offers this study its textual mooring has "memoir" in its title. From Berryman's description of the term above, memoir can easily be housed under the broad label autobiography. McArthur defines memoir as a "written record of people or events as experienced by the author; a form of autobiography that gives particular attention to matters of contemporary interest not closely affecting the author's inner life" (650). Consequently, I will choose to use the broader label, autobiography, in place of memoir.

Usually, most autobiographical writings explore the relationship between the "I" of the narrative subject and the "other(s)." The autobiographer, therefore, employs different strategies to distinguish the narrative self from every other character in the narrative. The cardinal questions the autobiography sets out to answer are: Who am I? And what distinguishes me from others (whether humans or nonhuman)? Once the readers or audience are able to relate to these questions, the intentions of the writer become known at the very beginning of the narrative, because, as one autobiographer observes, "[t]here is nothing more important than one's identity" (Keenan 141). Our ever-present desire to investigate our sense of self and to communicate it to other people is part of what makes us human. Most of us may probably never get around to putting down the stories of our lived experiences in ink, but this does not mean that we are not familiar with the autobiographical form. In fact, we all engage in the art of self-storytelling on a daily basis. Through interactions with fellow humans, revealing our innermost desires to them in order to express how we feel and what we have done recently, we perform exactly the same act as those of autobiographers, albeit in a nonscribal mode: we embark on journeys of self-discovery, reflect on and reshape our identities. Stories are primordial by every standard, not only as a means to organize our experience and understand the world, but as the process by which humans recreate themselves.

The act of (re)membering unconnected incidents and sharing stories is a universal human phenomenon, even though "[w]e know perfectly well that life certainly isn't a story, at least not in any simple . . . sense, and we also know that a person isn't a book" (Eakin 9). Through this means, we weave tales or stories to make sense of our experiences that are usually in a state of indefinable transition.

Reading other people's stories gives us the opportunity to accompany them on their journey to their inner being and identify with their feelings and experiences. But in spite of the high chance that our lives may be very different from the autobiographers', we read ourselves into their stories. Perhaps it is "precisely [this] process of . . . identification that sends readers to the biography section (which is where you find autobiography) in such large numbers" (Miller 3). As Martin Amis observes in his autobiography, daily encounters with fellow humans and other worlds make up experiences as humans: "[e]xperience is the only thing we share equally, and everyone senses this" (Amis 6). However, Maathai's narrative does not deal specifically with just her encounters with fellow humans; it equally deals with her observations about the relationship between humans and the other worlds—the wild, the landscape, and the aquatic. Interestingly therefore, the genre of the autobiography oscillates between two private poles—individuality and retrospection. Invariably, the unknowable authorial intent is revealed as the narrative begins to unfold, private lives intersect with the public, and the experiences of the "I" stand out from that of the communal. Autobiographical writings, therefore, map the trajectories of the self as autonomous and the self as relational. The point I try to make here is that, although the self is perceived as "separate and unique" (Friedman 34), it is constructed within a social space that performs a gatekeeping act. Autobiography cannot be constructed if "the individual does not oppose himself to others" and "does not feel himself to exist outside others, and still less against others, but very much with others in an interdependent existence" (Gusdorf 29).

This essay is rooted in the eco-critical tradition, but it does not intend to dabble into the theoretical contestations and the issue of methodology or the applicability of eco-theories to text. Eco-criticism, as many have noted, needs more "definitive structure, methodological definition and viable terminology" (Estok 204). I use eco-theories because there are now numerous variants of the tradition without a "single world view" (Slovic 1102). Eco-criticism deals with an anxiety that is real and frustrating; it draws attention to the visible disappearance of the nonhuman world. The diversity that characterizes the field of eco-criticism reverberates with the different labels by which the field has been identified: it has become a buzzword for what some critics prefer to call environmental criticism, literary-environmental studies, literary ecology, literary environmentalism, or green cultural studies (see Buell 11–12). From the theoretical contestations, conceptualizations, and the debate over what could be designated as ecological studies within the borders of literature, academics (critics and scholars) will continue to hypothesize and theorize in circles and there will be almost nothing left in our ecosystems to be saved. The utilitarian function of this field will only be meaningful if it is liberated from the confines of academia and deregulated so that even people outside the literati can understand how to read and salvage nature pragmatically. This is what eco-literacy should espouse: coming to terms with the realities of our parasitic relationship with the nonhuman world and the desperation to redeem it from its present ruins. The field will mean more if critics combine the analytic modes of academic discourse with more experientially based forms of writing that Scott Slovic has called "narrative scholarship." Eco-criticism is a universal call for the need to redefine the relationship between the human world and the "other" worlds. Significantly, for eco-literacy to function adequately well, we need more of teachers than scholars and critics. The study, therefore, examines the strategies Maathai employs in her memoir, *Unbowed*, to afforest her environment that is visibly balding from human exploitation of natural resources.

Like Tanure Ojaide, the African eco-artist and poet–scholar, Wangari Maathai, Africa's first female Nobel Laureate for peace, was "born at the right time" (Ojaide 121). The quote above remains one of Ojaide's most memorable remarks when considering the alarming pace at which the wild world continues to vanish. It helps him (re)member how green his homeland, Nigeria's Niger Delta, was before the advent of capitalist industrialism, powered by the colonial search for natural resources in Africa and territorial expansionism, which culminated in the politics of the balkanization of Africa at the Berlin Conference. Maathai was born in 1940 in the Kenyan village of Ihithe. She was born at a time when African cultural systems were gradually fading away because of the overbearing nature of colonial policies, which forcefully replaced traditional African modes of life with Western ones. Born at a period when "an old world was passing away" (Maathai 7), she is able to remember the lushness of her childhood homeland and the breakdown of the ecological stability of that homeland:

> At the time of my birth, the land around Ihithe was still lush, green, and fertile. The seasons were so regular that you could almost predict that the long, monsoon rains would start falling in mid-March. In July you knew it would be so foggy you would not be able to see ten feet in front of you, and so cold in the morning that the grass would be silvery-white with frost. In Kikuyu, July is known as *mworia nyoni*, the month when birds rot, because birds would freeze to death and fall from trees.
>
> We lived in a land abundant with shrubs, creepers, ferns, and trees, like the *miundu, mikeu,* and *migumo*, some of which produced berries and nuts. (Maathai 3)

The world Maathai describes here is not an attempt at a mythical reterritorialization of Ihithe. Invariably, this Ihithe does not exist as a timeless archetype; its whole existence can tangibly be located or traced within a visible historical process. Maathai's childhood memories seem real and powerful as political resource and historical truth.

The lustrous and green world of Maathai's childhood is characterized by subsistence abundance. She makes one point very emphatically: her people, like other Africans elsewhere, are not wealthy in the capitalist sense of the word, but they never starved because "hunger was virtually unknown" (Maathai 4). Her memoir *Unbowed* recreates in the present the idyllic and innocence of rural life and the strength of familial cum communal bond in her growth process. The tone of nostalgia in the narrative is very strong, and the charm with which she evokes the past is not only skilful, it equally foregrounds an ambience of immediacy. This in turn creates an atmosphere for the reader to easily understand how and why Maathai's childhood homeland is almost lost to both colonial capitalist exploitation of natural resources and postcolonial lust for material acquisition and mindless appropriation of collective wealth for bureaucratic and private utility.

The kinship between the Ihithe people and their environment is established from birth. A ritual of human-nature-environmental relations is usually performed at the arrival of a newborn. This ritual is a very powerful spiritual-cultural ordinance, which reminds humans of their moral-ethical responsibility to their environment. The items for this inaugural ritual are derivable from the "other" worlds—the soil, animals, and the product of the soil. Invariably, the Kikuyus owe their environment a duty to always protect it in order to sustain a tradition that is only conducted through the amalgamation of the items mentioned above. This ritual is geared toward incorporating the newborn into the human world and to make him/her understand that s/he is obligated to protect that world. From Maathai's narrative, this obligation is not a collective responsibility, but a private duty; hence, it is collectively performed on the individual:

> In anticipation of the birth, the expectant mother would fatten a lamb that slept and ate inside her home. While the women gathered the ritual foods, the child's father would sacrifice the lamb and roast a piece of the flesh. The bananas and potatoes would also be roasted and along with the meat and the raw sugarcane given to the new mother. She would chew small pieces of each in turn and then put some of the juice into the baby's tiny mouth. This would have been *the* first meal of any *Kikuyu* child. Even before breast milk, *he/she* would have swallowed the juice of green bananas, blue-purple sugarcane, sweet potatoes, and a fattened lamb, all fruits of the local land. (Maathai 4)

This cultural order makes every Kikuyu person as much a child of the native soil as of his/her father and mother. Interestingly, therefore, nothing is more beautiful for the Kikuyu than protecting and cultivating the land. Ngugi wa Thiong'o's narratives and plays make this point very emphatic. In fact, *Unbowed* reaffirms and makes eloquent the relationship between humans and their environment, fictionally explored in Ngugi's imaginative craft. Maathai further demonstrates the potency of this relationship when she remarks that "Earth and water, air and the waning fire of the sun combine to form the essential elements of life and reveal to *them their* kinship with the *environment*" [emphasis mine] (47).

Communal focus is one of the major continuities in African and other Black autobiographies. This focus on community is explored in different forms, ranging from a focus on the writer's nuclear and extended family to the immediate community and to a community of writers. *Unbowed* spans beyond the writer's immediate and extended family and friends, it equally explores the ecology and its politics in Kenya. One may therefore be tempted to assert that *Unbowed* is more of an eco-biography as I have argued elsewhere.[1]

This chapter focuses on how Maathai writes the ecological history of Kenya in her memoir. The narrative is characterized by transitional shifts: from the story of an individual to that of an activist; a community, the ecology, and to that of the Kenyan nation. I will pay particular attention to how the traditional ecological consciousness of Kenyans was submerged in the deforestation that gave way to the colonial demand for raw materials in the country. I equally consider how gender compounds Maathai's resistance to environmental degradation in the colonial and postcolonial Kenya. Through the autobiographical mode, Maathai demonstrates that through the years of colonial capitalist exploration and exploitation of the landscape for cash crops, and postcolonial greed for material acquisitions, the Kenyan ecology has morphed through economic cultures, and adjusted itself to socioeconomic evolution, man's consumerism, and his galloping greed. Maathai's memoir records and recreates particulars that may stir the imagination of the reader with places and ambiances that retain a very special atmosphere; not always easy to describe. The pastoral ideal she (re)members in her memoir is evolving and not completely lost to time, but she substantiates her ecological anxiety with photographs, which exaggerate and validate her fears and reemphasize the need to protect the nonhuman world.

Since this essay is analytical, I rank-shift Maathai's position in the narrative from the cardinal to the ordinal. The ecology of her birthplace becomes cardinal. Through this reading strategy, I intend to bring to the foreground the fact that the subject of Maathai's memoir is not just Maathai, but also ecology. The autobiographical mode offers her the cultural and folk paraphernalia to dialectically reappraise the plight of the Kenyan people with regard to government's policies for landscape preservation, acquisitions, and appropriation in her homeland, and recreate a vanishing idyll—the Edenic beauty and virginal purity of her nativity. Maathai's capital intention in *Unbowed* is to recover her vanishing homeland, which she realizes through childhood memories. This gives credence to Azade Seyhan's contention that, "life stories offer a diversity of strategies for writing about loss and critical insights into the vicissitudes of personal and communal remembrance" (70). Seyhan's argument is important in understanding the politics of *Unbowed*. This is so because it enunciates the fact that though the object of nostalgia is physically lost in time and almost displaced in history, the reinvention of the homeland, through writing and activism, relocate the past not in the physical geography, but in the geography of memory. And more importantly, it equally admonishes Africans to be ecological in the exploitation and consumption of environmental/natural resources.

Unbowed rearticulates the way the modern man exploits resources and demonstrates that we now live in an age of uncertainty—an age that evokes both a sense of hope and one of deep concern. Nevertheless, the hope of sustaining a balance in our ecosystem remains alive, because like never before, we continue to witness so many distinct efforts to shape a better and more peaceful world for all. From different media, we notice governments partnering with civil society to enhance the well-being of citizens and the global community through shared knowledge and technology, common markets, and commitments to environmental protection. We also hear myriad civil society voices standing shoulder-to-shoulder with governments for a more humane society and a secure planet.

The human crave to satisfy his/her yearnings and the need for progress and development continue to hurt the nonhuman world. Invariably, natural resources are depleted at an alarming pace without a commensurate means for their replenishment. Growing desertification is not only irrevocably changing the natural environment, but also resulting in a decrease in the capacity of ecosystems to support the subsistence needs of the ever-growing population of the human world. *Unbowed* makes it very glaring that the threat of unmitigated climate change looms large, and it challenges the adaptive capacity of human and natural systems.

Freshwater supplies continue to decline; similarly, increases in droughts and floods are projected to affect local production, especially at the subsistence level.

The pressure humans put on their world and the wild because of their unsymbiotic ecological habits and insatiate environmental needs, the number of ecological refugees—people forced to flee their homes for environmental reasons—continues to rise with the passage of time. This is not a nascent phenomenon. Maathai captures this point whole during the colonial era, where land is reappropriated to enable white settlers to acquire large spaces for cash cropping, leaving the host communities with almost nothing. The Niger Delta people of Nigeria easily come to mind when issues like this are discussed, because they are a vibrant example of a group suffering the burden of forced relocations. Rob Nixon adds a new dimension to the crisis of ecological refugees when he remarks that there are those who suffer "displacement without moving" (19). Although the United Nations[2] has estimated the figure at 250 million people in Africa alone, I think the number of ecological refugees continues to soar with the passage of time.

Maathai's ideological position on human/environmental relations is fascinating. She understands the infinite relationship between sociocultural practices of a people and the space they occupy. She enchantingly weaves myth into history to enunciate this fact. This is further amplified by the signification of the metaphor of Mount Kenya and the fig tree. Exploring archives, and archiving and other forms of memory work provide insights into how the local understand itself. In other words, we examine public memory as part of a more complex epistemology of self, community, space, and place that inhabit the local. The narratives we weave about this process do not therefore simply make room for local voices; we want to know how the local speaks as well as why and how people give voice to the past that dwells within and among them as individuals and as communities. In his magisterial study *Time Maps: Collective Memory and the Social Shape of the Past* (2003), Eviatar Zerubavel suggests that societies emphasize the unchanging materiality of place as an anchor between the past and the present. Souvenirs, natural endowments, and relics serve as bridges that allow us, regardless of our current location, to take a cognitive journey back in time and across space to the point where we acquired the object. Although these interconnections are important, Zerubavel's work strictly divides materiality from the mental work of memory, forged against the constancy of place.

From Zerubavel's argument, the two most dominant symbols in Maathai's narrative are Mount Kenya and the fig tree. These two natural-cum-environmental endowments occupy a reassuring space in Maathai's growth process. They symbolize hope and the continuity of human existence. They connect the past to the present, and connect both to the future. But above all, they equally demonstrate the relationship between mortals and supernatural forces. When the Kikuyu erect their buildings, they face Mount Kenya; when they pray, they face this mountain, a symbolization of God among (wo)men. Maathai faced this mountain and observed the power of God in her life when she was informed that she had been named the Nobel Laureate for Peace for the year 2004.

Maathai often begins her tales with a story about a fig tree in the village where she grew up. Her mother and other grown-ups make it categorical for young adult and children that the fig tree was sacred; "it was a tree of God" (Maathai 63). Everyone in the community considered this tree sacred and observed it as such. Near the tree, there was a stream with clear, clean water that ran abundantly. As a child she played in the water, observing the metamorphosing process of frog eggs and tadpoles. She hardly knew then of the intimate biophysical relationship between fig trees and water—their roots draw water up to the surface. She only knew that the two existed together and that the tree was sacred. However, after she pulled through her education at college in the United States, Maathai returned to her homeland, her anchorage, the site from where she visualizes and measures the world. She becomes terrified on discovering that the fig tree has been felled and in its place stood a church. Ideally, the church should represent the power of God's surplus abundance. Paradoxically, the church engenders new and frustrating burdens for the Kikuyu people—drought, hunger, poverty, and the absence of divine and spiritual sustenance. The tree had been cut down and the stream had dried up. She tells this story with theatrical immediacy and vividness, which artistically collapse the durational gap between experience and narration. This in turn creates just a little ideological and emotional distance between the narrating persona who, ideally, is supposed to be the subject, and the fig tree, which is now the subject. This narrative immediacy helps Maathai in establishing autonomy in these two natural endowments, thereby placing primacy on them as agency. This narrative strategy helps to illustrate the power of culturally grounded knowledge, and in particular, the significance of a traditional African worldview. This worldview is one that establishes a connection between nature, humans, and the divine.

Semiotically, the church[3] remains a colonial capitalist instrument for devaluating African belief systems founded on pragmatic interrelatedness of all the worlds. Ideally, the church should provide man with a kind of transfiguration, which will in turn realign him with God. Maathai's memoir offers a travesty to this position. From the perspective of *Unbowed*, the presence of the church in her homeland violently uproots man from the presence of God and, by extension, divine protection. The destruction of the sacred fig tree marks a turning point for the ecological history of the Kikuyu. This is so because Maathai makes glaring the relationship between the worldview one celebrates and the way an individual is intricately related to her/his world. She suggests that her traditional African (Kikuyu) worldview respects the three-way relationship between nature, humans, and the divine, and that this worldview is what had protected the environment for ages. With the adoption of European values, the fig tree, she said, "no longer called for the respect, inspired awe, it was no longer protected" (Merton and Dater). The inability of the colonialist to sustain the standing cultural order gave room for environmental invasion. This therefore means the Western worldview has failed to come to terms with the reciprocal relations between humans and nature, which in turn gave room for the mindless exploitation and destruction of the environment as a signifier of human progress. Colonialism therefore remains a violent cum strategic attack of the ways of life of colonized peoples.

Most societies across the world with acute cases of poverty usually suffer the burden of ecological imbalance. Through her informal cultural learning and childhood observations about the species relations, Maathai easily identified the root cause of the galloping poverty associated with her people. Much of our understanding of poverty on national and regional scales comes from poverty assessments that have traditionally referred to material or monetary measures of well-being. Over the past century, however, a more multidimensional understanding has emerged that recognizes the social and psychological nature of the burden of poverty. This wider perception is reflected in Amartya Sen's description of poverty as a lack of capabilities that enable a person to live a life s/he values, covering the domains of health, education, income, human rights, and empowerment. Participatory poverty assessments have borne out some dimensions of this definition. Apart from material deprivation, being poor is a matter of sickness and chronic pain, loss of familial and social roles, lack of access to information and institutions, and a lack of self-confidence. The sociocultural identity of a people is determined by the physical space they occupy—that is, the environment. This wholesale depletion of natural resources steaming from the capricious shift from a livestock, food crop–based economy to that of a cash crop altered the lifescape of the people, foregrounding the absences of basic requirements for human survival—no firewood to cook meals, water is in short supply. There is the absence of land to cultivate food crops for subsistence, and the incessant felling of trees for space for cash crops altered the ecological balance of the Kikuyu. If all these vital resources for human existence and survival are absent at any given time in the history of a people, poverty becomes manifested in their sociocultural relations.

The fiercest environmental crisis the world has ever experienced remains a product of our time and the consequences of our inordinate ecocidal attitude to nature. Regardless of the different development trajectories, most countries of the world are being forced to reflect on their responses and contributions to a global strategy of mitigation, environmental degradation, and climate change and to redefine their environmental utility. Maathai is one individual who has responded pragmatically. Global warming may likely bring a rise in global temperatures of 2–3 degrees centigrade, and the resilience of most ecosystems has been exceeded at the dawn of the twenty-first century owing to an unprecedented combination of climate change and other global change drivers, such as land use change, pollution, and overexploitation of resources. Water scarcity has become the calibrating index to measure the looming environmental crisis in world consumption of natural resources.

Unbowed makes it explicit that the ecological systems that have been the basis of life for most Kenyan societies are in a state of disrepair. Fragmented by the assaults of a myriad of human projects, the inherent resilience of these systems to repeated and prolonged stresses continues to be seriously undermined. There are already signs of this degradation in the form of global changes in climate, hydrological patterns, and other critical ecological functions, as well as the desertification of millions of hectares of once-productive land. At a steadily increasing pace, species of plants and animals are vanishing as a result of the loss of their natural habitats or fall prey to human enterprise. For example, in the Niger Delta, numerous species of birds now sustain their lives in permanent migratory mode to avoid eco-death caused by oil exploration and exploitation. These are not just individual resources that we are losing for human consumption and one-sided progress, but are threads that make up the web of life.

There is an irony in the pattern of the impact of ecological collapse in the Kikuyu nation and the world at large. The Kikuyu people are involved in production deriving from their natural resource base, and live in close association with the natural environment on which they depend for their livelihoods and cultural lives. This is why the environmental crises Maathai identifies forcefully hit them in a mega proportional way.

A close reading of *Unbowed* and the understanding of the political economy of hunger will reveal that a large number of the Kikuyu population lives in chronic poverty. This is as a result of the decline in the availability of minor forest produce, owing to the deforestation and degradation of forests as being the most important factor threatening their food security. Although the immediate effects of ecosystem change will be on rural dwellers like people in Maathai's homeland, the impact will eventually be much broader, with the declines in food and water supplies likely to spawn acute contestations and violence in rural and urban areas alike.

The most fascinating aspects of *Unbowed* are the strategies Maathai deploys to regulate the ecological imbalance of her society and her immediate response to devastating (post)colonial environmental challenges. Her strategies are rurally entrenched in the cultural metrics of her people. She draws a parallel between the looming poverty in rural settlements and the vanishing green such settlements were noted for until the sudden change in human resources consumption and depletion. This story of the fig tree is an affirmation of the value Maathai places on culture, not just in abstract terms, but also in how it is intricately linked to survival. Postcolonial and Afrocentric scholars have written about the impact of racism on the mind, body, and spirit. In this way, they have suggested the link between de-centering people and how that loss can contribute to killing a part of them. Maathai amplifies this by positing that the displacement of African people from their worldview, which is harmonious and nonexploitive, can literally kill them, as the absence of the natural resources needed to sustain life, such as the unavailability of water, complicates the identity of the African people. *Unbowed* enters into an important dialogue with colonialism. It is however, narrowed to the problem of eco-racism. Maathai puts into use her experiences with civic organizations like the National Council of Women of Kenya (NCWK) and the Environmental Liaison Centre (where she was a member of the board) to launch the Green Belt Movement.

To liberate women from the double burden of womanity, Maathai maximizes the project of replenishing the landscape by planting trees through an adult literacy program where women realize their yoke and respond accordingly. Besides the burden of motherhood, African literature of the second half of the twentieth century is characterized by the agony of independence, which gives expression to the humiliation and despair the Africans experienced. Maathai's memoir reaffirms these experiences by retelling the African predicament. It also captures the double oppression of women—part of the oppressed population and specifically as women—and provides useful insights on their mobilization, particularly rural women. Moreover, it underscores the point that it is not enough to have ideas; ideas must be backed by conviction and translated into action. And more importantly, *Unbowed* presents the Green Belt Movement as a model: one that may not survive elsewhere considering the sociocultural dimension from which it is organized, but at least it offers an important approach in tackling acute environmental crises.

When Maathai first drew government's attention to the plight of the Kenyan people as a result of environmental injustice and its responsibility to help restore and sustain what is left of the ecosystem, she was ignored and dismissed as reactionary. Maathai was not alarmed at the government's reaction to her anxiety over the ecological injustice it was perpetrating. She kept her focus and held on to her mission from the very first time she dabbled into environmental activism, which was specifically meant to facilitate the recovery of the original land base of the Kikuyu, while preserving and restoring traditional practices of sound land stewardship, community development, and strengthening the spiritual and cultural heritage of her people. Her work is based on grassroots organizing of her local community, it focuses on education and the dissemination of information beyond specialized groups and into the larger mainstream media, and it is committed to social justice. The women involved—and many others like them in other communities in Kenya—have achieved national and even international reputations because they dared to speak out. The resolve to protect their families and communities, and the refusal to be shut down by governments, corporations, and legal systems, are remarkably unique. Whatever their educational levels, these women tirelessly educated themselves about community organizing, environmental science, legal precedents, media representation, corporate loopholes, and many other subjects in order to fight the battles that were crucial to their collective survival. After all, Maathai makes the point lucid when she muses about the irrelevance of diplomas in the struggle to rehabilitate the earth.

The Green Belt Movement (henceforth GBM) remains one of the most successful attempts by Africans to rediscover the relationship between humans and the environment. The methods the Movement adopted in regreening and belting the environment are not only trado-African, they equally enunciate African development practices hinged on reciprocal consumerism that is neither antagonistic nor destructively conflictual. However, the GBM success lies in its affecting real environmental change as well as real political and social change in Kenya. The success of the Movement is connected to its approach, which is anchored on a philosophy that reflects values and principles that integrate people to be responsible for their world. Through the GBM, Maathai addressed the root causes of real problems, not just in terms of structures, but also in terms of agency. She realized this by challenging political, economic, or gendered power systems while simultaneously teaching people to recognize and insist on their right.

Familiarizing people with the realities of their predicaments created as a result of human yearnings to satisfy his desires for conquest and power, *Unbowed* advocates the importance of understanding the relationship between man and the other worlds. This is what I designate as ethical-cultural literacy. Within the frame of this literacy lies the idea of eco-literacy—that is, the understanding of one's responsibilities to the environment. As noted earlier, the most fascinating aspect of *Unbowed* remains the way in which Maathai incorporated environmental change into social and political change. Through the GBM, Kenyan women rejected the bureaucratic uncertainties that threatened traditional lifeways or folk traditions and contaminated sacred land. The GBM started its activism in rural areas and took it to civic centers where the women and men struggled to desperately save what was left of the ecosystem. One of the two most outstanding battles the Movement engaged in was the insistence on contesting the Moi government's construction of a high-rise building in Nairobi's famed Uhuru Park—a site that remains a constant reminder of the deadly battles Kenyans fought to preserve and sustain their humanity as a free people. Within Uhuru Park, Maathai maps a space that is labeled Freedom Corner, a sanctuary for the women when government policies become overbearing. That space functioned as congregational spot for these women, especially when their husbands and sons were illegally incarcerated by the government. The park is a national identity marker for Kenyan nationalism. That park replicates Philadelphia, the city of brotherly love and home of freedom, where the founding fathers of the United States of America authored the Declaration of Independence. Philadelphia is like a sanctuary for reflection on issues bordering on nationhood, the journey of liberation for every American citizen, the route taken and strategies deployed to sustain the equality of all men.

The other battle was against the ruling party awarding public land for private development to political cronies. About 2,500 acres of the pristine Karura Forest were to be developed with estate homes and offices. Government officials barricaded the forest from protestors, but Maathai and her friends waded through marshlands to access the forest and plant trees. In a later attempt to plant more trees, she and others were attacked and she sustained a near-fatal blow in the head. Violent confrontations continued until after 2002, when restoration of the forest began in earnest. Like the title of the book suggests, Maathai was undefeated all through her journeys and battles, and she never groveled, even when her life was under severe threat.

Maathai's approach to rescuing what is left of her homeland broadens the field of eco-activism by deploying an African adult literacy educational scheme that provides a model of committed and unswerving leadership for liberationist environmental adult education—an approach that reconciles promise with reality. Through the GBM, Maathai employed adult education as a method to approach community development as a decolonization process. The Movement also used adult education to foster the revitalization of indigenous culture, self-ethnic identity, and women's empowerment. The prime position the African women occupy in the Movement is important because their lived experience situates them in a way to understand interlocking systems of oppression. Wangari Maathai's approach grounded on the agency of the GBM remains a profound success, especially her linking environmental protection with social, political, and economic issues. Initially, she addressed a locally identified problem—firewood shortage—by using adult education to build knowledge and capacity with local women in order to identify the root causes of the conditions they faced. Ultimately, her work and the activities of the Movement used adult education and a liberatory agenda to address the impact of colonialism. The primary aim of the agenda was to counteract environmental racism and re-center the African knowledge base that had fostered sustainable land use and healthy living for generations. It is vital to understand that the political, sociocultural, and economic conditions in Kenya that necessitated the founding objectives of the GBM were the result, in part or full, of British colonial rule. Invariably, the GBM constitutes a kind of counterhegemonic force or site where an alternative public sphere[4] is constructed.

The exploitive tendencies of the colonial regime resulted in environmental degradation, loss of indigenous knowledge, disempowerment of people, and the marginalization of women. While African people reclaiming their lands and culture have made tremendous progress, the effects of colonial domination are still palpable (Hickling-Hudson). Maathai's approach to healing the Kenyan balding landscape is Afrocentric because it revolutionises an indigenous knowledge-based system to counter a Western-imported crisis in Africa. Afrocentricity is therefore a transforming conduit through which all things that were old become new and the people must respond to this transformation by adjusting their ways of life to this psychic transfiguration, which is not wholly physical, but geared toward protecting the indigenousness of the African identity. Consequently, this becomes everywhere sensed and everywhere present. A new reality is invoked; a new vision is introduced (Asante *Afrocentricity*, 3–4). The GBM approach in the rescue of the residual ecological image of their once-virile environment could be easily housed under Afrocentricity as a concept.

Scholars in this tradition maintain particular responsibilities to the practice of knowledge construction within the paradigm. Asante opines that "[t]he Afrocentrist seeks to uncover and use codes, paradigms, symbols, motifs, myths, and circles of discussions that reinforce the centrality of African ideals and values as a valid frame of reference for acquiring and examining data" (*Kemet*, 71). Consequently, the cardinal goal of scholarship within this tradition is to reconstruct, reinforce, and restore African-centered knowledge.

While all Afrocentric scholars appraise their work from the perspectives of Africa and the African experience, some employ additional paradigms to further understand the experience of Africans or members of the Diaspora. Womanist scholars are particularly interested in the experience of African women and women of the African Diaspora. This study is not womanist-centered, but it is imperative to note its relevance as base for Maathai's activism. Women and children are usually the hardest hit when issues of environmental degradation are discussed in most places of the world because they continue to hold responsibility for all functions of running the familial base. A close examination of GBM as an environmental justice movement will demonstrate that gender issues are central to the movement. My analysis so far demonstrates that women's responses to environmental injustices in the Kenyan communities have resulted in their empowerment and leadership development. Maathai's private agitations and those of the women in the GBM vehemently show that both individual women and female communities have initiated the process of overcoming (hu)man's contamination and destruction of natural, residential, and sacred spaces. In *Unbowed*, women bear the burden of emotional response as well as physical action, often while endangering their own bodies, relationships, careers, families, and lives. *Unbowed* has tactically expounded the borders of environmental justice literature, thereby reemphasizing the fact that it is multicultural, it emphasizes social justice, and it identifies environment as the inextricable combination of human culture and natural setting. It also attends to issues of race, class, and gender as often as it acknowledges the influence of place.

The Green Belt Movement began as a local tree-planting campaign, evolved into a grassroots organization with a focus on environmental conservation and helping communities improve their quality of life, and eventually grew into a multifaceted international movement:

> I founded the Green Belt Movement 30 years ago to respond to environmental challenges, which I observed both during my childhood and while working at the University of Nairobi and the National Council of Women of Kenya. These challenges included loss of indigenous forests and local biodiversity, soil erosion, lack of clean drinking water, malnutrition and lack of firewood. I realized that to live in a clean and healthy environment ought to be a human right. (Maathai 92)

From its conception to date, GBM continues to negotiate its goals from a populist dimension, and its commitment to grassroots action is not only rural, but polydynamic. Thus, Maathai still describes the GBM as an "indigenous initiative" grounded on ethnocultural knowledge base.

The literatures on the field of environmental politics or studies continue to connect environmental problems to sociopolitical crisis, or link environmental activism to social movements. Interestingly, therefore, environmental rights cannot be wholly advocated in the absence of human rights. From the perspective of *Unbowed*, it is glaring that both are intricately connected. To achieve environmental justice, the rule of law and human rights are fundamental. This is why eco-literacy as an interventionist scheme must be deeply entrenched in human development as part of our unwritten curriculum, both in the formal and informal educational modes. This will in turn foreground the relationship on issues bordering on power, politics, economics, and culture dynamics, particularly in postcolonial contexts. It could equally provide colonized worlds with the tool to reappraise colonialism, especially environmental racism, and the continuous Euro-American domination of postcolonial peoples. Indeed, this may precisely be the sermon the Nobel Committee foregrounded when it awarded the 2004 Nobel Peace Prize to an environmentalist. As a colonized people, Africans should not continue to approach environmental problems from a mechanistic and compartmentalized dimension, but rather seek to understand the social, political, and economic dimensions of environmental problems.

The twenty-first century for African peoples is very vital because Africa remains the one continent that was not an active participant in the industrial revolution. Presently, the continent remains a consumer in this new information age. What Africa has in abundance is its eco-power, where lies the resources needed to reposition the continent in global politics. But disappointingly, this eco-power does not only continue to disappear with the passage of time, it has equally become a serious subject of violent crises. O'Sullivan et al. describe the twenty-first century thus:

> Our movement into the twenty-first century is momentous not because it is a millennium turning point or a movement into some kind of postmodern history, nor because we are moving from an industrial age into a new information age. The period in which we are living is not simply a turning point in human history; it is a turning point in the very history of the earth itself. We are living in a period of the earth's history that is incredibly turbulent and in an epoch in which there are violent processes of change that challenge us at every level imaginable. The pathos of the human being today is that we are totally caught up in this incredible transformation and we have a significant responsibility for the direction it will take. What is terrifying is that we have it within our power to make life extinct on this planet. Because of the magnitude of this responsibility for the planet, all our educational ventures must finally be judged within this order of magnitude. This is the challenge for all areas of education. For education, this realization is the bottom line. When setting educational priorities, every educational endeavor must keep in mind the immense implications of our present moment. This demands an attentiveness to our present planetary situation that does not go into slumber or denial. It poses significant challenges to educators in areas heretofore unimagined. Education within the context of "transformative vision" keeps concerns for the totality of life's context always at the forefront. (2)

Environmental change should be predicated on social change. By social change, I mean the need to be ethically responsible to issues bordering on individual responsibility to human existence and environmentalism outside statutory order. While it is true that some environmental problems confronting our world occur naturally, humans have the propensity to facilitate or decelerate change in various dimensions. However, humans owe the environment a duty to protect and keep it alive, thereby establishing the fact that "[w]e have a responsibility to future generations, not to mention the rest of the species we share the planet with, to ensure a healthy and sustainable world" (Kushner 168).

Unbowed not only demonstrates that memory appeals to us partly because it projects an immediacy we feel has been lost from history, but it also reinforces the significance of collective memory and cultural pluralism, highlighting the primacy of both human culture and natural setting within the environmental justice themes. Not only does the book retell (post) colonial ecological tragedy of staggering proportion, it equally demonstrates how Maathai responds to this tragedy quickly and pragmatically. Human desire for progress most times inflicts pains on our world; in fact, they are an attack on our ways of life. Consequent upon this, there is the need to balance consumerism and production with the sites of production. This will in turn make mankind eco-sensitive to the environment, which is hardly remembered, considering human capitalist instinct. Eco-literacy therefore means acknowledging the symbiotic relations between the human world and the other worlds.

Maathai's memoir contains anthropological and sociological data and details on Kenyan societies, both rural and urban, which can be very useful for researchers. *Unbowed* espouses the relationship between localized environmental issues and the broader national developmental issues. As one who understands the politics of the relationship between resource consumption, utility, and the consequences of not replenishing nature when exploited, Maathai discovers that the primary solution to the looming problem of poverty that assaulted Kenyans is to afforest the landscape, which will in turn regreen the environment. Her philosophy makes one fact explicit: trees are the crux of a successful natural environment, and could not only benefit humans and their subsistence needs, but also the broader ecosystem. The memoir equally has a pronounced environmental justice viewpoint, as depicted by Salzman and Thompson (2007) in *Environmental Law and Policy*. Although their analysis focused primarily on environmental justice issues in the United

States, such as the planning of low-income housing near Superfund areas, Maathai's vision of environmental justice tapped into a larger narrative of postcolonialism.

Most studies on the impact on colonized spaces hardly discuss the problems of environmental racism and the overbearing nature of Western capitalism on the people. *Unbowed* interrogates these issues in a manner that leaves that part of the narrative bare with the violent tremors that continue to manifest the disequilibrium in the distribution of resources. *Unbowed* identifies the widespread view that the planet is a resource to be exploited according to human needs and desires, but most importantly identifies the need to cultivate moral-ethical and ecological attitudes in our exploitation of natural resources. Gore makes this fact apt when he laments that "to some people, nature is like a giant data bank that they can manipulate at will" (203). The capitalist commoditization of the environment is an endangerment to the possibility of human progress. And to rebuild the world, environmental activists must first respect and legitimize local knowledge; that is, the knowledge of the people who understand the tenor and pulse of a space. Maathai's project is a success because she has local knowledge of the space and the world she is regreening and belting. This knowledge is not only transformational, it is equally re-generational because it collapses the gap between promise and reality.

Notes

1. "The Vanishing Eden: The Politics of Recovering in Tanure Ojaide's *Great Boys: An African Childhood*" in *East-West Cultural Passage*, No. 6, 2007: 42–60.
2. World Bank. *World Development Indicators*. Washington: World Bank, 2007.
3. See Kofi Awoonor's 2004. (1976) "Cathedral" in *A Selection of African Poetry, New Edition*. Introduced and annotated by K. Senanu and T. Vincent. p. 209.
4. Most of the discourses on contemporary theorizations on the public sphere are based on the conceptual and ideological positions expressed in Jürgen Habermas' book *The Structural Transformation of the Public Sphere—An Inquiry into a Category of Bourgeois Society* (1989), which is an English translation of his original work in German published in 1962. In this book, the German term *Öffentlichkeit*, which means "public sphere," encompasses a variety of meanings. It implies a spatial concept, the social spaces or sites where meanings are articulated, distributed, negotiated, and consumed, as well as the collective body constituted by, and in, this process, "the public" (Negt and Kluge).

Works Cited

Amis, Martin. *Experience: A Memoir.* New York: Vintage, 2001. Print.

Asante, Molefi Kete. *Kemet, Afrocentricity and Knowledge.* Trenton: Africa World Press, 1990. Print.

____. *Afrocentricity: The Theory of Social Change.* Chicago: African American Images, 2003. Print.

Berryman, C. "Critical Memoirs: Theories of Autobiography." *Mosaic: A Journal for the Interdisciplinary Study of Literature* 32 (*1999*): 71–85. Print.

Buell, Lawrence. *The Future of Environmental Criticism: Environmental Crisis and Literary Imagination.* Oxford: Blackwell, 2005. Print.

Colin, Scipio A. J. Interview with Jennifer Kushner. Williams Bay, WI. June 19, 2007.

Eakin, Paul John. *How Our Lives Become Stories: Making Selves.* Ithaca and London: Cornell UP, 1999. Print.

Egya, Sule E. "Eco-Human Engagement in Recent Nigerian Poetry in English." *Journal of Postcolonial Writing.* 49.1 (2013): 60–70. Print.

Estok, Simon. "Theorizing in a Space of Ambivalent Openness: Ecocriticism and Ecophobia." Web. 11th February 2010. <http://isle.oxfordjournals.org>.

Friedman, Susan Stanford. "Women's Autobiographical Selves: Theory and Practice." *The Private Self: Theory and Practice of Women's Autobiographical Writings.* Ed. Shari Benstock, Chapel Hill: University of North Carolina P, 1988. 34–62. Print.

Gore, A. *Earth in the Balance: Ecology and the Human Spirit.* New York: Rodale, 1992. Print.

Gusdorf, Georges. "Conditions and Limits of Autobiography." 1956. *Autobiography: Essays Theoretical and Critical.* Trans. James Olney. Ed. James Olney. Princeton: Princeton UP, 1980. 28–48. Print.

Hickling-Hudson, Anne. "Cultural Complexity, Post-Colonialism and educational Change: Challenges for Comparative Educators" *Review of Education* 2006. 52: 201-218. Print.

Keenan, C. "On the Relationship between Personal Photographs and Individual Memory." *History of Photography* 22.1 (1998): 60–64. Print.

Kushner, Jennifer. "Righteous Commitment: Renewing, Repairing, and Restoring the World—Wangari Maathai and the Green Belt Movement." Diss. Paper 23, 2009. Web. 22nd May 2010. <http://digitalcommons.nl.edu/diss/23>.

Maathai, Wangari. *Unbowed: A Memoir.* New York: Anchor Books, 2007. Print.

McArthur, T. *The Oxford Companion to the English Language.* Oxford: Oxford UP, 1998. Print.

Merton, Lisa and Alan Dater. 2008. *Taking Root: The Vision of Wangari Maathai.* DVD. Directed by Lisa Merton and Alan Dater. Marlboro, VT: Marlboro Productions.

Miller, Nancy K. "Autobiographical Deaths." *Massachusetts Review* 33.1 (1992): 19–47. Print.

Negt, Oskar and Alexander Kluge 1993 Public Sphere and Experience. Minneapolis: UMP, 1993.

Nixon, Rob. *Slow Violence and the Environmentalism of the Poor.* Cambridge: Harvard UP, 2011. Print.

Ojaide, Tanure. *Poetic Imagination in Black Africa.* Durham: Carolina Academic Press, 1996. Print.

O'Sullivan, Edmund, Amish Morrell, and Mary Ann O'Conner, eds. *Expanding the Boundaries of Transformative Learning: Essays on Theory and Practice.* New York: Palgrave, 2002. Print.

Salzman, J. and B. H. Thompson. *Environmental Law and Policy* (2nd ed.). New York: Foundation Press, 2007. Print.

Sen, Amartya. *Identity and Violence: The Illusion of Destiny.* London: Penguin, 2006. Print.

Seyhan, Azade. *Writing Outside the Nation.* Princeton: Princeton UP, 2001. Print.

Slovic, Scott. "Ecocriticism: Containing Multitudes, Practising Doctrine." *The Green Studies Reader: From Romanticism to Ecocriticism.* Ed. Laurence Coupe. New York: Routledge, 2000. 160–62. Print.

———. "Letter." *PMLA* 114.5 (Oct. 1999): 1102–03. Print.

United Nations. The Millennium Development Goals Report, 2007. New York. Print.

Zerubavel, Eviatar. *Time Maps: Collective Memory and the Social Shape of the Past.* Chicago: U of Chicago P, 2003. Print.

10

Nature and Social Responsibility in Rachel Carson's *Silent Spring* and Tanure Ojaide's *The Tale of the Harmattan*: Cross-Border Studies in Social Responsibility

Roselyne M. Jua, Department of English, University of Buea, Cameroon

> There was once a town ... where all life seemed to live in harmony with its surroundings. The town lay in a checkerboard of prosperous farms, with fields of grain and hillsides of orchards.... Then a strange blight crept over the area and everything began to change.... Everywhere was a shadow of death. (Carson 1–3)

So begins Rachel Carson's narrative of a fabled town in America, but it might well be Tanure Ojaide's Niger Delta. Like Carson, Ojaide sets out in *The Tale* to seek what has silenced the voices of the spring. The harmattan becomes a sustained metaphor for the devastation that has come to characterize the land (the Niger Delta in particular) and the corruption reflected in the people, especially the government; but in a convoluted sense, it is also representative of the lost years of youthfulness, abandon, and plenty, which can now no longer be experienced. In telling the tale, Ojaide puns and asks whether this is the *tail* of the harmattan. Are we at the end? Is there any hope? Or is there no light at the end of the tunnel? In investigating and analyzing these questions, this paper examines how Carson raises awareness against all ecological desecration and how Ojaide employs irony and metaphor to embrace the dichotomy that his tale encapsulates.

This chapter examines how Rachel Carson, a white American Scientist, and Tanure Ojaide, an African poet, raise awareness against all forms of ecological desecration in their works. A reading of Carson's *Silent Spring* and Ojaide's *The Tale of the Harmattan* proves that these intellectuals are aware of the hazardous use of nature by man, and through their different texts (Carson's being a series of scientific essays on the environment, and Ojaide's a collection of poems) raise awareness for man to redeem nature. It is for this reason that I agree with Linda Lear who writes that "Carson's thesis that we were subjecting ourselves to slow poisoning by the misuse of chemical pesticides that polluted the environment" (x) can be considered a call for revival and the rethinking of man's activities with regard to the natural environment. How these writers use their different genres, their different locales (Carson, the United States, and Ojaide, Nigeria) to discuss issues of the environment becomes the motivation behind the research. Carson and Ojaide, in the works under study, emanate from traditions/societies that have long recognized that Man is an integral part of his/her landscape; the tapestry of their works illustrates that the world is interconnected and the resonance of issues no matter the technological skills Man has acquired in the intervening years.

By training a scientist, Carson nevertheless devolves on the prose narrative to convey to a wider audience her social consciousness on DDT poisoning, while Ojaide appropriates the more elevated poetic form to depict the despoliation of the Niger Delta and the loss of cultural values through the farming of oil by faceless multinational corporations and a greedy corrupt government eager only to amass wealth. Both can therefore be considered social critics. According to Romanus Okey Muoneke in *Art, Rebellion and Redemption,* a creative writer and a scientist may all be social critics as he argues that "by means of their craft, writers [the writer] aim to deliver or save their societies from destruction or disintegration or failure. They aim to liberate their people from ignorance and illusion and from possible difficulties and dangers that threaten them" (3). This view by Muoneke seems valid, as Carson and Ojaide seem to abrogate the mission of conscientization of the public about Man's treatment of the natural environment. From this perspective, these intellectuals respect the platonic purpose of literature as their works in every way go beyond aesthetic pleasure to real utilitarian and functional goals.

The paper adopts eco-criticism as framework for its analysis. This is so because of the theory's capacity to discuss cultural productions (literature, music, painting, and essays to mention just these) and their relationship with the ecology. Cheryll Glotfelty has argued that eco-criticism "negotiates between the human and non human" (xix); since literature is the artistic representation of human activities, eco-theory helps to expose and explain man, art, and their relation with the natural environment. This kind of criticism is what this research sets out to interrogate in this paper—exploring not only the literariness of literature, but also its role and contribution to environmental redemption.

Though green theory in literary studies seems to be very recent, Ojaide's corpus reminds us that he has gone green even before it became fashionable to preach it, as he dreamed of a world that was just, sustainable, and peaceful. Interesting to note is the fact that Carson raised concerns about the environment at a time when it was hardly thought of. Lear wonders how the book was received upon publication in 1962 in these words: "It is hard to remember the cultural climate that greeted *Silent Spring* and the fury that was launched against its quietly determined author" (xi). This shows that this work and its author, though groundbreaking in its pro-nature discussion, was not welcomed in the mid-twentieth century. Like John the Baptist in the wilderness, Ojaide laments in "Quatrain Suite":

> The map of my homeland has changed.
> The cartographers blot out forests and rivers.
> Oil wells and flares dot the new landscape—
> now nobody recognizes the beauty queen's face.
> . . .
> The apiapia cries hysterically, flying over its former haunt:
> "It's another planting season and what a cheerless sight,
> hardly any farmers!" They fled to be servants in the city.
> Who blames bird or migrant, the soil one barren crust?
> . . .
> Evergreens bald, every head bowed in disgrace.
> No season grows back flared or suffocated leaves
> And the cycle of self-succeeding generations dies.
> Green is now a scarce commodity in the rainforest. (*Tale*, 17–18)

These lines carry the speaker's lament for all that has been lost. The tone is sorrowful as change though inevitable is destructive and nature is eroded by man's activity. The lack of recognition of the "queen's face" from any observer today shows the extent to which human activities have transformed the earth from a partner to a victim. This same picture of lament for what has been lost is at the center of Carson's work, as she writes in the opening essay:

> There was once a town . . . where all life seemed to live in harmony with
> its surroundings. The town lay in a checkerboard of prosperous farms,

with fields of grain and hillsides of orchards. . . . Then a strange blight crept over the area and everything began to change. . . . Everywhere was a shadow of death. (1–3)

One realizes that the narrator is nostalgic about a past that can no longer be regained. It is important that, although a natural scientist, Carson opens her book in a folktale style. The lamentation of the narrators demonstrates to us that their concern for the desecration Mother Earth is suffering. Carson and Ojaide are both preoccupied with the disharmony that has come to be because of man's activity with nature. David O. Orr in *Earth in Mind: On Education, Environment, and the Human Prospect* holds that "[e]xcessive logging, corporate monocultures, agriculture, urbanization, road building, recreational development, and air pollution are reducing forested areas around the world" (64), a premise which, if applicable, justifies why the speakers in both the verse of Ojaide and the narrative of Carson are lamenting. The whole cause of this disharmony is Man, and thus there is the need for Man to revise his/her relationship with nature. The civil rights activist Ken Saro-Wiwa fought for major political and social changes for the "Ogoni"; Ogoni denotes the intimate relation between the people and the land as he asserts in *A Month and a Day*: "[T]o the Ogoni, the land and the people are one and are expressed as such in our local languages. It emphasizes, to my mind, the close relationship between the Ogoni people and their environment" (2). He sought restitution and compensation, not the paltry "renovated school buildings . . . teachers, and donated school furniture and science equipment" (Hunt 247) that Shell Oil doled out to the Ogoni. He got instead the hangman's noose. He could do so because of the intimate relationship that exists between the African and his environment; he fed off it and preserved it, and it in turn protected and sheltered him. Everything the African used prior to his contact with the Western world was biodegradable; civilization has brought in its wake nothing but chaos and destruction. The recent oil disaster in the Gulf of Mexico and how it is affecting human and natural life is a case in point and so worth noting here for any doubting Thomases.

Saro-Wiwa's words bred fear in Royal Dutch/Shell Nigeria as recorded in Owen Wiwa's interview with Brian Anderson, its Managing Director, in *The Politics of Bones*. Anderson ensured that Saro-Wiwa remained jailed when he refused "to write a press release on MOSOP letterhead saying that there is no environmental devastation in Ogoniland due to Shell's activities" (Hunt 247) and also to call off worldwide anti-Shell campaigns.

These campaigns spelled ruination to the Sani Abacha regime in Nigeria, and on November 10, 1995, Saro-Wiwa was executed on a trumped-up charge. These same words spelled hope and redemption to the embattled Ogoni who had lost so much in the despoliation of their land and the stark poverty to which they were relegated, even as they sat on pools of oil while others fed fat and grew rich from their land. Vampire-like, the government and the multinationals fed on the Ogoni as they suck the life-force out of the people. It is worth recalling here that Shell finally owned up to their destruction with a big cash packet. Therefore, the very words that spell wealth and life on the one hand, spell poverty and death on the other. In "Oil Remedies," oil, which in all its forms should be the balm of the people, has indeed become the bane of the people, the symbol of Western imperialism and a recolonization of the African:

> Produce of blessed palm tree, testimony
> of industry of men and women; oil confers wealth.
> We knew our brides by the lavish oil
> that massaged their bodies to glow with allure—
> Oil is the lamp we keep at the crossroads
> for humans and spirits to find separate ways.
> The same oil that makes every meal a feast
> for the palate and completes every rich dish!
> The oil we know has always been the lamp—
> friend of the eyes, it fuels a bright spectacle.
> Then came subsoil oil, no longer red but black,
> converted by entrepreneurs into capital fuel.
> This oil bleeding from the earth flowers light
> and they sing hymns to fan its incandescence.
> It is we who live in the dark that give out light.
> they make bonfires of our blind ancestors' gifts
> After hauling away priceless pools of abundance
> and leaving with us silent and roaming epidemics. (27–28)

Ojaide here evokes the simplicity and innocence of impoverished African ancestors who sat ignorant on wealth, conserving it for predators that now devastate the land, pollute the environment, and hoard the spoils. In doing so, he employs literature as therapy and it can therefore be suggested that he seeks to amend through his craft, poetry, what the young guerrillas of the Movement for the Emancipation of the Niger Delta do in fact and symbolize metaphorically through their adoptive acronym,

MEND. Ojaide's metaphorical portrayal of this impoverishment of the land in the eyes of the local singer is given cause, as Carson sees the same age in world history in these words:

> It is also an era dominated by industry, in which the right to make a dollar at whatever cost is seldom challenged. When the public protests, confronts with some obvious evidence of damaging results of pesticide applications, it is fed little tranquilizing pills of half truth. (13)

Ojaide's speaking like the voice of Carson here helps us see the reasons for the impoverishment of the earth: first, Ojaide's speaker laments that industrialization has made oil not to have the value it once had. There is no doubt that Carson sees industrialization as an oppressor to nature in our times. Second, money has become a god; and third, the promoter of all these is the capitalist who sees people who cry out against such mishandling of nature as threats that must be eliminated.

In providing light, oil dispels darkness and catapults us into a *new dawn*, the metaphor through which Ojaide portrays the eternal conflict between good and evil, between white and black, right and wrong. Oil has caused untold suffering and destruction in the same manner as the law courts in Charles Dickens' *Bleak House* (Dickens is a recognized social critic of nineteenth-century England and its institutions). And like the Lord High Chancellor oblivious to the "ruined suitor . . . from Shropshire [who] breaks out in efforts to address the Chancellor at the close of the day's business, and who can by no means be made to understand that the Chancellor is legally ignorant of his existence after making it desolate for a quarter of a century" (Dickens 3), the Nigerian government and multinationals seemed unaware of and insensitive to Saro-Wiwa's call and the plight of the people. Becoming more self-protective of their affluence, like other African leaders, the Abacha government is like the rich capitalist that Carson describes in the case of the United States of America. This is testimony to the fact that the exploiters of nature in this evil form are a handful of capitalists in a production-led country like the United States, and her compradors in consumer countries like Nigeria seek wealth and care less about nature and fellow man. With this arises the ethical question. According to David E. Cooper et al. in their *The Environment in Question: Ethics and Global Issues*, "What ethics is about in the end is seeing outside your own sector of self interest, of class interest. . . . An ecological conscience requires an unprecedented mix of science and conscience, of biology and ethics" (136). Thus, Ojaide's delicate task as he navigates the troubled waters of the Delta, as had been Saro-Wiwa's, is how to raise the consciousness of the international conglomerates and an embattled government to their ecological responsibility without bringing the waters to a boil (as they have).

Again taking up the clarion call through his poetry to explore the devastation of the land and the untold suffering of a now dispossessed people, Ojaide illumines not only his literary commitment as advocated by Wole Soyinka (1968), Ngugi wa Thiong'o (in Sander and Lindfors), and Americans like Henry David Thoreau, Walt Whitman, and Herman Melville, but reasserts the interconnectivity between literature and the environment and also social/shared responsibility as he proceeds to reinsert man into the ecological equation. Survival as a major preoccupation resonates in Carson's and Ojaide's works under study here, as they address and assess what effect the past has on the present and possibly the future of the Delta[1] and urbanized America. Ojaide sees not only the stunted growth of the people but also the blighted productivity of the earth's flora and fauna, and in light of the trinity of man, vegetation, and animal life, senses in "The Goat Song" (10) that this aberration can only spell death because:

> The blackened stream is ancestral blood
> tapped away by giant pipes into ships
> to rejuvenate foreign cities, invigorate markets;
> distant places lit with wonders; here, a blackout.
> . . .
> The big family is dying out—irokos fall; game
> leave in droves, and humans flee to hunger.
> Soon the whole landscape will be a cemetery
> south-south of the carousing palace of the king.
> The carrion lord cares not for the rot he stirs;
> he pranks with consorts in the death-field—
> Government and the coalition of global lords
> have snatched away what ancestors sat upon. (Ojaide *Tale*, 10–11)

Poetry has gone green and is "crying for salvation," to use the phrase of Cameroonian folk star Prince Afo-Akom. The big family here equated with the dying iroko tree, which in African mythology is not only king of the forest but embodies the forest itself, adumbrates in Ojaide's Whitmanesque composition, the scalping of the people. The oil-rich Delta, which should have been the breadbasket of the people, has become their grave, a dead-end in the manner which Gloria Naylor had proclaimed of the wall for the inhabitants of Brewster Place in *The Women of Brewster Place*:

> No one cries when a street dies. There's no line of mourners to walk behind the coffin wheeled on the axis of the earth and lidded by the sky. No one is there when a street dies. It isn't dead when the last door is locked, and the last pair of footsteps echo up the sidewalk, reluctant to turn the corner and melt into another reality. It dies when the odors of hope, despair, lust, and caring are wiped out by the seasonal winds; when dust has settled into the cracks and scars, leveling their depths and colorations—their reasons for being; when the spirit is trapped and fading in someone's memory. (Naylor 191)

Cut off from a thriving economic zone by the wall, the dead-end street signifies the prevalence of institutionalized racism within the imperialist American society; an analogy (not so farfetched) that would hold true for the Delta inhabitants who have been completely disenfranchised, since Ojaide summons the specter of slavery, the Middle Passage, and the dehumanization of African slaves on the plantations of the South, by evoking "the blackened stream [which] is ancestral blood tapped away by giant pipes into ships"Not only is the cultural way of the Delta disappearing, but the Delta has become an endangered people. It is an analogy that also speaks to the brain drain African nations undergo.

The voice of the speaker in the above poem expresses almost the same concern like Carson in the fourteenth essay, which she entitles "One in Every Four"; this grim picture begins to show the negative impact of Man's abusive use and exploitation of nature. While the blackened stream of ancestral blood flows through the Niger Delta, Carson's society has to grapple with diseases such as cancer. She writes:

> The battle of living things against cancer began so long ago that its origin is lost in time. But it must have begun in the natural environment. . . . The environment contained these hostile elements before there was life; yet life arose, and over the millions of years it came to exist in infinite numbers and endless variety . . . life reached an adjustment with destructive forces as selection weeded. (Carson 219)

Carson's concern here is to adequately justify the view that nature is active and not passive. It seems, as far as the authors we are studying are concerned, that nature is speaking back to man. This excerpt taken from this fourteenth essay does not only focus on nature's response to fertilization, industrialization, and capitalism but, from its title, reveals nature's negativity, too, on man. The coming of the disease cancer, which "kills one in every four" of its victims, is nature's response to pesticides whose effects are so negative to man that Carson calls it biocide. Human activity on nature is thus unfair at all times and space.

The foregoing examples illustrate that Carson and Ojaide stand in the company of other writers throughout the ages. The difference is that some of these writers seemed to have gained the ears of their governments and brought about reforms. While the United States remains slow and skeptical about environmental and green reforms in general even today, and some writers, whose concerns have been green since the nineteenth century, have seen very little space in popular discourse in Africa, these writers have been persecuted and even sent to the gallows without trial. There is a need for a new voice, a different *song*, which also requires careful reading to decipher the author's intent.

This is what makes Carson and Ojaide unique. Reading Carson's and Ojaide's works from this perspective, one perceives that they have long lamented environmental catastrophe, but received no attention. These writers see a tomorrow that politicians and industrialists failed to believe. The Delta, Ojaide's point of reference in particular, and Africa in general, like the United States, is, to Carson, caught in the same web. Posturing as griot, Ojaide chants "the gifts in line"[2] to tell the story, for as Leslie Marmon Silko states, his task is to "pass down an entire culture / by word of mouth / an entire history / an entire vision of the world / which depended upon memory / and retelling by subsequent generations" (6). Carson, on her part, ends "A fable for Tomorrow" in these words: "What has already silenced the voices of spring in countless towns in America? This book is an attempt to explain" (3). Thus, like Ojaide the African poet, Carson the zoologist heralds the defense of the oppressed, and more so in this case, nature.

In this three-part story, Ojaide, in "When Green Was the Lingua Franca," mythologizes the people as he sings the blues—a lamentation of life's hazards and a celebration of life—as he recreates the past and reminds us about the missteps taken to the present deplorable state of affairs. This is a world gone topsy turvy.

> My childhood stretched
> one unbroken park,
> teeming with life.

> In the forest green was
> the lingua franca
> with many dialects.
> ...
> Undergrowth kept as much
> alive as overgrowth, the delta
> alliance of big and small,
> markets of needs, arena
> of compensation for all ...
> Then Shell broke the bond
> with quakes and a hell
> of flares. Stoking a hearth
> under God's very behind!
> ...
> Explosions of shells to *under*
> mine grease-black *gold*
> drove the seasons mental
> and to walk on their heads. (Ojaide *Delta Blues*, 12–13)

But in the retelling and reenactment, he inadvertently participates in the rape of the very people he set out to protect. Shell Oil, the neon-like insignia also coated by a shell, can display only indifference. He reopens old wounds, which bleed anew as the layers of degradation endured are peeled back and aired in *The Tale of the Harmattan*. If these are songs of death, they are also songs of hope centered in the *leitmotif* "harmattan," which despite its cold and wind and dust in West Africa assures and maintains the cycle and circle of human, vegetable, and animal life. This is a record of the tragedy and at the same time an endeavor to bridge the divide and restore what has been lost, as suggested by the epigraphs taken from Banna Kanute's *Sunjata* and Jorge Luis Borges. Does the paradox continue when we consider that our griot himself abandoned the homeland for the greener pastures of the West?

Carson, on her part, laments the past as she sees the United States as a land still even when the times change. With a tone full of nostalgia, she regrets that:

> Over increasingly large areas of the United States, spring now comes unheralded by the return of the birds, and the early mornings are strangely silent where once they were filled with the beauty of bird song. This

sudden silencing of the song of birds, this obliteration of the color and
beauty and interest they lend to our world have come about swiftly, insidi-
ously, and unnoticed. (Carson 103)

The picture painted here is like the dryness and emptiness expressed
in Ojaide's *The Tale*. The harmattan in the title becomes a sustained metaphor, signifying the devastation that now characterizes the land and government's corrupt and irresponsible practices, coupled with the rise of the
strong industrial power and the ruler ship of money in the capitalist world.

In a convoluted sense, the snapshots are nostalgic of the years of
beauty, youthfulness, abandon, and plenty depicted in *Great Boys*, which
can no longer be enjoyed, as Ojaide moans in *Delta Blues*:

> This share of paradise the delta of my birth
> Reels from an immeasurable wound.
> The inheritance I have been blessed with
> Now crushes my body and soul. (21–23)

Death and destruction have become the hallmark of the land. The
fishermen have disappeared; no swimmers can be spotted in the now-pol-
luted rivers, and the pomp and pageantry of the regattas have ceased. The
glory has indeed departed from the land:

> It is harmattan, time to prepare every hearth
> to combat northeast winds, fierce warriors
> . . .
> Season of brush fires, kites fly overhead
> in festive formations in smoke-smothered skies;
> . . .
> But this season's like no other in the minstrel's memory;
> the rubber tappers are frustrated with anemic trees
> suffering hardship and baldness from a neighbouring
> business that devours whatever stands before it.
> The exciting spirit of the harmattan is lost on us,
> there's nothing to celebrate with bonfires
> because the regular visitor failed to arrive
> with the good luck that follows its wake –
> the swarm of generous djinns that invade us
> barred from the land by free marketer of oil.
> In place of heat from the log-stoked hearth,
> we burn from gas flares and oil blowouts

on insomniac nights in the big compound.
we no longer swathe ourselves from cold
In one blanket, warm and inhaling body odour;
the sparkling hearth telling the tale of the
harmattan. (Ojaide *The tale*, 23–24)

The country has been taken over by a procession of "oil-soaked water spirits," and the Delta is wobbling. In telling this tale of corruption, waste, and degradation, Ojaide puns deliberately on *tale* and *tail*, designating an end and yet a continuum—what I call the paradox of his harmattan. Is there hope, a light at the end of the tunnel? In investigating and analyzing questions of ecological responsibility, Ojaide's tale bristles with irony and metaphor as it embraces the inherent dichotomy of waste and progress, of life and death.

Indeed, the land, formerly protective and nourishing, where groups "came together as one" with "love in everyone's heart" (Ojaide *Delta Blues*, 10) is now marked by ethnic dissensions from which there is no respite, no safe harbor. It is now a tomb: to "go towards the sea is death" and to flee "inland is also death."[3] Clearly one can suggest that Ojaide's poetry thus filters his sometime paradoxical stance toward the advent of oil companies as he depicts the possibility for growth, but *inter alia* registers the degradation of nature and the debasing of a people and culture. This is the dilemma of modern man caught in the web of modernization and globalization who acknowledges that even as he is at the cutting edge of technology, that edge may very well be the brink of a precipice.

Composed of three segments, each segment suggests an end in itself, and yet is as fragmented as the people whose tale it tells. Painting pictures of abundance and greed, of warmth and paralysis, of waste and death, Ojaide punctuates his mosaic with "dots in a circle" as if to suggest that to obtain completion one must make connections to recapture not only the innocence but the grandeur of the Delta's lost youth.

As mentioned previously, Carson's style is prosaic and in some cases relates to the art of storytelling. This compelling technique by a natural scientist expresses her foresight to what the environment was supposed to become, since the mid-twentieth-century *Silent Spring* is a collection of seventeen essays where the writer views "the postwar culture of science that arrogantly claimed dominion over nature as the philosophic root of the problem" (Lear xvi); the problem being that the earth now constitutes a great danger to its occupants. We come to understand that the issue is not a fatality because, as she puts it, "No witchcraft, no enemy action had silenced the rebirth of new life in this stricken world. The people had done it themselves" (Carson 3). Man's manifested greed or domineering attitude toward nature stands entirely to blame and not religion as some eco-critics have strongly argued.

This paper set out to underscore the centrality of nature's destruction in the world, and from the texts analyzed—an American essay and an African poetry collection—it seems clear that the discourse of environmental awareness had long been the call of authors from former colonized societies like Nigeria and imperial societies like the United States of America. An eco-critical reading of both works—fiction and nonfiction—reveals that the writers share the same concerns, even though at different times and space. This means that the issue of nature's degradation knows no boundaries. It seems a collective struggle and cry for all to contribute to redeem our world, the world our children and children's children will inhabit.

Notes

1. As with Ken Saro-Wiwa, all references to the Delta refer to the people and their environment.
2. "The drum beats itself" (Ojaide *Delta Blues*, 10).
3. Ojaide states in *The Tale of the Harmattan* that "Warri has never really been a beauty" (30).

Works Cited

Achebe, Chinua. *Things Fall Apart*. In *The African Trilogy*. Reading, Berkshire: Cox & Wyman, 1988. Print.
Ashcroft, Bill, Gareth Griffiths, and Helen Tiffin. *The Empire Writes Back: Theory and Practice in Post-Colonial Literature*. London and New York: Routledge, 1989. Print.
Carson, Rachel. *Silent Spring*. Boston and New York: Houghton Mifflin, 2002. Print.
Cooper, David E., et al. *The Environment in Question: Ethics and Global Issues*. London: Routledge, 1992. Print.
Dickens, Charles. *Bleak House*. Boston: Houghton Mifflin, 1956. Print.
Fanon, Frantz. *The Wretched of the Earth*. Transl. Constance Farrington. New York: Grove Press, 1981. Print.
____. *Black Skin, White Masks*. Transl. Charles Lam Markmann. New York: Grove Press, 1982.

Glotfelty, Cheryll and Harold Fromm. *The Ecocriticism Reader: Landmarks in Literary Ecology.* Georgia: U of Georgia P, 1996. Print.

Gikandi, Simon. *Reading Chinua Achebe.* London, Portsmouth and Nairobi: James Currey, Heinemann and Heinemann Kenya, 1991. Print.

Hunt, J. Timothy. *The Politics of Bones.* Toronto: McClelland & Stewart, 2005. Print.

Lear, Linda. "Introduction." *Silent Spring.* Ed. Carson, Rachel. New York: Mariner Books, 2002. x–xix. Print.

Muoneke, Romanus Okey. *Art, Rebellion and Redemption.* New York: Peter Lang, 1994. Print.

Naylor, Gloria. *The Women of Brewster Place.* New York: Viking Penguin, 1983. Print.

Ojaide, Tanure. *Delta Blues and Home Songs.* Ibadan: Krafts Books, 1998. Print.

———. *God's Medicine—Men & Other Stories.* Lagos: Malthouse, 2004. Print.

———. *In the House of Words.* Lagos: Malthouse, 2006. Print.

———. *The Tale of the Harmattan.* Plumstead: Kwela Books and Snailpress, 2007. Print.

———. *Great Boys.* Trenton: Africa World Press: 1998. Print.

Okoro, Dike. "Ojaide Sings The Tale of the Harmattan from Cape Town." Web. 18 Nov. 2009. http://www.africanwriter.com/ojaide-sings-the-tale-of-the-harmattan-from-cape-town/.

Orr, David W. *Earth in Mind: On Education, Envirnment, and the Human Prospect.* Washington: Island P, 1994. Print.

Said, Edward. "Literary Identity and Re-Configurations of Cultural Nationalism." *Figures, Configurations, Transfigurations.* Race & Class. 32.1 (1990): 1–16. Print.

Sander, Reinhard, and Bernth Lindfors, eds. *Ngugi wa Thiong'o Speaks: Interviews with the Kenyan Writer.* Oxford and Nairobi: James Currey and EAEP, 2006. Print.

Saro-Wiwa, Ken. *A Month and a Day: A Detention Diary.* Jersey: Safari Books, 1999. Print.

Silko, Leslie Marmon. *Storyteller.* New York: Seaver Books, 1981. Print.

Soyinka, Wole. "The Writer in a Modern African State." *The Writer in Modern Africa.* Ed. Per Wastberg. Uppsala: Scandinavian Institute of African Studies, 1968. 14–21. Print.

11

Poetic Rites, Minority Rights, and the Politics of Otherness in Tanure Ojaide's *Delta Blues and Home Songs*

James Tsaaior, Pan-African University, Lagos

Deeply etched within the textual interstices of Tanure Ojaide's poetic universe are the thematic trajectories of the ritualized despoliation and violation of the Niger Delta environment. Consistent with this environmental degradation are the hyphenation of minority rights and the divisive and retrogressive politics of otherness orchestrated by successive irresponsible and irresponsive Nigerian governments and their multinational oil collaborators. Ojaide executes a subversive poetic project against Nigeria's postcolonial political leadership, which has colluded with international monopoly capital to exploit, oppress, and marginalize the Niger Delta and other minorities. Within this agonistic schema, the poet assumes the rites of the bardic tradition as the custodian or repository of the people's heritage, contests and subverts the hegemony of imperial essences, and affirms the dignity and humanity of the people with keen artistic insights. As the veritable heir to society's epistemological networks and hermeneutic grids, the poet bears the moral burden to crystallize these asymmetrical hegemonic patterns quintessential of society, and distills alternative strategies to transcend the warped ethos. This paper negotiates Tanure Ojaide's poetry within the fabrics of environmental degradation, minority rights, and the politics of otherness practiced by the center against marginal and peripheral categories like the minorities that populate the Niger Delta, employing *Delta Blues and Home Songs* as a paradigm. It submits that Ojaide's oeuvre is angst-ridden and his poetic afflatus and sensibility evince a corrective and rehabilitative vision that hopes to reverse the calculus of political and economic power to privilege the minority who are, in fact, the majority.

What should constitute the veritable role of poetry and the inalienable responsibility of the poet to society has, ostensibly, become a settled epistemological mould. What has, however, dominated and will continue to dominate and govern literary and critical discourse is the location of the poet's creative afflatus and sensibility. This is because the constitution and construction of the poet's mind necessarily substrate and mediate the distillation of thematic foci and the magnitude of the poet's commitment to his art and society. Implicitly implicated here is the intrinsic value of art, particularly poetry, and its social relevance to societal engineering processes. Poetry in this perspective is not a hermetic enterprise, what Peter Barry characterizes as the "independent existence" of the poetic text (9). In other words, text which enjoys independent existence is latent with coherent semiotic systems and stable structures but without referents to the surrounding social circumstances critical to its constitution, production, and circulation as an artistic commodity.

Poetry here is not conceived as a transcendental theological doctrine but as an undifferentiated episteme that draws its vitality and inspiration from the milieu that endows it with beingness. For the poet is the repository of the individual and communal voice, memory and re-memory. He is also the custodian of the fund of society's ontology of values and mores. He represents the open wound of collective conscience, piously rankling and applying the therapeutic, healing herb to the weeping wound in society's experiential trajectories through the continuum of history. This is the creative burden of the poet. As observed elsewhere,

> [t]he rite to appropriate the poetic word and write, it will seem, is a right that rests exclusively with the initiates of the poetic cult. It will also seem that the poetic muse incarnates only scions that are endowed with circumcised minds, and harnessed hearts. Only the elect, it will seem should as such belong to this noble poetic pedigree and be conferred with the prerogative of wielding the poetic word. (Tsaaior)

But poetry should neither be a cult nor an esoteric experience. Also, the republic of poets should not be populated by ascetics or hermits but ordinary individuals imbued with a keen sense of society, history and life.

Fundamentally too, poets, through the materiality and efficacy of the creative wor(l)d, are quintessential midwives of transition and revolution. Chidi Amuta argues that these frontline countries' "liberation struggle was waged in the context of a clear anti-imperialist ideological standpoint" through the "mass mobilization of culture and literature in the service of the struggle for freedom" (56–57). Similarly, Clive Willis underscores the revolutionary potentials of poetry in the Lusophone countries of Angola and Mozambique in their "protracted armed struggles" (80) as an imperative for national liberation from Portuguese imperial domination. In the kinesis of human history, the transitional imperatives and revolutionary potentialities of poetry can be concretely located within the interstices of radical instabilities and what Femi Ojo-Ade calls "a corpus of contradictions" (127) within society and the appropriation of poetic rites and public space by poets to articulate the complex of sociocultural concerns and econo-political lineaments that define societal structures.

The Sociology of Poetic Craft and Postcolonial Angst in Ojaide's Poetry

Thus, whether they occupy the sensitive office of the traditional songbird, town-crier, griot, prophet, marabout, or that of the peripatetic and (post) modern poet, the poet's social responsibility to society as the oracular voice and compass of public morality remains. This enduring responsibility orders on the very sociology of artistic craftsmanship and, in this case, poetry. And with fidelity and piety, the poet must conscientiously embrace this high office with searing vatic insights and visionary fervor, a compelling vision that must transcend mere doctrinaire metaphysics of presence and barren mystificatory dialectics to a frontal engagement with the real issues of the day gnawing at the very viscerals of society. It is within this epistemic trajectory that the social specificity of the role and responsibility of the poet can be defined. For the poet must necessarily and inescapably bear the existential burdens of society and its vicissitudes of history. But even if he is unwilling to identify with the society, the society is willing to identify with him in the agonistic process of fashioning up a coherent voice for him and providing the herb for the healing of the society's infected soul. He may choose to preserve or subvert societal institutions, mores, values, and ideals, but must remain steadfast in his responsibility to society and its continued health in its strivings to fulfill its destiny.

Ojaide's poetry can be located within a postcolonial matrix. It is a poetic engagement that interrogates the Nigerian nation, founded upon a fraudulent federal structure but whose real operative mechanism is unitary. In this lopsided, unjust, and oppressive arrangement, the true tenets of federalism have been negated and compromised by an overarching federal government at the center. This centralized governmental structure owns all and controls all the resources from the regions, aggregates them into a whole, and routinely retails them to the same regions that have produced the resources in the first place. This is a radical disjuncture from other federal-state arrangements where the center is a beneficiary from the component parts that control their resource bases and merely contribute to the center for the purposes of maintaining national security and ensuring the territorial integrity of the state.

The Nigerian experiment, Ojaide argues through his poetry, demonstrates how best not to engineer a federation as it is a perversion of the *grundnorm* federalism. It stands federalism on its head and concentrates enormous powers in the center, thereby making Nigeria a centrist nation-state. This vulgarization of federalism through an absolutist and totalizing construction of state structures of power and hegemony is consistent with colonial and imperial arrangements, which Nigeria, as constituted at present, typifies. To accomplish the imposition of hegemony, the hegemons—in this case, Nigerian political oligarchs—appropriate the dictatorship of the ordinary citizens through the truncation of their fundamental rights to democracy, constitutional freedoms, power of free expression, and so forth, and institute their dictatorship. In the Niger Delta and other minority communities in Nigeria, this hegemony has been expressed through the alienation of the people from their mineral resources, and their exploitation by the state that should protect them but rather kills them instalmentally through environmental despoliation caused by multinational oil corporations like Shell.

Antonio Gramsci, the Italian theorist of hegemony, uses it as a concept that indicates the legitimacy of the political leadership of the people who should reside in their chosen representatives and democratic institutions but who are often hijacked by a powerful class of people to exclusively privilege themselves (Gramsci 22). Gramsci's work became popular during the fascist regime in his native Italy, but also strikes synonymy with Marxist and working-class peoples who want to assert their energies in a democratic revolution. This perception is also corroborated by Louis Althusser, the French philosopher, who asserts that hegemony by a totalitarian state is maintained through ideological state apparatuses. This translates to a stranglehold on the social structures of society through its key structural formations, which include the family, the media, religious organizations, the law enforcement agencies, the military and, most importantly, the education system, as well as the received ideas they propagate (Althusser 135).

While this hegemony and the ideological foundations on which it rests can deploy persuasive means, it can also apply violent means to establish itself and compel compliance to its regime. In the colonial and imperial dispensation, this hegemony was imposed through what Frantz Fanon refers to as "a great array of bayonets and cannons" (36) and also, Edward Said apprehends as "persuasive means" (131).

The Nigerian experience, which Ojaide negotiates in his poetry, has been aptly described as internal colonialism. This internal colonizing experience and culture have been perpetrated by a decadent political class formation, mainly from the majority ethnic extractions of the Hausa-Fulani, Igbo, and Yoruba. The minority groups, which include the Delta peoples, are marginalized in the scheme of national invention, as they are constituted as peripheral others. The politics of otherness practiced by the majority groups alienate the minorities from their resources, impoverishes them, and degrades their environment through oil spills, gas flaring, and air pollution, among other oil exploratory activities. In many cases, though, the minorities have also thrown up hegemons who actively collaborate with their counterparts in the majority ethnic groups to exploit and oppress their marginalized kith and kin in what is now known as the Nigerian project.

In his theorization of otherness, Homi Bhabha argues that essential differences are constructed between the self and the other in the maintenance of such identities based on oppositional binaries. The other is constituted as peripheral to the self and so becomes "a reformed, recognisable Other, as a subject of a difference that is almost the same, but not quite" (86). In Nigeria's political and socioeconomic patterns, the minorities are the others who have been socialized by the dominant groups, and their difference has become a liability. The hegemony of the ruling class has foisted on them an orgy of oppression, repression, exploitation, and other deprivations. Thus, within postcolonial discourse, the writer/artist imposes on himself the task of rigorously questioning hegemonic assumptions and practices, whether within or without, and through such a transgressive vision and rebellious tradition, hopes to retrieve society from the precincts of disintegration and destruction. This is precisely what Ojaide seeks to accomplish in his poetry.

Tanure Ojaide's poetic oeuvre is a monumental creative sacramental to the prohibitive social role of the poet to his society. And consistent with every meaningful social contract, Ojaide's corpus of poetry is an eloquent testament of a poet's unalloyed commitment to his people and society in the face of overwhelming impossibilities and reassuring possibilities, coherences and incoherencies, and adversities and prospects, as well as crippling predicaments and enabling opportunities. Thus, whether in *Children of Iroko and Other Poems* (1973), his maiden poetic outing, *Labyrinths of the*

Delta (1986), *The Endless Song* (1987), *The Fate of Vultures* (1990), *Delta Blues and Home Songs* (1997), or *In the Kingdom of Songs* (2000), Ojaide's poetic hemisphere heaves with passionate commitment to his Niger Delta peoples and the respect for their minority rights and the protection of their environment in a heterogeneous Nigerian nation-state. It is against this studied backdrop that this paper navigates Ojaide's deployment of poetic rites in the defense of the rights of the Delta minorities and the politics of otherness they are enmeshed in, refracting these issues through the prism of the poetic canvas of *Delta Blues and Home Songs*.

Ojaide's Poetry and the Minority Rights Question in the Niger Delta

As a pluralistic entity, Nigeria is an amalgam of heterogeneous peoples, multivalent cultures, ethnicities, and identities. Nigeria represents an ethnonational mosaic whose diverse polyphonic voices compete for a meaningful space to be heard. Since the 1914 amalgamation of the northern and southern protectorates by British imperialist and colonialist fiat, this pluralism has become synonymous with Nigeria. But concomitant with the politics of cultural pluralism is the constitution of the Nigerian state into the binary opposition of majorities and minorities. In this uneven, undemocratic, and exploitative sociopolitical arrangement, the Hausa-Fulani, the Igbo, and the Yoruba are privileged as the majorities, while the rest of the ethnic nationalities who actually constitute the majority are de-privileged as the minorities. It is to this subjugated and marginal category that the Niger Delta peoples have the misfortune of belonging.

The cumbersome burden of the poetry of Ojaide, and in this case, *Delta Blues*, is to negotiate and to plough the furrowed contours of this region, which is, paradoxically, so rich and yet so poor, so blessed and yet so accursed. Caught inextricably in the sticky web of these panoply of contradictions and the virtual absence of a national ethos, Nigeria's developmental arrest has been accentuated by what Femi Osofisan calls a corrupt and decadent officialdom "who control the nation's resources" (35–36). He further states:

> This nation is still in the process of becoming; our national ethos is still undefined, chaotic, self-contradictory in many respects. But the artist can help create a new ethos, and help transcend these contradictions, because he is easily the magician of nascent dreams, and is therefore the best midwife to a culture like ours struggling for a lasting parturition. (Osofisan 35–36)

This is the poetic project Ojaide has enlisted himself for, the revolutionary ethos he has espoused, to write back from the margins of the marginalized minorities to the center of the privileged majority. Central and strategic to the universe of *Delta Blues* is the pivotal question of minority rights within a pluralistic and polyvalent nation-state like Nigeria, which is in a perpetual state of becoming, and particularly with the fraudulent federation it operates. Within this exploitative political schema and socioeconomic calculus, the resources of the minorities are appropriated by the majorities to develop the latter and impoverish the former. As Crawford Young observes, this politics of Selfness and Otherness is quintessential of societies with plural cultural heritages and traditions of ethnicities like Nigeria (12). He further crystallizes the hermeneutic significance of cultural pluralism, its immanent referents, and concrete sociopolitical patterns at three componential levels:

> Plurality is with relationship to an authoritative arena, the sovereign territorial state (polity, political system), which provides sharply demarcated boundaries within which groups define themselves and each other, and their interaction occurs. Two or more socially and politically significant aggregates, differentiated by cultural criteria ... whose competition, interaction, and conflict constitute one important ingredient in the overall pattern of political transactions in the polity. The basis for these solidarity groupings are commonalities or affinities of ethnicity, language, race, caste, assume blood tie, custom, and territory. (Young 2–3)

Young's components of cultural pluralism achieve striking synonymy with Nigeria's essential character as a nation of nations. This multiple cultural heritage, which Young also acknowledges is "not necessarily permanent, frozen collectivities, but in a state of flux in response to long-run forces of social change" (12–13), has been negated in the Nigerian situation. In radical contradistinction to an open-ended, fluid, and constantly negotiated and renegotiated performative cultural identity formation process that encourages paradigms of continuous interactions and meaningful cultural affiliations among the diverse ethnic nationalities, Nigeria conceptualizes its cultural multiplicity in essentialist and binarist terms. This mummified cultural ethos constructs rigid, ossified, and Manichean hierarchies between the majorities and the minorities in a vertical and asymmetrical relationship, which feeds on internal colonialism and imperialism, power accumulation, oppression, repression, and the blatant exploitation of the natural resources of the minorities by the majorities.

These dominant issues are at the core of the Niger Delta condition and constitute the poetic fulcrum of *Delta Blues and Home Songs*. Spatially set in the Niger Delta in Nigeria's South-South geopolitical region, this area is famous for its idyllic and arcadian surroundings populated by ageless swamps, calm creeks, and astonishing estuaries. It is also home to a congregation of swaying streams, graceful rivers that teem with shoals of fish, and a verdant vegetation of tall, imposing, and intimidating forest trees. The Niger Delta is also a neighbor to the majestic Atlantic Ocean, which generously bathes its long stretch of shoreline with refreshing waters. It is this aquatic splendor and ethereal milieu of near primeval innocence that Ojaide weaves into his poetry. As Ojaide himself observes,

> [t]he poet responds to the environment around. This simultaneously spatial and temporal environment is an aggregate of his or her response to immediate and distant happenings, which may concern the individual or group, or in the wider contexts of nationality, race, or humanity. (*Delta Blues*, 8)

Fundamentally too, the Niger Delta area is also a reservoir of priceless resources. In the bowels of this rich, fertile, and alluvial soil sojourns crude oil in prodigious deposits. It is this invaluable resource known otherwise as black gold that translates to oil. It is this oil that lubricates the heart and arteries of Nigeria's monocultural economy. It is the same oil that also coagulates and burns these arteries and veins through the exploratory activities of multinational oil conglomerates, such as Shell, Exxon Mobil, Chevron, and Elf. The once salubrious landscape has become degraded, polluted, and endangered by oil spills and gas flaring, among other environmental hazards. This has, in turn, taken its devastating toll on the flora and fauna of the Niger Delta. As Ike Okonta and Oronto Douglas observe,

> oil producing communities therefore see Shell as the number one culprit in the economic and ecological war currently being waged against them . . . slowly but relentlessly such oil production activities as gas flaring, oil spillage, indiscriminate construction of canals and waste dumping have brought the human ecosystem of the Niger Delta to the point of near collapse. (12)

Ojaide himself chronicles this harsh and brutal reality in the poem "When Green Was the Lingua Franca." According to the poet, Man and

Nature were locked in a harmonious, communal relationship, which was mutually beneficial to both. Nature's elemental temperaments and man's corpus of needs were held in delicate balance through a dialectical interaction between man and epiphenomena. Ojaide states tellingly of the disruptive presence of big business:

> Then Shell broke the bond
> with quakes and a hell
> of flares. Stoking a hearth
> under God's very behind! (*Delta Blues*, 13)

Appropriating the etiological tale, which deplores women of driving God farther to the heavens with the end of their pestles, Ojaide acquits women of the charge and excoriates Shell: "Stop perjuring women for / their industry, none of them / drove God to the sky's height / it wasn't the pestle's thrust / . . . that caused the eternal rift" (13). Employing a counterdiscursive strategy, Ojaide interrogates this hegemonic epistemology, which is decidedly prejudicial to feminist ideology, and accuses Shell whose "[e]xplosions of shells to *under*/mine grease-black *gold*" which "drove the seasons mental / and to walk on their heads" (1998, 13). In Ojaide's transgressive and anti-imperial discursive counterhegemony, Shell Oil is solely responsible for the degradation and despoliation of the Niger Delta environment and the resultant disharmonious and disjunctural rhythm in the seasonal tide.

Besides Shell, the poet turns his searing and penetrating poetic lenses at successive collaborationist governments in Nigeria, which perfidiously turned the other way when Shell was employing unethical and unacceptable methods in its oil exploratory activities in Nigeria's Niger Delta. The poet considers this as a rite of treachery and betrayal by Nigeria's decadent, irresponsible, and irresponsive governments, which lacked legitimacy as they were largely military dictatorships whose interregnum trampled roughshod on the inalienable, fundamental rights of the minorities. These despotic governments were dominated by the military oligarchy, largely composed of the majority ethnic nationalities, though with the backing of some minority individuals and groups. In the poem "Seasons," Ojaide interrogates rebelliously this political engineering process that privileges the nation of majorities to the mutual exclusivity of the minorities. According to the poet:

> Our towns rose from riverbanks of barter.
> Once the waters sustained colouring from oil slick,
> Our constitution could not remain the same again –
> We selected delegates to take our prayers to Abuja,
> but guns scared them from the promised land. (Ojaide 15).

The poet implicates the military establishment, which (mis)ruled by subverting the constitution and by sheer might of the muzzle of the gun and, in the process, undermined the rule of law, violated fundamental freedoms of the people and hyphenated their humanity. In an argument reminiscent of the nationalist fervor, which galvanized political autonomy from colonial Britain in 1960, the poet laments in unmistakable funereal cadences: "We clubbed the pythons" of British imperialism "we believed meant evil, but / forget we were nursing cobras in our closets; / we pay for not heeding our forebears' voices" (15). Here, the poet directs his critical barbs at the national petit bourgeoisie that emerged at independence to succeed the retreating colonial overlords. Ojaide etches his rehearsed piece of poetic vitriol on the taut bow-string of his imagination and declares:

> No one doubts anymore where the Niger flows.
> If we had a centaur for president, we wouldn't lose
> customs as we have done to the emperor of cackles!
> Life would be worse in drought, but it won't be better in
> floods; the seniority debate disables. (Ojaide 16)

Then the poet tolls the knell:

> We spent more than thirty years of marriage/debating whether
> we should live together or split—
> we are fast passing the season of childbearing.... No one doubts
> anymore the fortune slipping away. (Ojaide 16)

In Ojaide's estimation, Nigeria's state of arrested development is a metaphoric representation of a barren marriage which is rancorous pointing portentously to the inefficacy of the union. The prophetic insights of the poet are here foregrounded as he has accurately predicted the political reforms conference in Abuja, which has been debating Nigeria's future as a corporate entity.

The politics of oil and the institutional malfeasance associated with it forms the pulsating trajectory that courses through Ojaide's *Delta Blues*.

The fundamentality of oil to the continued sustenance of the Nigerian federation cannot be ignored. As I have observed elsewhere, oil is:

> a natural mineral resource that possesses prodigious value and presides over life and living in Nigeria and the economics and politics associated with this invaluable priceless resource ... oil as life-blood lubricates, but also burns the arteries of the nation, endows life but also murders, prospers the nation but also causes adversities.... Oil which majorly sustains the economy and holds the component parts in (dis)harmonious communion as a single entity has the paradoxical potentials of wounding and healing, of sickness and therapy. While it enriches a few, it impoverishes a chunk of the population. While it erects mansions and other magnificent edifices, it pollutes and degrades the environment that houses it. While it launches a particular class into a blissful, carnivalesque mood, it etches indelible tattoos of poverty, mourning and moaning on other faces. Oil, thus, salves the soul of a nation but at the same time gnaws lethally at it. (Tsaaior 17)

The contradictory potentialities of oil and the politics it intensely generates as well as the congealed unsavory repercussions associated with its exploitation constituted the vanguardist activities of Ken Saro-Wiwa, the late writer, environmentalist, and minority rights crusader who was hanged in 1995. His killing represents what Neil Lazarus (1990) refracts as a nation's "mourning" in the "morning" of a revolutionary struggle for a safe environment for the Niger Delta. This concern is central to Ojaide in *Delta Blues* and it forms the focal point and organizing principle of his poetic *weltanschauung*. He states succinctly:

> My concern about the injustice and unfairness of the treatment of the Niger Delta people has always underscored my blues ... Ken Saro-Wiwa's championing of the cause of minority rights and environmental protection that I believe in and his judicial murder by the Sani Abacha regime gave rise to *Delta Blues and Home Songs*. (Lazarus 52)

The murder of Saro-Wiwa, leader of Movement for the Survival of Ogoni People (MOSOP) and his eight compatriots haunts, relentlessly, the pages of *Delta Blues*. This is much, as the murder by the hangman's noose drew virulent condemnation and opprobrium from the Commonwealth of Nations, the United Nations, and other international bodies and organizations. In concrete, metaphoric strokes, Ojaide mourns this perfidy against the people in the poem "Wails," which is modeled after his native Urhobo *Udje* dance songs. He, metaphorically, refers to Saro-Wiwa as "the elephant" whose absence will be conspicuous when "[a]nother ANA meeting will be called" (Ojaide 17), referring to the Association of Nigerian Authors to which Saro-Wiwa once presided over. In a sepulchral, disconsolate mood, the poet announces with tearful cadences, " I must raise the wail / so that each will reflect his fate / Take care of your people / they are your proud assets" (Ojaide 17–18).

Ojaide discovers in the courageous and irrepressible minority rights leader a veritable human shield against totalitarian regimes just like the elephant shields its young ones from the predator's rampages. The poet concludes climactically:

> Streets echo with wails.
> A terrible thing has struck the land,
> Everyone is covered with shame or sorrow
> This death exceeds other deaths,
> They have murdered a favourite son,
> . . . they have hanged a favourite son
> and eight other bearers of truth. (Ojaide 18)

Delta Blues is not only a poetic rite for minority rites but, specifically also, a general rite for the nine Ogoni activists. Ojaide engages this recent undulating historical past with poetic passion in other poems like "Immortal grief," "Sleeping in a Makeshift Grave," "Elegy for Nine Warriors," "Journeying," "Fresh Casualties," and "Remembering the Town-Crier," the last poem in the first of the two sections. In all these poems, Ojaide sculpts a poet-persona in Saro-Wiwa who is intimidating like an elephant, tall and imposing as Iroko, the hardy mangrove forest tree (even though the subject was actually diminutive), and an oracle whose intellectual stature towered above his murderers. Saro-Wiwa emerges as the authentic hero of the people who trod the alternative path paved by Isaac Boro, another Niger Delta activist.

In all these, it is, however, in *Delta Blues*, the eponymous poem, that Ojaide crystallizes his thematic treatment. The poem is a micro-historical rendering of the Niger Delta condition, periscoping the paradisiacal nature of the area before the "[b]arrels of alchemical draughts flow" almost irreparably assaulted "[t]he inheritance I sat on for centuries" (Ojaide 21). In this delectable area, the poet announces, "hosts and guests flourished /

on palm oil, yams and garri" and "[t]his home of plants and birds / least expected a stampede" from the oil prospecting merchants and conglomerates (Ojaide 21). First, it was palm oil for which the Royal Dutch company under Taubman Goldie obtained a charter in 1886 to exclusively exploit, and now Royal Dutch Shell, its heir, with crude oil as the major article of trade. The poet laments this checkered historical heritage foisted on the land:

> My nativity gives immortal pain
> masked in barrels of oil
> I stew in the womb of fortune
> I live in the deathbed
> prepared by a cabal of brokers
> breaking the peace of centuries
> and tainting not only a thousand rivers,
> my lifeblood from the beginning
> but scorching the air and soil.
> How many aborigines have been killed
> as their sacred soil was debauched
> by prospectors, money-mongers? (Ojaide 22)

Lurking behind and indelibly inscribed within the matrices of Ojaide's poetic lines are layers and vistas of epistemologies that yield a harvest of elastic hermeneutic stretches and significations. Thus, what looks deceptively like a bare, austere stylistic deployment bereft of ornamentations and aesthetic embellishments is actually an uncluttered and uninhibited poetic style that is devoid of unnecessary encumbrances. In the politics and ideology of Selfness–Otherness and its dialectic, Ojaide elects to flow in the turbulent currents of history with his marginalized minority people. This concern dominates and rules the texture of the last section of the collection titled "Home Songs." These are Urhobo folksongs that unearth and celebrate the people's rich cultural heritage and traditional oral forms, which form their grammar of values, architecture of knowledge systems, and architectonics of moral beingness.

These songs are laced with cultural markers and tropes, which resonate the ontology of the Delta people and acclaim the virtues of family life and public morality, as in "Climbing the Family Tree," and "Ayayughe." Others are satiric renditions, such as "Poachers," "Odebala," "My Relatives-in-law," "My Townsman in the Army," "Professor Kuta," and "Lordship of the Leopard" which lampoons decadent and dictatorial regimes. As Ezenwa-Ohaeto observes of Ojaide, "[T]he most important aspects of his poetry is [sic] its satiric quality. He satirises the army, prevalent notions in his country and numerous corrupt practices ..." (326). Some of the songs also mobilize the protest mode in the tradition of anti-populist government policies and programs. Ojaide's poetry is, as such, eminently political in mood and temperament with a visible ideological complexion. This is evident in the entire volume, especially in poems such as "Dance of Defiance," "Fragments," "I, Oniniwherhe, the Ant," and "Children of Notoma Street, Warri." All these poems chronicle the vicissitudinal realities of life in the Niger Delta.

Conclusion

Delta Blues and Home Songs constitutes a poetic continuum in the tradition of humanist intellection and populist ideology. In it, Ojaide boldly and courageously appropriates the poetic rites in the defense and protection of the minority rights of the Delta peoples as a peripheral and marginal category, a rite which rehumanizes, ennobles, and retrieves the dynamic agency and subjectivity of the Delta personality. Ojaide weaves a rich tapestry of heroic poetic lines that deify charismatic personages like Ken Saro-Wiwa, the late writer, environmentalist, and minority rites upholder and his eight Ogoni compatriots who led MOSOP against the imperialist tendencies of Nigerian governments and the exploitative machinations of international monopoly capital masquerading as oil companies in the Niger Delta. Included in the roll also is Wole Soyinka, the Nobel laureate for literature and NADECO chieftain, and Gani Fawehinmi, the political and social activist lawyer.

Ojaide's remarkable achievement in this volume peaks significantly at two paradigmatic levels: first, his consistency of poetic vision, evidenced in the distillation of thematic networks that unabashedly negotiate and interrogate the grids of binary relations that mediate Nigerian nationhood and privilege the majorities but ascribe subaltern status to the minorities. At another level, he combines an apocalyptic and *angst*-ridden poetic outlook with an abiding and persevering sense of millennial optimism that heaves with vast possibilities, even in the face of overwhelming contradictory circumstances. What emerges is a poetic idiom whose *angst* is tempered in the forge of thematic appositeness, relevant and compelling imagery, as well as an affirmatively austere stylistic deployment, which throws into relief the dominant concerns of the poetry.

Works Cited

Althusser, Louis. "Ideology and Ideological State Apparatuses." *Lenin and Philosophy and Other Essays.* New York: Monthly Review Press, 1971. Print.

Bhabha, Homi. *The Location of Culture.* London: Routledge, 1994. Print.

Barry, Peter (ed.). *Issues in Contemporary Literary Theory.* London: Macmillan, 1987. Print.

Fanon, Frantz. *The Wretched of the Earth.* Trans. Constance Farrington. New York: Groove Press, 1968. Print.

Gramsci, Antonio. *Selections from the Prison Notebooks.* London: Lawrence and Wishart, 1971. Print.

Lazarus, Neil. *Resistance in Postcolonial African Fiction.* New Haven and London: Yale UP, 1990. Print.

Ezenwa-Ohaeto. "Funso Aiyejina and Tanure Ojaide." *Perspectives on Nigerian Literature: 1700 to the Present Vol. 2.* Ed. Yemi Ogunbiyi. Lagos: Guardian Books, 1988. 321–326. Print.

Ojaide, Tanure. *Delta Blues and Home Songs.* Ibadan: Kraft Books, 1998. Print.

_____. *A Creative Writing Handbook for African Writers and Students.* Lagos: Malthouse Press Limited, 2005. Print.

Ojo-Ade, Femi. "The Black Man's Burden: Christianity in Black African Fiction." *Essays in Comparative Africa Literature.* Ed. W. Feuser and I. N. C. Aniebo. Lagos: CBAAC, 2001. 125–156. Print.

Okonta, Ike, and Oronto Douglas. *Where Vultures Feast: Shell, Human Rights and Oil in the Niger Delta.* San Francisco: Sierra Club Books, 2001. Print.

Osofisan, Femi. *Literature and the Pressures of Freedom.* Ibadan: Opon Ifa Readers, 2001. Print.

Said, Edward. *Culture and Imperialism.* London: Vintage, 1994. Print.

Searle, Chris. "Mobilisation of Words: Poetry and Resistance in Mozambique." *Marxism and African Literature.* Ed. G. Gugelberger. Trenton: Africa World Press, 1985. 150–164. Print.

Tsaaior, James Tar. "Mantids of Mankind Without Mission, Vision and Ambition." *The Post Express Literary Supplement.* A Review of *Mantids* by Nengi Ilagha. March 18 (2000): 19. Print.

_____. "Oil that Lubricates and Burns the Arteries." *The Post Express.* A Preview of *All for Oil* by J. P. Clark Belkederemo. Sept. 22 (2000): 17. Print.

Young, Crawford. *The Politics of Cultural Pluralism.* Ibadan: Heinemann Educational Books, 1993. Print.

12

Transcending the Discontents of Global Capitalism: Toward the Dialectics of De-commodified Environment in *Daydream of Ants and Other Poems* and *The Eye of the Earth*

Uzoechi Nwagbara

> The inheritance I sat on for centuries
> Now crushes my body and soul. (Ojaide, *Delta Blues* 21)

> Earth is nothing more than
> A cauldron of dry dreams. (Osundare, *The Desert Cometh* 237)

Introduction: The Siege of Global Capitalism, Eco-poets, and the Nation

This chapter provides an aesthetic framework for understanding the ways in which global capitalism (globalization) has reshaped the topography and benchmarks of environmental, ideological, political, and socioeconomic relations, both at national and global spheres, as well as exerted adverse pressures on the continental bliss of developing nations—particularly Nigeria. Consequently, Tanure Ojaide's and Niyi Osundare's collections of poetry, *Daydream of Ants and Other Poems* (1997) and *The Eye of the Earth* (1986), respectively, shall be used as texts to unearth the dimensions of the environmental upshots of the presence of the multinationals (cultural agents of global capitalism) on Nigeria's (the Niger Delta's) environment. As global capitalism problematizes the dynamic of subordination and domination of nations as well as reinforces the logic of core-periphery thesis, the lingering aftertaste is that periphery nations are continually in the shadow of multinational corporations, which manifests in the commodification of the environment as well as marketization of socioeconomic relations. Behind the mask of globalization, the multinationals undermine the Niger Delta's environment, biodiversity, and people. Although the volumes refract the commoditization of Nigeria's environment, they also essentialize the poetics of transcending this environmental malaise, which resonates with negating the actualities of commoditized environment on the heels of global capitalism for a reinvented Nigeria.

Since Nigeria's political independence in 1960, the nation is mired in the crisis of leadership and nationhood precipitated by the bungling mode of governance instituted by the political class and their compradors, the multinational oil corporations, to perpetually hold the people down as well as to frustrate the nation's attempt to be developed and valued in the comity of nations. This has also impacted negatively on the nation's environment. More than five decades since Nigeria gained political independence, there seems to be palpable dissonance between the hopes as well as aspirations that the people had as it became politically independent, and what has become of self-rule in the nation. This disequilibrium between people's hope and what is the actual nature of political leadership has animated a brand of literary experience that reverberates with what Emmanuel Obiechina called literature of "post-independence disenchantment" (). This literary pattern animates the Ojaidean "activist role of the verbal art" (in Shantz "Beyond Socialist Realism," 111), a revolutionized kind of writing Osundare defined as "man meaning to man" (*Songs*, 3). It is the type of literature that gauges Nigeria's burden of memory in the wake of bungling leadership as well as environmental-unfriendly politics that percolates its nationhood.

In maintaining that the paradigm that espouses the continued significance of the people's hope at Nigeria's attainment of political independence is no more valid, as well as the urgency of nationalist aesthetics given the actualities of postcolonial Nigeria, recent poetic voices in the nation are geared toward unearthing this departure. Thus, Nigeria's political experience has thrown up the saliency of what could be described as an aesthetic paradigm shift (in the Kuhnian sense), a departure from anti-colonialist–committed literature, to literary engagement with the inanities of "internal colonialism" speckled with globalist project. This unsavory landscape that finds accommodation in the timbre, tenor, and texture of eco-critical Nigerian literature, is described by Chidi Amuta as "the politicisation of the Nigerian literary imagination" (92). Given this backdrop, the postcolonial Nigerian condition as well as "the global economy and the forces of globalisation have become prominent characteristics of the current paradigm of world politics" (Monshipouri, Welch, and Kennedy 966). Modern Nigerian (eco)-poets have risen to this occasion.

Oil politics is one of the main hues of Nigerian political woes. This is so given what oil represents in the country. Virtually all political operations in the nation stem from oil, which accounts for nearly all of Nigeria's GDP (Obi; Ojakorotu; Nwagbara "Political Power," "Poetics of Resistance," "In the Shadow"). Oil is the main reason for the presence of the multinationals. Beyond the rhetoric of magnifying as well as intensifying the level of interaction and interdependence among nation-states and societies as markets become available on a worldwide scale, the real face behind the mask of globalization is commodification of periphery nations' environment and oil politics of disempowering periphery nations. In instantiating the globalized dynamics of environmental (ecological) and political drama unfolding in Nigeria (the Niger Delta), Cyril Obi in his piece "Globalisation and Environmental Conflict in Africa" offers this perspective:

> Environmental conflict in the Nigerian oil industry, particularly in the oil-rich region of the Niger delta, is 'globalised' in the sense of the presence of global actors in the local communities; the integration of the communities via oil production into the global economic system and the connections being forged by local social movements to the global human rights agenda; and international human and environmental rights groups in the fight against the state-global oil alliance. (40)

The seamless, unrestricted movement of labour and capital across nations that global capitalism purportedly embodies has animated debates and writing on the issues of social justice, environmentalism, corporate social responsibility, "environmental apocalypse," "ecological war" and eco-criticism, among others. Part of this debate finds provenance in eco-poetry. The poetics of *Daydream of Ants and Other Poems* as well as *The Eye of the Earth* is anchored in eco-poetry as shall be demonstrated in this chapter.

In defending his position on the impact of capitalism in our world, Johan Norberg in his acclaimed treatise *In the Defence of Global Capitalism* (2003) states that the distribution of capitalism in the last decades has brought down poverty rate globally as well as spawned opportunities around the world—particularly in developing nations. Life expectancy, living standards, and environmental health of communities have been positively affected by the forces of globalization. Thus, hunger, inequality, social stratification, and infant mortality have been normal as a consequence. This is in view of the urgency of globalization that inheres in economic and technological development grounded on the anvil of free-market economy. Further to this, developing or poor countries that include Nigeria have benefited from this, as their liberalized economies underwrite impressive results, while the nations that are not on the liberalization bandwagon are in the lurch of Oguibean "[un]connectivity" rider (Oguibe 175). Ultimately, Norberg's admonition here is that the world needs more and more globalization for world economic prosperity.

In revolt against what Norberg called man's "new liberty and internationalism" (ix), a metonymy for globalization, the skepticism about globalization (Okunoye "Alterity," "Writing Resistance"; Okuyade "Rethinking Militancy"; Olaoluwa; Nwagbara "Poetics of Resistance") is underscored by its potency to erode cultural values as well as environmental wholesomeness of periphery nations, as the concept behind the system is underpinned by fierce frontier capitalist operation as well as underdevelopment agenda. In interrogating the evil buried under the veneer of globalization, both in his *An Inconvenient Truth* (2006) and *Our Choice* (2009) Vice President Al Gore, as well as Alan Weisman in his *The World Without Us* (2007) and Caroline Fraser in her *Bewildering the World* (2009), unequivocally questions the impact of humanity's business on our planet. In addition to these books, volumes of books, essays, and collections of poetry have been churned out by African as well as international writers and observers about the dangers of man's business in our environment.

From Henry Thoreau's *Walden* (1854) to Richard Carlson's *Silent Spring* (1962); from J. P. Clark-Bekederemo's *A Reed in the Tide* (1965) to Gabriel Okara's *The Fisherman's Invocation* (1978); and from Ken Saro-Wiwa's *Songs in a Time of War* (1985) to Tanure Ojaide's *Labyrinths of the Delta* (1986), *Daydream of Ants and Other Poems* (1997), and *Delta Blues and Home Songs* (1998), the complicity of man in the despoliation of the environment is central. In this mould, from Niyi Osundare's *The Eye of the Earth* (1986) to Adiyi Bestman's *Textures of Dawn* (1998) and to Nnimmo Bassey's *Intercepted* (1998), there is an abiding commitment to interrogate man's business in our world as well as its effects on our environment, ecology, and biodiversity. Similarly, in the millennium, works such as Ibiwari Ikiriko's *Oily Tears of the Delta* (2000), Uzoechi Nwagbara's *Polluted Landscape* (2002), Uche Umez's *Dark through the Delta* (2004), and Ogaga Ifowodo's *The Oil Lamp* (2005) among others are cast in the mould of eco-critical poetry. In these poetry collections, there is an ideo-aesthetic consciousness to depict man's collusion in the destruction of our environment and its commodification premised on the logic of globalization. Thus, recent experiences have inspired extending an awareness of the link between the human presence and Nature in

[the] poetry ... an assessment of the damage done to the society. This translates into an almost obsessive concern with the human quest to survive in an environment that was once rich and capable of supporting life. ... This constantly provokes nostalgic reflection on the lost beauty and natural wealth of the region (Nigeria) following the discovery and exploration of oil. (Okunoye 4)

Given the above, Nigerian eco-critical poets that include Ojaide and Osundare have given the ecological neglect of our environment and its commodification as well as our endangered Nature a central place in their poetry.

In challenging the cultural siege and marginalization agenda engendered by global capitalist logic, the Nigerian writers see this as social responsibility on their part to contribute to the issue of "truth-telling" (Lodge 4) about Nigeria's postcolonial condition as well as to offer insights into the evils of cultural deracination couched in this system. As Onyemaechi Udumukwu contends in his *Social Responsibility in the Nigerian Novel*, "social responsibility is predicated on the basic assumption that the writer is endowed with a communal voice" (5) to chronicle the rhythm of the time in a humanizing manner. This position is in sync with Edward Said's assertion that every work of art should be put in its world in order to unearth the muted interactions that inform it (in Udumukwu *The Novel and Change in Africa*, 20). Thus, Ojaide and Osundare are preoccupied with "representations of colonialism, nationhood, postcolonity, the typology of rulers, their powers, [and] corruption" (Aijaz 124) in a world inextricably tied to the politics of global capitalism. One of the main concerns of this paper is to interrogate the interplay between poetry and environmental politics as Nigeria grapples with the postcolonial condition, primarily shaped by the ruse of global capitalism.

Speaking on the message behind his book, *Writing in a State of Siege*, Andre Brink asserted that "[t]here lies a peculiar satisfaction in countering the tactics of secrecy with exposure: the dark fears nothing quite so much as light" (35). Although the writer in Nigeria is not in the South African situation, he is no doubt in a similar terrain, where global politics has made existence for the masses, including the writer, unbearable. This is the same point made by Coetzee in his acclaimed *Doubling the Point*:

For the writer the deeper problem is not to allow himself to be impaled on the dilemma proposed by the state, namely, either to ignore its obscenities or else to produce representations of them. The true challenge is: how not to play the game by the rules of the state, how to establish one's own authority. (364)

The above national quandary requires a "commitment to political critique and social action" (Morrison 114), which will mark a departure from the destruction of the environment to "fertility and increase" (Ngumoha 131) in our environment.

In using their poetry as actions in the world—the world of global capitalism—Ojaide and Osundare contend that there is a possibility of this if environmental politics is interrogated via the conduit of poetry in order to rise above the challenges posed by the commodification of sociomaterialist relations as well as man's original neighbors (Ojaide 1994), flora, and fauna. In Ojaide's interview with Charles Bodunde in 1999, the eco-poet admitted his inexorable drift toward ecological and environmental concerns in his works:

> The Delta has a special appeal to me ... the vegetation, the evergreen, the heavy rains almost all year round but you know this has been complicated by the coming of the oil companies. I knew when they came. I was only a boy then but I knew. There has been a great change in the environment since they came ... long before Ken Saro-Wiwa started to talk about the Delta, as far back as 1973, I was already talking about Ughelli and the other areas; about how they are producing so much and getting little back. Now the environment is destroyed with gas being flared, the farms are not good; fishes are driven from rivers, everywhere is polluted. And yet, government does nothing to help the people. (Bodunde "Tanure Ojaide Poetry," 196)

The above globalized environmental slough is what the repertoire of Ojaide's poetry negates: "There are indications that ... African poetry will continue to be radical. ... Poets will continue to portray the bleak socio-economic landscapes with negative and ugly images and dream of light at the end of the tunnel" (Ojaide "New Trends," 17). Within this frame of thought, Osundare inscribes the political content of poetry into the goings-on in the society for human "consciousness raising" (the Freirean conscientization schema), an actuator of political consciousness and activism that is capable of illuminating people's views about the menace of oil politics. Thus, poetry is about man meaning to man (Osundare *The Eye of the Earth*, 3). To this end, as Osundare contends, "the deep structures of our cultures and the literatures they produce unite us. It is the politics of the surface which divides and alienates us" (in Ohaeto 95).

Theoretical Clarification: Commodification of the Environment as Default, Eco-criticism as Counternarrative

This study is predicated on the bifurcation: the commodification of Nigeria's environment and eco-critical poetry aimed at resisting the commodification of the environment mediated by globalization. Globalization and global capitalism will be used interchangeably in this paper, as both words portend the same thing. Globalization as a term is enmeshed in definitional welter (Monshipouri, Welch and Kennedy; Obi). However, for a grasp of the definitional contours of the concept for our analysis in this paper, globalization (global capitalism) entails "the aggregation of compliant nations of the world into a community wherein their territorial boundaries dissolve into ideological insignificance while retaining their political sovereignty as independent nations" (Obioha 2). This is about the creation of "new conditions of proximity, intensity, and even intimacy with what used to be distant faraway worlds" (Aina 5). In this instance, globalization is about homogenizing the world economic system as well as information technology and allied concept for ease in global business transactions among nations. However, this process resonates with the reinvention of the world into "developed and developing countries, industrial and industrialising nations and core and periphery" (Saurin 679) for the marginalization of the periphery nations as well as economic, ideological and political benefit of core nations.

The term commodification finds provenance in the Marxian dialectics. It originated from the word commodity. As a Marxist notion, commodification argues that every human dealing or relationship is based on socioeconomic as well as materialist gains. Therefore, the idea behind global capitalism is the quest for domination and economic power that arguably endorses virtually all human relationship as Marxist dialectics instructs. So, in this regard, commodification is the act of measuring the worth of a person or an object in terms of its monetary or social value. It can also be defined as the act of relating to objects or persons in terms of their financial and social worth and benefit (Azumara 16).

As a consequence, for the eco-poets, man's activities on the planet are fundamentally hinged on the commodification of relations (life) and environment (both human and nonhuman) are inextricably linked to exploitative relationship. Accordingly, various forms of resistance dialectics, specifically environmentalism, eco-poetry, deep ecology, eco-feminism, and eco-criticism, among others, stem from an ideological worldview to resist the ruse and dogma of commodification of relations mediated through globalization or capitalism.

The concept of eco-criticism or eco-poetry was first developed in a seminal study by Cheryll Glotfelty and Harold Fromm, tagged *The Ecocriticism Reader: Landmarks in Literary Ecology* (1996). In their contention, eco-criticism is "the study of the relationship between literature and the physical environment" (Glotfelty and Fromm xviii). It is about literature of the environment. Traditionally, the environment is used to depict the green world as well as wild/natural places. But in taking this further, the environment according to Armbruster and Wallace entails this:

> [the] environment need not only refer to 'natural' or 'wilderness' areas ... environment also includes cultivated and built landscapes, the natural elements and aspects of those landscapes, and cultural interactions with those natural elements. (4)

Thus, the present study is predicated on the commodification of the natural world as well as human relationships through global capitalist practice. Eco-poetry is steeped in negating this condition. Thus, the unequal level of development between core and periphery nations is associated with the rhetoric of globalization, which comes in deferent hues. One of the areas that commodification of relations has shattering consequences to the periphery nations is the environmental and the natural world. This is the case in Nigeria—particularly the Niger Delta, where global capitalists represented by the multinationals (such as Shell, Elf, Chevron, Agip, and others) in cahoots with the political elite have wreaked havoc on the ecology, biodiversity, marine life, and environment of the people as well as mangled the economic well-being of the inhabitants of this region of the world, all in the name of international business and oil exploration.

Robert Bullard in his *Unequal Protection: Environmental Justice and Communities of Colour* (1994) avers that most of the resistance movement to save the earth and to resist ecological devastation have emerged under the rubric of de-commodification of relations and the environment. Jeffrey Shantz asserts that

> commodification of relations crushes Nature as well as robs man of his natural inheritance; it is an ideological veneer by the powerful (the core nations) for economic, political, ideological and social control. In this sense, the commodification of Nature has become an ideological cover for those members of 'humanity' who, in asserting positions of privilege, have constructed not only Nature but fellow humans—typically the poor, blacks ... as mere resources to be exploited. Significantly, it is precisely

among these inferiorised positions that the impacts of ecological destruction are most severely experienced. (Shantz "Scarcity," 149)

In revolt against this cultural trap, the eco-poets, Tanure Ojaide and Niyi Osundare, "are turning to cultural expressions opposed to the processes and effects of capitalist globalization" (Shantz "Beyond Socialist Realism," 121) as well as poetic engagement, which negates the actualities of globalisation.

Ojaide and the Dialectics of Alternative Order: Negating the Discontents of Global Capitalism in *Daydream of Ants and Other Poems*

G. G. Darah in his piece "Revolutionary Pressures in Niger Delta Literatures" brings to the fore the negation dialectics of Ojaide's poetry:

> The poetry of Tanure Ojaide . . . fits into the tradition of outrage against political injustice, exploitation and environmental disasters. On the basis of sheer output, Ojaide is the most prolific in the Niger delta region. From his titles, one can discern an abiding concern with the fate of the Niger delta people. . . . ("Examining Canonisation," 12)

In corroborating the above, Ojaide in his own words assays this notion:

> contemporary trends are enlarging the African literary canon. African writers have been responding to the impact of migration and globalisation on their people and continent. Ecological and environmental matters, sometimes arising from the actions of the multinational companies, are at the core of . . . Tanure Ojaide's [works] on the environmental degradation of the oil-rich Niger delta area of Nigeria [emphasis mine]. ("Examining Canonisation," 15)

Ojaide is a pragmatist as well as realist artist who does not pander to the allure of art for art's sake thesis. He endeavors to make social facts find expression in his poetry as well as other aesthetic engagements. This is what Abdul Jan Mohammed calls "a profoundly symbiotic relationship between the discursive and the material practices of imperialism" (54).

The concept of negation is what Ogaga Okuyade in relation to literature responding to the inanities in the Niger delta, characterized as "counter-narrative" (4). Therefore, Tanure Ojaide's poetry of negating the crude logic of imperialism is a "locus for identity politics" (Okuyade

"Recent Nigerian Bards," 14) that is a nationalist agenda, mediated by means of a counternarrative embedded in counterhegemony project. Ojaide's poetry seeks answers to social and environmental problems in its unique way of negating contradictions. This is in consonance with Charles Bodunde's contemplation that Ojaide "envisions a break from the savage cast of... ruler[s]..." (204). Similarly in Ojaide's view, the ruling class referred here make the environment, fauna, flora and people "die in droves in their crossfire..." (Ojaide *Daydream of Ants*, 69).

For Ojaide, this process amounts to negating "the unhappy shift" (Bodunde "Tanure Ojaide Poetry," 196), which reverberates with Marxist "metabolic rift" thesis, the period of "Lemon Memory" (*Daydreams*, 65) that contrasts with "When Green was the Lingua Franca" (*Delta Blues*, 12). Ojaide extends the logic of negation that literature accentuates:

> Literature has to draw attention to [the] increasing gap between the haves and the have-nots. Literature has become a weapon against the denial of basic human rights. ... It is understandable why the African (Nigerian) artist is utilitarian. (*Poetic Imagination*, 42)

The above is what Ezeliora (47) considers being "the pragmatic framework of poetry" that is capable of interrogating social and environmental realities.

In the verse: "The Diviner's Chant," Ojaide's negation rhetoric is gradually rising in stridency in order to upturn environmental as well as social justice:

> Mask of the vain drum
> Speaking through the nose
> I understand you
> Liars of ages
> Hiding under a sleek tongue
> I detect you
> Robed scarecrow
> Parading for a beauty
> I detest you
> Teeth of the vicious
> Flashing stolen pearls
> I smell your stink
> Hand holding the hilt
> You will vanquish with blades
> But will die of a bloodless conscience

> Robber baron
> Championing charities
> I see the stakes to which you will be tied
> Workers will chase out drones
> The world evacuates its dross
> Let it not clog our front! (55)

Through the use of imagery, Ojaide harps on what Sule Egya (345) tagged "images of the oppressor," whom Ojaide calls "baron robbers" in another collection of his, *Delta Blues and Home Songs* (22). These "robber barons" are a metonymy for globalists whose conduct have commodified our environment. Thus:

> capitalist social relations, and specifically the introduction of commodity relations into ... the encompassing appropriation of nature through human labour, permitted through homogenization of the 'logic' of capitalist accumulation and the corporatist conjoining of labour and capital in mass consumption regimes, has consequently raised rather poignant questions regarding possibilities for ecological survival of complex life on this planet. (Shantz "Scarcity," 145–146)

In the above poem, Ojaide envisions the crushing of the oppressors, the "robber baron" who will be pulverized by "workers," the people, in their united stand against environmental injustice and prebendal buccaneering.

Similarly, in another versification, "Technology," attempt is made to instantiate the havoc precipitated by technology, a correlate of globalisation, as well as to interrogate the ruse behind global connectivity, which has brought untold misery to the periphery nations:

> Once foragers brought home food
> And robbery was sanctified by hunger,
> The ban on trespassing collapsed;
> The world swamped with hostility.
> This started cold-headed strategies:
> The bush-rat dug a dungeon
> Of infinite outlets;
> The tortoise stuck to a mobile phone fortress
> To go through hazards of life;
> Ants raised a hill
> To cover their habitat of holes. . . .
> You can see what we were born into! (13)

In continuing the debate above, what we were born into is "the feverish race towards planetisation otherwise known as globalization" (Olaoluwa 242), which has fuelled "polarisation both within cities and between" (Hill 246) as well as ossified the protracted period of violent conquest and environmental pillage. Through the imagery of "mobile phone," "tortoise," "bush-rats," as well as words such as "robbery" and "trespassing," the ruse behind the theory of global capitalism is appreciated. In African oral art, the creature tortoise epitomizes grand sleight and skilful cunning that Ojaide likens to the globalists, who use the veneer of Baudrillardian "hyperrality" to deepen their exploitative mission in the developing nations. This is done via the commodification of the environment, the logic of which is supported by marketization of social relations and labor justified by the corporeality and pressures of international business and cooperation. The mobile phone is a term that resonates with modern technology—information technology—that legitimizes "trespassing" through its "cold-headed" means of homogenizing world information flow. Commenting on this mould of thought, "Ojaide's narration of the nation is essentially from the point of view of the Niger Delta crisis and by so doing, he interrogates the basis for the invention and sustenance of the nation" (Olaoluwa 242). It is to this end that Ojaide's poet-narrator, Aridon, in his "Aridon's Call" is bent on negating this despicable order:

> My horse mounted,
> I obey the wind
> Blowing inside me.
> I shut my eyes
> And take a deep breath
> For a clear goal.
> The frontierless land
> Will change into a rock
> Under my feet—
> I want it to accelerate
> My pace
> And fortify my song.
> Once Aridon calls,
> Mine is to steer
> Tirelessly ahead.
> My horse is mounted
> For a lifelong ride. (Ojaide 9)

The above poem is quoted wholly to underscore Ojaide's commitment exemplified through his poet-narrator, Aridon, to break from the order of exploitation and dominion instituted by global capitalism. Thus, the narrator amounts "the wind / blowing inside" to prospective commitment and vision for a new world when the Niger Delta (Nigerian) environment will be free from imperial deadweight and environmental devastation.

In seeking alternative order that finds expression in de-commoditized nature and environment as well as vision of power devolution that globalization makes unattainable, Ojaide's poet-narrator in another verse, "The Daydream of Ants," avers trenchantly:

> We are in league with powers
> To wreck one vision
> With lust for more visions
> To refashion a proud world—
> With the same hands
> That raise a storm of dust,
> We paint towers of magnificence. (*Daydream of Ants*, 15)

The vision encased in "to wreck" amounts to the ideology to tear down the edifice of global capitalism, which brings perils to the marginalized nations down as well as makes their environment comatose. Ojaide's narrator is seeking for a concerted effort to upturn social justice and fair environmental dealings in the region. The march from "dust," a synecdoche for all the havoc caused in the nation, to "towers of magnificence," a metonymy for the much sought-after epiphany of a reinvented green world, is at the heart of Ojaide's meditation in the poem. This process incarnates with "refashion[ing] a proud world": this is the essence of the poet's vision.

In continuing the negation process as well as diffusion of powers from monolithic base, the West, to all nations of the world that are tied to what Olu Oguibe (175) calls "connectivity and the fate of the unconnected," Ojaide in another poem, "The Power of Victims," addresses this point:

> And these are the tolls of dominion:
> Victims reeling with vengeance.
> Cutting through stones to pathways,
> Arching wide rivers with rainbows,
> Launching dreams to people the moon
> And clearing space for inevitable confrontation,
> We straw our way with victims. (34)

The "tolls of domination" (the price) of re-enslaving the Saidian Order through global capitalism, are catalogued in the above extract—which is annealed in the dialectics of "confrontation" with the imperialists for Nigeria's renaissance. This is because in the conception of the globalists, "Nature is reintroduced to us as 'environment', a realm of capitalist profit and personal indulgence. Environment, nature's 'brand name', becomes little more than a stockpile of 'resource', reconstructed as a warehouse of riches solely for the gratification of ceaselessly multiplying human wants" (Shantz "Scarcity," 145).

Here lies the urgency of the "de-commodification of social life" (Mouffe 92) as well as the environment. Ojaide in another verse captured the materialization of this de-commoditizing wind that is blowing:

> My people brandished a phallus,
> Knife-carved, oversized banana,
> to break the curve of the uterus.
> Public sight, an erection
> That the childless one bore
> To carry her marriage dream
> Into cries of jubilation. ("The Other Writing" 19)

"Phallus" in the above extract symbolizes strength, vitality, and power "to break the curve of the uterus." The sense that the curved uterus invokes is infertility, barrenness and environmental slough that find abode in childlessness, a metonymy for damaged earth and nature in the wake of oil exploration. But in order to break from this misery, the "oversized banana," a phallic, sensual image of fecundity and agility, is being employed to usher us into a new dawn—the era of a regreened cosmos. This metastasis will ultimately find expression in jubilation as the globalists and their cohorts, the Nigerian political class, will be crushed.

Both in "Opinion Page" and "Reclamation," Ojaide offers variations of negation poetics. In "Reclamation," Ojaide's narrator's heart yearns for a time to bring justice in a sinful world: "My heart burns for a desire/that must be fulfilled" (68). This vision and desire for fulfillment finds corporeality in "Opinion Page," where global capitalists who are named "tortoises" (Ojaide's phraseology for underhand dealers) are being disparaged, disgraced and flogged:

> Passers-by to the market in the morning saw Tortoise being flogged. "The scoundrel deserves it," They chorused, "for the taboo." As they came back

in the evening, he was still being flogged with a leather thong and he bled
profusely, sweating and gasping for breath. . . . (47)

The above poem marks a crescendo in Ojaide's contemplation of negation dialectics against the pressures of environmental commodification. Versified as a story, "Opinion Page" adumbrates the final showdown against the oppressor by the oppressed as well as reverberates with the rise of the Saidian Other as the "tortoise" was "sweating and gasping for breath": an indication that the end of globalist oppression is afoot.

The Eye of the Earth and the Poetics of De-commodified Nature

In his seminal book, *The End of Nature* (1989), Bill McKibben makes an apocalyptic, prescient statement: "we are at the end of nature" (1989: 8). Similarly, in Niyi Osundare's *The Eye of the Earth*, the volume's poetics inheres in rather offering another layer of our endangered earth as well as commodification of nature through global capitalist operation:

> *The Eye of the Earth* introduces Nature as the basis of social and economic practices. Osundare posits that the manner of relation to earth determines forms of social practices. Where, for instance, labour approaches Nature in a communal medium, [. . .] However, where Nature and labour are reified and appropriated with all strategies including the instrument of money, an impersonal and exploitative capitalism emerges. These extremes of social practices are portrayed in *The Eye of the Earth*. (Bodunde "Niyi Osundare," 85–86)

Echoing similar view, Emmanuel Ngara in his metacritical analysis of *The Eye of the Earth*, asserts that the volume is replete with ideological concerns that resound with man's materialist and capitalist pursuits (Ngara 176) as well as unveils Osundare's poetic vision: the de-politicization of man's cruel dealing in our environment, which adversely affects nature and our biodiversity.

In his interview with Ogoanah, Niyi Osundare presented this perspective on art (literature):

> [A]rt has a purpose. I believe in the social status of art. . . . It must be used to advance the cause of humanity. . . . I believe that if art has any sake at all, it is human. I am a humanist. The content is as important as the work. A work of art is not a technical jargon. Cleanth Brooks refers to a poem

as 'well-wrought urn'. But that talks about appearance per se. A container without content is empty. As concerned, committed artists, the basis of all art is justice. (Ogoanah 5)

With the sense of commitment to rid our planet of commodification of social relations as well as marketization of nature, Osundare affirms this in his "Our Earth Will Not Die":

> Our earth will see again
> eyes washed by a new rain
> the westering sun will rise again
> resplendent like a new coin.
> The wind, unwound, will play its tune
> trees twittering, grasses dancing;
> hillsides will rock with blooming harvests
> the plains bating their eyes of grass and grace.
> The sea will drink its heart's content
> when a jubilant thunder flings open the skygate
> and a new rain tumbles down
> in drums of joy.
> Our earth will see again
> this earth, OUR EARTH. (51)

From the standpoint of envisioning a clean environment as well as de-commoditized nature in Nigeria (the Niger Delta), Osundare considers the capitalist torrents ravaging our world—Nigeria—to be a thing of the past if humankind could engage with the ruse of this macabre practice. This period will come with "a jubilant thunder" that will renew our earth, thereby making it witness once more the pristine era of de-commoditized social and labor relations: a time when "alluvial joy" (Osundare 1) lighted up our terrestrial efflorescence that has come under heavy onslaught by the activities of the globalists. The image of "thunder" incarnates with the act of fighting by the marginalized in order to break loose from the trammels of globalization. Some of Ojaide's verses articulated earlier sing from the same songbook as this poem: they all coalesce to paint a picture of "jubilation" that the natives would have as they break loose from the trammels of global capitalism.

In another poem, "They Too Are the Earth," Osundare's de-commodified poetics gets into high gear:

Are they of this earth
who fritter the forest and harry the hills
are they of this earth
who live that earth may die
are they? (45)

In preserving the earth from globalist plunder, Osundare questions the basis of destroying the earth (Nature), as well as leaves a moral scar on the conscience of the buccaneers. This interrogation process of negation via questioning the culprits in the destruction of our world finds continuation in "Dawncall": "Mark this misty mob breaking out / of the mouth of a yawning earth / And this earthworm/whose blood will break the fast of earth / when this dawn is done" (Osundare 40). The "dawn" here emblematizes Osundare's vision of regreening our earth after the bangs of globalization. This will be achieved through questioning the very foundation as well as morality of global capitalism. Words such as "mob" and "blood" exemplify Osundare's poet-narrator's commitment to wrestle power with the globalists in order to break the "fast" of domination and commoditized relations.

In getting back what we have lost, as Osundare articulated in the verses such as "Forest Echoes" by using phrases such as "perfumed memories" (Forest Echoes 3) and "bouncing boughs interlock overhead" (Forest Echoes 3), his vision of return to pristine period is given resonance. Also, in the poem "Harvestcall" that uses locutions such as "garnished in green" (Osundare Harvestcall 18), "where yam wore the crown" (18) and "coy cobs rocked lustily" (19), Osundare envisions a way of getting back man's inheritance. Osundare adds zest to his social vision to see change premised on reconstructing Nigeria's landscape via revolution (if possible):

A desperate match
stabs the night
in the gloomy alleys
of NEPA's darkdom
the distance glows
with sparks of amber blood. (25)

The image that "desperate match" creates is that of rage and desperation to counter the inanities that global capitalism practice has engendered, which has become "night"—imagery of disempowerment, suffering, darkness, and vitiation. The use of the word '"NEPA" as understood in the above excerpt entails the complicity of Nigeria's political class in the heist being carried out in our environment by the ruling class in cahoots with their compradors, the multinationals. The word NEPA is characteristically Nigerian in scope and reach. The image that the word "blood" invokes dovetails with images captured in earlier cited poems, whose imagistic intensity finds continuation in Fanon's third phase (fighting phase) theorizing: a time to fight with every weapon in the arsenal of the oppressed against the oppressor (globalists) for the liberation of the native (Nwagbara "Poetics of Resistance," 13).

Lumped together, Niyi Osundare in "Who Says That Drought Was Here?" brings to the fore the summary of his regreening vision, which is couched in a longer interrogation:

> With these green guests around
> Who says that drought was here?
> And anthills throw open their million gates
> and winged termites swarm the warm welcome
> of compassionate twilights
> and butterflies court the fragrant company
> of fledgling flowers
> and milling moths paste wet lips
> on the translucent ears of listening windows
> and the copper face of the gathering lake
> and weaverbirds pick up the chorus
> in the leafening heights . . .
> Soon crispy mushrooms will break
> the fast of venturing soles
> With these green guests around
> who still says that drought was here? (35–36)

The optimism painted in "Who Says That Drought Was Here?" that foreshadows "a constant reflection of the dialectical change from stasis to dynamic motion, from passive death to active life . . ." (Bodunde "Niyi Osundare," 99) is taken to another level of contrast and reassurance in "Our Earth Will Not Die":

> Lynched
> the lakes
> Slaughterd
> the seas

> Mauled
> the mountains
> But our earth will not die
> Here
> there
> everywhere
> a lake is killed by the arsenic urine
> from the bladder of profit factories
> a poison stream staggers down the hills
> coughing chaos in the sickly sea
> the wailing whale, belly up like a frying fish,
> crests the chilling swansong of parting waters.
> But our earth will not die. . . . (50)

In most of the verses in the collection, Osundare poeticizes heartrendingly about the wanton destruction of our natural neighbors: the flora, fauna, and rivers by global capitalists. With the effect of graphology, Osundare brings to the limelight the saliencies of power versus weakness hypothesis that globalisation sustains. This is manifest in the visual paraphernalia associated with the way the above lines were arranged to illustrate bifurcation in terms of might and weakness. The doing words (verbs) such as "lynched," "slaughtered," and "mauled" are imaginatively employed to signify strength—they are doing words of action and power that make "the lakes," "the seas," and "the mountains," which represent nature, drained. The verbs signifying "might" make our natural bequest atrophied; they make them "stagger down the hill." In spite of the bleak horizon, Osundare sustains his incurable optimism in the triumph of good over evil in the title of the poem, which is lodged in the final line: "but our earth will not die."

Writing in his *The Necessity of Art*, Ernest Fischer declares that:

> capitalism turned everything into a commodity. With a hitherto unimaginable increase in production and productivity, extending the new order dynamically to all parts of the globe and all areas human existence, capitalism dissolved the old world into a cloud of whirling molecules, destroyed all direct relationships between producer and consumer and flung all products onto an anonymous market to be bought or sold. (50)

To this end, commenting on the environmentalist and de-commodified stature of *The Eye of the Earth*, N. N. Alu avers:

> *The Eye of the Earth* is very special, fashioned on his perception of man in nature. The image of the poet is more than an interpreter of a complex and rich tradition of his people who share a collective philosophy. He celebrates the work nature of his people with special emphasis on their reverence for nature, defending the traditional myth on which the community lives together resisting collision. The volume is seen as one of the fiercest indictments of modern economic culture of the people and alien destructive forces. It takes a pictoral account of aggression on man and the earth.... (70)

Thus, there is no gainsaying the fact that Tanure Ojaide and Niyi Osundare in the two volumes analyzed have utilized the instrument of poetry to engage with the inanities in Nigeria wrought by global capitalists in partnership with Nigeria's political leaders. Their attempt to address Nigeria's environmental and ecological concerns mediated via the conduit of global capitalism as well as commodification of nature finds ample expression in eco-critical literature, which is literature of the environment.

Conclusion

In ending this chapter, it has been argued that both volumes, *Daydream of Ants and Other Poems* and *The Eye of the Earth*, sing from the same songbook: they both orchestrate the poets' aesthetic commitment to unearth the dangers inherent in global capitalism as well as man's business in our environment, which is largely responsible for the loathsome state of our planet. Thus, in transcending the ruse and impact of global capitalism in Nigeria (the Niger Delta), the poets investigated in this chapter aesthetically envision the vehicle of eco-poetry (eco-critical literature) or eco-criticism to take us to this dream of a new world filled with Green Wave rhetoric as well as de-commodified social and labor relations. This aesthetic vision as the poets refracted will be a process that finds corporeality in transcending the discontents of global capitalism as well as de-commodification of Nigeria's environment that is at present in the shadow of globalization and environmental brigandage. Therefore, Ojaide's and Osundare's artistic visions encapsulated in dialectics of transcending Nigeria's environmental malaise is appropriate ideo-aesthetic, philosophical pontification for countering the effects of commoditized environment as well as socioeconomic relations. Both poets contemplate freedom from globalist wrecks and feint via eco-poetry for the nation's emancipation. Put simply, the commodification of our environment traumatizes our "inheritance..., body and soul"

(Ojaide *Daydream of Ants*, 21). Thus, the aesthetics of de-commodified environment (nature) is crucial for Nigeria's renaissance.

Works Cited

Aijaz, Ahmad. *In Theory: Classes, Nations, Literatures*. London: Verso, 1992. Print.

Aina, T. "Globalisation and Social Policy in Africa: Issues and Research Directions." *Working Paper Series*, 6/96, Dakar, Senegal, 1996. Print.

Alu, N. N. "Style and the New Poetic Revolution in Niyi Osundare's Poetry." *African Research Review*, 2.3(2008): 62–84. Print.

Armbruster, Karla and Wallace, Kathleen. (eds.). *Beyond Nature Writing: Expanding The Boundaries of Ecocriticism*. Charlottesville: U of Carolina P, 2001. Print.

Amuta, Chidi. "Literature of the Nigerian Civil War." *Perspectives on Nigerian Literature 1700 to the Present Vol 1*. Ed. Yemi Ogunbiyi, Lagos: Guardian Books, 1988. 85–92. Print.

Ardono, Theodor. *Negative Dialectics*. Frankfurt: Suhkamp Verlag, 1966. Print.

Azumara, S. O. "Marxism and African Literature: Commodification and Ideological Conditioning in Achebe's *Things Fall Apart*." *Lagos Papers in English* 12 (2010): 12–29. Print.

Bodunde, Charles. "Niyi Osundare and the Materialist Vision: A Study of *The Eye of the Earth*." *Ufahamu: Journal of the African Activist* xxxv.ii (1997): 81–100. Print.

———. "Tanure Ojaide Poetry and the Delta Landscape: A Study of *Delta Blues and The Home Songs*." *Writing the Homeland: The Poetry and Politics of Tanure Ojaide*. Ed. Onookome Okome. Bayreuth: Bayreuth African Studies, 2002. Print.

Brink, Andre. 1983. *Writing in a State of Siege: Essays on Politics and Literature*. New York: Faber, 1983. Print.

Coetzee, J. M. *Doubling the Point: Essays and Interviews*. Massachusetts: Harvard UP, 1992. Print.

Egya, Sule. "Imagining Beast: Image of the Oppressor in Recent Nigerian Poetry in English." *Journal of Commonwealth Literature* 46.2 (2011): 345–358. Print.

Ezeliora, Osita. "Aspects of African Mythopoeic Assumptions: Representations of 'the Departed' in Nigerian Poetry." *Okike* no. 44, February (2000): 46–68. Print.

Fischer, Ernst. *The Necessity of Art: A Marxist Approach*. Northampton: Peregrine, 1924. Print.

Glotfelty, Cheryll and Harold Fromm. *The Ecocriticism Reader: Landmarks in Literary Ecology*. Georgia: U of Georgia P, 1996. Print.

Gore, Al. *Earth in the Balance: Forging a New Common Purpose*. London: Earthscan, 1992. Print.

Hill, Dileys. *Citizens and Cities: Urban Policy in the 1090s*. Hertfordshire: Harvester Wheatsheaf, 1994. Print.

Lodge, David. *The Novelist at the Crossroads, And Other Essays on Fiction and Criticism*. Reading: Cox and Wyman, 1986. Print.

McKibben, Bill. *The End of Nature*. New York: Random House, 1989. Print.

Mohammed, Abdul Jan. "The Economy of the Manichean Allegory: The Function of Racial Differences in Colonialist Literature" *Critical Inquiry*, 12 (1985): 59-87. Print.

Monshipouri, Mahmood, Claude Welch, and Evan Kennedy. "Multinational Corporations and the Ethics of Global Responsibility." *Human Rights Quarterly* 25 (2003): 965–975. Print.

Morrison, Jago. *The Fiction of Chinua Achebe*. Hampshire: Palgrave Macmillan, 2007. Print.

Mouffe, C. "Radical Democracy: Modern or Postmodern?" *The Politics of Postmodernism*. Trans. P. Holdengraber. Minneapolis: Minnesota UP, 1988. 31–45. Print.

Ngara, Emmanuel. *Ideology and Form in African Poetry*. London: James Curry, 1990. Print.

Ngumoha, Emma. "The Poet as Rainmaker: Fertility and Pluvial Aesthetics in Osundare's *The Eye of the Earth*." *Tydskrif Vir Letterkunde* 48.1(2011): 124–132. Print.

Norberg, Johan. *In Defence of Global Capitalism*. Washington: Cato Institute, 2003. Print.

Nwagbara, Uzoechi. "Political Power and Intellectual Activism in Tanure Ojaide's *The Activist*." *Nebula: A Journal of Multidisciplinary Scholarship* 5.4 (2008): 225–253. Print.

_____. "Poetics of Resistance: Ecocritical Reading of Tanure Ojaide's *Delta Blues and Home Songs* and *Daydream of Ants and Other Poems*." *African Study Monographs* 31.1 (2010): 17–30. Print.

_____. "In the Shadow of the Imperialists: A Philosophico-Materialist Reading of Tanure Ojaide's *Delta Blues and Home Song* and *Daydream of Ants and Other Poems*." *SKASE Journal of Literary Studies* 3.1 (2011): 76–96. Print.

Obi, Cyril. "Globalisation and Environmental Conflicts in Africa." *African Journal of Political Science* 4.1 (1999): 40–62. Print.

Obiechina, Emmanuel. *An African Popular Literature: A Study of Onitsha Market Pamphlets*. Cambridge: Cambridge UP, 1973. Print.

Obioha, Uwaezuoke. "Globalisation and the Future of African Culture." *Philosophical Papers and Reviews* 2.1 (2010): 1–8. Print.

Ogoanah, N. F. Interview. "I Am a Humanist": Niyi Osundare on the Poetry of Niyi Osundare." *West Africa Review* 4.1 (2003): 1–12. Print.

Oguibe, Olu. "Connectivity, and the Fate of the Unconnected." *Relocating Postmodernism*. Ed. Ato Quayson and David Goldberg. London: Wiley-Blackwell, 2002. 174–183. Print.

Ohaeto-Ezenwa. *Contemporary Nigerian Poetry and the Poetics of Orality*. Bayreuth: African Studies Series, 1998. Print.

Ojaide, Tanure. *Poetic Imagination in Black Africa*. Durham: Carolina Academic Press, 1996. Print.

———. "New Trends in Modern African Poetry." *Research in African Literatures* 26.1 (1995): 4–21. Print.

———. "Examining Canonisation in Modern African Literature." *Asiatic* 3.1 (2009): 1–19. Print.

———. *Daydream of Ants and Other Poems.* Lagos: Malthouse Press, 1997. Print.

Ojakorotu, Victor. 2008. "The Internationalisation of Oil Violence in the Niger Delta of Nigeria." *Alternatives: Turkish Journal of Int'l Relations* 7.1 (2008): 92–117. Print.

Okuyade, Ogaga. "Recent Nigerian Bards and Minstrels: Forms of Counter Narratives." *California Linguistics Notes* xxxv.2 (2010): 1–31. Print.

———. "Rethinking Militancy and Environmental Justice: The Politics of Oil and Violence in Nigerian Popular Music." *Africa Today* 58.1 (2011): 78–101. Print.

Okunoye, Oyeniyi. "Alterity, Marginality and the National Question in the Poetry of the Niger Delta." *Cahiers d'etudes africaines* 191 (2008): 1–18. Print.

———. "Writing Resistance: Dissidence and Visions of Healing in Nigerian Poetry of the Military Era." *Tydskrif Vir Letterkunde* 48.1 (2011): 64–85. Print.

Olaoluwa, S. S. "Where Do We Go from Here? Niger Delta, Crumbling Urbanscape, and Migration in Tanure Ojaide's *When It No Longer Matters Where You Live.*" *Nordic Journal of African Studies* 18.2 (2009): 175–195. Print.

Osundare, Niyi. *The Eye of the Earth.* Ibadan: HEBN, 1986. Print.

———. *Songs of the Marketplace.* Ibadan: New Horn Press, 1983. Print.

Robert, Bullard. *Unequal Protection: Environmental Justice and Communities of Colour.* San Francisco: Sierra Club, 1994. Print.

Saurin, Julian. "Globalisation, Poverty and the Promises of Modernity." *Millennium: Journal of International Relations* 25.3 (1996): 675–88. Print.

Shantz, Jeffrey. "Scarcity and the Emergence of Fundamentalist Ecology." *Critique of Anthropology* 23.2 (2003): 144–154. Print.

———. "Beyond Socialist Realism: 'Socialism by Tendency' in the Poetry of Tanure Ojaide and Wole Soyinka." *NAWA: Journal of Language and Communication* June 2007. Print.

———. "Beyond Socialist Realism: Glocal Concerns and African Poetry." *Literary Paritantra (Systems)* 1.1,2 (2009): 110–112. Print.

Udumukwu, Onyemaechi. *Social Responsibility in the Nigerian Novel.* Port Harcourt: Sherbrook Associates, 1998. Print.

———. *The Novel and Change in Africa.* Port Harcourt: U of Port Harcourt P, 2006. Print.

13

Poetics of Environmental Agitation: A Stylistic Reading of Hope Eghagha's *Rhythms of the Last Testament* and *The Governor's Lodge and Other Poems*

Macaulay Mowarin, Delta State University, Abraka

> The art of portraying the true state of affairs in the Nigerian society through literary creation is a form of environmentalism against the ecological imperialism spreading in Nigeria. (Nwagbara)

Introduction

This paper addresses the theme of environmental and ecological disaster in Nigeria's Niger Delta from a stylistic viewpoint. It focuses on how Eghagha employs the rhetorical strategies of imagery, metaphor, personification, syntactic repetition, and pronominalization in the two collections of poems titled *Rhythms of the Last Testament* and *The Governor's Lodge and Other Poems* to foreground the theme of environmental degradation in the region. Eghagha's two collections of poems are some of the eco-critical poems that have complemented the political and literary space of the region that has become radicalized within the past four decades. Eghagha employs these rhetorical strategies to foreground the abject poverty, disease, and internal refugee status pervading the region. Eghagha also uses these rhetorical devices to project himself as an apostle of hope for the enthronement of environmental justice in Nigeria's Niger Delta in the near future.

The environment is one of the "glocal" issues that now occupy the front burner of discourse by environmental and human rights activists and creative artists in Third World countries in particular and across the globe in general. The cause of unsustainable oil exploitation by multinational oil companies in the Niger Delta region of Nigeria is environmental degradation. The war of verbal weapons against political misrule and oil exploitation in the Niger Delta region is prominent among the second generation of Nigerian poets, who are also known as Alter-Native tradition poets such as Niyi Osundare, Tanure Ojaide, Odia Ofeimum, and Hope Eghagha.

This paper undertakes a stylistic analysis of how Hope Eghagha employs some rhetorical strategies to foreground the theme of environmental and ecological disaster in the Niger Delta region of Nigeria. The rhetorical strategies include imagery, metaphor, personification, lexical and syntactic repetitions, and pronominalization. The analysis will focus on poems from two collections of poems: *Rhythms of the Last Testament* and *The Governor's Lodge and Other Poems*. The aftereffects of environmental and ecological degradation highlighted by Eghagha in his poems include endemic poverty, numerous diseases and infections caused by contaminated water and polluted air, and internal refugee status. Eghagha did not display himself as a mere chronicler of environmental degradation in the region but was also as an apostle of hope for the amelioration of the despoliated environment and for the enthronement of environmental justice for the people in the region—a region that Eghagha (*Rhythms of the Last Testament*) categorizes as "goose in the flames of hunger".

Background

This section of the chapter focuses on environmental injustice, the Niger Delta, Poetry of Commitment in Africa, and nature poets. A major issue that has been resonating across the globe within the past four decades is that of environmental injustice, which is occasioned by the nefarious acts of authoritarian governments and military juntas, mostly in Third World countries. Instances of environmental and ecological inequitableness include land appropriation of powerless indigenous minorities, "transitional toxic waste dumping and natural resource exploitation" (Adeola 9).

Most cases of unsustainable natural resource exploitation and toxic waste dumping that cause environmental degradation and land appropriation are prevalent in poverty-Stricken, powerless indigenous minority communities in developing countries. Land is appropriated from the impotent indigenous minority by authoritarian rulers, mostly under the guise of proposed establishment of heavy industries, hydroelectric dams, and exploitation of mineral resources (Amnesty International; Donnelly; Adeola, "Endangered Community"; Ojakorotu). Instances of environmental and human right violations include timber harvesting in the Amazon rainforest of Latin America and sub-Saharan Africa, dispossession of land from the aboriginals in

Australia and Native Americans in North America, and mineral extraction and exploitation in Africa and South America (Renner; Adeola). Renner succinctly describes the inability of these peasant minorities to resist human rights injustice and its concomitant environmental evil thus:

> Their capacity to resist and defend their interest is extremely weak. These groups not only depend on marginal lands for subsistence but they are also socially, economically and politically disenfranchised. They are often too powerless to struggle for the preservation of natural system upon which their livelihood and survival rests. (59)

These nefarious acts that have resulted in the violation of nature are still being perpetuated unabated by governments who incarcerate, murder, and execute human and environmental rights activists across the globe. Adeola gives instances of these ignominious acts thus:

> Among the recent cases of environmental injustice and human rights violation in the third world are: the murder of Wilson Pinheiro and Francisco "Chico" Meridas in the Amazon rain forest, the massacre of Father Nery Lito Saler and several others in the Philippines and the public hanging of Ken Saro Wiwa and eight other members of the Movement for the Survival of the Ogoni People (MOSOP). (40)

In Nigeria, the late Ken Saro-Wiwa, the dogged environmentalist and creative artist, is now regarded as the symbol of the struggle for environmental justice in the environmentally degraded and penury-infested Niger Delta region of the country.

Environmental and ecological injustice in the Niger Delta is one of the local issues with global implication. The term glocalization has been coined for such concern, and Shultz succinctly describes it thus:

> Recent social and artistic movements emerging through opposition to capitalist globalization have emphasized the convergence of local and global concerns, what some have termed 'glocalisation' or 'glocality'. From this perspective, attention is given to locally rooted experiences, and especially experiences of struggle and resistance, that have global implications or address global concerns. . . . These are not universalist or universalising discourses which seek to present themselves as world historical or epoch-making. These 'glocal' themes include pressing concerns for the natural environment and local communities.(123)

Apart from the environmental and human rights activists who are fighting tenaciously against these acts of environmental injustice, literature is also now being used by creative artists, especially in Africa, as an instrument of social change.

Due to the fact that the Niger Delta region of Nigeria borders the Atlantic seabed, half of the region is permanently submerged in water; therefore, the oil and gas–rich region is ecologically very fragile. The population of this region is estimated to be about 12 million (1996 census) heterogeneous people who speak about 100 of the estimated 400 languages spoken in Nigeria (Darah; Hansford et al.).

The activities of oil and gas exploration and exploitation by multinational oil companies like Shell, Chevron, Agip, Mobil, and Texaco have already exacerbated the stress on the region's already fragile environment. The attendant stress on the environment includes severe damage to the flora and fauna of the area, wanton damage to arable land resources and to aquatic life due to environmental despoliation, abject poverty of the indigenes who live in squalor, and lack of basic infrastructure like potable water, electricity, good roads, and good educational institutions (Darah; Osaghae; Ojakorotu).

The unwillingness of the Niger Delta internal colonialists, which include the Federal Government and its international oil allies known as Joint Venture Partners, to develop and address the environmental concerns of oil and gas exploration on the region, as articulated by environmental and human rights activists, resulted in brutal repression by the nation's security operatives. The repression reached its apogee with the murder of Ken Saro-Wiwa and the eight other Ogoni activists. What is more, the murder also marked a paradigm shift by the agitators, as new groups that adopted violent tactics emerged. Two of the new groups are the Niger Delta People's Volunteer Force (NDPVF) and the Movement for the Emancipation of the Niger Delta (MEND). They adopted guerrilla tactics of negotiations, which include kidnapping of expatriate transnational oil company employees, bunkering of oil pipelines, seizure of oil rigs and installations, armed confrontation with the state security forces, and general militarized operations (Ojakorotu; Osaghae 96–98).

The radicalization of the agitation for environmental justice in the Niger Delta also percolated to literary works by Nigerian poets such as Niyi Osundare, Tanure Ojaide, and Hope Eghagha. Hope Eghagha is a prolific poet, essayist, novelist, and playwright. He is presently a Professor of English at the University of Lagos, Akoka, Lagos State, Nigeria. His published works include *Death Not a Redeemer* (1998; play); *Rhythms of the Last Testament* (2003; poetry); *This Story Must Not Be Told* (2003; poetry); *Emperors of Salvation* (2004; novel); *Reflections on the Problems of Leadership in Contemporary Nigerian Literature* (2004; monograph); *The Governor's Lodge and Other Poems* (2003; poetry). As a prolific essayist, Eghagha is a visiting member of the *Guardian Newspapers* editorial board, Lagos, Nigeria.

The second generation of Anglophone African poets are committed to describing and foregrounding the desperate situation in Africa. Olaoluwa (2008) describes Alter-Native poetry as one of commitment in Africa literature in Africa. The issue of commitment in African literature in general and African poetry in particular is encapsulated in the response of African poets to the sociopolitical happenings in their respective countries. Osundare described the hallmark of this generation of poets thus:

> Theirs ... is the literature of social command extremely sensitive to the social realities around them, but without losing sight of the aesthetic imperatives of their works. Thus this generation shocked African literature with a combativeness and radicalism never experienced before. The thematic preoccupation remains the desperate situation of the Africans, the stylistic hallmarks are clarity and directness of expression, formal experimentation, and a deliberate incorporation of African oral literary mode. ("African Literature Now," 27)

In Nigeria, this generation of poets is known as Alter-Native tradition poets, while in South Africa, they are called the Soweto/black–consciousness poets. This second generation of writers has spanned about four decades. So, they can be bifurcated into earlier and later groups. This later group now constitutes an emerging generation. The earlier members include Odia Ofeimum, Niyi Osundare, and Tanure Ojaide. The later members include Onookome Okome, Ezenwa-Ohaeto, and Hope Eghagha, among others. Critical works on the emerging group have been few and skeletal. Criticisms on the plethora of the emerging generation of poets have been adverse due to their lack of artistic craftsmanship, their deficiency in grammar, and their inability to use language dexterously. Jeyifo, the renowned Africa literary critic, describes the defects in the poetry of these emerging poets thus:

> In our new dispensation of post-civil war poetry, where there are constant flashes of inspiration, the perspiration is notably scanty especially in the relationship of new poets to words. For while language may be

the enabling medium of all literature, it is the special forte for poetry, simultaneously, the bulwark and love of the new poets and the trap, the Achilles heels of would be poets. (610)

Hope Eghagha is one of the few poets of the emerging generation that is not trapped in the language-deficit conundrum due to his training in English as well as his mastery of poetic craft.

Nature has been the most inspiring source of the radicalized poets from Nigeria. Nwagbara observed that Osundare and Ojaide are regarded as the two consummate nature poets on environmental and ecological issues in Nigeria. He further adds that Osundare's *The Eye of the Earth* has been regarded as his most environmental collection of poems. Ken Saro-Wiwa's collection of short stories, *A Forest of Flowers*, can be described as eco-critical stories since they focus on Nigeria's political corruption, which is the architect of environmental degradation and abject poverty in the Niger Delta region. As far as poetics of resistance against happenings in the Niger Delta is concerned, Ojaide is the ultimate nature poet and Eghagha closely follows in Ojaide's footstep.

In his analysis of the relationship between poets and nature, Mensah (283) observes that poets can be bifurcated into simple and sentimental ones. He defines simple poets, who are at home with nature, thus: "The simple poet, as a child of nature, is bold, direct, imaginary and yet takes nature a little bit for granted because it is there." Sentimental poets on the other hand, bemoan the loss of nature due mostly to urbanization and Western civilization. Due to this fact, they idealize nature and develop a nostalgic feeling for it. Mensah describes this group of poets thus: "The second kind of poets represents a time when nature is no longer at its primitive nature" (228).

Rhetorical Devices

Eghagha can be described as a sentimental poet, since his poems focus on the degraded Niger Delta region. His function as a simple poet is ironically used to project the people's concordance with nature and their folklore, streams, and fauna and flora, which the poet projects as his childhood experience during the pre–oil exploitation era in the Niger Delta region. This was most probably in the first half of the twentieth century. He contrasts this environmentally harmonious setting of the past with that of the chaotic present through the apt deployment of images of disease and environmental disaster ravaging the region. This is due to unsustainable oil exploitation and to the concomitant environmental degradation. The contrast enumerated above is aptly depicted by the poet in the poem "Black Gold" in the collection *Rhythms of the Last Testament*. The poet-persona projects himself as a simple poet in the first two stanzas of the poem thus:

> i remember the green leaves, the pods, the tubers we ate the fatlings from moon to moon, the earth danced to its music, the fishes need no nets to grace our pots. (Eghagha *Rhythms of the Last Testament*,)

The image of the environmentally affectionate natural setting of the farms and the healthy aquatic life in the creeks, streams, and rivers of the Niger Delta above is further stylistically foregrounded with the use of the pronominals in small letters—"i" "we" and "our"—which project a people living in concordance with nature and happily engaged in their fishing and farming activities.

The poet then transforms from a simple to a sentimental one by aptly enumerating the "ecological encroachment by multinational [oil] corporations on farmland" (Shultz 128) in "Black Gold":

> Black gold . . .
> The scourge of mansa musa
> Come cudgeling us again
> now
> fish come belly bobbling
> deep cuts on your faces
> a testimony of burnt insides
> yet they use the excuse
> of our size
> to beat us. (Eghagha *Rhythms of the Last Testament*, 34)

The head word of the nominal phrase "the Scourge of mansa musa" (Black gold in *Rhythm of the Last Testament*) foregrounds the imagery of plague and epidemic now ravaging the Niger Delta due to the adverse effect of unsustainable oil exploitation and its concomitant devastated environment. The imagery of "mansa musa" symbolizes the internal colonialists of the Niger Delta. Mansa Musa was a great Malian empire warrior during the precolonial era; he was regarded as a symbolic representation of the expansionist policy of the rulers during his era. Due to the connivance of the respective military juntas and authoritarian civilian regimes symbolized by mansa musa, with officials of multinational oil companies, the latter were nonplussed by the environmental impact of indiscriminate oil drilling activities as long as they can remit a part for their gargantuan profit to the internal colonialists to meet their voracious appetite. So, the spate of oil spills and gas flaring contaminated farmlands, creeks, rivulets, and rivers, which now contain waters of foaming gore inundated by fish that "come belly bobbling." The dead fish foregrounds the imaginary creeks, which have become belligerent to aquatic life due to environmental despoliation.

Eghagha also employs the imagery of hunger and deprivation in "Baptism" in *Rhythms of the Last Testament* to stylistically foreground the inevitable accompaniment of environmental despoliation on the people of the Niger Delta:

> Born anew
> In the waters of hunger
> tattered souls, famished flesh
> down from the twelve floor. (Eghagha *Rhythms of the Last Testament*, 31)

The transformation from "waters of nourishments" in the environmentally friendly Niger Delta region before it was environmentally devastated, to "waters of hunger" due to oil spills–induced environmental pollution resulted in the spate of hunger, disease, and penury now ravaging the Niger Delta, since the main means of livelihood of the peasant fishermen has reached a cull-de-sac due to loss of aquatic life. Okome aptly describes the pathetic situation thus:

> Today, Shell oil exploration has left the vast agrarian swamps and mash lands of the Niger Delta devastated and inhabitable. There are often reports of acid rains in the area... In most of the communities, the aquatic life, the mainstay of the rural fishing communities, has been completely destroyed. As one local chief pointed out to us in a personal conversation, life is now meaningless without the primordial occupation of fishing. (x–xi)

"Tattered soul" and "famished flesh," which are two noun phrases in paradigmatic relation, vividly contain imageries of disease and hunger engendered by the "waters of hunger."

Water is critical to life in the Niger Delta region and once it is contaminated, livelihood in the region becomes crisis-ridden. Apart from disease that afflicts aquatic life, indigenes in the region are also afflicted and

Eghagha graphically grafts imagery of disease on the indigenes in "A Night in Warri" in *Rhythms of the Last Testament* thus:

> Around the land
> The bar snaked
> Its tang on the open-eyed refugees
> This lock
> Left leg on hold
> Right leg too loose
> dangling species
> of men whose mother
> urinated black water
> for locomotion. (Eghagha 60)

Waterborne disease ravaging the Niger Delta region is aptly captured by the imagery of "mother" who urinated "black water." Also, the imagery of the indigenes as "open eyed refugees" in the poem is also a graphic illustration of how they relocate from their ancestral natural habitat to a new and strange one due to a devastated environment.

As a nature poet, Eghagha also uses imagery of natural disaster afflicting the earth to illustrate the nefarious politics that resulted in an environmentally devastated Niger Delta that grafts the imagery of disease in the poem titled "The Rulers" in *The Governor's Lodge and Other Poems*:

> How many children
> have you denied milk
> with the curse of your.
> earth-scorching polices
>
> homo many bodies
> with curse of your
> earth scorching polices
>
> how many wars
> have you caused
> with the curse of your
> earth scorching polices
> The figures are part of our history. (Eghagha *The Governor's Lodge,* 72)

The poem, which is structured in rhetorical questions, is inundated with the imagery of natural disaster in each of its verses and it is symbolized by the noun phrase "earth scorching policy" of the rulers, which had resulted in the devastation of the environment and the aftereffects are numerous diseases, interethnic strife, and wars in the heterogeneous Niger Delta region. "Earth scorching policy" emanated from the connivance of the region's internal colonialists with operators of transnational companies who engage in unsustainable oil exploitation and gas flaring that has resulted in a devastated environment. The refusal of the avaricious rulers to plough back part of the wealth derived from the sale of crude oil for the development of the region was one of the main causes of abject poverty and penury ravaging the region. It was also the cause of the violent agitation and confrontation with the military by the activists in the region.

Another image of natural disaster deployed by the poet to depict the devastated Niger Delta environment is that of the sand bar, which usually clogs the natural flow of water in the poem "Sand Bars" in *Rhythms of the Last Testament*:

> sand-bars green floods
> hallelujah to sand-bars
> sand-bars
> sand-bars down floods
> hallelujah to the messiah
> Sand-bars huge monstrous
> gobbling men of chests
> sand-bar bars us
> from flooding the city
> with freshness
> sand-bars blocks us.
> from our dreams
> locked in the hearts of mart yrs
> Sand-bars
> let us shout no hallelujahs
> to the sand-bars
> of our land
> sand-bars?
> sand-bars
> sand-bars
> the sound of barristers
> offer no hope.
> to men gripped by sand-bars
> sand-bars
> sand-bars?
> we need them no more
> let the floods come wash a new. (Eghagha, 17)

The jagged graphology of the poem is of stylistic significance since it foregrounds the abnormal situation in the Niger Delta region due to environmental degradation. In the poem, Eghagha categorizes the rulers and their ally, who are officials of international oil companies, as sand-bars since they act as forces that disrupt natural seasonal changes. The impediment of the sand bars to natural flow of water, which is the cause of environmental disruption, is supposed to nourish the earth. "Sand bars" are harbingers of gas flaring that devastated the environment. So, the Niger Delta has retrogressed since sand bars "block us from our dream" and "bar us from flooding the city with freshness." Eghagha portrays himself as not merely a chronicler of the aspects of environmental degradation on the Niger Delta due to political misrule by avaricious rulers but also as a committed poet with a vision for social change thus:

> sand-bars
> sand-bars
> We need them no more
> Let the floods come wash anew. (Eghagha *Rhythms of the Last Testament*, 17)

Eghagha employs the imagery of the flood flowing through its natural course as the symbol of hope for an amelioration of the devastated environment. This will usher in a breath of fresh air and a new lease of life to the indigenes of the Niger Delta. So, man's attempt to impede the natural force of nature is always transient. Natural forces symbolized by justice will always prevail.

The image of fire also pervades most poems in the two collections of poetry. This imagery is of stylistic significance, since fire, as well as the carbon dioxide it emits, is one of the main causes of global warming. In "The Divorce" in *Rhythms of the Last Testament*, Eghagha aptly depicts how spilled crude oil ignites into a flame that devastates the environment as well as its inhabitants thus:

> spilled black gold
> flames the hand
> Stinking flesh of brotherhood
> Lost antennae
> Tears of old age. (Eghagha *Rhythms of the Last Testament*, 31)

The putrefying imagery of burned human beings stares the reader in "stinking flesh of brotherhood."

In "The Last Lover" in *Rhythms of the Last Testament*, the poet also depicts imagery of the fire of Jesse thus:

> The fire is now ash
> we swim into tomorrow's Sea
> your laughter is lip laughter
> your smile bites
> fear into my face
> inside your insides
> anger is red like
> the oil fire of Jesse
> heart is black like Jesse's smoke. (Eghagha *Rhythms of the Last Testament*, 9)

The imagery of "Fire of Jesse" vividly reminds the reader of the Jesse oil fire disaster that emanated from burst oil pipe lines near Sapele in Delta State, in 1998 during the era of General Abdulsalami Abubakar. Almost two thousand young men, women, and children trying to scoop petrol lost their lives. Since then, there has been numerous cases of burst pipeline–induced fire incidents. Fire that emanates from burst oil pipeline degrades the environment, causes loss of lives, and inflicts fatal burns on survivors. Apart from the fact that many people, mostly youths, are either burned to death or maimed, the environment is also devastated due to the large plume of smoke bellowing from the burst oil pipeline.

In the poem "Fire in the Market Place" from *The Governors Lodge and Other Poems*, the imagery of fire is employed by the poet to highlight the ramshackled structures called "markets" due to government officials' refusal to build standard markets:

> The market place is not
> A house of infernos
> Yet this sprawling pile-upon-pile
> Has given birth to three consumptions
> Within the life span of Mr. rat.
>
> It eats up the dreams of debtors
> Whose wares have gone mountain-high
> Or the goodwill of creditors
> Each time the typhoon scours
> The earth of the market place
> It is transition time for some
> Those whose heart-strings
> Find anchor on prosperity of the market

> Again and again
> The fire licks up clothes
> Brand new and second hand
> Wood and metal jewelry
> Sometimes it eats up flesh
> Flesh of men and rodents
> But always the dream of prosperity. (Eghagha *The Governor's Lodge*, 46)

The frequency of the fire incidents is captured by imagery of Mr. Rat thus:

> Yet this sprawling pile-upon-pile
> Has given birth to three consumptions
> Within the life span of Mr. rat. (Eghagha *The Governor's Lodge*, 46)

This imagery gives one a mental picture of at least four fire incidents within a year. Eghagha personifies typhoon, which is a natural disaster, in the second verse to give a graphic illustration of the fire incident's devastating effect. The imagery gleaned from the typhoon is heart rendering. The nonchalant attitude of government of officials toward proffering solution to the problem of frequent fire disasters is highlighted by the poet thus:

> each time
> administrators pledge action
> and go to sleep
> until fire resurrects them again. (Eghagha *The Governor's Lodge*, 46)

So, the frequency of the fire disasters that destroy the environment with its plume of smoke and further impoverishes the already poverty-stricken traders of the region is attributed to the insensitivity of the government as far as developmental projects in the region are concerned.

The dual function of fire as the agent of environmental degradation and fuel for cooking is also exploited by Eghagha in his depiction of the reaction of women against the exploitative tendencies of operators of transnational oil companies. Fire is depicted as an invaluable asset of the women struggling for justice in "The Women's Anger" in *The Governor's Lodge and Other Poems*:

> The women descended like rain
> On the Farm of the Men
> The purloiners of black floor

> They bathed in the open
> They sat inside the engine room
> even the pilot took to his heels.
> Hunger has no brother
> Anger has no friend. (Eghagha *The Governor's Lodge*, 61)

The imagery of rain foregrounds Eghagha's use of natural phenomenon to fight for an amelioration of the desperate situation in the Niger Delta region. What propelled the women into taking their rash and dangerous action is hunger and anger, which are encapsulated in the refrain. Then Eghagha employs the positive effect of fire from gas-flaring on the women's action thus:

> It was fire from heaven
> Though it did not burn the farm
> Fires from black gold
> Lit up the villages
> Brightened the face of the women
> Days and nights
> Their husband did not
> Recognize their new wives
> The women were born again
>
> Hunger has no brother
> Anger has no friend
>
> Servants of the purloiners
> Came with armed men
> To attack naked women
> But their guns refused
> To obey the deadly sermons
> And the soldiers fled. (Eghagha *The Governor's Lodge*, 68)

The biblical images encapsulated in lexical groups in paradigmatic relationship are "fire from heaven," "born again," and "deadly sermon," and they create a mental picture of divine assistance in the action of these old women.

In the last stanza, Eghagha personifies "hunger" and "anger" thus:

> when next hunger drives
> the women into oil farm

> the men will join them
> then
> hunger will eat up thieves
> anger will burn the farm. (Eghagha *The Governor's Lodge*, 68)

This poem is a most graphic illustration of the struggle by people of the Niger Delta for a sustainable environment and for a fair share of the revenue from crude oil from the "internal colonialists."

As a sentimental poet, Eghagha also employs the imagery of the "earth" to illustrate the environmental injustice in the Niger Delta region in the poem "The Color of My Earth" in *Rhythms of the Last Testament*. The poem opens with the poet-personae depicting the surface of the Niger Delta, which connotes earth as "black gold"; what is more, it is also a synonym for crude oil:

> my earth color
> is black
> gold is the sun.
>
> my earths color
> gives us food
> yet they spit
> on its squatting face
> and smile across
> the Atlantic
> . . .
> my earth
> mother to all
> victim to green men. (Eghagha *Rhythms of the Last Testament*, 34)

The imagery of the sun is instructive here. Just as the rays of the sun nourish and sustain life on earth, so does black gold sustain the nation economically. Ironically, the earth is treated with contempt while the internal colonialists cart away its wealth. The earth is personified as a subjugated individual due to the nefarious acts of the internal colonialists and their collaborators. The poet-personae's earth is not only treated with contempt but it is also brutalized by green men. "Green" is the symbolic color of environmental friendliness. The imagery "green" in this poem is used ironically to illustrate the soldiers who brutalize the impoverished indigenes of the region and protect officials of international oil companies who engage in sustainable oil drilling that has devastated the environment. The "green men" constitute the military wing of the internal colonialists.

> O God give my earth
> a new color
> those who slap
> can be slapped
> before they face
> the gavel of
> the chief judge. (Eghagha *Rhythms of the Last Testament*, 34)

Finally, the poet invokes divine intervention in the struggle by the earth for its right. In "A Night in Warri," graphic imagery of a subjugated people and their captors symbolized by snake and gun-toters give a graphic picture of how the people of the Niger Delta are held hostage to enable unsustainable oil exploration to continue unabated.

> around the land
> the bar snaked
> its tang on the open-eyed refugees
> this lock
> this grip
> left leg on hold
> right leg too loose
> dangling species
> of men whose mothers
> urinated black water
> for locomotion
>
> gun totters
> curfew totters
> bribe totters in the curfew
> in the dialect that slap
> petrol on fire. (Eghagha *Rhythms of the Last Testament*, 60)

In the poem titled "In the Dock" in *Rhythms of the Last Testament*, Eghagha employs nature imagery to graphically illustrate the trial, incarceration and execution of Ken Saro-Wiwa and the other eight Ogoni human rights and environmental activists in November, 1995 thus:

guilty
the opaque voice
the wigged kangaroo
judgment
delivered Pilate again
yet the nine men
must go into the dungeon'
must go into the dark riverside
home to shark-crocodiles. (Eghagha *Rhythms of the Last Testament,* 13)

Eghagha utilizes nature imagery to give a graphic illustration of the events that took place from judgment to execution. The judge is categorized as "the wigged Kangaroo" and the men were incarcerated in the "dark riverside," while their executors are "shark-crocodiles." It is impossible to obtain justice from a Kangaroo court. Right from their trial, their being pronounced guilty was inevitable; what is more, the image of the "dark riverside" where they were imprisoned and the presence of the ferocious predator "shark-crocodile' are so mind-chilling that their execution became inevitable. Their execution on Friday November 9, 1995, is now tagged "the black Friday." Rather than quell the peaceful agitation for equitable distribution in the Niger Delta, their death radicalized it. The struggle reached a "point of no return" as Ken Saro-Wiwa presaged in *Once in a Darkling Cloud* which was quoted by Okome thus:

The Niger Delta agitation is a clear case as the people concerned have a distinct historical silhouette. Such a demand becomes all the more compelling when the area is so viable, yet the people are blatantly denied development and common necessities of life. If Nigerian government refused to do something to drastically improve the lot of the people inevitably *a point of no return will be reached.* (30)

"Wawi's Legacy" in *Rhythms of the Last Testament* projects the late Ken Saro-Wiwa as a legend, since he fought doggedly for the emancipation of his people from the clutches of the internal colonialists:

you must sharpen your axe to hack off Wawi's head.
Wawi's neck is made of steel
you must sharpen your spears
to pierce his heart

> his heart is insulated
> you must crack the skull
> with the back of guns
>
> but his brain is on paper
>
> you must burn his soul
> with incarceration
> with death.
> His spirit is the people. (Eghagha *Rhythms of the Last Testament*, 13)

"Wiwa's Legacy" is one of the few poems in the collection suffused with metaphorical language. It is in a series of definitional, animistic, and mixed metaphors.

In the title of the poem, Eghagha portrays himself as a gifted wordsmith by engaging in morphological innovation. This can be attributed to the poet's training in English. Eghagha morphologically dislocates the proper noun and then genitivizes it to derive Wawi's from *Wiwa*. The genitivization changes the word class of the proper noun to a common one. The stylistic significance of the change in word class to a common one is that it foregrounds Ken Saro-Wiwa as a mere symbol of a people's struggle. So, as long as all the people of the region have not been exterminated, the fire of the struggle cannot be extinguished because "his spirit is the people."

Ken Saro-Wiwa is projected as a legend in this poem not only due to his dogged struggle but also due to the nervous courage with which he faced ignoble death without flinching. These worthy attributes of Wiwa are foregrounded in the definitional metaphors:

> Wiwa's head is made by steel
> His heart is insulated
> But his brain is on paper. (Eghagha *Rhythms of the Last Testament*, 13)

The concretive metaphor "His spirit is the people" gives physical attributes to the abstract noun "spirit." This mixed metaphor, since it is both definitional and concretive, is of stylistic significance because it foregrounds the theme of hope that the incarceration, torture, and execution of human and environmental activists in the region will not truncate the eventual emergence of environmental justice and socioeconomic development in the Niger Delta region.

Apart from the use of metaphors, pronominalization is another rhetorical device employed by Eghagha in his poetry to foreground the theme of environmental degradation and injustice in the Niger Delta region. In "The Last Lover" in *Rhythms of the Last Testament* (9), Eghagha exploits this rhetorical device of pronominalization to depict the titanic struggle between the victims who are also the oppressed of environmental injustices and the perpetuators of environmental degradation and injustice. The later are the rulers as well as their international oil company collaborators.

> the fire is now ash
> we swim into tomorrow's sea
> your laughter is lip laughter
> your smile bites
> fear into my face
> inside you insides
> anger is red like
> the oil fire of Jesse
> heart is black like Jesse's smoke
>
> you called me a baboon
> you called me Okrika
> I come from a firm homestead
> I shall not call my senior a parrot.
>
> you are my last lover
> I reject your cast-iron phallus
> in masquerade of green
> if I step out of your arms
> without a tear of sorrow
> if I blossom after the greedy storm
> if I embrace with soul and body again
> it is because
> your seed was a seed of webbings
> with no track for
> the path that builds
> nests and homes
> for the weak birds
> of my race. (Eghagha *Rhythms of the Last Testament*, 9)

The poet-personae is symbolized by the pronominal "I." Since "I" occurs six times in the poem, the reader is able to see graphically through the poet-personae's eyes the deprivations, insults, and his imprisoned state as articulated by the lexical collocate "a seed of webbings." "I" is an anaphoric reference to "me," which is used three times, and "I" also an anaphoric ally refers to "my," which also occurs three times. The three pronominals are generic terms, which refer to the dispossessed and disease-ravaged indigenes of the Niger Delta who are victims of environmental degradation. "You" is used two times in the poem, and the pronominal is a generic term that represents the internal colonialists and the executives of the multinational oil companies who engage in unsustainable oil exploitation with impunity as long as they satisfy the avaricious and atavistic appetites of the rulers. "You," also an anaphoric ally, refers to "your," which is used five times in the poem. The titanic struggle and opposition between "I" and "you" is symbolized by the use of the pronominal "we." The flaming fire of love between these two opposing forces is "now ash." The struggle for environmental justice and a fair share of the oil revenue has resulted in torture, incarceration, and even execution.

Eghagha also employs deictic to illuminate the opposing class of people in the poem. The pronominal, "I," "me," and "my" also refer to the deictics "the weak birds of my race," "a baboon," and "okrika"; while "you" and "your" deictically refer to a heart that is "black like Jesse's smoke," "anger," and "a parrot" that is "red like the oil fire of Jesse"; and finally "You" is a "seed of webbings," since the impoverished indigenes are now entangled in the mesh of these wicked rulers.

In "Black Gold," Eghagha engages pronominalization to foreground the majority-versus-minority dichotomy among ethnic groups, which has resulted in environmental injustice in the Niger Delta, thus:

> yet they use the excuse
> of our size
> to beat us. (Eghagha *Rhythms of the Last Testament*, 34)

Eghagha's assertion above that the people of the Niger Delta are deprived of basic necessities of life due to the fact that they are minorities was also articulated by Darah thus:

> According to the political cartography of the Nigerian ruling class, the nations in the Niger Delta are "minorities" which must be confined to the margins of power in order for the "majorities" to survive. (4)

The pronominal "they" symbolizes the majority ethnic groups in Nigeria, while "our" also refers to "us" who constitute the minority. Unfortunately, the ethnic groups in the Niger Delta constitutes part of the minority, and that is why they are perhaps deprived a fair share of the oil revenue.

Eghagha also employs several rhetorical strategies of syntactic and lexical repetition to foreground the theme of environmental despoliation in the Niger Delta region. In "It Will Happen Again" in *The Governor's Lodge and Other Poems*, Eghagha employs parallel structures to show how the indigenes of the region tried to struggle for environmental justice despite the fact that they are under the clutches of their internal colonizers thus:

> they saw the wickedness of your smiles
> they saw the poison of your kindness
> they waited patiently like the dog and its precious bone
> they soon grew trees of political power
> and cut at a place for themselves. (Eghagha *The Governor's Lodge*, 10)

The four parallel structures begin with the anaphora "they" that represents indigenes of the Niger Delta region. The anaphora "your" represents "the internal colonialists." The structural difference between the parallel structures is of stylistic significance because they indicate semantic differences. The first two parallel structures, on one hand, have SPCA structure; they portray the ability of the indigenes to decipher the deceitfulness of the internal colonizers. The third parallel structure, on the other hand, has SPAA structure, and it is in this structure that the indigenes hatched a plan to act against the deceitfulness of the internal colonialists. The last parallel structure contains two main clauses and it shows how they regained their autonomy from the clutches of the internal colonialist. So, these sets of parallel structure project hope for the emancipation of the people and eventual regeneration of the environment.

In "In the Dock," Eghagha uses parallel structures to stress the inevitability of the nine Ogoni activists being sentenced to death thus:

> Yet the nine men
> Must go into the dungeon
> Must go into the dark riverside
> Home to shark-crocodiles. (Eghagha *Rhythms of the Last Testament*, 13)

The two parallel structures, which begin with the model auxiliary "must," create images of fear with lexical paradigms "the dungeon" and "The dark riverside," which is the residence of the most ferocious creatures in the ocean and creeks—sharks and crocodiles. There is much in Eghagha's use of repetition that is in the avant-garde tradition. One of them is the use of "guilty," which is in the first line. This can be termed as "'isolation." The word "guilty" projects the preconceived notion of the trial judge in the kangaroo court to sentence the wise men to death.

Conclusion

So, a stylistic analysis of the rhetorical strategies adopted by Eghagha in his eco-poetry foregrounds the poet's artistic enterprise in his fight against environmental and ecological imperialism in Nigeria's Niger Delta region. Through the poet's use of imagery, metaphors, parallelisms, lexical and syntactic repetitions, and pronominalization, Eghagha's earth-centered poetics highlights the fact that the devastation of the environment equally resulted in the destruction of the people's means of livelihood due to the loss of the region's biodiversity. Eghagha also used the rhetorical devices to stylistically foreground the aftereffect of an environmentally despoliated environment, which include abject poverty, malnourishment, and disease. Torture, incarceration, and even execution, which are among the strategies adopted by the Niger Delta's internal colonialists to gag human and environmental justice, are also adroitly depicted with the rhetorical strategies. The innovative use of graphology and repetition in the two collections of poems, which are in the avant-garde tradition, are distinctly Eghaghaesque. As an eco-poet, Eghagha projects himself as a committed poet who uses his craft to struggle for change from the present parlous state of the environment to an environmentally concordant one in the Niger Delta region.

Works Cited

Adeola, F. O. "Environmental Injustice and Human Rights Abuse: The States, MNCs, and Repression of Minority Groups in the World System. *Human Ecology Review* 8.1 (2010): 40–56. Print.

_____. "Endangered Community, Enduring People, Toxic Contamination, Health and Adaptive Responses in a Local Context. *Environment and Behaviour* 32.2 (2000): 209–249. Print.

Amnesty International. *International Human Rights Abuses*. Washington: News Conference Lexis New Life, 1998. Print.

Darah, G. G. "Revolutionary Pressures in Niger Delta Literatures." 2009. Web. 10 May 2011. <http://www.uni-leipzigde.de/-bickel>.

Donnelly, J. *International Human Rights*. Boulder: Westview Press, 1998. Print.

Eghagha, H. *Rhythms of the Last Testament*. Lagos: Concept Publication, 2002. Print.

_____. *This Story Must Not Be Told*. Lagos: Concept Publication, 2003. Print.

_____. *The Governor's Lodge and Other Poems*. Lago: Decocraft Communications, 2004. Print.

_____. *Promotions and Other Dreams*. Lagos: Concept Publications, 2005. Print.

Hansford, K. et al. "An Index of Nigerian Languages" *Studies in Nigerian Languages*. Ed. J. E. Hansford. Jos. Accra Summer Institute of Linguistics, 1976. 60–72. Print.

Jeyifo, B. "Osundare as Nature Poet: A Simple Sentimentality." *The Peoples Poet: Emerging Perspective on Niyi Osundare*. Ed. Abdul Rasheed Na'Allah. New Jersey: Africa World Press, 2003. 609–618. Print.

Mensah, K. A. N. "Osundare as Nature Poet: A Simple Sentimentality." *The Peoples Poet: Emerging Perspective on Niyi Osundare*. Ed. Abdul Rasheed Na'Allah. New Jersey: Africa World Press, 2003. 287–298. Print.

Nwagbara, U. "Poetics of Resistance: Ecocritical Reading of Ojaide's *Delta Blues and Home Songs* and *Daydream of Ants and Other Poems*." *African Study Monographs* 31.1 (2010): 17–30. Print.

Ojakorotu, V. "The Internationalization of Oil Violence in the Niger Delta of Nigeria." *Alternatives Turkish Journal of International Relations* 7.1 (2008): 92–117. Print.

Okome, O. *Before I am Hanged. Ken Saro-Wiwa: Literature, Politics and Dissent*. New Jersey: Africa World Press, 2000. Print.

Olaoluwa, S. S. "From Simplicity to Performance: The Place of Second Generation Anglophone African Poets." *English Studies* 89.4 (2008): 461–481. Print.

Osaghae, E. "Ethnicity and its Management in Africa: The Democratizations Link. *Centre for Advanced Social Sciences Occasional Monograph* 2 (1994): 6–15. Print.

Osundare, N. *The Eye of the Earth*. Ibadan: Heinemann, 1986. Print.

_____. "African Literature Now: Standards, Texts and Canons." *Glendora Review* 1.4 (1996): 25–31. Print.

Renner, M. *Fighting for Survival: Environmental Dealing, Social Conflict and the New Age of Insecurity*. New York: Norton, 1996. Print.

Shultz, J. "Beyond Socialist Realism: 'Socialism by Tendency' in the Poetry of Tanure Ojaide and Wole Soyinka." *NAWA: Journal of Language and Communication* 1.1 (2007): 121–133. Print.

14

Niger Delta Dystopia and Environmental Despoliation in Tanure Ojaide's Poetry

Obari Gomba, University of Port Harcourt

Oil is central to the dystopian condition of the Niger Delta. It is also the motif which best embodies the narratives on subjection and degradation in the Niger Delta. The Niger Delta is the oil-rich region of Nigeria. It is the coastal area that "lies between the estuaries of the Benin River to the west and the Cross River to the east of the Niger River itself" (Daminabo 285). It stretches along the Atlantic Coast and also several miles inland; it is criss-crossed by a network of rivers and a density of mangrove forests. Above all, it is the home of a huge deposit of oil and gas, and the hotbed of resource conflict.

In political terms, since 1999, the exigencies of oil politics have expanded the scope of the Niger Delta beyond cartographic or bioregional delineation. The Niger Delta has come to consist of 9 of the 36 states of Nigeria. In spite of this "new" political design, the intensity of conflict has continued mainly, with the echoes of history, on the swathe between the estuaries of the Benin River and the Cross River. This is the old turf, which had been colonially designed, in the build-up to the making of Nigeria, as the Oil Rivers Protectorate and/or the Niger Coast Protectorate. It is this belt of continuous oil conflict that has provoked the narratives in Ojaide's poetry. This paper will discuss a number of Ojaide's poems on oil conflict in order to accentuate the density of dystopia, subjection, and environmental degradation in the Niger Delta. It will also reveal that Ojaide's depiction of place is steeped in the Otherness, which has been consistently stoked by the incongruities of the postcolonial nation-state.

Niger Delta Dystopia / Abuja's Other

In situating the indices which, as Bassey states, have made the Niger Delta an "oil-fuelled disaster" (90), Ojaide's poetry sometimes posits a contrapuntal depiction of Niger Delta locations and Abuja. This pattern enables the reader to see the contrast between the dispossessed and the power center, in the light of the Otherness. Taking "Four Pieces" for instance, the speaker creates a counterpoint when he notes that the Niger Delta's "Jewelry of honour" is "sold to stave off drought / in [the] inland capital" (Ojaide 9–11). The speaker declaims the action of those who have "introduced a bill" that has enabled the transfer of Niger Delta wealth to service inland powers, "to throw enough green over desert dust" (35–7). Abuja is that inland capital which takes from the Niger Delta through the sleight of law, and it is also a figuration for the power of the ethnic majorities. Al Gedicks avers that oil provides "80% of government's revenue and accounts for 95% of exports" (42). But the ethnic minorities "have not benefited from the extraction of this oil wealth" from their land (Gedicks 42); they lack "functional hospitals and schools, paved roads, steady electricity and even running water" (Gedicks 42). Ojaide's poetry beams a light on this situation.

As in "Four Pieces," "The Goat Song" accentuates the contrast between the Niger Delta and Abuja: "they are rounded into a guarded prison / South-south of the mountain palace / where the king and his consorts carouse" and run "a bacchanalia that breaks the rock of reason" (Ojaide 3–6). The seat of power is so redolent with abuses; the "capital so afflicted with flatulence / only thunder can halt insatiable hands . . ." (6–8). The poem laments that the Niger Delta has become "a guarded prison" (3), designed by the king (and the lords) of "the mountain palace" (4). This mode of contrast is recast over and over in Ojaide's poetry, especially in the poems that depict the dystopia of Niger Delta locations. In the lamentations, which are provoked by the underdevelopment of Niger Delta communities, the personae are often wont to point to the contrasting image of Abuja.

It must, however, be noted that there are moments when the argument on the development needs of the Niger Delta runs into ambivalence as in such poems as "Reclamation" (Ojaide 2–7), "I Grew Tired of Towers" (Ojaide 13–31), and "Priests, Converts and Gods" (Ojaide 12–13) The attitude of the personae in the said poems toward development and modernity is cloudy; this attitude is capable of misleading the reader and misrepresenting the true import of Niger Delta agitation. In "Reclamation," the persona declares:

> I must grow back the forest
> cleared to build the schools
> for children of born singers;

> I must dig back Delta creeks
> from the football fields—
> let every dugout be afloat again. (Ojaide 22-7)

Similarly, when the persona in "I Grew Tired of Towers" returns from, say, the United States to the Niger Delta, he rues that modernity has robbed the region of its idyllic ambience, and that this situation has occurred at the behest of "developers and Government caring that / the people be not left in the bush" (Ojaide 19–20). When one reads "Reclamation," "I Grew Tired of Towers," and even parts of "Priest, Converts and Gods," it will seem that the communities of the Niger Delta have no need for modernity. It will seem that developers and government have an uphill task to bring modern facilities to a region that prefers to be stuck in its woods. It will appear that even when Niger Delta sons and daughters travel to developed locations, particularly in the West, they scramble home to feed their nostalgia for the bush. This somewhat anti-modern posture does not reflect the yearnings of the region. Granted, there are positions against certain aspects of modernity (like the assault of Christian values on tradition and the assault of industry on the environment), but aspects of modernity like education and sports are to be strengthened, not repudiated. The Niger Delta has been incorporated by the accidents of history into a modernity that is driven by modern capital. "In the south," says one of Ojaide's poems, "campfires of oil barons litter the landscape; / stoked all year round by helmet-wearing graduates / who consider themselves lucky" because they are "paid foreign currency / instead of naira; an astute ploy to buy their loyalty" (Ojaide 23–26). The intent and activities of the oil barons are detestable. But the Niger Delta is not bothered by what currency the oil workers receive. The region is rather bothered that its own children do not get to wear the helmets or earn the dollars. The region is bothered that whereas its resources are taken away and its environment is degraded, it does not get its due from the proceeds of the oil industry. Some of the benefits that ought to come to the region are employment, education, healthcare, and roads. While the Niger Delta persona celebrates the unsoiled sections of his environment (in "Less than Halfway to Erhuware"), he knows his development needs. Take the persona in "Noble Inheritance" who, unlike the one in "Reclamation," celebrates the value of modern education by showing the success of Aminogbe's children. He says:

His children went to school, saw the road ahead
and took it through the farthest crossroads—

they bought pens with their mother's pittance
and put on paper their inherited tales and songs;

they keep alive the life and history that
their father's caste chanted to be remembered. (Ojaide 42-7)

This poem records that the children of the Niger Delta really appreciate modern education, and they have put it to great use. The problem is that the facilities are far below standard, like the school in the fifth section of "Essi Layout," which is described as "the refuse-dumped school" (Ojaide 76). The greatest challenge of the region is that modernity and its waves of development have been travestied by the profiteering of transnational corporations and the Nigerian state. As the persona in "A Half-million Troops" puts it, "profiteers / come to sell travesties of development" (85–86). This has made the region a victim of "the fairy tale of oil," the contrast between potential and denial (Watts 37).

There is no doubt that the region has embraced modernity with little reservation. And the people have always seen education as the arrowhead of development. In "Mukoro Mowoe," the hero is praised for mobilizing the people to support educational development: "You clutched to your chest the lugubrous gifts / of your people so that they would not lose / their blessing for lack of foresight" (Ojaide 21–23). Mowoe is depicted as a visionary leader who reads the sign of change for his people: "you saw through granite clouds a resplendent sun / & you slept less and less to cover the landscape of / a destined mission" (24–26). The people too are praised for following Mowoe's light, a march into modernity. "At home and in distant outposts / men and women wrested out of penury three or six pence / for the college and scholarship funds you proclaimed" (27–30). The poem further says that the people "knew they had to reciprocate [Mowoe's] sacrifice / & they filled the coffers of the commonwealth / to be counted among keepers of the new light" (27–31). Mowoe, the Urhobo statesman, is celebrated for being an agent of modernity. He is a typology for several of his kind who inspired development in the communities of the region. He is remembered once again in "An Old Yearning Grips Me" (11–12) where the persona shows that his nostalgia for the past includes a yearning for the earliest goods of modernity and a repudiation of its ills. The trouble is that the people's hope has been dashed by the realities of the present. It appears that the region has been naïve to expect so much from a system that owes its existence to colonialism. Truth has come home to roost and the Niger Delta laments its loss (as in "The Fortune"). With the benefit of hindsight, the Niger Delta has come to see that the system of modernity, into which it has been incorporated, is programmed to keep it at the margins of development. The irony is that the wheels of the western economies and the systems of postcolonial Nigeria are oiled by the resources of the marginalized region.

In "My Heart," the speaker decries the condition of the Niger Delta. He says: "I am hungry for what grows in the heart . . . / hungry to see the Delta get a fair share" (Ojaide 16, 18). "We Are Many" and "The Cross" tell of the generational losses which the region has suffered. The "incubus of power" (in the poem "We Are Many"; Ojaide 18), which squeezes the region dry, is not only foreign, there are the ethnic majorities. "The Cross" says that "The brutish majority" (Ojaide 13) want the "blood" of the region "to keep the country one" (Ojaide 7). There are some sites in the region which buttress this point. Ughelli, Idjerhe, and Warri are but examples. The lamentions of these communities are not peculiar to them. They shed the tears of the region. These tears foreground the poles of conflict, the binary of "We/Us" and "They/Them."

The speaker in the poem entitled "Ughelli" mourns the lot of the community. The speaker is pained to "see" Ughelli "dry-skinned when her oil rejuvenates hags," to see Ughelli left "in darkness when her fuel lights the universe." to see Ughelli "starve . . . despite all her produce" (Ojaide–3). Ughelli is "dehydrate[d] before the wells bored into her heart"; she is "naked despite her innate industry"; she is "without roads when her sweat tars the outside world"; she is "homeless when her idle neighbours inhabit skyscrapers"; she is "lonely when sterile ones use her offsprings as servants"; she is "the artisan" who is treated "as a non-person when drones celebrate with her sweat" (Ojaide 4–9). All the images speak of dispossession: "the palm's oil" has been made "to be the fig tree's," "the goddess of wealth" is not "complimented for her gifts / but [is] spat upon by raiders of her bosom" (10–12). The land "earn[s] so much" but she is "denied all except life—; she is "sucked anaemic by an army of leeches, / it is a big shame" (13–16). "Ughelli" speaks for the entire Niger Delta. It wails the plight of the dispossessed. It shows, as Bamikunle puts it, the image of "the owner [who is] neglected" when her wealth is transferred to "make others comfortable" (Bamikunle 77). All that is left for the region is the story of pain and penury.

Consider "Idjerhe," which represents the fire disaster that killed about 1,000 residents of Idjerhe/Jesse in 1998. Like Ughelli, Idjerhe is stripped of its abundance by an industry that leaves death and sorrow in its wake. The speaker in "Idjerhe" notes that Idjerhe has become a community where "wraiths speak a delta of woes" (Ojaide 1); a community of "Soot-clad scarecrows and scorched cadavers" which "the unknowing world insults . . ." (2–3). Idjerhe has fallen into calamity but the community is accused of "'stealing fuel'?" (4). And the "salaaming man" accuses "festering flesh and kilned bones" of sabotage: "'You people say you are marginalized, but that's / no reason to destroy Gov'ment property'?" (5–7) Those who traduce Idjerhe ignore the sorry state of the land. "Marginalization wobbles rickety in rags staring / at piped-out dreams! Government is an ogre. / A curse on a callous heart. Bespectacled blindness" (8–10). The victims are denied help. "The mass-graved and palpitating patients need balm / But none [comes] from Abuja . . ." (11–12). The government and the firm are seen to be snug in the convenience of falsehood; the "conglomerate allies were too happy to bear false witness / against a restless group that dared to raise its head and voice" (23–24). The incident that is depicted in "Idjerhe" had actually occurred on 17–18 October 1998 in the days of Gen. Abdulsalami Abubakar who, as it appears, is referred to in the poem as "the salaaming man" (5). The poem is highly suggestive. The innuendo draws its strength from the sound elements in Gen. Abubakar's first name. It could be inferred that Gen. Abubakar is also called "Bespectacled blindness" (10) because the General is always bespectacled. Given these inferences, it could be said that the poem represents Gen. Abubakar's government as an extension of the tradition of ogres in power: "Government is an ogre" (9) which rules from "Abuja" (12).

Gen. Abubakar's days were days of political instability and petroleum difficulties, stretching from the inglorious days of Gen. Abacha. They were, arguably, also days of racketeering, and petroleum was crucial in the scale of profit. The poem shows why the oil firms and the government have cunningly allowed the cause of the Idjerhe inferno to remain nebulous till this day. The smokescreen is said to have enabled the state to put the blame on the Idjerhe people; it has also enabled the state and the oil firm(s) to shirk from making a commitment to the hurt. The state, the oil firm(s) and their allies might have craftily got away with a crime for which many have held them responsible, even if it is only on the basis of negliegence. One of such strong testimonies comes from a former Chief of Army Staff, Maj. Gen. David Ejoor (retired). Maj. Gen. Ejoor states, in *Environmental*

Testimonies, that "evidence abounds that the fire was caused by the oil companies and the Government" (ERA 84). Maj. Gen Ejoor argues that an oil cartel had been responsible for the pipe breakage. This corroborates the position in Ojaide's poem. The "bunkerer" could not close the joint valve (near Idjerhe) before daybreak. As the villagers became aware that petrol had flooded their farms and river, they set about helping themselves with the scoop. This might have given the oil firm the pretext to impute blame on the people of Idjerhe. Gen. Ejoor says that the company and the government dispatched a helicopter to the site of the spill. "The officials in the helicopter warned the people in English to disperse or something would happen to them. Most of the crowd did not understand what was being said and the sight of the helicopter added more fun to the fetching of the liquid gold . . ." (ERA 84). The officials might have been piqued. Maj. Gen. Ejoor says they "followed up their threat with firing nerve gas at the crowd, which made it impossible for them to run" (ERA 84). The people were emasculated. "Those who attempted to run could not move their limbs with agility. Then the horror came; the place was set on fire with the intention of killing everybody present and to prevent anybody from giving evidence" (ERA 84).

The disaster was terrible. And government is said to have pushed the blame. This "accounted for the two nerve-ranking [sic] statements by the Head of State, to the effect that there would be no compensation to Idjerhe people" (ERA 84–85). For this, Ojaide's poem calls the Head of State "the salaaming man" (5) who has "a callous heart" (10). The attitude of government is detestable and callous. Ejoor further says that the Military Administrator of Delta State at the time had ensured that truth was muffled by "scaring off survivors from giving evidence . . . hence many victims ran away from the hospitals" (ERA 85). The actions of the state suggest that Idjerhe and the rest of the Niger Delta are merely expendable in the scheme of oil profiteering. Gen. Ejoor notes that the "horror meted to the Urhobo people in Idjerhe could [have been] avoided if the Government and the oil companies [had] regarded the local peoples as Nigerians . . ."; if the "local people" had not been "regarded as nuisance"; if the "Government and the oil companies [had] good Urhobo (public) relations senior officers, and not just only Hausa, Igbo and Yoruba technocrats"; if the "warning given from the helicopter" had "been in Urhobo language, to be understood by Idjerhe people" (ERA 85). Gen. Ejoor says that the "oil companies have covered up their injustice of stealing petrol by using the helicopter to murder 1000 people; and that it has become imperative for the government to "realize that people from areas where national wealth is made are Nigerians . . ." (ERA 85). Gen. Ejoor's testimony conforms to Ojaide's "Idjerhe." They foreground the conflict of interest existing between the oil producing areas and the Nigerian state. The political system has aided reckless industrial activities at the expense of the oil-producing areas. It is a question of power. Ojaide poem sets Abuja as the symbol of the power, which revolves around the ethnic majorities. The poem casts Abuja in antithesis to Idjerhe. This is also the pattern that gives a force of value to the poems on Warri. In a great number of such poems, the conflict is between "Us" and "Them," and this perception is hinged on the counterpoint of underdevelopment and development.

Warri is more recurrent in Ojaide's poetry than any other Niger Delta location. The poems in which Warri is placed contrapuntally with Abuja show the positions of both cities in the scheme of things. "Curfew City" and "Essi Layout: Six Sketches" are two examples of such.

Warri is in a condition of unrest in "Curfew City," and the state has called in its soldiers. The city falls under a kind of siege because the soldiers tramp the land like an army of occupation. The persona holds Abuja responsible: "not until cadavers litter the delta will the jackals / be called back to their crowded barracks in Abuja" (Ojaide 16–17). Even the excitement of yuletide is hampered by the militarization of Warri. There is the anxiety that soldiers "could turn [the city] into a mass grave" (19).

In "Essi Layout: Six Sketches," the persona's visit to Abuja is a stimulus of pain. He says: "I had just come from Abuja to the Delta / still reeling from PTF's brazen robbery" (Ojaide 27–28). The Petroleum Trust Fund (PTF), which ought to be an instrument of development—dating back to the days of Gen. Abacha—is another conduit for the transfer of wealth from the Niger Delta. Whereas this conduit of accumulation favors Abuja, it leaves Warri and the rest of the Niger Delta undeveloped. The poem shows the grim picture of Warri as a city in "abject neglect" (Ojaide 3); "a city choked by ignorance" (13–35); "a city with grievous tenement problems" (36–51); "a city of easy sex and population explosion" (52–68); "a city of stench, refuse dumps and infrastructural decay" (69–77). There are several other poems that corroborate "Essi Layout: Six Sketches." Warri is equally depicted in "Dirge I" (Ojaide 102–103), "Warri Has Never Really Been a Beauty," "From Warri," "The Area Boy," "Everybody Has Turned Hunter," "Do Something," "Warri Night," "For These Moments," "One Day in Warri," and "In Search of a Fresh Song." These poems, which cut across a number of collections, speak on a wide range of issues: the upsurge of crime and violence in the city, the restiveness of youths, unemployment and the Area Boy syndrome, ethnic tension and conflict, militarization, degradation of the environment by oil firms, and so forth. All these conduce to make Warri a dystopian space from which the persona in "City in My Heart" flees: "I come . . . driven out / by dirt and doubts from Warri's delta lows" (Ojaide 2–3). Warri is portrayed as a perilous place to live. Its dystopian propensities stir up tension in the city. It also stirs up despair and hate. Warri is a cross-current of nervous conditions, which does not only create implosion, it sharpens the people's grouse against Abuja. Warri is Abuja's other, and both cities are locked in the conflictual symbolism between the Niger Delta and the rest of Nigeria.

Abuja is the seat of power and of might, it holds the instruments of control. It is the paradise of accumulation. The flatulence of power and riches has given Abuja the Ozymandian aspiration of absolute rule. But the city stews in its own perversions. The poem entitled "When We Hear Name of President" says Lagos was the first to wear the trappings that Abuja now has: "First na lagoon be graveyard, / then hillside of new capital" (Ojaide 55–56). The speaker sees the "new capital" as another graveyard, which has come to replace the "lagoon." Of course, the enrichment of Abuja has turned the Niger Delta into a graveyard, but the poem sees Abuja's program of control and accumulation as the making of a grand graveyard. Abuja is a travesty of national hope, so says the speaker in "The League of Heroes." The city that ought to be the symbol of security and prosperity for all the component units has become the pain of the oil-producing areas.

Abuja symbolizes both the transfer of wealth from the Niger Delta and the overbearing dictatorship of the center. "First came the politician, / then the army officer, and now / both flashing chronic baldness" on the account of "meals flavoured / with barrels of refined oil / in Abuja's deferred dreams" (Ojaide 92–97). Abuja's profiteering and flatulence is depicted once more in "Praying for Answers." The poem denounces the perversions of the city, which is governed by a "voracious pack, burghers who bugle Abuja / and have no recess from looting and scandals . . . (Ojaide 2–33). They pillage the wealth of the Niger Delta "in the name of a constitution they hold no dearer / than naira bills stuffed in Ghana-must-go bags" (34–35). Like "Praying for Answers," the voices of protest and denunciation are very strong and loud in poems like "A Bird's Tale" (Ojaide 65–77), "Enter My Dream," "Libation," "Dateline: Abuja," "When It No Longer Matters Where You Live," "Nobody Talks of El Nino," "Abuja," "The Chieftain and His Tribe," and "On Solidarity Marches." Each of these poems accentuates the features of Abuja—its greed, its corruption, its obdurate power, its opulence, and its accumulation. There is also the indication that the fortune of the Niger Delta is tied to Abuja. Since Abuja holds all the instruments of control and accumulation, the Niger Delta will only exhale whenever Abuja is "cured" of its systems of perversion. However, the poem which is simply entitled "Abuja" shows no prospect for positive change. The picture is bleak. The speaker in "Abuja" describes the city as the place "where all cardinal points meet in a capital" / . . . where rocks raise homes to the sky / . . . where the savannah rolls over the soil" (Ojaide 1–3).

Affluence and diabolical power intermingle in the city. It is "the coven where witches plot the demise of others / this is where chiefs celebrate on the sweat of slaves / this is where range chickens consume and scatter leftovers" (Ojaide 4–6). It is the place "where the hyena's den is guarded by rings of packs / this is where the hyena cornered the hare / and swallowed it, leaving no scent for a trace" (7–9). It is the city "where the boa-constrictor strangles its catch / . . . where robbers boast of their callous acts / . . . where the national flag covers a cesspool (10–11, 13). The images of power in the lines above evoke abuses and wastages. In this poem, Abuja is depicted as a dystopian space in its own right. It is the paradise of looters and abusive power. The bird in "A Bird's Tale" notes that "Abuja is bloated with looted oil and gas / a shameful ring to the nation's anthem" (Ojaide 73–74). Abuja is represented as a perversion of values that traps even the "representatives" of the people; the representatives fall for the lure of corruption; and they are shown to be "carousing in faraway Abuja" (in "Testimony to the Nation's Wealth"; Ojaide 8).

Subjection and Subjected Environment

A World Wildlife Fund report released in 2006 simply referred to the Niger Delta as one of the most polluted places on the face of the earth" (Watts 44). This situation has given the force of value to the images of environmental degradation in Ojaide's poetry. The bond between the people and their environment is a key formative in the poems of Ojaide. The significance of this relationship is depicted with a spiritual tenor in "Map of Time" by which the divinity of the river is made to mask its economic value. On the other hand, it can be said that the people, who take cowries and other items of worship to the River god, seem to acknowledge that the deity has been a factor in their socioeconomic wellbeing. "Labyrinth of the Delta," the title-poem of Ojaide's second collection, puts it very clearly.

The poem is like "Map of Time," a call to worship, couched in Urhobo frames of signification. The speaker in "Labyrinths of the Delta" raises a clarion: "Let us go to the River" (Ojaide 22). The people are to go there with the items for worship: "With drums, goats, and cowries; / Let us go, draped in our favourite madras, / Powdered and perfumed . . ." (23–25). The poem implies that the people owe the River the debt of faith. The speaker says:

> Let us go to her
> She called us this way,
> And we came, absorbing accents
> Into our tongue. (26–29)

It is noteworthy that the speaker has been diligent to ascribe the pious capital letter to the "River," and there is also a shift in gender. The import of veneration is maintained. The deity is still one with the environment—that is, to celebrate the deity is also to celebrate the environment and its provisions. The reason for the people's worship is woven into the matrix of their history. In their flight from the tyranny of Benin, they are said to have launched themselves into the unknown: "'Where are we going?' children asked their parents. / 'Where you will grow up, a place destined for us'" (Ojaide 8-9). Their desperate flight and blind faith is said to have been rewarded. "O Water Bride," says the speaker, "Moving without a boat in deep waters, / You heeded the anguished cries of our souls, / Ferried us fugitives across the midstream torrents . . ." (30–33). The Water Bride is said to have helped the people in their precarious crossing into the present homeland. "You made us calabashes on the water / And delivered us on the bank, giving us / The virgin beauty of the Delta" (34–36). The Water Bride is the same as the River in this poem.

The third segment of the poem exalts the soil (land) in the same measure: "You stood here, waiting since the beginning of time, / O soil, to give yourself to us, and here we are" (Ojaide 45–46). The land is the bounty of sunlight (47), a network of rivers (51), well-ordered rainfall (55–57), abundant wildlife (58–61), and a "tropical garden where you picked for free / whatever appealed to your constitution" (79–80). In fact, the speaker calls the Niger Delta "Our God-built home" (50), which serves a great concourse of deities, people, fauna, flora, and aquatic life. The concourse suffers a major upset when "Conquistadors drove . . . stakes into the labyrinths of the Delta . . ." (91, 94). That initial upset has formed the plinth for the consistent assault on the Niger Delta environment. The region has suffered centuries of abuse, and this has stretched from the earliest encounter with imperial Europe to the present. In the later poems of Ojaide, there is a depiction of the corrosive effects of industry and mercantilism on the environment.

"Ivwri" actually gives a face to the destroyers of the environment. The poem points to the processes that have affected the environment. The environment is said to have been sustainable "[b]efore overbreeding / tore the tangles with machetes and matches," and "before Shell BP flared / the forest into a wasteland . . ." (Ojaide 179–182). The poem points at the people who are driven by new waves of modernity and industry to mismanage the environment; it also points ultimately to Shell BP which stands as the imperial offspring of the conquistadors. In a similar vein, Shell BP also stands accused in "Reclamation" where the speaker declares: "I must keep off Shell BP / to decontaminate soil and water" (Ojaide 28–29). Shell BP does not only stand for itself; it also stands for the oil industry and its enterprise of assault on the people's environment. "Shell controls over 70 percent of the oil activities in the Niger Delta area. This explains why the company is the most implicated in incidents of environmental pollution" in the region (Omoweh 129). Other companies—such as Chevron, Mobil, Texaco, and Elf—are also guilty of environmental abuses but Shell is the standard-bearer of the fold (Omoweh 129). This is why the speaker in Ojaide's poem seeks to bar Shell BP from the region.

Ojaide continues the discussion in *Delta Blues* in poems like "When Green Was the Lingua Franca," "Delta Blues," and "Visiting Home." The first of the three poems sounds like the poet's own personal testimony: "My childhood stretched / one unbroken park, / teeming with life" (Ojaide 1–3). The land was viable before the rise of industry; "In the forest green was / the lingua franca / with many dialects" (4–6). The "many dialects" (6) is a metaphor for the bounties of the environment in the persona's childhood. The environment has been degraded; its provisions are being eroded. Here again, the persona accuses Shell of exploiting the environment with no consideration for the wellbeing of the owners of the region:

> Then Shell broke the bond
> with quakes and a hell
> of flares. Stoking a hearth
> under God's very behind! (Ojaide 43–46)

There are "Explosions of shells to *under* /Mine grease-black *gold*," which has driven "the seasons mental," and the explosions have made things ". . . walk on their heads" (Ojaide 53–56). Shell's assault on the environment is described as the "execution" of the environment (58–60). The provisions of nature have become "victims of arson" (61). There is a particular reference to the Ethiope waterfront where prospectors "beheaded" trees and "poisoned" streams "in the name of jobs and wealth" (64–68). Of course, the oil industry is the arrowhead of degradation, but other elements have joined the pillage. So the persona tries to address the situation, and he is bothered that others will mistake him for a madman (69–70). He laments that the environment has become a shadow of its past: "Now I commune with ghosts / of neighbours and providers" (77–78). These ghosts are the provisions of the environment that have had their "healing hands of leaves / and weeds . . . amputated" (79–80). The features of the environment are now ghosts of their luxuriant past.

"When Green Was the Lingua Franca" shares the same pattern of representation with "Delta Blues." Both poems depict a contrast between the past and the present, and they show the changes that have been wrought on the environment by oil exploration. "Delta Blues" opens with a lament. The speaker in the poem wails, as the voice of the land, against the degradation of the environment: "The share of paradise, the delta of my birth / reels from an immeasurable wound. / Barrels of alchemical draughts flow" through the environment (Ojaide *Delta Blues*, 1–3). "Chemicals and oil flow "from this hurt [environment] to the unquestioning world / that lights up its life in a blind trust" (4–5). The barrels service the interest of hegemony to the detriment of the Niger Delta. "The inheritance I sat on for centuries / now crushes my body and soil" (6–7), the poem says. The voice that speaks in "Delta Blues" is in a single mould with the environment. The condition of the environment affects the condition of the speaker. The irony is that oil is also a product of the environment. But the exploiters have come to prize this product above the entire environment. The exploiters show that their only concern is the extraction of oil, and they extract it with the backing of state laws. It does not matter to them that they are killing the environment by the processes of their reckless enterprise. The natural owners of the environment are in double jeopardy: they have no control over oil profit, and they have come to lose the natural provisions of their environment to the industry. In lines 25–33, the speaker rues the condition of the land. "My nativity gives immortal pain / [and it is] masked in barrels of oil" which hurt. The speaker laments: "I stew in the womb of fortune / I live in the death bed / prepared by a cabal of brokers" (Ojaide 25–29). The cabal of profiteers are "breaking the peace of centuries" and are "staining not only a thousand rivers, / my lifeblood from the beginning / but scorching the air and soil" (30–33).

Things are deplorable in the speaker's environment. But the speaker does not break his bond with his home. In fact, the pain of his nativity fires him to greater commitment. This explains the commitment of the persona in "Visiting Home" who returns to the "ruins of [his] old homesteads" (Ojaide *Delta Blues*, 3). He says "I stand before the homeland's spring: / I can neither drink of its present state / nor will I throw away the calabash" (22–24). He decides to "fashion ways to drink of it / without its dirt . . ." (25–26). There is a similar bond with the environment in the poem entitled "I Grew Tired of Towers" where the persona returns to the Niger Delta, to his nativity where "the water resources [have been] taken over / by oil companies" because "Government needs revenues" (29–30).

It is obvious that the personae in Ojaide's poems are constantly troubled by the environmental degradation, which has been caused by the interest of government and oil firms in the Niger Delta, as in two other collections, *The Tale* and *Waiting*. In the first poem of *The Tale* entitled "The Goat Song," the persona laments the havoc of oil activities on the environment. He says: "the trees" lose "their coiffure" (Ojaide *The Tale*, 40); "irokos fall" and "game / leave in droves" (43–44); and "humans flee to hunger" (44). He also describes the pollution of streams: "the blackened stream is ancestral blood / tapped away by giant pipes into ships" (33–34). The point here is that the environment has been the live wire of the people, its blackened stream is "ancestral blood" (33). This means that "stream" is the same as oil in the context of the poem. But it is presently tapped by mercantile interest. Indeed, the poem is laden with pain, and it opens the door to an avalanche of lamentation and anguish in the rest of the collection.

The questions that are raised are these: Is it possible for industry and modernity to treat the environment with care? Could there be a better way to extract oil in the Niger Delta? Are there examples to prove that development can be sensitive to nature? It is shown in "Transplants" that the persona finds that development does not necessarily have to be destructive. "I see transplants of my youth's landscape", says the poem, "first at Hawthorden and now at Steepletop: / the pristine streams, the multi-ethnic population / of plants, costumed birds, and graceful game" (Ojaide *The Tale*, 1–4). The visit of the persona to Hawthorden and Steepletop stir up memories of the once beautiful environment of the Niger Delta.

Hawthorden and Steepletop prove that development is not a negation of environmental protection. Enterprise must understand the need for "all members of the natural world—humans, animals, plants, rocks, oceans, winds—[to] live healthier and happier lives in a vigorously healthy earth" (McDowell 26). It is fallacious to think that reckless industry is an advancement of "homocentrism," or that paying attention to the condition of nature is a mere "counterculture" in opposition to "intractable homocentrism" (Buell 114). The truth is that reckless industry is sheer profit-centrism at the expense of human concerns. There is no centrality of man in any system that pillages the provisions of nature. Homocentrism must ally with nature-centrism. There is no excuse for the industrial nihilism of oil extraction in the Niger Delta: "Iroko and Mahogany are hardly seen; the forest fell / foul to fires of oil blowouts and poach raids / . . . the creeks I fished in without care now clogged" ("Transplant"; Ojaide 9–10, 12). There is the echo of this lament in "Priests, Converts, and Gods." The speaker in the "Priests, Converts and Gods" only rephrases the words in "Transplant" He says: "the streams and creeks" are "clogged to keep ocean tankers full, / we no more boast of fresh water or the abundance of fish" (Ojaide 27–28). He describes the situation as hellish: "The priests that came from abroad warned of the inferno / that would consume those who did not heed their commandments— / they were wrong in attributing hell to another life" (31–33). Hell is right "here [where] victims already suffer daily pangs from profiteers; / condemned to burning winds of gas flares and streams / of boiling oil so combustible they burn all in their wake" (34–36). The poem argues that exploratory activities have turned the Niger Delta into Hell Fire. The people are already in Hell Fire; they do not have to fear another.

What really deepens the pain in this poem is the contrast between the past and the present. The burden of memory, which is also noticed in "Transplant," foregrounds the violation which the environment has suffered, and it highlights the persona's nostalgia for the bountiful and idyllic era that predated petroleum exploration. Granted that this kind of nostalgia sometimes tilts toward over-romanticization, as in "Lesson from Grandma's Night-time School" where the persona overcoats the beauty of the past:

> We reaped bushels of goodwill without effort
> because no one ate outside the gathering—
> a morsel multiplied into meals
> to sate a thousand stomachs. (Ojaide 27-30)

The persona also adds: "We consorted with birds and animals, / communed with plants on fresh draught / that rain and sunlight provided for growth"; and there was *"no cause for anxiety in the commonwealth"* (Ojaide 31–34; italics mine). Although the hyperbolic thrust of the foresaid lines tends to overstate a paradisal past, there is no gainsaying the gulf that has come to exist between the idyllic past and the present nihilism. In "Womb-Wrapped," the speaker puts it thus: "As I deep feet and hands into the herb-dark stream / of my birth, I hear oil blowouts closer and closer" (Ojaide 13–14). The environment is constantly assaulted. "The stream shrinks and stands still / at the sight of a snaking oil slick" (17–18). And the villain is named: "Wearing Shell-coated gear, / the arsonist escapes fingerprinting" (25–26). We find this same tenor in "Quatrain Suite" (Ojaide 17–20) and "For My Grandchild" (Ojaide 1–6). The latter drives the issues deeper, and it shows how the activities of oil profiteers have eroded the basic subsistence of local economies. This point crops up again in "Market Day," which depicts the collapse of local commerce: "In this market I can no longer get my needs / the same market that filled my forebears" (7–8). The assault of oil production has affected traditional means of livelihood, and it upsets natural lines of productivity.

In the title-poem, "The Tale of the Harmattan," the speaker argues that pollution has altered the cycle of the season: "the regular visitor failed to arrive / with good luck that follows its wake" (Ojaide *The Tale*, 21–22). The significance of harmattan is based on the belief system of the people. The speaker notes that "the swarm of generous djinns that invade us" are "barred from the land by free marketers of oil" (23–24). The time-honored activities, which connect the harmattan to other seasons in the cosmology of the people, have been truncated by the violence of petroleum exploration on the environment. This is also a blow on culture. The speaker says the spirits (djinns), that come with the season, have been barred (23–24). This connects to "At Kaiama Bridge," which shows the travail of even divinities: "flotillas of river spirits / who for centuries brought their spectacle to town / in yearly masquerade . . . retreat seaward" (Ojaide 1–3). The spirits are said to be in hasty flight. They leave "for the freedom and health of the open sea" (19–20); they leave as "a procession of oil-soaked water spirits / wailing their way out" (46–47). In the worldview of the peoples of the Niger Delta, the people and their deities are bound inextricably with the environment. This tells why the deities are said to be just as hit by environmental degradation as the humans.

As the deities are dislodged from their natural habitat, we also see, in "At Kaiama Bridge," the condition of the people: "No boats of fishermen plying / the water ways; no regatta and no swimmer in sight" (Ojaide 47–48). The people are alienated from their environment. In "Swimming in a Waterhole," for instance, the children who have grown to love rivers and lakes can no longer swim in the waters where their parents swam. They now swim in burrow pits, which are polluted: "gas flares, oil slicks, and hyacinths converge / to turn acid rain and all the methane seeps" into their bodies (17–26). The images are the same as those of "At Kaiama Bridge" where "oil spillage has fuelled water hyacinths / to multiply"; and "Refugee gods are taking the last route / before the entire waterway is clogged" (25–28). Some other spirits "return to the hard soil posthaste because . . . / the waters have turned to a poisonous brew" (11–12). They should have known that even the land is not free from pollution. The land is just as hurt as the waters. Aquatic life is just as hurt as fauna and flora (in "Without the Trees"). There is no hiding place for humans or gods in the face of the onslaught of oil profiteers. The gravity of this situation is possibly the provocation for Ojaide's concern from his earliest poems to *Waiting* and *The Beauty*. In fact, a number of his recent poems are somewhat repetitive, perhaps for the sake of emphasis.

"The Fate of Our Lingua Franca" (Ojaide *Waiting*, 69) actually echoes the title of an earlier poem ("When Green Was the Lingua Franca") in *Delta Blues*. The concern in both poems is the same, except that in the more recent poem, the persona takes on the metaphor of Aminogbe (the traditional minstrel of Urhobo cosmology). "Aminogbe recounts his childhood delights: / wild apples, cherries, grapes and breadfruit / garnered from the forest[s]" (Ojaide *Waiting*, 1–3) of the region. He expresses nostalgia for his childhood, for the period when he drew from the bounties of his environment, for the period when his grandmother could draw from the abundance of the land to feed the house. He rues the pollution of the environment and strange "ailments consume the populace" (37). This pollution is said to have come from oil explorers who pursue profit at the expense of the people; "oil companies care not for the dying" (40). The persona is very angry and he places a curse on oil profiteers; he says "let murderers sleep not," let them "die [as] vultures" (44). They are murderers because they kill the environment and its dependants (55). There is a pathetic picture in the third segment of the poem. The introduction to the segment states that "Aminogbe comes to . . . a tributary of the Okpari River and he is "admiring the river before an oil company came to poison it with toxins . . ." (72). Aminogbe names the villain once again: "*Shell's oil spill snakes towards our feet, / The forest sighs in agony; the refuge fume*" (86–87). Shell is mentioned as a partner to government: "*Shell and Government stoke the flames*" (96–97). The culpability of Shell is trumpeted here as in the earlier poems such as "Ivwri," "Reclamation," and "Womb-wrapped." Those poems also connect to "Noble Inheritance" as well. The words of "Noble Inheritance" embody a sense of mission. The persona declares his commitment to "a delta of many creeks [that he has] to ply and keep clean from Shell's spilled toxins" (Ojaide *Waiting*, 74–75). Shell's villainy is highlighted here. And it runs through other poems like "The Fallout" and "Dirge II," even though the personae do not come as open as that of "Noble Inheritance." "The Fallout" mourns: "trees beheaded remain dirt, dead / as the rivers poisoned with oil slicks" (49–50). And "Dirge II" avers that "gas flares snuff life out of lively plants" and "oil spills kill the riverine population / that give so much life to the living" (68–70). There are "[w]ails for broken mirrors of rivers"; there are wails "for the lost gold of full moons"; there are wails "for the silver needs of rainfall, / and for the garden's loss of verdure" (71–74). These are all elements that constitute the poem's images of the lingua franca of the environment. "The lingua franca of green gone, / the choral music of the forest silenced / ears glued to endangered species" (75–77). The people feel the pain of the environment. "We can hear their pain and sorrow," says the persona, "and so let our wails rise high / in one dirge for all the dead" (78–80). The poem outlines aspects of environmental abuses in the Niger Delta, and it wails the condition of things. It buttresses the fact that environmental degradation is an index of underdevelopment and violence. The activities of the oil industry have wrecked havoc on the environment: "gas dey burn for our sky whaam wham / our river rotten (Shell dey shit for inside)," says the speaker of "When We Hear Name of President" (13–14). The subjection of the environment is a clear evidence of the repression that the region suffers. Subjection creates a subjected environment. In the case of oil production in the Niger Delta, Gedicks says "there is an inseparable connection between the assault on the environment and the assault on human rights" (41).

Works Cited

Bamikunle, Aderemi. "Literature as a Historical Process: A Study of Ojaide's *Labyrinths of the Delta*." *African Literature and African Historical Experience*. Ed. Chidi Ikonne, Emelia Oko, and Peter Onwundinjo. Ibadan: Heinemann, 1991. 73–82. Print.

Bassey, Nnimmo. "Oil Fever." *Curse of the Black Gold: 50 Years of Oil in the Niger Delta.* Ed. Michael Watts. New York: powerHouse Books, 2008. 90–91. Print.

Buell, Lawrence. *The Environmental Imagination: Thoreau, Native Writing, and the Formation of American Culture.* Massachusetts: Belknap Press, 1995. Print.

Daminabo, Amanyanabo Opubo. "The Niger Delta in the Era of Globalisation." *The Future of the Niger Delta: The Search for a Relevant Narrative.* Ed. Abi Alabo Derefaka and Atei Mark Okorobia. Port Harcourt: Onyoma Research Publications, 2008. 285–292. Print.

Environmental Rights Action (ERA). *Environmental Testimonies.* Benin City: ERA/FoEN, 1999. Print.

Gedicks, Al. *Resource Rebels: Native Challenges to Mining and Oil Corporations.* Massachusetts: South End Press, 2001. Print.

McDowell, Michael. "Talking About Trees in Stumpton: Pedagogical Problems in Teaching Ecocamp." *Reading the Earth: New Directions in Study of Literature and Environment.* Ed. Michael P. Branch, Rochelle Johnson, Daniel Patterson, and Scott Slovic. Idaho: U of Idaho P, 1998. 19–28. Print.

Ojaide, Tanure. *The Beauty I Have Seen: A Trilogy.* Lagos: Malthouse, 2010. Print.

———. *Children of Iroko and Other Poems.* New York: Greenfield Review Press, 1973. Print.

———. *Daydream of Ants and Other Poems.* Lagos: Malthouse, 1997. Print.

———. *Delta Blues and Home Songs.* Ibadan: Kraft Books, 1998. Print.

———. *In the House of Words.* Lagos: Malthouse, 2006. Print.

———. *In the Kingdom of Songs: A Trilogy of Poems: 1995–2000.* Trenton: Africa World Press, 2002. Print.

———. *Invoking the Warrior Spirit.* Ibadan: Heinemann, 1998. Print.

———. *I Want to Dance and Other Poems.* San Francisco: African Heritage Press, 2003. Print.

———. *Labyrinths of the Delta.* New York: Greenfield Review Press, 1986. Print.

———. *The Tale of the Harmattan.* Cape Town: Kwela Books, 2007. Print.

———. *Waiting for the Hatching of a Cockerel.* Trenton: Africa World Press, 2008. Print.

Omoweh, Daniel A. *Shell Petroleum Development Company, the State and Underdevelopment of Nigeria's Niger Delta: A Study in Environmental Degradation.* Trenton: Africa World Press, 2005. Print.

Watts, Michael. "Sweet and Sour." *Curse of the Black Gold: 50 Years of Oil in the Niger Delta.* Ed. Michael Watts. New York: powerHouse Books, 2008. 36–47. Print.

15

Eco-survival in the Poetry of G. 'Ebinyo Ogbowei
Bernard Otonye Stephen, Niger Delta University, Wilberforce Island

Introduction

In 2009, Gilbert 'Ebinyo Ogbowei released his fourth collection of poetry entitled *Song of a Dying River* and it was among 161 entries for that year's national literary competition, the Nigeria-NLG Prize for Literature. The collection made it to the final short-list of nine entries from which the winner would have emerged. However, in spite of the failure of the panel of judges to choose a winning entry, the nine books of poetry were adjudged the most outstanding in the genre for the year. Interestingly, that was not the first time Ogbowei's work got that far. Previously, in the maiden 2005 poetry edition of the competition, Ogbowei's entry, *Let the Honey Run and Other Poems* (2001), made the list of top eleven poetry collections. Ogbowei's two other published works are *The Town Crier's Song* (2003) and *the Heedless Ballot Box* (2006). With four notable poetry collections to his name, and the manuscript of a fifth already completed and awaiting publication, it is obvious that Ogbowei has established himself as a compelling voice in third-generation Nigerian poetry. It is imperative, therefore, to take a closer look at the subjects and themes that engage this poet's creative imagination. Consequently, this study attempts to examine aspects of Ogbowei's poetry, which deal with issues of the environment, using eco-critical criteria.

Ogbowei is among a growing number of poets that have come out of Nigeria's oil-rich Niger Delta region. Expectedly, much of Ogbowei's poetry is colored by personal experiences and his vast knowledge of the region, especially crude oil exploration activities by multinational conglomerates and the attendant ecological challenges the people face. Apart from the Niger Delta question, Ogbowei's literary canvas also features images of the myriad social, economic, and political problems bedeviling the

Nigerian state. However, from the range of subjects he deals with, it seems Ogbowei is at his best when he writes about the Niger Delta. In this regard, Ogbowei's poetry belongs to a corpus of works with the Niger Delta as centerpiece. Among many others, I have in mind the writings of pioneers like J. P. Clark-Bekederemo and Gabriel Okara; the gripping outpourings of Tanure Ojaide and Ibiwari Ikiriko; and the significant voices of Nnimmo Bassey, Barine Ngaage, Joe Ushie, Sophia Obi-Apoko, Ogaga Ifowodo, and Ebi Yeibo. The common denominator in the recent writings from the region is the interrogation of the socioeconomic, political, and environmental problems occasioned by the exploration of crude oil in the region. The problems which, in broad terms, include ecological destruction, pollution, loss of farming and fishing grounds, the disappearance of migratory birds in the skies, extinction of animal and plant species, joblessness, youth restiveness, and militarization of the region are too compelling to be ignored by any serious-minded writer. There is evidence in Ogbowei's poetry to suggest that he takes these issues seriously. It is no wonder then that environment-related issues, in terms of the survival of human and nonhuman life in the Niger Delta ecosphere, feature prominently in Ogbowei's poems. This is what makes the examination of Ogbowei's poetry from an eco-critical perspective relevant. Besides, the much that has been written on Ogbowei's poetry remains disturbingly skewed in favor of political concerns; we are yet to fully come to terms with this poet's environmental sensibility. Therefore, there is the need to appraise Ogbowei's eco-friendly poems to espouse what they say about the transformations that have occurred in the Niger Delta biosphere as a result of human activities. Thus, a reading of select poems from Ogbowei's published collections is premised on his eco-poetics.

The Eco-critical Perspective

Studies have shown that literary analysis from the perspective of ecological considerations is a relatively new intellectual engagement in the global literary establishment. It is even more so in Africanist literary scholarship. To delve into the evolutionary trend of eco-criticism would do little to address the kernel of the present study; a great deal of literature already exists on the subject in that regard. However, it is essential that we attempt an outline of the theory that frames our analysis. In eco-criticism, ecological concerns are given primacy. There is a conscious attempt to examine nature as something that is real, something having a life of its own, different from life seen from an anthropocentric perspective. In this regard, nature is privileged, brought to the forefront of human consciousness so that nature transcends the idea of a mere concept. In the new thinking, the shift in consciousness regarding the relationship between man and nature, Byron Caminero-Santangelo suggests that what is required is "to decentre humans" and give nature "'back' its subjectivity" (699). This approach is necessitated by what has been considered man's self-centered attitude to matters of the environment. According to Love, there is the notion, albeit an erroneous one, "that human beings are so special that the earth exists for our comfort and disposal alone" (229). The problem is that humans conduct their affairs to the detriment of the environment, and therefore have failed to recognize the need for the common survival of human and nonhuman elements alike. Harold Fromm articulates this idea quite clearly in the essay "From Transcendence to Obsolescence: A Road Map." Fromm writes:

> [T]he roots of his [man's] being are in the earth; and he has failed to see this because Nature, whose effects on man were formerly *immediate*, is now *mediated* by technology so that it appears that technology and not Nature is actually responsible for everything. (35; original emphasis)

Fromm's argument is that, driven by technology and industrialization, man has failed to fully appreciate the place of nature in his life. Consequently, man's neglect of nature—together with his insatiable, self-centered and destructive appropriation of nonhuman life in the environment—is driving "man's nurturing environment . . . to stop nurturing and start killing" (Fromm 34). For this reason, it is expedient to reexamine the reciprocal relationship between man and the environment. Thus, part of the motivation for an eco-centered literature, Love has said, is to extend "human morality to the non-human world . . ." (229). This would make it possible for the eco-conscious writer to assume "the consciousness of the whole earth" (Love 237). Clearly then, the eco-critical literature is one which responds to the problem of the environment. In the words of Cheryll Glotfelty and Harold Fromm, an earth-centered literary work depicts how "human culture is connected to the physical world, affecting it and affected by it" (xix).

To account for the broad aims of eco-literature, Glotfelty and Fromm state further that eco-criticism is akin to feminism in terms of the phases of development. The phases, according to the duo, include the study of the representation of nature in literature, the revival of the art of nature writing, and the turn to theory. For writers, the mapping of the phases makes little difference compared to the perspective they adopt. Every writer adopts an approach that suits his purpose. Some writers adopt a human-centered approach; others take the position of speaking for nature. In a synthesis of various eco-critical perspectives, Hubert Zapf, among others, identifies the sociopolitical, cultural-anthropological, and ethical perspectives as common orientations. Of these, the sociopolitical dimension seems relatively more connected to a broad range of concerns at the heart of the literature of the environment. According to Zapf, from the perspective of the sociopolitical, literary texts are deemed eco-friendly if they pay "attention to natural phenomena" with regard to "their degree of environmental awareness, their recognition of diversity, their attitude to non-human forms of life, or their awareness of the interconnectedness between local and global ecological issues" (51). Given Africa's peculiar history, Zapf's conceptualization—the sociopolitical paradigm—bears more relevance to African literature of the environment, going by William Slaymaker's study of black Africa's response to the subject.

That African writing has been engaged with the environment in different ways is not in doubt. However, because of the paucity of criticism on African eco-literature, we are yet to fully reckon with the treatment of the environment in our literatures. Available literature suggests that, as noted by Slaymaker, making the connection between the sociopolitical and the ecological in the criticism of African eco-centered literature will yield better insights. Of course, Ogbowei's eco-centered poems belong to a body of works in which ecological concerns are bound up with sociopolitical themes. In each of his published volumes of poetry, there are poems that speak to environment issues. Ogbowei vivifies the natural world so that the poems foreground nature; they privilege ecocentric values and call attention to the myriad human-induced environmental problems bedeviling the Niger Delta—the region where most of the poems are set.

Ogbowei's Eco-poetics

One cardinal distinguishing feature of imaginative composition on the Niger Delta is the dramatization of the environmental crisis in the region. Often the depiction is deeply political in calling attention to the region's environmental crisis. It is, therefore, difficult for the writer to turn away from such a pervasive problem, which clearly puts human and nonhuman life at great risks. Critics and commentators on Ogbowei's poems have approached the works from their satiric and political thrusts in excoriating the moral bankruptcy that pervades the Nigerian society. Apart from brief passing remarks on the environmental themes embedded in the works, nothing substantial has been done in the direction of Ogbowei's ecological concerns. There is ample evidence that Ogbowei not only makes references to the environment, but makes a case for its protection and sustenance. For Ogbowei, the survival of the ecology beyond the activities of man is crucial; so, even poems that are not overtly centered on ecological concerns, in places, relate to the environment through symbolic or metaphorical associations. In a number of poems, we witness Ogbowei's lamentation for the despoiled environment and the effect on both human and nonhuman life. Kontein Trinya has remarked in a recent essay that Ogbowei deploys images "carved out of the environment" (409); this is true, but it does not reveal much—Ogbowei certainly connects with the environment in far more complex ways than previously thought, especially when considering Trinya's essay. Most of Ogbowei poems falls within the latitude of eco-poetry given their strong ecological message. For instance, in his fourth collection *Song of a Dying River*, the title poem, "Song of a Dying River" (Ogbowei 17), as well as "Vultures" (41–42), "The Plundered Province" (47), "This House Full of Strife" (68–69), "What Tale Trinya" (30–32), and "Dancing Cats" (35), in various degrees captures the poet's response to the unmitigated ecological disaster ravaging the Niger Delta. The poems also encode Ogbowei's environmental vision, namely: the survival of the Niger Delta ecosphere together with all life forms.

In Ogbowei's eco-poems, the negative impact of crude oil exploration in the Niger Delta assumes a life of its own. In the title poem, *Song of a Dying River*, the persona—speaking for all living creatures—laments the growing environmental disaster in the oil-producing region through gas flares and oil spills. In his imaginative projection, Ogbowei draws a comparison between the ecological crisis in the Niger Delta and the 1989 Exxon Valdez supertanker oil spill disaster, which destroyed a staggering number of aquatic lives. The poem paints a gloomy picture of a potent threat to life generally, as our attention is drawn to the image of "two disoriented dolphins / squeezed out of our dying river / by a burning christmas tree / grown monstrous hot and bright" (Ogbowei *Song of a Dying River*, Stanza 2, lines 7–9). We also witness "two cold cormorants / drowning in our oil-clad creek" (3, 2–3). Clearly, life is bleak in these circumstances. First, the metaphor of a "dying river" speaks to a festering environmental problem which may result in the decimation of countless animal and fish species. Second, the river is dying because of the harmful substances discharged into it. Being symbolic of life, a river that is dying is indicative of its dwindling capacity to sustain life. Now, here lies the problem: that which supports life is literally in the throes of death; therefore, the continued dependence of life forms on the river hangs in the balance. This is the tragedy. But that is not all. The poet, being very sensitive to the survival of the environmental, is also disturbed by the polluting presence of "a burning christmas tree," which adds to the problems of the environment. By calling attention to the problem, the poet invariably plays the role of an environmental activist keen on protecting the environment. Elsewhere, in the poem "Vultures" (Ogbowei *Song of a Dying River*, 41–42), the imagery of a decimated ecology assumes a profoundly frightening dimension. It is obvious that man's quest for material advancement through the application of technology has created more problems than solutions for nature and its capacity to sustain life. The exploration of crude oil is made possible by advances in technology, but sadly it has left the environment in ruins. Industrial wastes and other forms of contaminants have saturated the environment, forcing humans, animals, fishes, and other creatures to literally gasp for breath. Their life-support system—the environment—is made increasingly uninhabitable, and with its life-giving substances fast depleting, even basic food and water have become difficult to come by. This is the scenario we witness in "Vultures" as we follow hungry and thirsty leopards, buzzards, and vultures on a desperate search for food and water. But these are not the only creatures we meet. We also notice fishes and other sea creatures in a life-and-death struggle to survive. As we survey the "slick-spoiled shores" (Ogbowei *Song of a Dying River*, 5.5) of "the moaning marshland" (5.4) of the Niger Delta, one notices:

> a dead gull
> a dead turtle
> fish washed up the shore
> a motorboat strike
> a maimed manatee. (4.1-5)

The scene, of course, looks like "a raucous vulture restaurant" (Ogbowei *Song of a Dying River*, 4.5). The evidence is everywhere; the activities of multinational oil companies adept at "scavenging profits from . . . / . . . the demonized delta" (6.5) have left "dead leafless trees" (6.2) in their wake.

We have seen that Ogbowei's engagement with the environment goes beyond anthropocentricism. He is, of course, deeply disturbed by the ecological degradation in the Niger Delta. Even when Ogbowei's immediate concern is not the environment as mentioned earlier, ecological worries always creep in at the corners of his verses. We find this in poem after poem, as exemplified in two poems that are political in tone and in tenor. They are "What Tale Trinya" (30–32) and "This House Full of Strife" (68–69), respectively.

Particularly striking in "What Tale Trinya" are the fourth and fifth stanzas in which the persona, in a sudden change of subject—as we have seen in most of these poems—invites the reader to view "spills from ships / seepages from corroded pipes / leaks from storage tanks (Ogbowei *Song of a Dying River*, 4.1–3) and "blackened beaches" (5.1), as well as "reeking rivers and coated creeks" (5.2), all of which are the imprints of the oil industry. In "This House Full of Strife," as we continue our excursion with the persona, we:

> hear the moans of mugged mudflat
> the cry of the clobbered coat
> the plodding misery of parents
> working double shifts to drag offspring
> stuck in sloughs of poverty
> into luxury liners destined for affluent ports. (Ogbowei *Song of a Dying River*, 1.1–6)

The above excerpt raises the issue of poverty amidst plenty in this affluent but despoiled region whose environment is characterized by effluents and all sorts of pollutants. The expropriation of the natural resources of the people, together with the attendant ecological damage, has combined to impoverish the people. As crude oil is pumped out of the ground, farmlands and fishing waters are destroyed so that the people's primary means of survival—their traditional occupations of fishing and farming—are rendered useless. The result is that parents, mired in misery and poverty, find it extremely difficult to fend for themselves, let alone take care of their children. The persona empathizes with these people, and this brings to the fore the subtext of revolutionary reaction against oppression encoded in the poem. Here, Ogbowei seems to advocate violence as a survival strategy. We may note too that, in this poem, the poet's environmental concerns coincide with his sociopolitical projections. The last stanza of "this house full of strife" reads:

> watch the plundered province provoked to revolt
> cut herself loose from this house of hate
> this house full of strife
> where compassionate uncles and conniving cousins
> singing from the same song sheet
> bully mug lock the winkle picker
> survey carve up her cash cow
> parcel out her money-making mud. (Ogbowei *Song of a Dying River*, 6.1–8)

The "social and political implications of representations of nature," Byron Caminero-Santangelo has said, should be seen in the light of the "danger of subordinating human concerns to environmental concerns" (701). In other words, it is important to account for both human and non-human concerns, especially in the African context where neo-colonial hegemonic tendencies seem to mask the real impact of environmental issues on people's lives. We have seen that in Ogbowei's eco-poems, both considerations bear relevance: environmental themes are espoused in relation to the human condition. Note, for instance, how the "winkle picker" (a metaphor for everyday people in the region surviving on the land) and the multinational oil conglomerates scramble for a share of the "money-making mud" of the Niger Delta. Of course, we know as much as the persona that in such a contest the locals are the underdogs. Therefore, survival for the indigenous people means a halt in the pillage and destruction of their land.

Akin to the above poem is "dancing cat" (Ogbowei *Song of a Dying River*, 35), which also echoes the themes of unmitigated profiteering and ecological damage. In a telling allusion to the deadly Minamata environmental disaster in Japan, the persona bemoans the sorry state of the Niger Delta environment:

> they seek a repertoire
> fluid as profit-multiplying effluent
> snaking down amadi creek
> fouls up bonny river
> where dancing cats
> mime the mood at minimata bay
> a dizzling display of dreams drowned
> buried in the mud. (Ogbowei *Song of a Dying River*, 3.1–8)

Here again, we see that while the "profit-multiplying effluent" is good news for the oil-prospecting companies, it is bad news to oil-bearing communities like Amadi Ama and Bonny Town (host to Nigeria's Liquefied Natural Gas Company) in the Niger Delta state of Rivers, where the environment has been severely degraded.

In Ogbowei's other collections, we witness a similar preoccupation with the environment. The poet highlights the problem of environmental pollution, not only from oil exploration but also from everyday human activities. Two poems are representative of this. They are "Fortune" in *Let the Honey Run and Other Poems* (36–37) and "The Foul Radiance of Promise" in *The Town Crier's Song* (104–105). In "Fortune," like some of the poems we have examined, the persona is haunted by the environmental mess around him. In this particular instance, although the poetic experience is inspired by the symbolism of names, the persona cannot but turn his attention to the pollution of the "brass river" (Ogbowei *Let the Honey Run*, 1.7). The persona figures out that the reason "the waves speak a strange tongue to the shore / swoop down on swamp [and] drain her of all resistance" is to "cleanse her of abominable traces left by picnickers and / timid lovers" (5.1–4). Interestingly, apart from the "picnickers," the persona also speaks of "poachers"—a metaphor for oil companies—who leave "behind bloated corpses assailing the senses" (6.3–4). Now, it should be realized that the exploration operations of oil companies involve the explosion of dynamites, metonymically referred to as "shells exploding" (4.4), and this usually results in the death of fishes and other forms of aquatic life. This, to the poet, constitutes a huge environmental hazard and is therefore unacceptable.

Similarly, in *The Town Crier's Song*, the poem "The Foul Radiance of Promise" takes on the problem of human waste and its impact on the environment. In the poem, there is a connection between the persona's disillusionment about life in the city and the environmental hazards that impinge on his consciousness. The persona lists the problems that particularly bother him, namely: "the lingering slick/befouling creek road waterfront" (Ogbowei *The Town Crier's Song*, 1.3–4); "the whispering odour of decay" (2.6); the noise "of the outboard motorboat" (3.1); "the wash of waste upon this beach" (5.3); and the "condoms and poly bags playing squids at high tide" (5.6). It is easy to fathom how this litany of problems affects the environment. One only needs to take a trip to Creek Road waterfront in the South-South Nigerian city of Port Harcourt to experience the nauseating stench of human feces deposited by night soil men in a portion of the river bank that once served as a dump site, when pier latrines were in vogue. On the other hand, "condoms and poly bags" are nonbiodegradable products, which add to the problems of the environmental. Put together, these human activities are anti-environmental practices, and this is the message Ogbowei drives home.

Other poems with identifiable ecological themes are "Folasade" (*Let the Honey Run*, 50–52) and "Omens" (*The Town Crier's Song*, 29). In "Folasade," the persona characteristically leaves the subject of love to voice his indignation for the health hazards crude oil production engenders in the Niger Delta. Here is his complaint:

> i've sung songs to nigeria ebony woman
> nailed to a cross of hard currencies
> whose bruised breasts overpressed
> yield not milk but explosives and *kombe* beans
> necklets of cropped heads would feel faith too close. (Ogbowei *Let the Honey Run*, 9.5–9)

Stephen and Nwanyanwu's reading of the poem indicate that "nigeria ebony woman" in the excerpt connotes crude oil, whose extraction, instead of bringing nourishment to the land and its people, has wrought terrible environmental catastrophe (89). Equally striking is the first stanza of the second movement in the poem "Omens," which opens on a bleak ecological note. It reads:

> hawks and black herons
> joyous vultures riding the gale
> worms and bloated corpses
> millet and dyed chicks
> the ageing farmer the smalling farm
> hunger the telautograph. (Ogbowei *The Town Crier's Song*, 12.1–6)

The entire poem is replete with what may be described as bioimagery, images drawn from the natural world of plants and animals. This is a conscious attempt by the poet to relate to the environment, and it further emphasizes this poet's worries about man's relationship to nonhuman life in the environment. In fact, Ogbowei even questions the mindless slaughtering of animals like, "the he-goat and the ram" (Ogbowei *The Town Crier's Song*, 14.1) as well as "the turkey and the cock" / "one night before Christmas" (14.3–4). Here, animals are figured as victims of man's unrestrained consumption, part of man's onslaught on virtually everything in the environment.

In *The Heedless Ballot Box*, two poems—"This Old Stager" (38) and "Put a Handle on This Pain" (50)—require a close consideration to unearth the environmental themes. The former, a two-stanza poem, in part addresses the harmful effects of carbon monoxide on man and the environment. This is precisely what the speaking voice in the poem complains about in the first stanza when he says: "this thick acrid smoke / from open fires and stoves / burning inside hungry homes / leaves us whooping and tearful" (Ogbowei *The Heedless Ballot Box*, 1.1–4). If Ogbowei wants old habits and practices to change in order that the environment and the things thereof may survive, we also note that he as well advocates punishment for perpetrators of crimes against the environment as evident in the short poem "Put a Handle on This Pain." In this specific instance, Ogbowei's gaze turns to the festering environmental calamity visited on the Niger Delta by those he has variously called "scavengers" and "vultures." For Ogbowei then, to understand and resolve the burning environmental issues and ensure the survival of all life forms beyond crude oil exploration, would require the arrest and possible prosecution of those behind the environmental misfortune in the first place. We have to quote the poem in its entirety to underscore the proposed solution:

> put a handle on this pain
> that rends the delta
> clamp cuffs on hands
> scavenging profits from conflicts
>
> clamp cuffs on vultures
> gorging themselves on dollars
> the despoiled delta bleeds. (Ogbowei *The Heedless Ballot Box*, 1–7)

The pains of the people and the concomitant conflicts are products of progressively disappearing opportunities, which complicate the task of survival. The picture we get of the Niger Delta is one exposed to all kinds of problems. We are faced with an environment that has undergone drastic and negative changes so that the people's traditional occupations have been compromised in favor of foreign economic interests. This is the crux of the matter and, in the reckoning of the persona, the solution lies in arresting the perpetrators, as this would put a stop to the damage wrought on the environment.

We have seen that thoughts on the environment occupy a special place in Ogbowei's creative imagination. And this poet sometimes speaks of the environment in deeply symbolic terms. In short, it is sometimes difficult to tell the difference between the human and the nonhuman subjects. This is the scenario created in the poem "Lament of an Overcropped Land" (*The Town Crier's Song*, 108–109), which draws parallels between the land and woman. Parts of the poem read:

> like a land overcropped
> you'd leave me fallow
> to cultivate another
> lush and fertile
>
> but burning with envy and desire
> can i renegotiate sufficient vegetation
> to attract again the farmer
> who lashed and burnt
> intensively cultivating the fertility of my youth
>
> no this holding
> overworked overcropped
> is exhausted
> cannot regain its puberty (1–13)
> And the result?
> the critical value of the land
> diminishes with age (4.1–2)

Two levels of meaning are possible here. On the one hand, the poem may read like a comment on the plight of women regarding the transience of beauty. On the other hand, the deterioration of the fertility of the land occasioned by overuse constitutes another interpretation. Both interpretations seem valid given the underlying meaning of the poem, namely that the woman and the land are vessels through which nature brings forth life, and whatever brings about their misuse or abuse invariably affects life in some way. This, therefore, is Ogbowei's thesis: to continue to yield its bounties, the land and the environment thereof should be protected as a man would his wife.

Conclusion

In sum, our study has demonstrated that Ogbowei, in his eco-poetry, exhibits a remarkable empathy toward the Niger Delta environment. Part of

Ogbowei's commitment involves creating awareness by highlighting the region's devastating environmental crisis as well as advocating the possible ways of arresting the situation. The political-cum-environmental issues articulated in the poems make eloquent statements about the complex and delicate link between human and nonhuman life in the ecosphere. Navigating these competing, sometimes complementary, interests is a tough call for any writer, but Ogbowei seems equal to the task. Even though reading poems that are almost completely bereft of punctuation marks and capitalization may impede easy comprehension, the message still comes through. Ogbowei is one poet that cannot be overlooked.

Works Cited

Caminero-Santangelo, Byron. "Different Shades of Green: Ecocriticism and African Literature." *African Literature: An Anthology of Criticism and Theory*. Ed. Tejumola Olaniyan and Ato Quayson. Malden: Blackwell, 2007. 698–706. Print.

Fromm, Harold. "From Transcendence to Obsolescence: A Road Map." *The Ecocriticism Reader: Landmark Literary*. Athens/London: U of Georgia P, 1996. 30–39. Print.

Glotfelty, Cheryll, and Harold Fromm, ed. "Introduction." *The Ecocriticism Reader: Landmarks in Literary Ecology*. Athens/London: U of Georgia P, 1996. Print.

Love, Glen A. "Re-evaluating Nature: Toward an Ecological Criticism." Ed. Glotfelty and Fromm. 1996. 225–240. Print.

Ogbowei, G. 'Ebinyo. *The Heedless Ballot Box*. Ibadan: Kraft, 2005. Print.

____. *Let the Honey Run and Other Poems*. Ibadan: Kraft, 2005. Print.

____. *Song of a Dying River*. Ibadan: Kraft, 2009. Print.

____. *The Town Crier's Song*. Ibadan: Kraft, 2009.

Slaymaker, William. "Echoing the Other(s): The Call of Global Green Black African Responses." Ed. Olaniyan and Quayson. Malden: Blackwell, 2007. 683–697. Print.

Stephen, Bernard Otonye, and Austin Uka Nwanyanwu. *G. 'Ebinyo Ogbowei's Let the Honey Run and Other Poems: A Close Study*. Lagos: Malthouse, 2010. 89–94. Print.

Trinya, Kontein. "Shadows of Development in the New Poetry of the Niger Delta." *From Boom to Doom: Protest and Conflict Resolution in the Literature of the Niger Delta*. Ed. Chinyere Nwahunanya. New Owerri: Springfield, 2011. 398–410. Print.

Zapf, Hubert. "The State of Ecocriticism and the Function of Literature as Cultural Ecology." *Nature in Literary and Cultural Studies: Transatlantic Conversations on Ecocriticism*. Ed. Catrin Gersdorf and Sylvia Mayer. Web. 8 May 2012. *Google Books Search*.

16

Poetics of Environmental Degradation in Tanure Ojaide's *Delta Blues*

Olusegun Adekoya, Obafemi Awolowo University, Ile-Ife

Tanure Ojaide's *Delta Blues and Home* Songs (1998) comprises two parts of about the same length, namely "Delta Blues," which narrates the agonies and sorrows of Nigeria's Niger Delta and mourns the extra-judicial killing of Kenule Saro-Wiwa and eight other Ogoni environmental activists, and "Home Songs," which explores the folklore of the Urhobo even as it recalls moments from the poet's past and paints in light striated colors diverse aspects of social life. The present essay engages the first part of the collection and focuses on the tragic effects of the industrial exploration and production of oil on people and nature in the Delta region in Nigeria.

Ojaide performs for Saro-Wiwa and his dead comrades funeral rites that immortalize their names and inscribe their significance in the long struggle for economic and environmental justice and basic democratic rights by the beleaguered people of the oil-rich Niger Delta. Unlike "Lycidas," a pastoral elegy in which John Milton mourns the death of a fellow poet who drowned in the Irish Sea, "Delta Blues" is sung not just for the nine activists hanged during the military regime of General Sani Abacha but for all victims—living or dead—of the destruction of the ecology of the Niger Delta by the oil companies operating in the area. Whereas nature is the wild aggressor in the former, it is the innocent victim of the onslaught by feral agents of transnational capitalist oligopolies in the latter.

"Delta Blues" shares similarities of form, function, occasion, and theme with Akeem Lasisi's *Ìrèmòjé: Ritual Poetry for Ken Saro-Wiwa*. It also shares thematic concerns with Niyi Osundare's *The Eye of the Earth* (1986). The Yoruba elegiac hunters' chant (*Ìrèmòjé*) is an inalienable part of obsequies performed by Yoruba hunters to formally disengage a deceased hunter from the company of his colleagues who are still living. Originated by Ogun, the Yoruba God of iron, the ritual poetry is performed only at night in an antiphonal style. It is psychotherapy, a subtle strategy by which the sting of death is blunted or removed, the weakened human will to live on the earth is recuperated and made adamantine, and cosmic harmony ruffled by separation occasioned by death is reestablished. Death is defeated with the device of poetry: the magic in the word of power. It is believed that *Ìrèmòjé* chants, a potpourri of incantations, panegyrics, lineage chronicles, and biographical accounts accompanied by music, are capable of resurrecting a dead hunter and inducing him to come and receive his paraphernalia, which in the case of Ken Saro-Wiwa comprises his creative works (essentially novels and plays).

Burial of the dead in the wasteland that Nigeria has unfortunately become is necessary, and Lasisi justifies it: "If we do not bury the dead for the sake of God / We must bury the dead for the fear of stench" (Lasisi 5), for a clean and safe environment translates into a healthy human community. Poets, therefore, put their rhetorical skills at the service of their dead scribal colleagues in defense of life in its fullest fecundity, profundity, and diversity, as Ojaide does for Christopher Okigbo in *Children of Iroko* (Ojaide 1973, 41).

"My Drum Beats Itself," the first poem in *Delta Blues*, is an eminently deserved homage to "Ken Saro-Wiwa and the other eight Delta martyrs" to whose blessed memory the entire book is dedicated (Ojaide *Delta Blues*, 9). It shocks a reader into the sudden realization of the mysteriousness of the ordinary and compels an admission of the truthfulness of the animistic conceptualization of the cosmos. The grand commonplace of the piece is simply that "Delta Blues" is inspired by Kenule Saro-Wiwa, or, put in another way, it is the dead writer who beats the poet's drum, which itself is an apt metaphor for the poetic imagination and draws attention to Ojaide's representation of poetry as essentially an oral performance. The metaphor of a drum beating itself signifies the mystery that death itself connotes, but the poet's fear that the subject is too heavy for him to bear and execute and might result in his head exploding is another facetious conceit: a hyperbolic expression of the heaviness of the martyr's death in the mourner's heart.

Echoing John Keats' unheard melodies, which are sweeter than the heard (Keats 295), the poet thinks if he waits patiently and listens attentively in silence, as does Christopher Okigbo at "Heavensgate" (Okigbo 3), he might hear the former deep in his soul and receive rare boons from the supernatural in the same way that a diviner is employed by Orunmila (the Yoruba God of wisdom) as a medium to convey messages to a troubled client in search of an urgent solution. Such gifts are generally bestowed on brave needful questers at night because its silence boosts creativity, enables writers to concentrate on their work, and expands their imagination. Undoubtedly, the Romantic conception of poetry, which attributes a higher degree of sensitivity and perceptibility to poets who double as prophets than to ordinary mortals, informs the piece. In the lines "The deer knows why it only comes out / When the whole world's withdrawn to bed" (Ojaide *Delta Blues*, 10), "deer" metaphorizes the poet. Night means more than the moment at which the living and the dead commingle; it is also the time the dead return to the living through conception for it is the time for mating in most world cultures. We could extrapolate and surmise that Ojaide works and walks at night, an opportune time for meeting and communing with the dead, who abhor noise and the garish, obscene light of day, who are never dead if appropriate funerary rites are performed for them, and whose "little," he affirms, "will make abundance in my hands" (10).

Ironically and in tune with the joyous spirit of Urhobo *Udje* and Yoruba *Ìrèmòjé*—the rhyme of the terminal syllables in the names borne by the two forms of oral art is unmistakable—the tone of the poet in the opening poem is not plaintive but celebratory. The lines in the third stanza are punctuated with the triumphant shout of *Iye* (ovation that denotes life), which in superlative terms also brings the piece to a rapturous end. Just as *Ìrèmòjé* begins with a tribute to master poets of the past who have joined the ancestors (Ajuwon 2–5), "My Drum Beats Itself" commences with an invocation, and in it Ojaide seeks the help of a Muse, Kenule Saro-Wiwa, whose cruel murder inspired *Delta Blues*.

"When Green Was the Lingua Franca" is a Romantic form in which the poet visits his homeland, after an absence, to see the changes that have taken place in the intervening years and assess their effect on nature and his own relationship to it. It is also a mental journey to Ojaide's childhood when the forest was green and teemed with life and the creeks sparkled with a variety of exotic fishes with distinctive qualities that are appropriated as metaphors to express the beauty and diversity of the human world. That was before the blind assault on biodiversity in the Niger Delta and the pollution of its land and waters by oil companies. In "Journeying," it is Kenule Saro-Wiwa who revisits his youth on Niger Delta creeks "unclogged by a waterfront sleaze," which speculators will later reduce to "a desolate swamp" and consequently force "unemployed fishmongers and farmers" to "sit in his sand-wrecked boat waiting for the high tide" (Ojaide *Delta*

Blues, 30). One of the compelling reasons for composing *Delta Blues*, then, is Ojaide's desire to realize the dead writer's wish for the high tide—plenitude—and bring his struggle to fruition.

Erhuvwudjayorho in "When Green Was the Lingua Franca" symbolizes the Niger Delta, the native land, a microscopic but enormously endowed part of a big and emasculated country that denies it an opportunity for self-development. It is "a glamorous fish / but denied growing big" (Ojaide *Delta Blues*, 12). Earthworm metaphorizes comfort-seeking women who are enamored of an easy and cushy life. Beautiful *Uwara*, another metaphor for the Niger Delta, resists the oppressive antics of *Akpobrisi*, which represents the Nigerian government that colludes with the oil giants to suck the native land dry. Snails, *koto*, periwinkles, *Ikere* froglets, and skipper-fish abound. Literally, they nourish life and metaphorically function as its simple joys that confer on it significant meaning. Fruit-bearing trees such as apple, grape, cherry, and breadfruit, and cash crops such as cotton and gum are proofs of the rich, rooted, self-replenishing, and self-regulatory agricultural life lived in harmony with nature in the Niger Delta of Ojaide's childhood days (Ojaide *Delta Blues*, 12–13).

However, the poet discovers to his chagrin and regrets that numerous minatory oil spills and forest fires have hobbled his homeland and imperiled the two-fold mainstay of its economy: farming and fishing. As he puts it in the fourth stanza:

> Then Shell broke the bond
> with quakes and a hell
> of flares. (Ojaide *Delta Blues*, 13)

The "bond" equates the equanimous and harmonious relation forged over time between the people and the land, which was founded on the animistic concept of the cosmos.

The unity of people and land, the whole architecture of ecology, was wrecked, for example, when bulldozers working for Shell's Liquefied Natural Gas Company invaded the sacred cemetery known as Odiebite, which belonged to the Umu-Akasi and Umu-Okendia families of Ohali-Elu in Ogba/Egbema/Ndoni Local Government Area of Rivers State. "Sacred burial grounds were unearthed, caskets and coffins were over turned [overturned], some crushed and bones were also scattered around in contemptuous disrespect of the people's culture and way of life" (Bassey *Knee Deep in Crude*, 140). Dogs in the community had a feast-day. Neither Shell nor SAIPEM, an Italian firm contracted to construct a gas pipeline, was willing to pay money for reburial and other necessary rituals to placate the ancestors whose sleep and rest was rudely disturbed and whose spirits were disquieted, the consequences of which were children dying, strange sicknesses, and general restlessness in the land.

In his exceedingly moving testimony Victor Osiagor said, among other things:

> We are a small community and we want to be treated fairly by the companies and the Federal Government. We are a peaceful community, probably that is the reason they are treating us like fools. Just imagine what has been done to our cemetery. How can a stranger come to dictate to us in our land what is sacred or not? (Bassey *Knee Deep in Crude*, 143)

His conclusion is anchored in the necessity for sacrifices of atonement to reestablish communion with their ancestors: "They have uprooted our ancestors and if we don't perform these rituals as soon as possible, then we are a finished community because the land is polluted" (Bassey *Knee Deep in Crude*, 144).

What makes the act of desecration most annoying and painful is that, according to Agu Maxwell's testimony, it "is an intentional act. We told them but they didn't listen" (Bassey *Knee Deep in Crude*, 144). His conclusion is damning: "The whole NLNG [Nigerian Liquefied Natural Gas] project is a curse to us instead of a blessing. The digging of the pipeline has cut us off from all neighboring communities" (Bassey 2009, 144). The gas and oil companies would not dare violate the sanctity of cemeteries in Europe and refuse to pay adequate compensation or appease the aggrieved on whose ontological icons and religious symbols they had arrogantly trampled.

Commenting on Shell's Jones Creek major oil spill, Alfred M. Bubor said: "Our speedboat was bouncing on crude oil. . . . The spill affected all aquatic life in the area. It is no exaggeration. . . . Clearly there is a conspiracy to wipe our people out of this land with crude oil" (Bassey *Knee Deep in Crude*, 137). Raising the issue of double standards, he asked, "What rights have they to be careless on our land and be careful where they came from?" (139). The Federal Environmental Protection Agency (FEPA)—which unfortunately has been dissolved—and the Department of Environment Resources that were supposed to protect the people and ensure sustenance of best practices and maintenance of safety measures colluded with the oil companies to cheat the people. "They are all agents of destruction," said Bubor. His conclusion is pointed and rendered in English Pidgin, which indicates the high degree of passion involved in the protestation:

> We accept their apology but no be apology we go chop for the next six months. I advise them not to play any foul game of divide and rule, pollute and cheat. All we want is justice. (Bassey *Knee Deep in Crude*, 139)

The pipe that caused the disaster was 28 years old.

Environmental pollution resulting from activities of the gas and oil companies operating in the Niger Delta generates endless conflicts between the host communities and the oil corporations that often lead to internal displacement with its accompanying refugee problems. Both instances of pollution and conflicts are well documented by the Environmental Rights Action (ERA) and the Friends of the Earth Nigeria (FoEN) in Volume 1 of *Knee Deep in Crude: Environmental Field Reports* and *Reporting the Nigerian Environment*. Shell's one-year oil spill in the Aleibiri community and the crude clean-up method, a bucket-and-spade affair, which involved digging a hole in the spill site, burying items contaminated by the oil spill in it, and burning them, led to a forest fire that covered between 11 and 12 hectares of land. The fire destroyed all the farm crops and palm trees in the area and thereby erased the community's means of livelihood (Bassey *Knee Deep in Crude*, 13–19). It is instructive that Bob Van Dessel, a Dutch environmentalist, resigned from Shell because the company would not replace 20-year-old oil pipes (22).

Shortly after the Aleibiri fire of 25 March 1998 caused by contractors conducting a cleaning exercise, another fire erupted at Foutorogbene in July 1998, a few kilometers away from Aleibiri, again caused by the burning off of remaining crude after a clean-up exercise. The fire destroyed about 12 hectares of forest land with thousands of palm trees, local distilling camps, fishing camps, and fish ponds (Bassey *Knee Deep in Crude*, 59–60).

Even when Shell admitted that the oil spill on the Oleh/Omoloro Oil Field, in Isoko, in August 1991 was not due to sabotage but to the puncture of an underground pipe during drilling by Deutag Drilling Company, an agent of Shell, the company did not pay any compensation for the extensive damage to land, water, and property, and the spill continued to wreak havoc for months before any attempt at cleaning was made (Bassey *Knee Deep in Crude*, 98–100).

Similarly, a contractor working for Shell caused an oil spill that adversely affected several communities, including Ekeremor-Zion, Obotobo I, Obotobo II, and Sekebolo. The matter became a subject of litigation at the Ughelli High Court that gave judgment after 14 years of prosecution, but Shell still appealed against the judgment (Bassey *Knee Deep in Crude*, 22–23). Equipment failure caused a major blowout at Shell's Railway Manifold and the resultant spill polluted the environment, but Shell refused to pay any compensation (Bassey *Knee Deep in Crude*, 122).

However, it is not only Shell that is culpable for the crime of destruction of the natural environment in the Niger Delta. On 14 June 1995, the Idoho Platform, a main junction for transporting oil to Mobil's facility at Qua Iboe, ruptured and thousands of barrels of oil were spewed into the sea (Bassey *Knee Deep in Crude*, 22). Leakage from the Chevron oil wells at the Ewan oil fields in Ilaje caused an oil slick that destroyed fishing nets, farm crops, and livestock of the Ubale-Nla and Ikorigbo communities. The source of drinking water was polluted, which brought on skin diseases, especially among children. Chevron paid a meager sum of four hundred thousand naira to the community of about four thousand people as compensation.

On 28 May 1998, 42 communities in Ilaje embarked on a peaceful demonstration to demand for environmental justice on the Parabe oil facility. Chevron invited soldiers who swooped down from helicopters to dislodge the protesters and, in the process, two youths, Arolika Irowanu and Jolly Ogungbeje, were shot dead and about 30 others were injured. A few months later, hostilities broke out between the communities, on the one hand, and their Ijaw neighbors, on the other, and left about 625 Ilaje people dead and many buildings razed (Bassey *Knee Deep in Crude* 92–96). The history of oil production in the Niger Delta is a horrendous tale of spillages, pollution, violence, death, destruction, and environmental degradation. It turns the ecology of the region on its head and destroys the relative peaceful coexistence among the communities. "A 1997 report by World Wide Fund (WWF) estimated that cleaning up the Niger Delta environment would cost up to £4 billion" (ERA/FoEN, 81).

If the pun on Shell is occluded in the clause "Shell broke the bond," it is unmistakable in the following lines:

> Explosions of shells to *under*
> mine grease-black gold
> drove the seasons mental
> and to walk on their heads. (Ojaide *Delta Blues*, 13; his emphasis)

Armed conflict, mayhem, kidnapping, cultism, political thuggery, and other criminal and violent activities in the Niger Delta are traceable to greed for profit and the failure of the government and the oil companies to develop the land that supplies the subterranean resource that generates wealth for the entire country. The consequence is the emergence of several ethnic militias and liberation movements, such as the Egbesu, the Chikoko Movement, the Movement for the Survival of the Ogoni People (MOSOP), and the Movement for the Emancipation of the Niger Delta (MEND) in the region. Resource control, then, is the perennial cause of conflict.

It is difficult, if not impossible, for victims of state aggression to keep calm and retain their sangfroid and sanity, while their communities are being ravaged on such a massive scale. Both nature and people are made mad by the virulent attack and naked injustice. For leading MOSOP to protest the rape of the land, Kenule Saro-Wiwa and eight other Ogoni environmental campaigners were executed. They were not alone, for "the ogre / closes on every foothold" (Ojaide *Delta Blues*, 13). The penultimate stanza is quite explicit on the ruination of the Niger Delta through deforestation and pollution of its air, land, and waters. It reads:

> I see victims of arson
> wherever my restless soles
> take me to bear witness.
> The Ethiope waterfront
> wiped out by prospectors—
> so many trees beheaded
> and streams mortally poisoned
> in the name of jobs and wealth!
> And for fear of being counted
> in the register of mad ones,
> I failed to plant trees
> beyond my fenced compound
> in the desert-advancing land.
> For fear of others' rights,
> I left the majority to be massacred,
> a treeful carnage. (Ojaide *Delta Blues*, 13–14)

Lines such as the ones just cited portray *Delta Blues* as advocacy work and also as propaganda for environmental justice. In a subtle manner and in an ironic tone, the poet-persona invites victims of degradation of the oil-producing region to stand up and fight for cessation of exploitation, to repossess their patrimony and struggle for restoration of the land.

Unlike oil that is a nonrenewable energy, trees could be planted to replace felled ones. Africa Timber and Plywood depleted the Okomu Forest Reserve in the Ovia South-West Local Government Area in Edo State. It is estimated that the company felled a total of 5.6 million logs in a 50-year period of timber exploitation (Bassey *Knee Deep in Crude*, 50). Besides, it opened up the forest for illegal game hunting, caused enormous havoc to tree saplings and undergrowth as well, and failed to either launch a reforestation program or fulfill its promise to tar the 28-kilometer Udo–Nikorogha road. Lumbering and oil extraction operations in the Niger Delta are done without the least regard for the safety of the host community and the environment (Bassey *Knee Deep in Crude*, 45–58).

The use of personification for the mindless act of deforestation without a complementary program of reforestation not only expresses the intensity of the grievous harm done nature but also suggests that it is human beings who ultimately bear the brunt of the slash-and-burn onslaught. His green world having been ruined, the poet-persona communes with ghosts, which are not to be mistaken for benevolent ancestors, for they are simulacra of real revenants and represent angry, restless, and vengeful spirits of the elements of despoiled nature. If nature that supplies the material of culture is destroyed, it is humanity that will face gargantuan problems arising from depletion of earth's resources and terrible adverse effects of climate change and global warming. If the waters are polluted, it is people who will drink poison. Whatever violence is visited on the earth, like a boomerang, bounces back to attack the pride-propelled human aggressors who unleashed it, for the earth is our bedroom, dining-room, breadbasket, kitchen, living-room, toilet, school, hospital, and graveyard.

Earthquakes, flooding, hurricanes, landslides, outbreaks of epidemics such as AIDS and avian flu, and volcanic eruptions are constant reminders that mute matter matters a great deal, our disavowals notwithstanding, and we, human beings, are part and parcel of matter and often are rendered helpless when nature strikes us with all its elemental fury. Étienne de la Boétie in *Nostradamus* affirms the inevitability of the vengeance of Nature if humanity persists in abusing it:

> I tell you: if we're presumptuous enough to exalt ourselves above Nature because we consider ourselves the crowning glory of creation, Nature will avenge itself and destroy us. We're no more than ordinary natural

elements, despite our intelligence—our capacity for self-observation, which distinguishes us from cattle, should prompt us to recognize that fact. We haven't the strength to challenge Nature and gain the upper hand, strong as we are, yet that is what we daily attempt to do by subjugating, exploiting and despoiling each other. The history of nations demonstrates that they were never in direr straits than when someone made himself their master and abused them. We must harken to our innermost selves and recognize our own nature for what it is. Then we shall be just and good. (Boeser, 151)

Frederick Engels provides the same insightful perspective on nature and admonishes human beings thus:

Let us not, however, flatter ourselves overmuch on account of our human victories over nature. For each such victory nature takes its revenge on us. Each victory, it is true, in the first place brings about the results we expected, but in the second and third places it has quite different, unforeseen effects which only too often cancel the first.... (12)

With more advancement in the natural sciences and a better understanding of the laws of nature, Engels prognosticated, human beings would "know their oneness with nature" and reject "the senseless and unnatural idea of a contrast between mind and matter, man and nature, [and] soul and body" (13).

The primacy of nature consists in the fact that nothing lies outside its text. Even Karl Marx, in spite of his high humanism, asserts that "man is a part of nature." "The worker," he submits, "can create nothing without *nature*" (Marx 328, 325; his emphasis). Marx recognizes the priority of external nature with only one qualification that the priority exists within mediation. Objective nature that has not been mediated by a human being neither interests nor exists for him. He argues: "The material of nature alone, in so far as *no* human labour is embodied in it, in so far as it is mere material and exists independently of human labour, has no value, since value is only embodied labour." (qtd. in Schmidt 30; Marx's emphasis). His theory of value overestimates human labor, a defining element of all humanisms.

In Ojaide's "Seasons," the third poem, an attempt by the people of Niger Delta to draw the attention of government to their privation and to get the problems of environmental degradation, unemployment and lack of basic necessities in the region fixed is rebuffed: "We selected delegates to take our prayers to Abuja / but guns scared them from the promised land" (Ojaide , 15). That last phrase, "the promised land," an allusion to the land of Canaan, which God gave his chosen people, the Israelites (*King James Bible*, Gen. 12:7), raises the important question of injustice in the relationship between the Niger Delta and the rest of the country; for it offends against the principle of natural justice to leave the oil-producing states groaning in penury and sighing under the trammels of underdevelopment, while deploying the resources extracted from the zone to develop Abuja, the capital of Nigeria.

Whereas the federal government makes concerted efforts to check desertification through a vigorous tree-planting campaign in the Northern part of the country, its attitude of criminal indifference to reckless destruction of the natural environment by oil companies in the South-South zone that produces a disproportionate percentage of the wealth of the country is simply inexplicable and execrable. The rejection of dialogue by government and its collusion with the oil corporations suggest a continuation of the imperialist agenda of the colonial authorities. The so-called independent Nigerian state is doing a new political dance to an old economic tune played by the colonial powers. So, nothing fundamentally has changed in the pattern of administration bequeathed by the colonialists to the nationalist politicians who took over the management of the resources of the country.

Using images of predatory reptiles in the second stanza, Ojaide metaphorizes the latter-day colonialists as '"pythons" and their Nigerian collaborators as "cobras." Deployment of images of carnivorous animals continues in the third stanza in which the national government is perceived as "the hyena" and its agents—the bribe-bloated police and the morally tainted judiciary—as "vultures." They collectively oversee "a desolate country" (Ojaide *Delta Blues*, 15). As used in "Immortal Grief," the vulture image signifies corruption: feeding on offal. So "those / vultures already rotting before their inevitable end" (20) alludes to the four Ogoni chiefs who were killed by an irate mob for their alleged traitorous conspiracy with the despoilers of their land. The chiefs, like factors in the days of slavery, were perceived as quislings who had sacrificed the security of their land and the health and well-being of its people for the blood money offered them by the oil companies that resorted to the old colonial divide-and-rule policy. Independence, then, has brought neither observance of democratic rights nor liberation from economic deprivation, and the country continues to behave irrationally, like Ireland, the "old sow that eats her farrow" (Joyce

Ulysses, 524; *A Portrait*, 188). "The flag we fly is a whetstone for matchets [machetes], often / bloodied in closed-door rites," the poet laments (Ojaide *Delta Blues*, 15). Could this be an explanation for the reason why the Nigerian government that was celebrating 50 years of the country's independence at Eagle Square in Abuja on 1 October 2010 was given a horrendous birthday gift of two bomb explosions that killed 12 and injured about 40 people? The violent act was not just a mere expression of revolutionary anger but an absolute rejection of the order of things in the country.

Almost a century after the contraption called Nigeria was constructed by Lord Lugard, who amalgamated the Northern and Southern Protectorates, the country remains, as correctly and prophetically perceived by Obafemi Awolowo, one of those who worked for its political independence, a mere geographical entity that is divided along ethnic, linguistic, and religious lines and devoid of unity. The fate of the *àbíkú* (a child, in Yoruba belief, that dies as many times as it is born by the same woman in infancy) country still hangs in the balance, and fear of disintegration still holds the collective imagination of its frustrated citizens 50 years after the attainment of political independence. Ojaide purls a plaint:

> We spent more than thirty years of marriage
> debating whether we should live together or split
> we are fast passing the season of childbearing. (Ojaide *Delta Blues*, 16)

As far as the poet is concerned, Nigeria is a failing state, an "impotent" giant (Ojaide *Delta Blues*, 16), despite huge earnings from the sale of crude supplied by the Niger Delta. "The oil corporations are estimated to have pumped out oil worth over $350 billion since operations started in the region" (ERA/FoEN, 81).

A significant proportion of the money, of course, was stolen and stashed away in foreign bank accounts and, consequently, the opportunity for economic development was frittered away. The same idea is stressed in "Waiting for the Next World" in which the country is portrayed as a gluttonous prodigal: "If only I denied myself the festive table, / I would be leaner and healthier today" (Ojaide *Delta Blues*, 46). Access to oil money is not just the most important factor that motivates Nigerian politicians who seek elective office and adopt the Machiavellian principle that the end justifies the means, which transforms politics in the country into warfare; it is the supreme force that drives the Nigerian economy. A natural resource that is supposed to be a blessing turns out to be the country's curse. It changes even the Joint Task Force that is assigned the duty of providing security in the Niger Delta to an army of occupation that engages in illegal oil bunkering, pillages distressed communities, and rapes their women. Among communities that have been virulently attacked or sacked are Umuechem (1990), Ogoni (1993–1995), Odi (1999), Odioma (2005), and Ugborodo (2008).

Truly, money, the universal pimp, is the source of all evil. It destroys every relationship based on contestation for power, perverts all things for which it serves as a medium of exchange, and inverts all values, including spiritual ones. A good servant and a bad master, the universal whore transforms its adorers into beasts and savages. In George Bernard Shaw's view, "the road to riches and greatness is through robbery of the poor and slaughter of the weak" (234). The more the Niger Delta produces crude for Nigeria and the oil corporations, the worse the ecology of the region becomes, the greater the privation of the people grows, and the more appalling the moral degeneracy of the political leadership appears. It is, therefore, not surprising that a natural resource that should be a source of blessing metamorphoses into a source of grief and sorrow, alienates its supposed owners from themselves, from other ethnic groups in the country, and from their natural environment, and drives them angrily to the warpath.

"Wails," an elegy that is fashioned after *Udje* dance songs of the Urhobo, continues the lamentation of the murder of Kenule Saro-Wiwa, who was once President of the Association of Nigerian Authors. "*Udje* as an artistic tradition," G. G. Darah wrote, "had three aspects, namely, dance, poetry and music" (vii). A grand finale that marks the end of an agricultural year and ushers in a new one, the *Udje* carnival is analogous to the annual convention of the Association of Nigerian Authors. Both are essentially oral festivals at which artists perform their works and contest, winners of competition are announced, and rewards in form of praise or prize awards are given. It is at such annual rituals organized around contests that master poets emerge and are celebrated. The poem opens casually:

> Another *ANA* meeting will be called
> and singers will gather.
> I will look all over
> and see a space
> that can take more than a hundred—
> the elephant never hides. (Ojaide *Delta Blues*, 17; emphasis in the original)

Among many ethnic groups in the coastal states of Nigeria, a fallen elephant is used in funeral dirges as a metaphor for an important personality or a community leader who dies. Although Saro-Wiwa was a man of small physical stature, his acts of heroism qualified him for the hyperbole of a space that could take over a hundred lesser mortals, an idea that is expressed through the image of an elephant, itself an exemplification of the heavy influence of the African indigenous oral poetic tradition on written modern African literature. It is plausible to argue that the latter is largely a translation of the former and that both exist in a transitional state and enter into a symbiotic relationship.

Saro-Wiwa's absence or death, the poet confesses, gives him a feverish cold, which is not the iciness of death but the dread triggered off by its mere contemplation. However, the work of mourning performed by the poet is not only for Saro-Wiwa, a Man-Mountain among Lilliputians, but also for all the nine Ogoni activists who were killed in order to drive fear into their followers and stem the tide of agitation for economic justice and environmental protection in the land. So intense is the pain felt by the poet, consequent upon the felling of his "forest of friends" who are "bearers of truth" (Ojaide *Delta Blues*, 18) that he calls on *Aridon*, the Urhobo God of memory, and *Uhaghwa*, the Urhobo God of songs and performance, to help him execute the onerous task, a call that gives the lyric a quality that is normally associated with epic.

Another reason for performing the work of mourning is stated in the elegy: "The world needs to hear this" (Ojaide *Delta Blues*, 17), which is not too divergent from the motivation for writing the present essay. In the formulaic expression of traditional Yoruba raconteurs, it is not because of today but because of tomorrow that the poet sings. In other words, poetry serves as a reminder in order to prevent a recurrence of past evil, for human memory is short and needs constant jogging.

It is in the eponymous "Delta Blues," which shares great affinities with "When Green Was the Lingua Franca," that the poet really paints in bleeding colors the horrendous havoc wreaked on the nature-endowed Niger Delta by profit-driven international oil oligopolies. It is, then, clear why Ojaide perceives the Ogoni Nine hanged on the orders of the Nigerian military government under the aegis of the maximum ruler General Sani Abacha as "Delta martyrs" in the dedication (Ojaide *Delta Blues*, 9). Starting with a hyperbolic line that represents the region as paradise before the destruction wrought by oil exploration and extrusion, the highly emotive first stanza opens afresh the running sore:

This share of paradise, the delta of my birth,
reels from an immeasurable wound.
Barrels of alchemical draughts flow
from this hurt to the unquestioning world
that lights up its life in a blind trust.
The inheritance I sat on for centuries
now crushes my body and soul. (Ojaide *Delta Blues*, 21)

It is ironic that oil, the cause of much suffering and many woes in the Niger Delta, gives the smug world outside abundant energy to light its cities and work its machines. The international community is indicted for its conspiratorial silence and callous indifference to the plight of Niger Delta people whose subterranean wealth is carted away to develop other places, while they are abandoned to disease, deprivation, environmental pollution, and total neglect.

Ojaide also censures the unquestioning world for its complacency and double standards in its dealings with the oil companies. Whereas in the developed countries of the northern hemisphere safety rules are enforced, their violations are stiffly penalized, victims of oil spills are adequately compensated, and cleaning exercise is thorough, in the Niger Delta, sharp practices of the oil companies are tolerated, spillages go unpunished, and if compensations are paid at all, they are minuscule. To exemplify, British Petroleum was made to set aside $20 billion for damages caused by its oil spill in the Gulf of Mexico as a result of the 20 April 2010 explosion on the Deepwater Horizon drilling rig in which 11 workers were killed. The company agreed to contribute $100 million to a foundation to support the rig workers who lost their jobs because of the American administration's deepwater drilling moratorium. In addition, the company pledged $500 million for a 10-year research program to study the impact of the spill, the largest of its kind in the world. It also donated $32 million to Florida's marketing efforts and fifteen million each to Louisiana, Mississippi, and Alabama to help promote tourism in the affected regions (Krauss and Broder 1–3).

A contrary scenario presented itself when the Elf Gas Plant exploded at Obite on 20 March 1999 and many people were killed. On 28 March 1997, eight days after the explosion, three youths—Ugochukwu Agi, Marinho Okiridu, and Uche Azuma—were arrested by members of the Flush Team (a combination of police and naval officers) and severely tortured for calling for a meeting to discuss the gas explosion and the issue of compensation (Bassey *Knee Deep in Crude*, 82–83).

Quite similar was the incident that occurred when Sdem Erectors, a contracting firm with Ponticelli Nigeria Limited (a subcontractor of Elf), wanted to lay off some workers from Ogbogu who demanded "pay-off money." The workers took their case to the Ogbogu Youths Body who impounded a vehicle belonging to Sdem Erectors on 19 April 1999 to force the company management to come for negotiation. While a negotiation meeting was under way between representatives of both employers and employees, a fully armed band of the Operation Flush arrived in four vehicles, stormed the scene, and opened fire on the youths. Many teenagers were hit by bullets and 10 people were arrested. The ugly episode was a continuation of the brutalization and repression of the Ogba people (comprising Ogbogu and Obite communities) by the Nigerian Armed Forces. Ikiri Joe testifies:

> It is as though the whole of Ogba land is besieged by the military as if there is a state of war. All these actions cannot happen without the knowledge of the military government. They collaborate with the oil companies to treat us this way. We have become a conquered people in our land. (Bassey *Knee Deep in Crude*, 83)

For speaking up against environmental degradation in Oleh community, Daniel Ogodo, Abighe Oletu, Kenneth Oyeboro, Christian Tolota, Victor Utoro, and Alex Okpokpo spent over a year in police cells at Divisional Headquarters in Warri on trumped-up charges under inhuman conditions (Bassey *Knee Deep in Crude*, 101–102). Ewelesuo delegates that took the demands of their community to Shell in Port Harcourt on 14 September 1998, according to Mrs. Enere John, were brutalized by members of Operation Flush who arrested and robbed them of "all the money with us, took our belts, wristwatches, necklaces and rings. . . . They are thieves in uniform." (Bassey *Knee Deep in Crude*, 160). Mrs. Judith Asuni, an American-Nigerian environmental activist, was arrested and arraigned at a Federal High Court for allegedly being in possession of classified documents on the Niger Delta issue (ERA/FoEN, 18). The struggle for a clean environment in the region has taken a heavy toll on poor farmers, fishers, company workers, defenders of human rights, and journalists who have done a great deal of work in publicizing the daily struggles of Niger Delta people for environmental justice.

It is disturbingly ironic that the government that has the constitutional duty to protect and improve the Nigerian environment and safeguard its water, air, land, forest, and wildlife is the one that continually harasses and oppresses the courageous and sensitive souls and concerned nongovernmental organizations that mount a vigorous clean environment campaign and struggle to keep the oil-bearing Niger Delta safe from total annihilation by the destructive impact of oil production. The government fails abysmally to implement the plethora of legislation that is purposed to protect the Nigerian environment, regulate and control minatory human and industrial activities. Since corporations were not sanctioned in Nigeria for violating guidelines, procedures and standards on effluent limitation, greenhouse gas emissions, waste disposal through underground injection, management of industrial and hazardous wastes, and pollution traceable to gas flaring and petroleum production, a foreign waste disposal company saw the country as a haven for toxic wastes and made Koko in Delta State a dump site in 1988. Although a court order has outlawed gas flaring, it has been ignored with utter disdain by both the Nigerian government and the oil companies.

Gas flaring does not only amount to a wanton waste of a product that most Nigerians cannot even afford for domestic cooking; it is indisputable proof of the general incompetence of the political leadership in the country. Flaring "wastes US $15 million worth of gas daily" (Bassey *Knee Deep in Crude*, 79). Besides, the pollution of the atmosphere alone provides enough justification for legislating against the harmful and prodigal practice. In the opinion of Nurudeen Ogbara, environmental laws in Nigeria "are still tokenistic, inappropriate, unenforced, disjointed and devoid of requisite political will and zeal" (Ogbara, 50). A collective responsibility that should be borne by the entire polity, management of the Nigerian environment cannot be left to the whims and caprices of the National Environmental Management that replaced the Federal Environmental Protection Agency. Considering the interconnectedness of the environment, a safer, cleaner, healthier, more humane, and more pleasing living space demands global attention and multilateral agreements that are best served by the practice of true democracy and equitable international relations. Little careless acts in small corners of the earth add up to engender phenomenal environmental problems that heat up the world and cause climate change.

Perhaps lack of knowledge led the Abacha regime and other military administrations in Nigeria to deny the Niger Delta people environmental rights and oppress them, while acute consciousness of the interconnection between environment and sustainable development made the American government stand by victims of a major oil spill and fight for them. Well, dereliction of duty on the part of successive Nigerian administrations—military and civilian—has allowed paradise to be transformed into hell in the Niger Delta. Its agricultural produce—palm oil, yams, and cassava—is no longer buoyant and its aquatic culture is severely hurt. The birds of pulverized paradise take to the sea and "the animals grope in the burning bush" (Ojaide *Delta Blues*, 22) and its citizens who cannot endure the resultant hardship flee into exile, foreign havens, the fortunes of which are equally under threat in a globalized world tottering under the momentous pressure of climate change and economic meltdown, and those who are not so lucky and cannot escape suck, grin and bear it.

Constructed on the artistic principle of chiaroscuro, "Delta Blues" projects the oil-rich region as paradise with abundant forest, subterranean and water resources, while it portrays Northern Nigeria, the climate of which is dry and Sahelian as hell. The parched people of the latter who are constantly scorched and oppressed by heat waves envy the swamp dwellers of paradise who are protected from meningitis, rinderpest, sunstroke, and other dangerous diseases caused by excessive heat. What is missing in the portrait is the paradoxical force, dinergy, which pierces through the whole gamut of nature, negates every binary division, and transforms every paradise into a veritable hell.

The image of "the burning bush," a biblical allusion to the holy ground on which Moses stood and received Jehovah's call, is literally appropriated to express the devastation caused by forest fires in the Niger Delta where, unlike magic Mount Horeb, fires consumed vegetation, agricultural produce, livestock, fishing-nets, and distillers' camps. Moses was ordered to remove his shoes so that he would neither desecrate the altar of God nor defile His holy presence (Ex. 3:1–10), a religious injunction that is in consonance with the animistic spiritualizing of nature, which enhances conservation of earth's resources. Feet imprisoned in shoes can neither feel free nor fondle naked earth. The poet asks a hypothetical question:

> With what eyes will *Olokun*
> look at her beneficiaries,
> dead or still living in [on] the rack
> of uniformed dogs barking
> and biting protesters
> brandishing green shrubs? (Ojaide *Delta Blues*, 22, emphasis in the original)

The question intensifies the threnody of the partly laudatory and partly satirical elegy. Agents of the corrupt and oppressive military regime that inflicts unimaginable suffering on the Niger Delta people are contemptuously imaged as rabid "uniformed dogs" that bite the hands that feed them and kill the goose that lays the golden eggs.

In "Sleeping in a Makeshift Grave," the Niger Delta is represented as prize game over which the diverse ethnic nationalities in Nigeria that are imaged as hungry hunters quarrel and fight. In other words, it is the oil wealth that comes from the Niger Delta that paradoxically welds together the diverse ethnic groups that constitute the country and generates conflict among them as well. The poet has no problem sharing the wealth of the region with other parts of the country, but he objects to the carelessness with which it is produced, which leaves disastrous effects on the environment, and mismanagement of the proceeds from the nonrenewable resource, which undermines the strength of the polity and breeds class conflict and interracial hatred and strife. Hence, the slumbering giant is taken for dead and laid in a grave, which hints at possible future demise of the polity. A literary allusion to Alex la Guma's novel *The Stone Country*, the phrase "a stone country" recalls apartheid South Africa and its vicious racist policies and practices that forced the Blacks to take to armed struggle against the evil regime that dehumanized and reduced them to prisoners and slaves in their own land. The phrase connotes emptiness of compassion, empathy, and love, tender emotions that constitute the force that is supposed to serve as glue to bind together a multiracial, multilingual, and multireligious country such as Nigeria. Given the absence of this unifying force and of the practice of true federalism, the six geopolitical zones into which the country is divided war over which zone controls the center and gets to spend a huge proportion of the petro-dollars accruing from the Niger Delta.

There is no gainsaying that misrule by both civilian administrations and military regimes have destroyed the Nigerian environment. By environment, we mean space and all that is in it, namely: matter (organic and inorganic); human beings who are misled by pride, bred by knowledge to separate themselves from nature and by power to erroneously perceive themselves collectively as its controller and lord; animals (visible and invisible) that are placed by the human race on a lower level on the Great Chain of Being; plants, water, air, their interactions, activities and processes; and all ideas and objects produced by humans as they struggle relentlessly with nature in order to create culture and civilization.

To be in a healthy state, the environment must be always protected against all manner of pollution, be it air, human, land, noise, or water.

Naturally, creation without destruction is impossible, and accidents are inevitable in the creative process. However, what appears idiotic and mind-boggling is wanton destruction of the environment, coupled with senseless repetition of preventable accidents either because of sheer imbecility (lack of knowledge) or insanity. Perhaps the time has come for the World Health Organization to legislate that all political office-seekers from the ward to the national level should undergo rigorous psychiatric tests before they are allowed to contest elections, and annually after winners take the oath of office.

Butchery, such as witnessed in Nigeria under the despotic rule of General Sani Abacha, who is called a "barbarian chief" void of vision in "Elegy for Nine Warriors" (Ojaide *Delta Blues*, 26), becomes the norm once the mind of a ruler is fractured and muddled up. The hanging of Kenule Saro-Wiwa and his eight fellow travelers, therefore, is to be understood as an externalization of the turmoil in the dictator's mind and as an extension into the human world of the violence visited on material nature.

The pervasive stench of death in *Delta Blues* derives from the simple fact that the powerhouse, Aso Rock, the seat of the Nigerian government, from where energy is supposed to flow and radiate to all the parts of the polity, is itself half-dead. Of significance in this respect is the question that closes the third part of "Elegy for Nine Warriors":

> Is the prisoner who presides
> over cells and cemeteries
> not slave of his own slaves? (Ojaide *Delta Blues*, 26)

The problem assumes a global dimension once it is realized that the consumption and management of the resources of the earth are driven by greed, which capitalist ideologues argue is good. Simply put, then, problems of environmental degradation are ultimately traceable to the abysmal absence of vision on the part of controllers of the economic, political, scientific, and technological levers of the world.

A symbol of knowledge in most primitive myths, the sun is "blinded by a hideous spectacle" in *Delta Blues* (Ojaide *Delta Blues*, 26), an eclipse that further deepens the darkness that reigns in the land where justice and truth are abhorred and those who uphold and fight for them are dispatched without remorse. There is a hint at egregious evil and an abysmal lack of knowledge and vision in the metaphor of General Abacha's dark goggles, an article that prevents the wearer from accurately perceiving reality and the horror of his mis/rule. Ordinarily, a people perish for lack of knowledge, but when a political leadership consciously cultivates evil, the problem assumes monstrous proportions.

It is the light from the sun that makes life possible on the planet Earth and if that light dims or dies out, a terrible disaster is bound to follow for all living things in the world, including human beings, for the earth itself on which they depend for sustenance faces the threat of extinction. It is indubitable that human beings now constitute one of the endangered animal species on the planet Earth. Even if a habitable planet is found elsewhere in any of the galaxies in deep space and some people are transported there to preserve the race, it is expected that the same fate of extinction will eventually befall such a planet, judging by the inescapability of the problem of pollution that attends human inventiveness and historical progression. The mere attempt to explore space and make the discovery has caused its pollution. Whatever is touched by human beings inescapably gets contaminated, and it is one of the uncanny laws of Nature, our Mother, who has been forcibly undressed and sadistically raped and whose violated body has been gruesomely hacked to pieces. "A new child: oh, how much new filth has come into the world," Zarathustra exclaims grievously (Nietzsche "Thus Spoke Zarathustra," 403).

Amoral, the children even jeer at their mother's nakedness and incur her wrath. All natural disasters that occur in the contemporary world approximate the vengeance of Mother Nature on her prodigal children who lack filial love and waste her resources. They are self-inflicted wounds. Yet millions of people exist in the world today who are neither environmentally conscious nor sensitive and so do not correctly interpret the wounds. Some scientists even deny outright the truth of climate change and global warming, despite the melting of polar ice, desertification, flooding, and forest fires in diverse places and their tragic consequences in virtually all the corners of the world. Ojaide's anger breaks out in lines such as the following:

> These children who laugh at their naked mother
> incur the wrath of their creator-goddess.
> They forfeit their kinship, these bastards. (Ojaide *Delta Blues*, 27)

It is not the poet but their own insensitivity that excises them from the human community, for to be human is also to be humane, to feel, to love, to empathize, and to engage in selfless acts of sacrifice. Apt and exquisite is the word of abuse "bastards" that represents the ingrates: freaks and accidents of creation. The phrase "the fate of vultures" (Ojaide *Delta Blues*, 27), the title of one of Ojaide's collections of poems, is idiomatic and expresses the idea of death of corrupt betrayers. Vultures are carrion eaters, and in the natural order of things all predators ultimately serve as a prey to more powerful carnivores. Employing an ingenious technique of verbal inversion, the poet takes laughter from the dirty mouths of the blind mockers and turns the self-cursed clowns into objects of derision.

However, the question of what should be the proper attitude to the extra-judicial killing of the environmentalists and to natural calamities such as earthquakes, flooding, and volcanic eruptions transcends the binary and mechanistic division into comedy and tragedy, for all things are interwoven. Plenitude resides in a blend of the two literary genres or worldviews and in paradox; and "greatness," as conceptualized by Nietzsche is, "being as manifold as whole, [and] as wide as full" (Nietzsche *The Portable Nietzsche*, 446). Extremes meet and all contraries are inextricably mixed: "midnight too is noon; pain too is a joy; curses too are a blessing; night too is a sun . . . a sage too is a fool" (Nietzsche *The Portable Nietzsche*, 435). Laughter is the answer to all conundrums that perplex human beings and leave their brains in a muddle.

Given that "conclusions are consolations" (Nietzsche *The Gay Science*, 32), Zarathustra beseeches humans to learn to laugh, for "all good things laugh" (Nietzsche *The Portable Nietzsche*, 406). In the same vein, a Yoruba maxim posits that when an event is too tragic for weeping, the best thing to do is laugh. "There are heights of the soul," Nietzsche avers, "from which tragedy itself no longer appears to operate tragically." He theorizes that what human beings enjoy in tragedy—its painful delight—"is the philtre of the great Circe 'cruelty'" (Nietzsche *Beyond Good and Evil*, 44, 177). Laughter is therapeutic and should not be demeaned, even in utterly tragic situations. "Tragedy provokes laughter" (Ojaide *Delta Blues*, 27), therefore, is a cryptic and perspicacious aphorism that could come only from a profound poetic imagination that, rather than detest natural ambivalence, accepts and works with contraries of which nature is composed. The tragedy of Nigeria under General Abacha's rule was so monumental, it changed to droll comedy.

Although the language of the poet is abusive, what with a suffusion of pejoratively deployed words and phrases, such as "ghoulish," "cockroach," "thief, commander of roaches," "crow" (Ojaide *Delta Blues*, 25), "barbarian," "butcher," "Ogiso's grandchild by incest" (26), "vultures," "fool," "sorcerer,, "cobra" (27), and "demon" (28), they all demonstare the author's disgust with the government. His rage is provoked not just by the criminality and perfidy of the Nigerian government in alleged collusion with the exploitative and greedy oil corporations but also by the egregious socioeconomic injustice of which the Niger Delta people are victims. How could the people whose land exudes the wealth of the country be calm and cool "without government roads and light" (29)? So, the tone of anger and bitterness does not mar the poem; instead, it endues the elegy with power, just as John Milton's excoriation of corrupt clergy lends rhetorical force to "Lycidas."

"Witchcraft" poeticizes Nigeria as a "bewitched land" that is neither alive nor dead, in which people walk on their heads, eyes closed, "trip on stumps of beheaded dreams," fall, fart, and infect every available space with the contagion that spreads from the center of power (Ojaide *Delta Blues*, 32). The country is robbed of its fertility and vitality by an incubus that mates with her and ensures the perpetuation of debauchery and witchery.

As stated in "The Singer's Wish," the poet's self-imposed "curse" is that he can neither be indifferent to nor overlook Africa's "multiple afflictions," her decimation and degradation by internal and external enemies, and the widening wounds of the Niger Delta:

I cannot sleep over the soul's deep wounds;
nor can I throw down the hump, Africa's
crushing bundle, that I carry on my back. (Ojaide *Delta Blues*, 34)

An enumeration of victims of state aggression on the battlefield that the Niger Delta has become, "Fresh Casualties" (Ojaide *Delta Blues*, 37) foregrounds the idea that the denudation of the land continues apace. Among the victims mentioned are protesters mercilessly bludgeoned, left "half-dead" and reduced to a vegetable state; farmers and fishers impoverished through destruction of farms and creeks on which they respectively subsist; the diseased whose dry skins peel off or are covered with rashes after eating poisoned fish or drinking water contaminated by chemicals; martyrs of environmental campaigns; married women and single schoolgirls raped by lustful soldiers at gunpoint; the disabled incapacitated by industrial accidents; the psychologically afflicted; witnesses of horror who become hypochondriacs; and mercenaries and members of the armed forces hired by giant oil corporations to harass, kill, maim or drive fear into stubborn agitators who demand land rights and adequate compensation for losses suffered by their people on account of industrial activities of the oil companies.

Taking its cue from J. P. Clark's "The Casualties," which similarly catalogues the victims of the Nigerian Civil War (1967–1970), the title of the poem implies that what is going on in the Niger Delta is plain warfare. The war goes on and takes the form of kidnapping by ransom-seeking militants, even after the declaration of general amnesty and the launching of rehabilitation programs by government for those among the militants who laid down their weapons. Continuation of violence and acts of sabotage, such as oil pipeline vandalism and incendiary bomb attacks by the Movement for the Emancipation of the Niger Delta (MEND), connotes that the demobilization or pacification scheme is neither thorough nor complete; and it will not be until economic, political, and social justice is done to the casualties and the people's demand for resource control for self-development is recognized as legitimate and granted.

However, Ojaide is not a vengeance-seeking poet of the Niger Delta but a thorough-going humanist who is willing to forgive and save his enemy. In "I will Save My Enemy," he argues with the full force of logic that "inflicting shame on a defeated enemy / does not fit the battle-cry for human rights" (Ojaide *Delta Blues*, 38). So, the struggle for observance of democratic principles and good governance in the oil-rich region must not be confused or besmirched with acts of terrorism. On the contrary, it should be correctly perceived as the defense of biodiversity and the right to a clean environment and a healthy and fulfilling life. General well-being is the ultimate goal. "O Aridon," he cries out in the eponymous poem "The Fate of Vultures," "bring back my wealth / from rogue vaults" (Ojaide 1990, 11).

Just as Leopold Sedar Senghor rounds off "Prayer for Peace" with a saintly act of forgiveness and prays not only for his enemies but also for the death of the serpent of evil in his own heart, Ojaide pleads: "*Osonobrughwe*, give me a full cup of courage / so that I will not shame my worst enemy in death" (*The Fate of Vultures*, 38), the mean way the executioners did the Ogoni Nine. Friedrich Nietzsche upholds the same principle and frowns on the despicable practice of denigrating and humiliating people. Yet the German philosopher admonishes humans to be hard, for it is the strong that wins, and has Zarathustra declare pithily: "shame, shame, shame—that is the history of man" (Nietzsche "Thus Spoke Zarathustra," 200). Is there then, as insinuated in the phrase "crazy gods" that concludes "Fetish Country" (39), a streak of madness in manifestations of power by the world's tyrannical political leadership that trickles down to the common mob of humanity? The pollution of the earth has no ideological coloration and transcends the division of the world into politico-economic blocs.

All humanity in different degrees is responsible for problems of global warming and climate change.

The search for peace and social justice in the world is inseparable from the struggle for a clean environment, for the security of human life is contingent on the health of nature. To exemplify with food security, the impact of desertification and soil denudation on the environment through consumption of fossil fuels and livestock, which causes global warming, diminishes the size of arable land in sub-Saharan Africa. Conflict, environmental pollution, economy, and politics are intertwined and occupy the front burner of world affairs. Slush funds migrate from poor peripheries to centers of power in America, Europe, and Asia. They also move on a local level from Aleibiri, Awoba, Ewan, and Obogu to Abuja, Kano, Lagos, Port Harcourt, and Sokoto, and corrupt their handlers and possessors.

Moral depravity, the thematic preoccupation of the poet in "The Chieftain and His Tribe," "Abuja," "On Solidarity Marches," "Army of Microbes," and "Pregnancy of the Snake" has its source in the oil wells of the Niger Delta. The cause is still the consequence, and internal colonization is indistinguishable from the European. Both are plagues, wear the same cloak of blood and human flesh, and leave tales of pain, suffering, and woes. They ravage the Niger Delta and ruin its tillers. It is apodictic that Ojaide is "the mirror of their sufferings and the mighty sparrow of their melancholia" (Olafioye 122). The aftermath of the pillage is the erosion of traditional values and the entrenchment of the ontology of Social Cannibalism. As the poet epigrammatically expresses the moral dilemma, using a culinary image: "don't eat / and starve; eat and be sick" (Ojaide *Delta Blues*, 44). Only the food for vultures fostered by corruption is readily available in the country.

The question in *Delta Blues* "is it sweat, tears, or acid rain falling / from the brows of subjects" (50) asked in "A General Sickness" gives intimations that, indeed, it is a general ailment that afflicts both the earth and the world of humans. Highly ingenious, the pun on the word "general" captures at once the perennial nature of warfare in human history and the universality of the problems it engenders. The unceasing struggle with nature endangers humans in the postindustrial world. At last, the chicken has come home to roost. At Independence in 1960, Wole Soyinka made a prognostication through Spirit of Darkness in *A Dance of the Forests* that Nigerians would be "misled" (Soyinka, 74). The last two lines of "A General Sickness" attest to the irrefragability of the prognostication and of other frightening prophecies pronounced by spirits of the elements in the play on the tragic fate of humanity: "The head has choked us with poisons & the land rebounds with insufferable groans," Ojaide laments (*Delta Blues*, 50). The "head" refers not just to General Abacha, the ruling Head of State at the time of the political debacle poetized in Delta Blues, but also to the political leadership of every nation as well as scientific and technological knowledge, for climate change is the effect of industrial revolution, which itself is the child of the Enlightenment. Similarly, "land" is not only the Niger Delta nor Nigeria but also the planet Earth. Most of the key metaphors and symbols used in *Delta Blues* work on several semantic levels—the local, the national, the global and the universal. Avant-garde space scientists would add the multiverse.

In "Visiting Home," the poet-persona's thirst is not assuaged because he cannot bear to drink of polluted spring water. His choice—to "fashion ways to drink of it / without its dirt, drink it only clean . . ." (Ojaide *Delta Blues*, 45)—postpones the festival of life until after the restoration of the land and gives hope to the bereaved and the famished. What is to be done? Unambiguous is the poet's answer that the country must return from the oil wells to the abandoned green path and waterways once again: the cultivation of food crops to banish hunger and quench the thirst in parched throats. He is assertive: "I have to dig the land into deep-rooted crops / to erect barriers against claims of famine" (Ojaide *Delta Blues*, 45), famine being a metaphor for all life's inadequacies.

Therefore, the persistent and trenchant call for diversification of the Nigerian economy is not misplaced and must be urgently heeded if the empty barn of the country is to be filled to overflowing to meet the needs of citizens and strangers alike. Anthropogenic explanations of climate change, however, locate the source of the problem in agriculture itself in deep history, the clearing of forests for farming and livestock production, which started more than ten thousand years ago. Given the natural ambivalence that lies at the center of the ecosystem, a paradox that is insoluble in any finite sense, what human beings should aim at is a balance, not a negation, of the implacable centripetal and centrifugal forces that are perpetually at work in nature. They create the conditions that make human existence possible.

Ojaide lyricizes in panegyrics that revivify the African oral poetic tradition the relentless struggles of compatriots such as Gani Fawehinmi, Wole Soyinka, and members of the National Democratic Coalition who refused to partake of offal and instead joined forces with Niger Delta activists to fight the army of occupation who stole the collective voice of the people of

Nigeria. He represents them in "Exceptions" as "black ants," stinging the buttocks of the military despot that presided over the rape of the land. In other words, moved by human suffering and the groans of the earth, the mindless destruction of its resources and the waste of lives, few courageous Nigerians stood up to the monster, stared in *its* ghoulish face and fought for freedom, peace, and prosperity.

Although Ojaide, like Moses, is for liberation of the oppressed, he rejects the law of vengeance and confesses that he "can only kill in self-defence" (Ojaide *Delta Blues*, 54). All human beings, without exception, are biological and geological agents and participate in different degrees in the gradual killing of the planet Earth (ecocide). Our best solutions produce negative effects. Edward O. Wilson avers: "Humanity has so far played the role of planetary killer, concerned only with its own short-term survival. We have cut much of the heart out of biodiversity" (*The Future of Life*, 102). He proposes a universalistic solution: "We will be wise to look on ourselves as a species" (Wilson 2008, xii) "Technofixes," according to Mark Maslin, "are dangerous or cause problems as bad as the ones they are aimed at" (Maslin *Global Warming*, 147). A plant that serves as a pesticide could itself become a plague, as is the case with the introduction of water hyacinth into Nigeria. The weed now constitutes a serious hindrance to water transportation in the littoral states of Nigeria. "Water hyacinths," we are told in "The Desert's Not Infinite," a poem of hope and optimism, "closed waterways for boats" (Ojaide *Delta Blues*, 51).

The little choices we make, either as individuals or as communities, as we consume resources of nature for sustenance of life aggregate and destabilize the delicate balance of nature. Their impact is visibly scripted on rapidly vanishing glaciers on mountaintops and in the arctic region, on ocean beds and their biodiversity loss, and in the smoky atmosphere and the depleted ozone layer. It is time to eat humble pie, to tear down the wall of separation erected by deceptive knowledge between human beings and nature, to perceive ourselves collectively as an integral part of its complex chemistry, to work hard at salvaging the earth, and to forestall the real possibility of a self-induced extermination of our race. Literary art, as evidenced by *Delta Blues* that bears witness to the despoliation of human beings and the degradation of the natural environment, could help in the healing process by softening hardened hearts, raising consciousness of the natural environment, and directing alienated humanity to the path of reconciliation with earth: its patient, long-suffering, and occasionally vengeful mother. The Niger Delta, the main supplier of the wealth of Nigeria, is in the essay perceived as Mother Nature that bears the wounds of civilization. If the struggle between humans and nature cannot be abolished, in order for culture and civilization to continue, at least it can be reconceptualized and made less destructive to both parties. Poetry can vigorously participate in the search for a new way.

Works Cited

Ajuwon, Bade. *Ìrèmòjé: Eré Ìsípà Ode*. Ibadan: UP, 1981. Print.
Bassey, Nnimmo. Ed. *Knee Deep in Crude: Environmental Field Reports, Vol. 1*. Benin City: ERA/FoEN, 2009. Print.
———. "Appendix 1: Oil Sector and Localized Energy Conflicts." *Reporting the Nigerian Environment*. Environmental Rights Action/Friends of the Earth. Benin City: ERA/FoEN, 2010. 67–82. Print.
The Bible. King James Version. London and New York: Collins, 1957. Print.
Boeser, Knut. *Nostradamus*. Trans. John Brownjohn. Avenel: Gramercy, 1996. Print.
Clark, John Pepper. "The Casualties." *A Decade of Tongues: Selected Poems: 1958–1968*. London: Longman, 1981. 84–85. Print.
Darah, Godini Gabriel. *Battles of Songs: Udje Tradition of the Urhobo*. Lagos: Malthouse, 2005. Print.
Engels, Frederick. *The Part Played by Labour in the Transition from Ape to Man*. Moscow: Progress Publishers, 1980. Print.
Environmental Rights Action/Friends of the Earth Nigeria (ERA/FoEN). *Reporting the Nigerian Environment*. Benin City: ERA/FoEN, 2010. Print.
Joyce, James. *Ulysses*. London: Bodley Head, 1937. Print.
———. *A Portrait of the Artist as a Young Man*. 2nd. Ed. London: Heinemann, 1977. Print.
Keats, John. "Ode on a Grecian Urn." *The Penguin Book of English Verse*. Ed. John Hayward. London: Harmondsworth, 1975. 295–296. Print.
Krauss, Clifford, and John M. Broder. "BP Says Limits on Drilling Imperil Spill Payouts." NYTimes.com. 2 Sept. 2010. Web. 24 Sept. 2010. <http://www.nytimes.com/2010/09/03/business/03bp.html>.
La Guma, Alex. *The Stone Country*. London: Heinemann, 1974. Print.
Lasisi, Akeem. *Iremoje: Ritual Poetry for Ken Saro-Wiwa*. Lagos: Hybun, 2000. Print.
Marx, Karl. "Economic and Philosophical Manuscripts." *Early Writings*. Trans. Rodney Livingstone and Gregory Benton. Harmondsworth: Penguin, 1975. 279–400. Print.
Maslin, Mark. *Global Warming: A Very Short Introduction*. Oxford: OUP, 2004.
Milton, John. "Lycidas." *The Oxford Anthology of English Literature*. Vol. 1. Ed. Frank Kermode, et al. New York: Oxford UP, 1973. 1252–1257. Print.
Nietzsche, Friedrich. *Beyond Good and Evil: Prelude to a Philosophy of the Future*. Trans. Helen Zimmern. London: George Allen & Unwin, 1967. Print.

———. "Thus Spoke Zarathustra." *The Portable Nietzsche*. Trans. Walter Kaufmann. London: Chatto & Windus, 1971. Print.

———. "Preface for the Second Edition." *The Gay Science*. Trans. Walter Kaufmann. New York: Random House, 1974. 32–38. Print.

Ogbara, Nurudeen. "Environmental Laws in Nigeria." *Reporting the Nigerian Environment*. Environmental Rights Action/Friends of the Earth Nigeria. Benin City: ERA/FoEN, 2010. 43–57. Print.

Ojaide, Tanure. *Children of Iroko*. New York: Greenfield Review, 1973. Print.

———. *The Fate of Vultures and Other Poems*. Lagos: Malthouse, 1990. Print.

———. *Delta Blues and Home Songs*. Ibadan: Kraft, 1998. Print.

Okigbo, Christopher. *Labyrinths*. London: Heinemann, 1971. Print.

Olafioye, Tayo. *The Poetry of Tanure Ojaide: A Critical Appraisal*. Lagos: Malthouse, 2000. Print.

Osundare, Niyi. *The Eye of the Earth*. Ibadan: Heinemann, 1986. Print.

Schmidt, Alfred. *The Concept of Nature in Marx*. London: NLB, 1971. Print.

Senghor, Leopold Sedar. "Prayer for Peace." *Selected Poems*. Trans. John Reed and Clive Wake. London. Oxford UP, 1964. 48–49. Print.

Shaw, George Bernard. *Pygmalion and Other Plays (The Devil's Disciple and Caesar and Cleopatra)* New York: Dodd, Mead & Company, 1967. Print.

Soyinka, Wole. *A Dance of the Forests*. London: Oxford UP, 1963. Print.

Wilson, Edward O. *The Future of Life*. New York: New Millennium Audio, 2002. Print.

———. "Foreword." Jeffrey Sachs. *Common Wealth: Economics for a Crowded Planet*. New York: Penguin, 2008. xi–xii. Print.

17

For Common Corn: Eco-ing Bole Butake's Concerns in *Lake God, The Survivors,* and *And Palm-Wine Will Flow*

Joyce Ashuntantang

Bole Butake is the leading playwright in Cameroon. He has published nine plays and produced most of them for the stage. Most critics, including Bate Besong (1996), Eckhard Breitinger (2001), Eunice Ngongkum (2007), and Hilarious Ambe (2007), consider Butake a political playwright. Although *Lake God, The Survivors,* and *And Palm-Wine Will Flow* speak to the political changes that were occurring in Cameroon from the mid-1980s to 1990 when these three plays were written, a critical analysis of these plays reveal that Butake is also concerned here with the relationship between people and their environment. Nevertheless, John Takem argues, "No radical Anglophone literary dramatist has focused any of his writings exclusively on environmentalism" (53). However, Takem is quick to add that "some of Butake's plays do give a hint of the writer's environmental concerns, which were to become some of his major preoccupations in his grassroots Theatre for Development projects" (53). By contrast, I argue in this paper that Butake does not only hint at environmental issues in *Lake God, The Survivors, and And Palm-Wine Will Flow,* but that these environmental issues are central to the plot of each of these plays. In fact, Butake seems to be making the argument that unless community leaders take environmental issues seriously, the consequences may be devastating to their very existence.

Lake God opens with a narrator who seems to be the sole survivor of a disaster. He is suffering from acute grief and addresses the audience directly. From him they learn about the devastation caused by the Lake God:

> Man, woman, child
> Fowls, dogs, and cats
> Cattle, goats, and pigs
> Wild animals in the bush including
> Rats and flies . . . yes flies, even flies
> Every living creature
> The Lake God of death swept them all
> Into his kingdom in a swift silent whirlwind . . .
> Only yesterday I was a man!
> A husband with five wives and a compound
> Bustling with life and ringing with laughter and song. . . . (Butake 6)

After the narrator is done with his dirge, the stage directions read:

> Darkness and silence rain supreme. The lights turned on slowly, simulating dawn. All over the playing area are bodies of humans and animals lying still. It is a macabre and terrifying scene, one of the form stirs uneasily and with great difficulty. It is a woman about thirty years old. She rises slowly and lurches forward and falls on another figure, which remains frozen. She pulls herself together and examines the form, prodding it and turning it over. It is obviously lifeless. . . . (Butake 8)

When this play was first performed in 1986 by the Yaounde University Theatre and later published by BET & Co. in Yaounde, Cameroon, it was seen as a fictional representation of the Lake Nyos disaster of 1986 where a volcanic eruption in Lake Nyos emitted a huge amount of carbon dioxide, which suffocated 1,700 people and about 3,500 livestock in nearby towns and village in Menchum Division in the Northwest of Cameroon.

Despite the environmental issues embedded in this play, many critics have analyzed it more in terms of the "modernism versus tradition" theme prevalent in African literature. Hilarious Ambe confirms this when he writes that:

> the play is not just an attempt at offering a hypothetical input into the catastrophe; it explores the other components that continue to despise the harmonious growth and evolution of a people. The components hover around the playwright's typification and symbolic use of myth as a central dramatic metaphor to explain the ideological issues in the lake community's politics and economics" (53).

It is easy to attribute the tragedy that results in *Lake God* as the consequences of the conflict between Fon Joseph, the Christian monarch on the one hand, and the chief priest Shey Bonyo who represents the entire village. Central to this conflict is the Fon's disobedience in leading his people in a yearly sacrifice to Lake God after which he is supposed to consummate his love with the queen, thereby ushering in fertility and a good harvest in the lake community. As their traditional ruler, he is expected to do so but he has abdicated this role because he sees himself as a Christian monarch and does not partake in "pagan rituals." He is supported in this decision by the Roman Catholic priest who is his mentor and guide. In keeping with his Christian principles, the Fon succeeds in getting the government to ban Kwifon—a sacred secret cult doubling as the supreme council of the land. Counseled by Father Leo, he has also declared the Chief priest of the lake and diviner, Shey Bonyo, as *persona non grata*. Hence, when the Chief priest divines that the lake is boiling and the Fon needs to act quickly, he ignores the urgency and by the time "Kwifon" kidnaps the Fon to present as a sacrifice to the Lake God, it is too late.

Despite the significance of the myth of the Lake God in Butake's play, a careful analysis of *Lake God* shows that what actually drives the plot of the play is the dwindling corn harvests, which are threatening to cause starvation. Although Butake does not make specific the setting of *Lake God*, one can assume that it is set in the Northwest region of Cameroon where Lake Nyos is found. The presence of "Kwifon," the secret and sacred ruling council of the land, the appellation of the ruler as "Fon," and the names of the characters are all pointers to this assumption. For people in Cameroon, and especially those living in the North West region, corn is a staple crop. It is from corn that they make "corn fufu," which forms part of the daily diet. The cultivation of corn is predominantly done by women in this village. Unfortunately, Fon Joseph has entered into a new alliance with the Bororo-Fulani ethnic group, allowing them to settle in the village. What makes this a problem is that the main occupation of these new dwellers is cattle rearing. The Bororo-Fulani are nomadic herdsmen who are thought to have emigrated from the Middle East or northern Africa years ago in search of new grazing land for their cattle. Not only are the cattle a menace to the women whose farms are near the cattle grazing areas, the need for grazing areas for these cattle is also creating a shortage of farming land. It is this problem of mixed farming gone wrong which fuels the crisis in the play.

In the absence of the Kwifon, the women have no choice but to take their complaints to the Fon. When one of the cattle rearers, Dewa, allows his cattle to encroach on the farms of the women, they tie him up and take him to the Fon. Their reasons are many:

> "All the women who have farms in Ngangba will starve this year. Dewa's cattle have ruined all the corn"
> "When we went to his Kiban to demand an explanation, he laughed in our face and told us to take him to the highest court in the land."
> "And he said the cattle were not his but those of the Fon."
> "And he asked if we had seen his people buying land from Kombi ever since the Fon started selling land to them."
> And when we said he will be hearing from the Kwifon, he spat in our face and said the Fon had . . . the kwifon."
> "he challenged our men to build fences around our farms or the cattle rearers will take no responsibility for their laziness and poverty."
> (Butake 15)

Analyzing these statements one can begin to understand the gravity of the crisis facing these rural women. First, their crops in their farms are being destroyed by the cattle, and the cattle rearers fail to control the cattle. Also, starvation is looming large in the horizon because without a proper harvest, they cannot feed their families. The women also do not seem to have a means of solving their problem because the Fon has banned the Kwifon. The women also make it clear that the cattle rearer seems to be acting above the law since he arrogantly asks them to take him to the highest court of the land who is the Fon. This is not surprising since the women reveal that Dewa claims the cattle are those of the Fon and not his. Another charge against Dewa is that he has asked the men to build fences around the farms to protect them from the cattle, a practice which is not normally done. When the Fon asks Dewa for his own side of the story, his answers reveal that he doesn't think he has done anything wrong because he was on the land that the government has given to the Bororos via the Fon. The women's earnest desire remains the removal of the cattle from their farmlands. However, the Fon cannot allow the Bororos to leave because of his insatiable greed. He tells the women, "Progress here is tied to cattle" (Butake 19). Father Leo throws more light on this when he tells the women who attend his doctrine class that,

When I receive a little money from my country, I give it to your Fon who invests it in the purchase of cattle. That is how we have been able to move mountains. If the cattle leave, we will not be able to continue to give you services which you now have. A school for your children, a health center for the young and old and a big motor road. (Butake 33)

However, there is every indication that Fon Joseph sees a personal development in these benefits. He sees the development in the village as a path for him to be elected into parliament. This seems to be his major concern as he confides in Father Leo, "Father, if the cattle rearers are forced to leave, my chances will be lost. Development in the village will stop and the government might even revoke my first class chieftaincy" (Butake 37). With these revelations, it becomes clear that despite the Fon's Christian outlook and his refusal to be part of "pagan rituals," what really fuels his actions is rank materialism. Shey Bonyo, the Chief priest, reveals in the play that the Fon got the throne by bribing King Makers, a fact confirmed by Father Leo when he confides in Fon Joseph that "Your father never wanted you to become Fon. He thought I had too much influence over you" (Butake 38). To demonstrate that he is only concerned about his personal wealth, the Fon exploits the situation with Dewa to enrich himself. He does not only take the money from the women, but he asks Dewa to remove two cows from his herd and add to the Fon's. He insists that the cows must be female so they could procreate.

In his greed, the Fon pushes the problem of food sufficiency in this village to the crisis point. The ominous future as perceived by the women is one of hunger and starvation. To make matters worse, the refusal of the Fon to make sacrifices to the Lake God, a sacred duty, also denies the people ancestral blessings and a good harvest from the Lake God. Faced with this double threat to their continuous existence as a people, the women pragmatically work out modalities to ensure their men are galvanized into action by going on a sex strike.

Under the leadership of an old woman, Ma Kusham, they take the oath of the fibuen to deny their husbands corn fufu or sex until they can drive the cattle rearers from the village. It takes a couple of days for the men to realize that what they believed to be their personal problem in their household is indeed a general problem. They come to realize that each time they mention fufu or sex, their women talk about Ngangba— the farming location of the women. In Maimo's case, he slaps his wife for failing to provide fufu, but the reaction of his wife gets his full attention. According to him,

> [M]y wife wiped the tears from her face, looked straight into mine and said in a cold voice that if I really wanted to eat fufu, I should go to Ngangba and make the cattle leave the land instead of beating up a defenseless woman who has been trying to feed her husband and children. (Butake 30)

When the priest finds out what the women have done, he admonishes those of them who attend his church to give up their position. He goes further to remind them of hell fire and the need to rethink their position. He seems oblivious to the gravity of their problem when he tells them, "You all were in the Fibuen, participating in Satan's play and eating of his food and taking oaths. All for what? My children? Mere corn? Common corn?" (Butake 32). Father Leo totally misreads the situation. When the Fon tries to discuss the women's revolt with him, he asserts arrogantly, "I wouldn't call it a revolt. Just some uncoordinated action of ill-disciplined village women" (Butake 36). He is very convinced that he has successfully talked the women out of their anger. As he explains confidently to the Fon:

> I talked to the Christian women this morning in their doctrine class. It's all over. They promised not to disobey their husbands any more. . . . There is absolutely nothing these village women can do. If we could succeed in neutralizing the kwifon, that terrible secret cult what more of a handful of ignorant village women? I warned that without cattle there will be no development. (Butake 36–37)

Father Leo, the Catholic priest, is very confident that the women cannot be a bigger threat than Kwifon. The Fon, with the connivance of Father Leo, succeeds in getting the government to ban Kwifon. Also, through the influence of Father Leo, the Fon has refused to be part of any non-Christian activities sanctioned by Kwifon. It is thus with confidence that Father Leo reassures the Fon that:

> most of women in the village are good Christians. They have seen the good things that the church has brought. Even their men are more concerned about drinking palm-wine than eating foo-foo. They want their sons to have the kind of education their Fon has had. They see the happy

change that education can bring into their lives. Many of them even own cattle; and are interested in making money. (Butake 37)

Father Leo certainly gets it all wrong because the men who know their women better are taking the women's revolt seriously. The men believe that the Fon is to blame because he is being stubborn and not sensitive to the needs of his people. The men understand the psyche of their women and the inherent problems that the crop shortage and the absence of the annual sacrifice would do to their collective wellbeing in a way that Father Leo does not seem to comprehend. As Juliana Nfah-Abbenyi reiterates:

> It is the coming together of traditional/local ways of knowing and modern science/technologies that can best guarantee a productive but protected environment in Africa and third-world countries where the drive toward modernization and so called " progress and civilization" is pushing the limits of environmental degradation and the survival of its people. Their survival will continue to hang in a balance unless "progress and civilization" also means learning to aggressively combine local and exogenous ways of knowing. (710)

It is because the men of this village are imbued with the "local ways of knowing" that they come to the realization that they must find a way to reinstate the power of Kwifon so Kwifon can take control of the land and they can, in turn, take control of their households. The men need the chief priest, Shey Bonyo, who is the head of the Kwifon to lead, but Shey Bonyo has been declared a madman by the Catholic priest, Father Leo, and as such the Fon considers him *persona non-grata*.

While the men are strategizing how to defy the Kwifon's ban and get it to act, Shey Bonyo, the chief priest of the Lake God, is dealing with another problem—the lake which seems to be boiling and threatening to overflow its banks. The lake is central to the village in many ways including being the residence of the Lake God, the main deity of the people here. The Fon is supposed to lead a yearly sacrifice to appease the Lake God, but he claims he is a Christian Fon and will do no such thing. Despite the entreaties of the priest of the Lake God, the Fon does not budge and the priest is instead severely beaten by the Fon's guards. Six years before, the lake had disappeared and when the Fon refused to perform the annual sacrifice, Kwifon intervened. Because of Kwifon's intervention, the Fon reported Kwifon to the government authorities who, in turn, banned their activities.

The two environmental problems facing this village come together because in order to solve the problem of depleting corn harvests caused by mixed farming and the problems of a temperamental lake, Kwifon needs to act. Consequently, the seven pillars of the Kwifon defy the government ban, and get together and visit the Fon to force him to take action. They put the problem clearly to the Fon:

> There is trouble in the land
> The cattle are destroying farms
> The women are starving their husbands
> The Fon must do something. (Butake 42)

The Fon is certainly aware of the environmental problems that are responsible for the crisis, but he believes he has the situation under control. Thus, he argues:

> The land is for both cattle and crops. I have designated farmlands and separated them from grazing lands. If you allow your women to encroach on grazing land, the cattle rearers cannot take responsibility for anything. As for the starvation, you don't expect the Fon to run your homes for you. If you allow your women to starve you, that is entirely your responsibility. If there is nothing else you may now leave. (Butake 42)

What the Fon fails to acknowledge is that by making the land totally accessible to the Bororos, he has reduced the farmland the women have been accustomed to, and as such, he is continuously reducing their harvest with each piece of land he sells to the cattle rearers. He also has not come to terms with the basic principles through which the farmers can benefit directly from cattle rearing, thereby both the cattle rearers and corn farmers can happily cohabit side by side, consequently establishing a kind of symbiotic relationship between the duo. However, the most pressing problem facing the village seems to be that presented by the lake. Once again, the Kwifons state it clearly to the Fon:

> The lake God is angry
> The waters have been boiling for four days . . .
> We heard noise of thunder
> Coming from the depths of the lake. (Butake 43)

What the Kwifon wants at this time is for the Fon to lead the people in sacrifice to the lake God. The Fon equivocally states that he does not "participate in heathen sacrifice" (Butake 44) and threatens the Kwifon with police and death by firing squad. Kwifon leaves the Fon's presence in anger.

Since he will not lead the sacrifice to the Lake God, they plan to give him as the ultimate sacrifice to the Lake God. His wife rushes to Father Leo to inform him. On their way to the lake, there is an explosion from the lake, which kills the sacrificial train and everybody else in the village, including animals, but spares the chief priest, a man, a woman, a boy, and a girl.

Most critics who have concentrated on the mytho-poetic explanation of the Lake Nyos disaster in Lake God have missed the environmental problems that are central to this play and propel the plot. The play does not offer solutions on how the villagers can find a common ground in mixed farming or how to deal with a lake that seems to have carbon monoxide trapped at the bottom, but Butake shows that these are problems this community must face to live harmoniously in their land. In the postmortem provided by the survivors, a woman explains the source of the disaster succinctly. She holds:

> He [the Fon) sold the land to strangers
> And made alliance with rearers of cattle
> Which destroyed crops causing famine
> And suffering the people had never known
> He rejected tradition and denied the women a good yield even though
> They clamoured for a queen and the lake sacrifice
> And now this. (Butake 53)

Even though Butake does not provide a solution here, he continues, however, with the environmental problems that plague the survivors of this Lake disaster in his next play, *The Survivors*.

The Survivors has often been dubbed a revolutionary play castigating the kleptomania of a despotic regime, which shamelessly pillages relief supplies destined for the survivors of a natural disaster. The play drew a lot of attention when it was first performed in 1989. Coming three years after the lake Nyos disaster, many Cameroonians recognized the corrupt practices of the ruling government fictionalized in the play. As the lead character in the first cast, this writer is aware of the reception of the play by critics and theater goers. What most of them failed to notice at the time and even today, two decades after the publication of the play, is that Butake once more centers his plot on two environmental issues: pollution and the need to eat fresh healthy foods grown naturally.

The play opens with a radio announcement of a major disaster, which has occurred in a mountainous region leaving several people dead. The announcement assures the people that the government is sending military personnel and relief materials to the afflicted region. *The Survivors* has been labeled a sequel to *Lake God* because it seems to begin where *Lake God* leaves off. At the end of *Lake God*, there are five survivors of the environmental disaster: Shey Mbonyo, a woman, a man, a girl, and a boy who morph into Old One, Mboysi, Ngujoh, Bolame, and Tata in *The Survivors*. The famine and hunger which precedes the lake disaster takes a turn for the worse in this play.

The play opens with "complete darkness on stage, now and again broken by eerie sounds of owls and other night birds" (Butake 60). This macabre atmosphere completes the desolate picture of the five survivors who enter the stage chanting a dirge and dressed in rags, "giving the impression of extreme agony and desperation" (Butake 60). The major crisis facing the survivors is that there is absolutely nothing to eat and there is no clean water to drink. The desolate environment cannot nurture them and they seem to be trapped in this wasteland contoured with the potholes of a natural disaster. As they try to leave for a neighboring village, Ewawa, a menacing voice stops them with the words "Don't move! Don't move! Halt" (Butake 60). As Hilarious Ambe notes:

> The tactics of the voice in this opening scene is to terrorise and cow the already traumatised characters into a position of total submission. To go about this, the voice usurps space and speech and imposes its "regles du jeu"; and there is therefore, no room for talking or negotiations. This is the beginning of the putting in place of the machinery that would ensure total control. (71)

This confirms Old One's assertion that they are trapped and "there's no going forward. And there's no turning back. We are caught in the web of a spider. (63)

The survivors are now prisoners quarantined on a wasteland. Despite being destitute, the survivors are energized by the human will to survive. The children crave for water and food, and Mboysi cannot watch them waste to death after surviving the disaster. The survival of the children is tantamount to the survival of the future generation. When Mboysi decides to go see the person behind the voice to negotiate their freedom, she is made aware of another potential environmental hazard. The area may be contaminated. The officer will not let her into his space without spraying a disinfectant on her body. When she questions him on his action, he states "One must take precaution, you know. This area is dangerous and has been sealed off" (Butake 73). One would expect the government to evacuate the survivors if the area is supposed to be dangerous; instead, the Military officer is holding the survivors hostage for what he calls his "survival." He makes it clear that their presence on the desolate land guarantees the continuous donation of relief supplies; also, he does not reveal the fact that there are only five survivors. Like Fon Joseph in *Lake God*, the officer undermines the concerns of those he is supposed to protect. In contrast to the austerity of the survivors, the stage direction reveals that the military officer is living in comfort:

> A tent lavishly set with piles upon piles of cartons and sacks in the background. A well-fed man in mufti is sitting at a table ticking off items of relief supplies. There is a bottle of whiskey from which he serves himself generously from time to time. He is also munching all the time. There is a revolver placed prominently on the table. (Butake 71)

Mboysi confirms this when, after her visit to the Officer, she reports that "[e]ach time he calls me to his house, I see piles upon piles of cargo and cartons and sacks and all sorts of things" (Butake 77). Although the officer eventually gives Mboysi food and water for the survivors, the kind of food comes under sharp attack by the playwright. The food is not only unhealthy, but it is one they are not accustomed to. Officer gives them bottled water, biscuits, and other packaged Westernized food. What he does not realize is that human beings get acclimated to their fauna and flora. The survivors cannot survive on these kinds of food:

> While the children seem to settle for these things, the old man refuses them vehemently. Ngujoh on the other hand manages to eat them for survival but as he explains to Old One, "Do you think I eat because I like the food? No. I don't like it. I don't like what she brings to us from officer. Cold food that has no taste. Food that is cold on the tongue and never makes your belly warm and heavy. Food without foo-foo and vegetables and meat. Cold fish removed from a ngong-ngong that makes your intestines wriggle like earth-worms. You call that food? (Butake)

Ngujoh's comments open up the debate between fresh food and processed food. He craves common corn used to make fufu and eaten with vegetables. Fresh food does not only possess more flavor, it is healthier than canned foods since foods lose valuable nutrients when they are processed. Old One also complains of water in a plastic bottle. He prefers water in a calabash. Again, this brings up another heated environmental debate: whether bottled water is better than ordinary water. At the end Mboysi realizes that they have a choice to die fighting for their freedom or they may die as prisoners of the Officer. She uses the Officer's lust for her to trick him to hand over his gun, which she uses to kill him. Although Mboysi is later killed by another officer who appears on the scene, one hopes that the survivors will be allowed to leave the polluted area to go to Ewawa where they will not only breathe clean air but they can once more feed on common corn which can nourish both their body and soul.

Additionally, Butake's *And Palm-Wine Will Flow* seems to follow on the heels of *The Survivors*. The third play is set in the kingdom of Ewawa, the desired destination of the survivors in the previous play. In fact, their dialogue provides a snapshot of what seems to be a utopia:

> Ngujoh: We will get to Ewawa before the sun goes down
> Tata: Songs and children in the village square
> Mboysi: smiling faces! Open arms and music and dance
> Bolame: laughter and food
> Ngujoh: foo-foo, roast chicken and palm wine
> Oldone: I am looking forward to a very decent meal. My mouth waters at the mere thought. Foo-foo, roast chicken in palm oil and pepper, and palm wine! (Butake 68–69)

This image of a village paradise does not come true in the Ewawa of *And Palm-Wine Will Flow*. While *Lake God* and *Survivors* seem to dwell on problems dealing with lack of food and an environment turned into a wasteland, *And Palm-Wine Will Flow* shows a Fon who wastes the resources of his people in debauchery. The play is set in the fondom of Ewawa. The fondom is in the grips of a Fon and his council of elders who revel in corruption and alcoholism. Their activities have alienated Shey Ngong, the spiritual leader of the Fondom. The play, written in one movement, begins and ends at the grove of Shey Ngong where he performs rituals on behalf of the people of Ewawa. The play opens with Shey Ngong performing an incantation but he is interrupted by a voice that tells him everyone in the village is heading toward the palace to witness Kibanya's red feather ceremony, and as usual, there will be a big celebration afterwards and palm wine will flow. The Fon has abused the traditional feather reserved for heroes of the clan by giving it to the highest bidder. Shey Ngong is exasperated with the corruption, drunkenness, and greed that have pervaded the fondom, so he refuses to join what he sees as the madness of the Fon. He tells the voice "my obligation is to the gods of the land. My duty is to the gods. Not the Fon and the palm wine . . . the gorilla can do nothing to the Iroko tree" (Butake 88).

Exasperated by Shey's refusal to join the celebration, the Fon seizes farmlands from Shey's wives and gives them to Kibanya's wives. As one of the Fon's messengers comes to announce the Fon's pronouncement to Shey, the Earth Goddess mask in the grove is animated and pronounces the coming of a drought, "the sun shines on hills / the sun shines in the valleys / the sun shines in the depths of the streams / the sun shines" (Butake 94). Shey asks the messenger to take Earth Goddess's message back to the Fon. Events reach a climax in Ewawa when the Fon's watchdogs beat Nsangong, a respectable elder of the fondom, because he is Shey's friend. The people abandon their usual drinking spree at the Fon's palace in protest over this beating. To cleanse the land from these excesses, the Kibaranko goes on a cleansing mission to rid the land of all evil forces, including the Fon. He unleashes destruction as he heads for the palace, but by the time he gets there, the Fon is dragged into a room and the Kibaranko splits the Fon's throne in two, a symbol of the annihilation of the Fon. The Earth Goddess finally curses the Fon and he dies. The people now vow that they do not want a Fon anymore; power should not be in the hands of one man but given to a council of elders. However, all the people are summoned to the marketplace to discuss the best way to govern the Fondom. Butake combines Western theatrical idioms and different modes of orature-masks, incantation, and proverbs from his Noni tradition to establish his dramatic vision. Consequently, the natural and supernatural live in one continuum of reality. He broadens the scope of his characters by exploiting spirit possession. According to Firth, "Sprit possession is a form of trance in which the actions of a person are interpreted as evidence of control of his behaviour by a spirit normally external to him" (qtd. in Alembong 130). Invariably, Kwengong is both the Earth Goddess and Shey's first wife. The Tapper also doubles up as Kibarankor. As Bate Besong observes, "without coming to terms with Butake's syncretic imagination using traditional Noni mythic pattern in an otherwise realistic mode, and how it influences his art, it is impossible to apprehend his potential as an Anglophone Cameroon artist" ("Ontogenesis"; 7). Nevertheless, what also becomes clear in the analysis of this play is that Butake once more casts the problems of this village in environmental terms. His use of proverbs does not only establish the conflict in the play, they also reveal the people's identification with the totality of their landscape and, as Gerald Moore puts it, "explore their own existence in its terms." For example, the following set of proverbs pit the Fon against the Shey:

> The cockroach does not call a fowl to a wrestling match. (Moore 88)
> The gorilla can do nothing to the iroko tree. (Moore 88)
> The stream never flows uphill. The leopard and the goat have never been bed fellows. (Moore 14)
> The rat does not play with the Cat. (Moore 93)

Butake's strongest eco-criticism of the Fon, however, is his wanton cutting down of palm trees for palm wine. The Fon has reduced Ewawa to a veiled police state and dictatorship. He has subverted the rules of the land, which are based on meritocracy and the equal sharing of power. He disregards tradition by selling titles and positions in the council of elders to the highest bidders. By so doing, the Fon has succeeded to surround himself with fawning stooges like Gwei, Mformi Nyam, and Mformi Eleme, who do as he pleases. The loyalty of this group of "yes-men" is easily secured by continuous feasting and drinking of palm wine. What the Fon does not seem to realize is the adverse effect that his excesses can have on the land as a whole. It is not a coincidence that the plot reaches a crisis point when the Fon oversteps his own notoriety by seizing the palm bush. As the tapper reports to Shey Ngong, "The Fon has seized the palm-bush. His watch-dogs are there now. Getting drunk on the wine I tapped" (Butake 98). But these drunkards do not end in the palm bush. As Tapper further narrates,

> I found them in my hut, where I store palm-wine. They were already drunk. And they had finished a whole pot of wine which I tapped yesterday. When I asked them what they wanted, they laughed and said the palm bush has reverted to the Fon, its rightful owner. (Butake 99)

It is from this kind of frivolities that Shey Ngong, the priest of Nyombom, distances himself right from the beginning of the play. Even after the Fon seizes his lands and gives it to Kibanya's wives, Shey refuses to "pay respect to a man who respects only palm-wine and food" (Butake 97). However, the real crisis comes when the Earth Goddess pronounces the coming of a drought. Environmentalists will easily make the connection between the coming drought and the excessive cutting down of palm trees for palm wine. By felling down the palm trees at a continuous rate, the Fon has exposed the land adversely. Trees are known to absorb and store large amounts of water quickly during rainfall. Thus, when trees are cut, it disrupts the natural cycle of water flow, which in turn can lead to droughts or floods. Butake makes this connection earlier in *The Survivors* when Tata is thirsty and wants to go look for water. He explains, "But we can go down to the valley where there are palm bushes. Where I see palm bushes, there must be water" (Butake 62). Butake is therefore aware that the excessive cutting of palm trees will lead to dryness. Thus the pronouncement of drought by the Earth Goddess is not just a superstitious tradition, but it is ecologically logical. The only way to stop this destructive trend is to get the Fon out of the way. It is the job of the Earth Goddess to cleanse the land and rid it of any destructive tendencies that threaten the collective survival of Ewawa. Her fatal spell on the Fon is swift and needed:

> Die and deliver the land from the
> Abominations of drunkenness and gluttony
> (The Fon begins to reel until he collapses)
> Die! Chila Kintasi, die!
> And save the land from merry-making
> Die Fon! So we may think
> The people need your death to think
> Die! Die! Die!
> (The Fon lies still. Lights fade out). (Butake 110)

Although the Earth-goddess pronounces the spell, it is the masked spirit, Kibranko, who completes the annihilation of the Fon by symbolically breaking all pots and calabashes in the Fon's courtyard, breaks the Fon's throne into two, and sets the palace ablaze.

Eckhard Breitinger insightfully argues that "the thematic points of departure for most of Butake's plays are taken from current political issues . . . But the issues in which Bole Butake is really interested in go beyond pure topicality. The overall concern that can be traced in all his plays is "good governance" (9). I think Breitinger makes a valid point and one could add that Butake's plays show that he sees the "good governance" of the environment as pivotal to the collective survival of any community of people. He seems to advocate that where the leader undermines environmental factors that threaten the lives of members of the community as in *Lake God*, *The Survivors*, and *And Palm-Wine Will Flow*, the people must do whatever it takes to address the situation, because it is a matter of life and death.

Works Cited

Alembong, Nol. "Oral Traditions in the Literary Imagination: The case of Spirit Possession in Bole Butakes's *And Palm-Wine Will Flow*." Anglophone Cameroon Writings. Eds. Iyonga, Nalova, Bole Butake, Eckhard Breitinger. Bayreuth: U of Bayreuth, 1993. 76-83.

Ambe N. Hilarious. Change Aesthetics in Anglophone Cameroon Drama and Theater. Bayreuth: Pia Thielman/Eckhard Breitinger, 2007.

Besong, Bate. "Politics and Historicity in Anglophone Cameroon Drama." Diss. U of Calabar, 1996.

Breitinger, Eckhard. "Bole Butake's Strategies as a political Playwright." *African Theater: Playwrights & Politics*. Ed. Martin Banham, James Gibbs, and Femi Osofisan. London: James Curry, 2001.

Butake, Bole. *Lake God and Other Plays*. Yaounde: Edition Cle, 1999. (All quotations from *Lake God, The Survivors*, and *And Palm-Wine Will Flow* are from this text.)

Moore, Gerald. The Negro Poet and His Landscape. *Introduction to African Literature*. London: Longman, 1979.

Nfah-Abbenyi, Makuchi, Juliana. "Ecological Postcolonialism in African Women's Literature." *African Literature: An Anthology of Criticism and Theory*. Ed. Tejumola Olaniyen and Ato Quayson. Malden: Blackwell, 2007.

Ngongkum, Eunice. "Drama and Revolutionary Vision: Bate Besong's *Beasts of No Nation* and Bole Butake's *Lake God*." Lagos Papers in English Studies Vol. 2, (2007): 238–251.

18

Destabilizing the Images of the African Forest As a Conceptual Space for Renegotiating African Identities during the Zimbabwe Armed Liberation Struggle in the Film *Flame* (1996)

Urther Rwafa, Midlands State University, Zimbabwe

Introduction

In Africa, approaches to the appreciation of the ecosystem abound. Most of the approaches emphasize the urgency for the conservation of the environment. Numerous reasons could be adduced for the need to preserve the African environment. In the past, scholarships emphasized the fact that with the coming of colonialism, African people were displaced from their ancestral lands and trapped in areas that were not self-sustaining. The consequences of this displacement without permanent movement is what is responsible for the desertification or disappearance of what was left in the form of "sacred groves" needed to be preserved. Celia Nyamweru and Michael Sheridan suggest that "this relic theory based on the outdated notions of tropical ecology and African societies as static is now superseded by new approaches that emphasize that African ecosystems and social systems are dynamic at different temporal and spatial scales" (1). African conservationists have described, in different ways, negative dynamics occurring within the African environment that call for efforts at intervening and conserving the natural ecology. For example, "tropical deforestation" (Sheridan 9), and uncontrolled fires are held responsible for much destruction of African ecosystems. Aiah Lebbie and Raymond Guries add that communities' exploitation of African ecosystem for medicine has also contributed to the degradation of the environment and this resulted in the disturbance of the biodiversity of ecosystems (47). Nyamweru, Kibet, and Cooke view climate changes as exerting physical influences and changes on the African environment (64). Apart from climatic fluctuations or instability, Africans residing in the African continent also contribute to the destruction of the ecosystem through their engagements in uncontrolled cutting down of trees for purposes of building poles and firewood (Nyamweru, Kibet, and Cooke).

These threats to African biodiversity continue to revive interests in eco-conservation. Wily's study (2008) reveals how in sub-Saharan Africa, governments enact laws in order to conserve African forests. In addition to introducing laws to protect forests, African communities link religion to ecology (Deil, Culmsee, and Berriane) in order to highlight the need to preserve sacred groves that "mark grave sites of political or spiritual leaders [and] others that comprise archetypal forests from which social groups' first ancestors are said to have emerged" (Berhane-Selassie 105). Whether it is a religious, legal, or humanistic approach to the conservation of African forests, all these pragmatic approaches have one thing in common: they seek to address the question of putting in place recognizable policies of environmental management so as to help African societies realize economic benefits for their peoples.

However, African forests have also been appreciated for their spiritual and symbolic values offered to rural African communities. African forests and groves are also valued because of the political implications as power-laden landscape features related to "social dynamics and historical contexts" (Nyamweru and Sheridan 1). In fact, besides balancing biodiversity and satisfying certain material human wants, African forests command symbolical meanings associated with how they can be assigned meanings that transform them into conceptual spaces for the renegotiation of African identities. Like Sheridan asserts, the shift in viewing African forests as just physical entities called the African bush toward projecting forests as symbolic spaces introduces ambiguities in the meanings that African forests and their ancillary environs can engender. These new associations of forests with symbols and metaphors

> describe ecosystems as ongoing mosaics of processes (rather than endpoints) within the new paradigm [which] includes resistance (the degree to which an ecosystem absorbs disturbance without change), resilience (the rate of recovery to a former state), persistence (the period over which a given state exists), variability (the degree of change over time), sensitivity (the relative vulnerability of particular variables to change), and surprise (unexpected, stochastic, and nonlinear causation). (Sheridan 17)

The capacity of African forests to symbolize something else other than their natural self has been seized upon by creative and literary artists in Africa. In the African literary works of art, African environments that include the forests are imbued with meanings that become a commentary on the dynamics of power struggles and identity (re)formations and constructions in African communities during colonialism and postcolonial period.

The Representation of Forests in African Literature

In African arts, the image of the African forest, for example, suggests or commands not one, but several meanings. Ato Quayson, commenting on the portrayal of the African forest or bush in Nigerian literature, remarks that "the bush is the antithesis of settled communities and is conceived of as the problematic 'Other' harboring all sorts of supernatural forces" (46). An example of the ambiguity that is alluded to here is taken from Achebe's novel *Things Fall Apart*, which depicts the evil forest as a space of destruction of human identities. The evil forest is depicted as the abode of negative spirits into which societal abominations such as the birth of twins and individuals with other abominable ailments in nineteenth-century Igbo societies were abandoned to die or killed by the clan for fear of bringing misfortune into the community. At the same time, the same evil forest becomes the space where white missionaries or Western evangelizers settle and build their churches that would eventually pose a challenge to the Igbo way of life. In *Mayombe*, the African forest not only camouflages the freedom fighters that are contesting Portuguese imperialism and enable the freedom fighters to execute a successful war, it equally provides the contesting ideological expressions of freedom fighters to manifest. In Zimbabwe, the Zimbabwe African National Liberation Army (ZANLA) used the spaces of the rivers and mountains within the African forest as shields from Rhodesian forces (Samupindi). In some popular songs from Zimbabwe, the forest is a liminal space where identities are reconstituted and reconstructed. Thus, the forest performs the function of cover to fighters and at the same time the forest harbors lions that devour some of the freedom fighters (Vambe).

In some Shona folktales of Zimbabwe, the forest is depicted as a space providing game for hunters, but the same forest contains or is thought to harbor supernatural forces believed to cause harm to those who traverse it, so the capacity of humanity to overcome the adversities encountered in the African forest defines the hunters or fighters' heroism. In the film *Flame,* which offers this chapter its textual moorings, the significations associated with the images of Rhodesian and Mozambican forests that provided cover to the freedom fighters during Zimbabwe's armed struggle (1975–1979) embody a range of identities akin to a symbolical movement described by Northrop Frye as an "escape, remembrance, the discovery of one's real identity, growing freedom and the breaking of enchantment" (129).

Flame, the African Forests, and the Forging of Contradictory African Identities

Flame narrates the story of two girls, Nyasha and Florence, growing up in colonial Rhodesia in the late 1970s, and their resolve to join the liberation struggle and the subsequent betrayal of their goals by the nationalist leadership that reimposed patriarchal definitions on women after the war. This summary of the film hardly explains why the launching of the film in 1996 met with resistance from some sections of the Zimbabwean population. *Flame* encountered its public life in a controversial way. Its producer, Ingrid Sinclair, aimed to produce a film that would reveal the seamy side of Zimbabwe liberation struggle-cum-war, foregrounding the rape of women as cardinal to the plot structure of the film, which symbolically tends to "overthrow" the regimes of heroic images that the armed struggle had entrenched. Some ex-combatants, mainly from the ZANLA wing, staged a demonstration against what they perceived as the film's spectacular representation of excessive violence committed on female guerillas by male guerillas. The ZANU PF government felt uneasy with sections of the film that underplayed the representation of heroic aspects of the struggle. Objections to *Flame* also focused on the content of the film defined in racial and gendered power relations. However, what is often underplayed in appreciating the film is the role that the African environment played in forming the geographical background against which the themes of power struggles within the larger liberation struggles were played out. The geography of the film is both the physical forests as well as the complicated labyrinths of ideas based on culture that can also be used to describe forests as spiritual environments that humans have to negotiate in order to realize different aspects of their potential identities.

Interestingly therefore, in reexamining *Flame*, the essay articulates the images of the African forests and how they are associated in the psyche of an African audience as conceptual spaces for rethinking African identities. To give the chapter its desired conceptual bearings, I enter several caveats. The first one is that, although the film *Flame* employs numerous flashbacks and foreshadowings in the verbal and visual narratives, it is important to reconstruct a linear narrative journey of the freedom fighters from the geographical environment of Rhodesia, its forests that the sons and daughters of the land traveled, the rivers they crossed, and the places in the forests of Mozambique they used as bases for training, and to retrace the journey back into Zimbabwe as blacks returned home as trained guerrillas committed to wage a war of liberation under the cover of the camouflage provided by the bush. In order to reproduce an approximate mental picture of the different meanings of "forests" the film depicts, the article shall reconstruct and divide the movement of the film into four segments. The first is "Colonialism as forest" that produces stressful African identities; the second is "Traversing the physical forests of Zimbabwe" in which Florence and Nyasha, the two female characters, face trials and tribulations as they cross into Mozambique to be recruited and trained as freedom fighters. The third movement of the film is "Surviving the forests of Mozambique and the battlefields of Zimbabwe" in which, after completing training, Florence (now Comrade Flame) and Nyasha (now Comrade Liberty) engage the Rhodesian security forces. The fourth movement of the film is the "Return to Zimbabwe and Betrayal" in which the female comrades feel isolated from a predominantly male leadership that continues to arrogantly explore and access the fruits of independence.

The second caveat is that none of the themes explored in the film narrative movement related to the African forests can be discussed outside the frame of power relations implicated in the changing African identities between men and women who abandoned traditional roles and embraced new ones. Furthermore, the visual language of the film also enables one to explore the role of the physical geography of the African forests and other forms of "nature, religion, magic and politics [that] cushioned the course and effects of the forests" (Musiyiwa 65) on the military strategies and psychological fears of the guerrillas. In order to come to terms with the role of the African forest as a conceptual space for recreating new identities for Zimbabwean men and women who enlisted in the struggle, one also has to pay attention to the styles or techniques such as realism, popular songs, and visual pictures that the film harnesses as narrative.

"Colonialism as Forest": Reproducing Inferior Identities of Women in *Flame*

Flame is set around 1975 in Rhodesia when the war of the liberation of African people was intensifying. In narrative terms, *Flame* begins with cut-up pictures of the Pioneer Column crossing of the Limpopo River, marking the formal colonization of Zimbabwe. The lens then shifts, capturing rural Zimbabwe in the late 1970s when colonial discriminatory policies had divided Zimbabwe into black and white areas. In the black rural reserves, one easily notices the problem of overcrowding; the physical forest is receding from the settled communities because the rural communities have cut down trees for use as firewood. In her state of childhood reminiscences, Florence, who appears on the screen with her friend Nyasha, remarks that she thought that this situation "appeared normal." What has been normalized by colonialism are the inequities in the access and distribution of resources. Below the hierarchy of African men, who are also oppressed by colonialism, are African women whose mental worlds is implicitly described as a spiritual forest in which the main preoccupation were to bear children, till the exhausted land, and not to be encouraged to aspire to another alternative life beyond the kitchen. The colonial world is also a patriarchal one in which African men roam like lions, ready to pounce on young girls. Even when it is indicated in the film that this is all happening during the middle of the war, when the armed freedom fighters living in the mountains request food from villagers, it is the women who cook that food, act as couriers, and have to kneel when giving the food to the male comrades.

Within the narrative, the representation of the armed struggle in the early phase of the film, women's age-old roles as bearers of children are foregrounded. In the group of freedom fighters that the women feed, there is not yet even a single female freedom fighter, a fact that underscores the gendered roles of Africans during the struggle. In the cover of the dark and the thick forest at the night vigil or *Pungwe*, male comrades teach female peasants the goals of the war as if to confirm that women have a low level of consciousness about the necessity of the struggle. Women are simply excluded from active fighting, as they are marginalized into roles that do not rupture the patriarchal ideology informing the liberation struggle. Both women and men are under subjection under brutal colonial conditions. However, the toll is heavier on the woman. Colonialism is therefore depicted as an "ideological forest" or space for dramatizing power and powerlessness in which the marginalized roles of women are entrenched. African male freedom fighters consummate this perception of women as inferior, not only by asking them to be couriers, but also by viewing young girls as sexual objects. Cultural attitudes of African males are therefore also presented as a "forest" or conceptual space African women have to renegotiate in other to realize some alternative selves of black womanhood.

Traversing the Physical Forests of Zimbabwe in *Flame*

In the narrative movement of the film, Florence decides to go Mozambique to train as a freedom fighter because her father was killed by the white soldiers. The journey to Mozambique through the dangerous physical forests of Zimbabwe is depicted graphically in the film. Together with Nyasha, Florence goes through difficult trials and tribulations. The two girls cross rivers, the habitat of crocodiles, walk on beaten pathways with thorns, sleep under rocks, and plod through the forest lianas, while hiding from white soldiers patrolling the bush. Florence remarks that at first she was "frightened of the bush," but she later realizes that the African forest was the best friend of the comrades-at-arms. The forest provides camouflage from the pain they endure from the relative "security" of home where parents insist on promoting the observance of traditional roles of women as mothers, sisters, wives, and prostitutes (Gaidzanwa 40) The movement into the forest signifies for the two girls a journey into the unknown world, depicted in the film as signifying a break from the confined village consciousness. The journey into the African bush also underscores their isolation, and implies some form of spiritual dislocation. Not always aware of the directions that they took in the forest, Nyasha and Florence experience momentary "individual loss, or confusion or break in the continuity of identity" (Frye 104). Movement from home into the perilous African forest also symbolizes a descent from "this world into a lower one" (Frye 129). However, with all its frightening specters of wild animals, Rhodesian soldiers, and snakes waiting to strike, the move into the deep of the African forest ironically symbolizes for the girls a physical as well as spiritual threshold crossing.

Their traversing of the African forests imitates the mytho-poetic Shona folktale of Jikinya in which a young girl is lured into a forest by the sound of the drumbeat, only to realize that she has put herself into the jaws of wild animals. In the folktale, the young girl cheats her way out of danger by singing to the wild animals until they all fall asleep, and then she takes this chance to run back home to the communal fold. In *Flame*, Florence and Nyasha brave the lonely nights and the hazardous fords; in the process, their awareness of the need to liberate their country from colonial rule grows and emboldens them to continue with their journey to Mozambique. Their identities as mere village girls waiting for men to come and marry them transforms as they see themselves as prospective guerrillas. Therefore, for the two girls, the African forest re-configures or is a space upon which they redefine their identities. The ascent from the 'lower' world of the African forest marks a spiritual "remembrance, the discovery of one's real identity, growing freedom and the breaking of enchantment"(35) for the two girls who cross into Mozambique escaping from imprisonment by colonial policies at home, and the confining strictures of the phalocentricism of the African tradition.

The deliberate "loss" into the African forest is the condition of possibility for the generation of a new "national" consciousness in which the problems of women in a colonial context are seen as broad and requiring a broader confrontation with the ideological challenges posed by colonialism, African patriarchy, and also the need to overcome a personal sense of lack of confidence experienced by women subjected to oppression over many years. In short, for Florence and Nyasha, the very ability to traverse the African forest in pursuit of a higher goal makes the space outside the village a liminal one of pain and endurance as well as a space of "becoming and assuming double identities: one of vulnerability and the other that affirms the desire to engage the subterranean spiritual resources available in one's culture in order to strike back at the source of the threat to individual and community well-being" (Vambe 34).

Battlefields, Haunted Spaces, and Survival Strategies in *Flame*

In *Flame*, when Nyasha and Florence reach the ZANLA training base in Mozambique, their journey also affords them the opportunity to appropriate the concept of heroism found outside the narrow confines of the village. In Mozambique, Nyasha and Florence find out that there are also black women who have committed their lives to the struggle alongside their male counterparts to realize the freedom of Zimbabwe. But the military and training base in Mozambique that is controlled by male guerrillas is also depicted as a forested space with its own dynamics. Here, at the base, some female combatants have acquired not only new war names, their attitude toward life has become self-assertive and the female guerrillas feel free to articulate their vision of life. Others still view themselves as the underdogs of male guerillas. Furthermore in Mozambique, Nyasha and Florence have to overcome their surprise when they see that female guerillas trained just like their male counterparts. Most female guerillas wore trousers. In one instance, Nyasha says to Florence: "your father would have beaten you for wearing those." This statement is a clear indication that women have been socialized to think that they cannot express their freedom just like men. Nonetheless, the war front in the African forest opened up possibilities for change in female guerillas' identities. The irony is that the same war threatened to equalize and sometimes even closed up other *spaces* that were strictly reserved for men. For example, in the film, the rank of commanders of a battalion was usually reserved for a male guerilla.

During their first training session, Florence and Nyasha realize that to become a committed guerrilla, self-discipline is fundamental. Self-discipline was particularly important because it ensured the safety of individual guerillas as well as the safety of the whole group. As the women do drills, they sing:

Simudza gumbo	[Lift your leg]
Hau	[Hau]
Ndere musangano	[It belongs to the party]
Hau	[Hau]
Kana rikatyoka	[If it gets broken]
Hau	[Hau]
Ndere musangano	[It belongs to the party].

In the above song, the words *Ndere musangano* places the political party above the individual. In its pervasive form, the reference of the women's leg in the song as belonging to the party, *Ndere musangano* is the discourse of erasure (Handrinath) that dissolves any feeling of individualism a guerilla might harbor. The objectification of the female body by male guerrillas enforced traditional roles of women as sexual objects that the war was beginning to allow African girls to question. In *Flame*, the Mozambican forests provide cover to guerrillas from napalm used by Rhodesian soldiers. The irony is that the same African bush is used by male guerrillas to perpetuate inequalities between African men and women. In the film, the African forest paradoxically becomes the background for sexual molestation of African women. For example, when Comrade Che declares his love for Comrade Flame, Che—the male guerrilla—does not wait or allow Flame to voice her consent; he pounces on her in an act of rape that violates the sanctity of the female guerrilla and undermines the pretension of the nationalist discourse of freedom authored by male guerrillas. The sequence of this rape scene is brought to the fore when Comrade Che, who committed the inhuman act of rape, faces the ugly reality of his folly. Although Comrade Che apologizes by saying that "War changes everything. Sometimes we forget that we are human beings. I'm sorry for what I did," the act is actually geared to extinguish the self-esteem of the woman. But if one considers the commitment and respect for one another embodied in the song *Chirenje*, the behavior of comrade Che is put to test. In *Chirenje*, Zimbabwe is not for sale nor does it belong to rapists of the likes of comrade Che. The lyrics are captivating in their message:

Baba Chirenje	[Father of Chirenje]
Chirenje	[Chirenje]
Ukatamba neZimbabwe yanguwo	[If you play around with my Zimbabwe]
Ndinokuchekaka nebanga	[I will cut you into pieces with a knife]
Baba Chirenje	[Father of Chirenje]

Although Comrade Che plays with Comrade Flame's body, he is not punished by ZANU leaders. The result of this nonconsensual sexual encounter is Hondo, a male child born in war and also consumed by the same war, together with his father Comrade Che. The rape scene in *Flame* remains the most controversial aspect of the film when it was first screened in Zimbabwe. The rape of women, let alone fathering children with women, was widespread in the war (Simbanegavi). Whether performed consensually or not, the act of procreation during war inadvertently stigmatizes the woman. She was looked down on as loose and dangerous by both men and fellow female guerrillas. In *Flame*, Comrade Flame is castigated by Comrade Liberty as a bitch that "sleeps with everyone who smiles at her." But Comrade Liberty (Nyasha) herself is also not spared the physical violence from male guerrillas. She receives a hard slap on her cheek after refusing sexual advances from a male guerilla. In other words, whether a woman was educated or not, at the training camps in the deep forests of Mozambique and later Zimbabwe, there were struggles within struggles; Africans fought white Rhodesians at the same time African males sought to keep the African female guerrillas as his underdog. For female guerrillas, the African forest and the journey to Zimbabwe's independence acquired dual or double and contradictory meanings. The forests were as much a space for elaborating a newfound identity of being a fighter for freedom for black women as much as it was also transformed into a space where male guerrillas constantly attempted to reimpose their will on their female guerrilla counterparts.

In the same forest, gender inequalities were maintained and this is shown in the film where *Flame* depicts women carrying both their guns and the huge, heavy boxes with ammunition on their heads, while men only had their guns to carry. This depiction in the film is reminiscent of the domestic roles that society imposes when it makes it appear natural that at home women must carry gallons of water from the well. In the struggle for Zimbabwe, deep in the country's jungle, male comrades lord it over women in an attempt to consciously or unconsciously reverse the equal identity between a man and a woman that the reality of war imposes on its African protagonists.

A further complication that reveals the differentiated roles that women played in the Zimbabwean forests during the armed struggle is manifested through the simmering class consciousness among female combatants, a fact that enacts a struggle within the nationalist struggle in Zimbabwe's liberation war. In *Flame*, for most of the time, female guerrillas such as Nyasha or Comrade Liberty were chosen to remain at the base to study, and "type" for male guerrilla commanders in exchange for sexual favors. Comrade Liberty proudly reminds her fellow comrade, Flame that "while I was studying, Flame became a legendary soldier. She was not afraid to confront the enemy and those who sold out to the Rhodesian forces." Flame's identity as a woman who takes revenge by burning Chiwara's shop because Mr. Chiwara sold her father to the Rhodesian forces who then killed him reinforces the different identities that women are forced to assume. Flame is not only sexually desecrated by one male guerrilla, Comrade Che, during the struggle, but she is eventually sent to the dangerous warfront where many female guerrillas like her perished. In other words, African women remember African forests differently. These differentiations based on the class structure reemerge after independence, a new context or metaphorical forest in which only a selected group of guerillas enjoy the fruits of victory at the expense of others. Lyons (1997) asserts that the pain that women endured during the war and how they are sidelined in postindependence Zimbabwe make some female ex-combatants shy away from telling stories of heroism during the struggle. This is one of the reasons why *Flame* focuses on the dynamics of female identities in the Zimbabwean war.

The Depiction of the Return to Zimbabwe and Betrayal in Postindependence Zimbabwe in *Flame*

The narrative power of *Flame* in representing female identities in the war of liberation is manifested in the way the director effects the metaphorical transference of the concept of a real bush or forest and transposes it to refer to the postindependence cityscape of Harare. This technique is poignant because it metaphorizes the forest, thereby imbuing it with symbolic delicateness. In this depiction of Harare as a different kind of a forest where it is easy to lose one's identity or bearing, what is emphasized is the betrayal of Comrade Flame, and most of the guerrillas with whom she fought the Rhodesian army in the physical forest of Zimbabwe during the liberation struggle. In the film, the male African commander of the guerillas who announces that "Macomrades the war is over" indicates to the guerrillas that the war is over; the irony is that the male commander is referring to the end of the bush war because for Flame, the war did not end when the guns went silent. The male commander sounds patronizing and insulting to the female guerrillas when he goes on to congratulate the women who fought in the bush, saying, "It is women like this [pointing to a female guerilla] who have won the war. Women have sheltered us. They fed us, and they died with us." It is true that women fought side by side with men in the forest. Men and women endured pain. However, the journey back home is one in which the film dramatizes the tensions and conflicts between male and female guerrillas that the informing ideology of the struggle did not resolve in the forests of Mozambique and Rhodesia.

The ritual that signifies that the war is really over is dramatized by Comrade Danger who goes to his home and as he gets to those who remained at home announces that he has brought with him a wife. This wife is depicted as Comrade Flame. Home, with its insistence on cultural observances, resembles the labyrinth of the natural forest that Flame had learnt to negotiate in order to survive the war. At home, patriarchy still expects that Flame must kneel down in front of her in-laws, as a gesture that consummate the reimposition of traditional roles associated with home, which for Flame has become a new "cultural forest." In this forest, even Comrade Danger, the former male guerrilla, assumes a position of superiority and will not accept the fact that the experiences of war have inaugurated new political awareness in the mind of Comrade Flame. When Flame tells Danger that she needs to go to the city to look for employment, Danger responds by slapping Flame as if to say to her that she cannot organize her life without consulting the male who has the privilege of allowing or disallowing her to go. After independence, female guerrillas are tamed and domesticated using age-old values that assumed that the experience of the liberation struggle was meant to dislodge the white men from power but leave the subordinate status of women intact. As Lyons puts it:

> ... when female combatants returned from the war they faced a society which did not welcome the freedoms they had known. Many women found it difficult to marry or stay married. At home they found men and in-laws ready to label them murderers or prostitutes, while their male comrades were deemed 'heroes'. They were seen as too tough, too liberated and not good enough to be wives. (1)

The experience of Flame in the rural geography of her in-law's home is depicted as one with a single purpose: to ensure that women carry out, without question, whatever their former guerrilla husbands asked them to do. In this culturally reinvented "forest" in postindependence Zimbabwe, Danger could ask Flame "Is my food ready" without ever thinking that from the perspective of women like Flame, the war had equalized male and female social roles. Instead, Flame is pushed back into the position of an ordinary woman who fetches firewood, and cooks for a husband who occasionally beats her to assert his power in the new dispensation characterized by material inequalities. In the case of Danger, his material position is no better than that of Flame, yet he feels entitled to own Flame's body. Danger is in fact re-creating a dangerous cultural script that only the momentary period of the liberation struggle in the African bush had threatened to upset in favor of women. Flame's defiance, depicted when she chooses to go to the city, dramatizes the fact that she believed that she owned her life, and that she alone could decide what she could do with her body. This show of defiance is, however, deflated when she arrives into a more complicated maze of a "forest" represented by the city. In the city, the people are cold and dispassionate, and do not care less whether or not one fought to liberate Zimbabwe. Postindependence Zimbabwe is also a different kind of modern forest where hunting for a job does not require traditional weapons such as the gun that Flame had used in the forests of Rhodesia and Mozambique when she was "hunting" a white man in order to bring down the mountains of colonial separatist policies. In the film, Flame realizes that in the city, one had to "pass some exams," and those former guerrillas such as Comrade Liberty who were studying in the forests of Mozambique while the likes of Flame were fighting are the kind of hunters whose tools are suitable to secure them jobs in this new forest that is the city. In the new forest that is the city, survival depends on who you know, and not on comradeship that brought together the freedom fighters in the jungles of Rhodesia. In the city, social differentiations based on education accentuate the difference of identities between and among former female guerrillas, because one who was both a former guerrilla as well as educated stood a better chance to survive in this new jungle. In Flame, the Heroes Day in postindependence Zimbabwe is used to show that freedom fighters do not command similar identities at all times. Flame, Liberty, and a handful of the guerrillas who fought for freedom are in the film depicted as having been left out, and excluded in the feasting and celebration taking place at the Heroes Acre—yet another forest where more powerful male freedom fighters than female guerrillas who died in the struggle in the physical forest, are reburied decently.

Flame's Reinvented Images of Female Subordination and Betrayal in Postindependence Zimbabwe

It is important to underline the grievances that are articulated by female ex-combatants through *Flame*. The silencing discourses of colonialism and African patriarchy that Nyasha and Florence escaped from when they ran away from home to join the liberation forces in the forests of Rhodesia and Mozambique are culturally revived through the invocation of the language that equates women's respectability with marriage. It is true that the film attempts to carve new identities for the likes of Nyasha-alias-Comrade Liberty when for example, after the war Nyasha is employed as a secretary. But Nyasha is actually at the mercy of a male boss who knows the language of commanding things to be done his way.

The film vibrantly interrogates how former male combatants treat women when it depicts how Florence ekes out a precarious existence in the rural areas. Her husband does not look after the family as he spends his time drinking beer with friends. When Danger is confronted by his wife for his apparent lack of concern about the welfare of the family, he slaps Florence hard on the cheek and shouts at her, "you think I am a woman." *Flame* succeeds in portraying the sad story of female ex-combatants who, in contemporary Zimbabwe, are shunned by society and even by those who are closer to them (Bryce). Nyasha reveals this to Florence when she says that "I had to make it alone in a men's world. You know what they are saying? They say we are prostitutes." Against this backdrop, the belief in *simba remadzimai* (Women's Power) articulated by Comrade Flame is not fully realized in the film as well as in real life in Zimbabwe. To most women, the concept remains utopian idealism.

However, audiences derive solace in that throughout the different "forests" that the film has been depicting, most women try to imagine challenging patriarchy. The film succeeds in revealing that without changes happening in the mental or "spiritual forests" in whose space images of women as inferior beings are entrenched, the physical journey to Mozambique through deadly forests and the return to a treacherous Zimbabwe is bound not to guarantee freedom to women. The film suggests that this form of betrayal during the struggle fought in the geographical locales of Rhodesia and Mozambique as well as in the metaphorical forest of the postindependence Zimbabwe is a necessary condition of possibility for the emergence of a critical consciousness that can enable women to renegotiate their multiple identities in "multiple forests," whether these are physical, cultural, symbolical, or spiritual.

Conclusion: From Environmental Conservation to Celebrating Human Agency in African Forests

This chapter deploys the image of the African forest to discuss normative approaches to issues of environmental conservation. The aim was to show that in African imaginative compositions, themes related to the African environment are imbued with symbolical meaning so that they take on board more than one explanation or meaning. Whereas the discourses of ecology and ecosystems in Africa have tended to emphasize careful management and preservation of African forests, in African art forms such as *Flame*, one of the reasons why the African environment needs to be preserved is that during the liberation struggle, those forests functioned as both the background or physical space on which new African identities were forged. *Flame* dramatizes how in that war for the freedom of Zimbabwe, African forests also assumed a human character that often shielded or provided cover to freedom fighters from enemy fire. In my analysis of the depiction of the geographical space of the African forest in *Flame*, I emphasized the ambiguity of that physical space, which on one hand allowed the successful execution of a difficult war, but on the other hand was the nemesis of the freedom of female combatants because they were killed by Rhodesian soldiers as well as sexually preyed upon by their own male counterparts. *Flame* also allows one to rethink the African forest as a metonymy of something representing itself outside, especially in those scenes in the film when the Rhodesian bombers destroyed the vegetation. However, in *Flame*, the African forest acquires some metaphorical meanings that are symbolic and go beyond traditional efforts at conserving nature for immediate material benefits. My argument reveals that conceptualization of the space of the African forest as metaphor or liminal space creates meanings of those forests that destabilize our normative ways of appreciating African ecosystems, as authorized in the discourses of environmental management and conservation. As a figurative way of knowing, the metaphor in the film "preserves" the images of African forests by way of reordering and suggesting multiple meanings that echo in the cultural and political experiences of the African people.

Works Cited

Achebe, C. *Things Fall Apart.* Oxford: Heinemann, 1958. Print.

Berhane-Selassie, T. "The Socio-Politics of Ethiopian Sacred Groves." *African Sacred Groves: Ecological Dynamics & Social Change.* Ed. M. J Sheridan and C. Nyamweru. Oxford: James Currey, 2008. 103–116. Print.

Bryce, J. "Incendiary interpretations and Patriotic Imperatives: The Case of *Flame.*" *Versions of Zimbabwe: New Approaches to Literature and Culture.* Ed. R. Muponde and R. Primorac. Harare: Weaver, 2005. 25–39. Print.

Chikowero, J. "Simba Remadzimai: Contesting Historical Amnesia in Zimbabwean Women's Film: The Case of *Flame.*" *Imbizo. International Journal of Literary and Comparative Studies* 1.1 (2010): 134–143. Print.

Deil, U, H. Culmsee and M. Berriane. "Sacred Groves in Morocco." *African Sacred Groves: Ecological Dynamics & Social Change.* Ed. M. J. Sheridan and C. Nyamweru. Oxford: James Currey, 2008. 87–102. Print.

Denzin, N. *The Cinematic Society: The Voyeur's Gaze.* London: Sage, 1995. Print.

Gaidzanwa, R. B. *Images of Women in Zimbabwean Literature.* Harare: College P, 1985. Print.

Handrinath, R. *Audience-Citizens: The media, public knowledge and interpretative practice.* Los Angeles: Sage, 2009. Print.

Karnik, N. "The Photographer, His Editor, Her Audiences, Their Humanitarians: How Rwanda's Pictures Travel Through the American Psyche." *Association of Concerned African Scholars Bulletin* 50.51 (1998): 35–42. Print.

Lan, D. *Guns & Rain: Guerrillas and Spirit Mediums in Zimbabwe.* Harare: Zimbabwe Publishing House, 1985. Print.

Lebbie, A., and R. P. Guries. "The Role of Sacred Groves in Biodiversity Conservation in Sierra Leone." *African Sacred Groves: Ecological Dynamics & Social Change.* Ed. M. J. Sheridan and Nyamweru. Oxford: James Currey, 2008. 42–61. Print.

Lyons, T. "The Forgotten Soldiers: Women in Zimbabwe's Liberation War." *Southern African Report (SAR)* 12.2 February (1997): 23–36. Print.

Musiyiwa, M. "Eschatology, Magic, Nature and Politics: The Responses of the People of Epworth to the Tragedy of Operation Murambatsvina." *The Hidden Dimensions of Operation Murambatsvina.* Ed. M. T. Vambe. Harare and Pretoria: Weaver Press and Africa Institute of South Africa, 2008. 65–74. Print.

Nhongo-Simbanegavi, J. *For Better or Worse: Women and Zanla in Zimbabwe's Liberation Struggle.* Harare: Weaver, 2000. Print.

Nyamweru, C., S. Kibet, M. Pakia, and J. A. Cooke. "The Kaya Forests of Coastal Kenya: Remnant Patches or Dynamic Entities?" *African Sacred Groves: Ecological Dynamics & Social Change.* Ed. M. J. Sheridan and C. Nyamweru. Oxford: James Currey, 2008. 62–86. Print.

Pepetela. *Mayombe: A Novel from Angola.* Harare: Zimbabwe Publishing House, 1983. Print.

Quayson, A. *Strategic Transformation in Nigerian Writing.* Bloomington: Indiana UP, 1997. Print.

Samupindi, C. *Pawns.* Harare: Baobab Books, 1992. Print.

Sheridan M. J. and C. Nyamweru (eds). *African Sacred Groves: Ecological Dynamics & Social Change.* Oxford: James Currey, 2008. Print.

Sheridan, M. J. "The Dynamics of African Sacred Groves." *African Sacred Groves: Ecological Dynamics & Social Change.* Ed. M. J. Sheridan and C. Nyamweru. Oxford: James Currey, 2008. 9–41. Print.

Wily, L. A. "Are Sacred Groves in Sub–Saharan Africa Safe? The Legal Status of Forests." *African Sacred Groves: Ecological Dynamics & Social Change.* Ed. M. J. Sheridan and C. Nyamweru. Oxford: James Currey, 2008. 207–220. Print.

Vambe, M. T. *African Oral Story-Telling Tradition and the Zimbabwean Novel in English.* Pretoria: UNISA Press, 2004. Print.

Notes on Editor and Contributors

ADEKOYA, Olusegun (PhD), teaches Literature at the Department of English in Obafemi Awolowo University, Ile-Ife, Nigeria where he is a Professor. The author of the highly acclaimed book *The Inner Eye: an Oriel on Wole Soyinka's Poetry*, he has published three collections of poems, namely *Guinea Bites and Sahel Blues*, *Chameleon and Chimeras* and *Here and There*. The first Chairman of the Osun State Chapter of the Association of Nigerian Authors, he is married and has two sons.

ASHUNTANTANG, Joyce (PhD), actress, screenwriter, film producer and poet was born in Kumba town in South West region, Cameroon. She earned a B.A in English from the University of Yaoundé, Cameroon, a Masters in Librarianship from the University College of Wales, Aberystwyth, U.K., and a PhD in English from the City University of New York, Graduate Center. Her published works include a collection of poetry, *A Basket of Flaming Ashes (Poetry)* and *Landscaping Postcoloniality: The Dissemination of Anglophone Cameroon Literature*. Dr. Ashuntantang is currently Associate Professor of English and African Literature at the University of Hartford, Connecticut. She blogs her world at: www.joyceash.com.

AWHEFEADA, Sunny (PhD) is a Senior Lecturer in the Department of English and Literary Studies, Delta State University, Abraka, Nigeria. He was Associate Dean, Faculty of Arts at Abraka. He took Degrees in English from the University of Benin, Edo State and University of Ibadan in Nigeria.

CHUMA-Udeh, Ngozi (PhD) holds a double Doctorate in Educational Administration and African/Comparative Literature. Twice an international award winner, her first novel *Teachers on Strike* won the West African Literary Award in 2005 and her second novel *Echoes of a New Dawn* won the AAWW Masterpiece Award in 2010. Her latest collection of poetry is titled *Chants of Despair*. She is a member of Modern Language Association

(MLA), African Literature Association (ALA), Association of African Women Writers, Pan-African Writers Association and Association of Nigerian Authors (ANA). Presently she functions as the Head, Department of English, Anambra State University, Nigeria. Dr. Chuma-Udeh's dream is to pursue a most distinguished and remarkable career in the study and teaching of world literature.

ERNEST-SAMUEL, Gloria is of the Department of Theatre Arts in Imo State University. Her research interest is in Cultural, film and Media Studies. She is presently undertaking a Doctoral research in Media Studies.

FEGHABO, Charles Cliff teaches African and Diasporic literatures in the Department of English and Literary Studies, Niger Delta University, Wilberforce Island, Nigeria. He has almost completed his Doctoral research on the Literature of Nigeria's Niger Delta.

GOMBA, Obari (PhD) has studied at both the University of Nigeria and the University of Port Harcourt. He has a PhD in English, and he teaches Literature and Creative Writing in the Department of English Studies at the University of Port Harcourt. He has published four collections of poetry: *Pearls of the Mangrove, George Bush and Other Observations, Canticle of a Broken Glass* and *Length of Eyes*. He has contributed essays to journals and books. He has promoted scholarship as the Editor of *The Muse*: Journal of the English Association of the Department of English, University of Nigeria (2000); and as the Assistant Editor of *Working Papers*: Journal of the Department of English Studies, University of Port Harcourt (2011-till date). He has also been a key figure in the annual Garden City Literary Festival.

JUA, Roselyne M. (PhD), holds a PhD from SUNY Buffalo, New York, has taught courses in American, English and Women's Literature to undergraduate and graduate students at the Universities of Yaounde and Buea. She was recently appointed Director of Academic Affairs at the University of Bamenda. The author of *The Betrayed Town and Other Poems*, she has published in peer-reviewed journals, co-authored *To the Budding Creative Writer: A Handbook* and published two collections of Victor Elame Musinga's plays: *The Barn* and *The Tragedy of Mr No-Balance*. She is co-editing a critical text on *Anglophone Cameroon Drama and Theatre* and The Struggle for Space and Power by Four Women's groups in the North West Region of Cameroon through a CODESRIA NWG grant.

MOWARIN, Macaulay holds a (PhD) in English language from the University of Ibadan, lbadan, Nigeria. He lectures in the Department of English and Literary Studies, Delta State University, Abraka. Nigeria. His areas of teaching and research include; syntax, pidgin and creole, linguistics, stylistics and sociolinguistics. He is currently the Head, English and literary studies Department. Several of his publications have appeared in journals and chapters in books

NWAGBARA, Uzoechi holds both BA and MA in English from Abia State University and University of Port Harcourt Nigeria respectively. He also has MSc in Human Resource Management from University of Wales, UK, where he is currently doing a PhD in human resource management. He is a published poet, academic and writer; some of his publications have appeared in *Matatu, African Identities, Journal of Sustainable Development in Africa, Journal of Pan African Studies, Leadership* and *Journal of African Business, African Study Monographs*, among others.

OJARUEGA, Enajite is of the Department of English and Literary Studies, Delta State University, Abraka, Delta State, Nigeria where she teaches Literature-in-English. She has published scholarly articles in peer reviewed journals and she equally has chapter contributions in books. She is interested in Gender Studies and Contemporary African Literature.

Dr. OKUYADE Ogaga teaches popular/folk culture, African literature and culture, African American and African Diaspora Studies, and the English Novel in the Department of English and Literary Studies, Niger Delta University, Wilberforce Island, Bayelsa State, Nigeria. He is an ardent student of Postcolonial Studies, particularly narratives of growth, popular music, film and ecological studies. He is currently the Editor of *Island Review: Journal of the Faculty of Arts*, Niger Delta University. He guest edited two volumes for *Imbizo: International Journal of African Literary and Comparative Studies* on *Wole Soyinka and African creativity 25 years after the Nobel*. He has almost completed a special issue on third generation African Narratives which he is currently guest editing for *ARIEL: A Review of International English Literature*. He has chapter contributions and essays in both local and international peer reviewed books and journals. His articles have appeared in Journals like *African Literature Today, World Literature Today, ARIEL, MATATU, WASAFIRI, East/West Cultural Passage, IMBIZO, Latin American Report, AnaChronist, Interventions, Journal of Commonwealth Studies, Africa Today, MUZIKI: Journal of Music Research in Africa, The*

Australian Review of African Studies, Commonwealth Essays and Studies. He is almost through with editing a book project on the oeuvre of Tanure Ojaide: Between Verse and Prose: A Critical Study of Tanure Ojaide and his Art. He is the Editor of this Book.

OKOLO, Genevieve Ifeyinwa is a budding scholar. She holds a Doctorate Degree from the University of Ibadan. Her major research interest is in gender and sexuality discourses in African literature. She partly explores these in her creative and critical writings. She teaches African Literature at the Federal University Lokoja, Kogi State, Nigeria

OWHOFASA, Ovwoke Dorcas is a budding scholar. She is interested in how the environment is represented in postcolonial texts and she is an advocate of ecological justice.

RWAFA Urther is a Lecturer in the Department of Film and Theatre Arts Studies at Midlands State University in Zimbabwe. He holds a Diploma in Education (UZ), BA in Media Studies(ZOU), MA in African Languages (UNISA) specializing in film. He has graduated with a Doctor of Literature and Philosophy (UNISA) on film censorship in Zimbabwe. Rwafa has written numerous articles on film and the Rwandan genocide. He has also published articles about the Language of African films, popular music and the state of Theatre Arts studies in Zimbabwe and Africa.

STEPHEN, Bernard Otonye teaches African Literature and Gender Studies in the Department of English & Literary Studies at the Niger Delta University, Bayelsa State, Nigeria. His research interests focus on Gender and Masculinity Studies, and Literature and the Environment. He is the co-author of *G.'Ebinyo Ogboei's Let the Honey Run and other Poems: A Close Study.*

TSAAIOR, James Tar (PhD) is an Associate Professor and Chair of the Department of Mass Media and Writing in the School of Media and Communication, Pan-African University, Lagos, Nigeria where he teaches creative writing, media/cultural studies and postcolonial literature. He is also the Director, Academic Planning of the University and editor, *Journal of Cultural and Media Studies*. Between 2010 – 2011, he was a visiting Research Fellow, Centre of African Studies, University of Cambridge, United Kingdom and a participant in the International Faculty Programme, University of Navarre IESE Business School, Barcelona, Spain.

VAMBE, Maurice Taonezvi (PhD) is professor of African literature at the Department of English, University of South Africa. He has published quite a number of academic articles on popular culture, especially film and popular music. He is the author of *African Oral Story Telling Tradition and the Zimbabwean Novel in English* (Pretoria, Unisa Press, 2004). Vambe also co-authored *Close to Sources: Essays on Contemporary African Culture, Politics and the Academy* (Pretoria, Unisa Press 2009) with Abebe Zegeye.

Index

A

Abacha, 50, 61, 165, 166, 185, 244, 246, 273, 286, 289, 292, 298
Abomination, 79, 81, 317, 321
Abortion, 120
Abubakar, Gen. Abdulsalami, 226, 244
Abuja, 184, 239, 240, 244, 246, 247, 248, 283, 284, 297
Abuse/s, 3, 36, 112, 123, 131, 134–137, 236, 237, 240, 248, 250, 256, 270, 282, 294, 314
Academic discourse, 110, 142
Adaka Boro, Isaac, 50, 106
Administration, xv, 83, 88, 136, 283, 287, 289, 290, 291, 337
Affluence, 166, 248
Africa identity, 17, 75, 154
African culture, 4, 75, 78, 212, 341
African eco-criticism, 24
African environmental history, 17
African fiction, 1, 16, 189
African identities, iv, xvii, 319–320, 322–323, 339
African narratives, 339
African profit, 105, 111, 117
Agary, iii, xiv–xv, 95, 97–107, 109–122, 125, 129–130, 138
Agary, Kaine (*See* Agary)
Agbala, 77, 79, 80, 81
Aggression, 50, 111, 210, 280, 295
Agriculture, vii, 7, 9, 114, 164, 298
Agricultural harvest, 79
Alternative vision, 37, 41
Ambivalence, 240, 294, 298
Aminogbe, 241, 255
A Month and a Day, iii, 47, 50, 61, 62, 63, 73, 164, 174
Analytic, xv, 110, 142, 144

Ancestors, vi, 26, 27, 80, 81, 165, 167, 275, 277, 281, 320
Ancestral, 7, 37, 167–168, 223, 252, 307, 319
Ancestral lineage, 34
Angst, xvi, 112, 116, 175, 177, 188
Animals, vi, 23–24, 76–78, 84, 87, 91, 99, 114, 130, 143, 149, 253, 254, 264, 268, 283, 290, 291, 304, 311, 325
Antipastoral, 17
Apparatus, 41, 53, 70, 109, 178, 189
Archetypes, 28
Area Boy syndrome, 247
Arid, 4, 5, 18–19, 68, 106, 143, 144, 289, 299, 312
Armah, Ayi Kwei, 26, 28, 49
Armed, iv, 13, 55, 59, 65, 70, 97, 101, 125, 133, 151, 177, 218, 228, 280, 288, 291, 295, 319, 322, 324, 329
Ashawo pikin, 105, 111, 117
Atmosphere, 24, 64, 86, 87, 106, 143, 144, 289, 299, 312
Autobiography, xiv, 48, 72, 139–141, 159
Ayi Kwe Armah (*See* Armah, Ayi Kwei)

B

Barn, 80, 298, 338
Bastard, 117–118, 293–294
Bell Oil Company, 42
Benin River, 239
Benzene, 119
Betrayal, 1, 12, 115, 119, 183, 322–323, 329–330, 332–333
Biodiversity, 32–33, 38–39, 96, 155, 191, 194, 198, 205, 236, 275, 296, 299, 319–320, 334

Bioregional, 32, 239
Blackmailed, 119
Born throw-ways, 111
Branch Michael, viii, 45, 93
Buell, Lawrence, xviii, 122, 159, 257, 344
Bush, 18, 19, 38, 76, 78, 79, 84, 85, 91, 92, 201, 202, 241, 253, 290, 304, 316, 317, 320, 321, 323, 325, 327, 329, 330, 331, 338
Business tourism, 37
Butake, iv, xvii, 303–318

C

Cameroon, iv, xvii, 161–167, 303–305, 311, 315, 318, 337–338
Capitalist, ix–xi, xiii–xiv, 4, 8, 10, 49, 54, 65, 95, 142, 144, 148, 157, 158, 166, 171
Capitalist industrialism (*See* capitalist)
Cartographic, 239
Celebrity paradise, 38
Chants, 169, 187, 274, 337
Chaotic, xi, 111, 133, 180, 220
Character, iii, xii, xiv, 2–4, 6, 8, 13, 15–16, 23, 26–28, 34, 40–41, 44, 51, 59–60, 71, 102, 107, 111, 116–117, 121, 127, 140, 181, 305, 311–312, 315, 323, 333
Characterized (*See* Characterizes)
Characterizes, 50, 76, 141, 161, 171, 176
Characteristically, 208, 268
Characteristics, 2, 69, 192
Characterization, xiv, 4, 15, 18, 28
Character development, iii, xii, 15
Cheated, 25, 33, 113
Cheryll Glotfelty, x, 124, 162, 198, 261
Chevron, 53, 182, 198, 218, 250, 279
Chief Tobi Ishaka, 42, 43
Children, xvi, 5, 10–11, 18–20, 55, 77, 80, 82, 86–87, 102, 105, 110–111, 117–118, 123, 125, 127, 131–132, 135, 137, 147, 154, 173, 179, 188, 223, 226, 240–242, 249, 255, 257, 265, 274, 277, 279, 293, 301, 307–308, 312, 313–314, 324, 328
Christianity, vi, 189
Chronicle newspaper, 55, 58
Chronological, xv, 110, 117

Chuma-Udeh Ngozi, 337
City, xi, 16, 20–22, 25–26, 27, 35, 42–43, 57–58, 103–104, 114–115, 118, 120, 122, 126, 130–131, 152, 163, 224, 225, 246, 248, 257, 267, 300–301, 330, 331, 337, 338
Cityscape, 20, 330
Clan, 76, 78, 80, 84, 86, 315, 321
Climate, 81–82, 86, 145, 149, 163, 281, 289, 290, 293, 297–298, 300, 313, 319
Coastal, xi, 18–19, 109, 113, 239, 286, 335
Cocks, 24, 88
Colonial Era, xiv, 49, 75–76, 79, 82, 98, 146, 221
Colonialism, 3–10, 12–14, 16, 23–24, 29, 48, 49, 65, 94, 96, 98, 108, 148, 150, 153, 156, 158, 159, 179, 181, 192, 195, 243, 318, 319, 321, 323–324, 326, 332
Commonwealth, x, 185, 211, 242, 254, 339, 340
Communal existence, 21
Community, vi, vii, xvii, 4, 12, 15, 23, 32, 41–43, 51, 58, 66, 70, 76, 79, 83–84, 93, 105, 110–111, 113, 115, 119, 121–122, 127, 129, 130, 137, 144–147, 151, 153, 197, 210, 216, 236, 243–244, 274, 276–279, 281, 286–288, 293, 303–311, 317, 321, 326
Compensation, 12, 109, 112, 119, 164, 170, 245, 277–279, 287, 295
Conduit, 154, 196, 210, 246
Conflict, xii, 16, 35, 61, 66, 72–73, 85, 105, 109, 166, 181, 193, 212, 237, 239, 243, 246–247, 269, 271, 278, 280, 291, 297, 300, 305, 305, 316, 330
Confrontation/s, xvi, 70–71, 109–110, 153, 203–204, 218, 224, 326
Confusion, 110, 325
Conquistadors, 98, 249–250
Consciousness, iii, ix, 49, 56, 61, 70–71, 80, 116, 119, 134, 144, 162, 167, 194, 196, 219, 261, 267, 289, 299, 324–326, 329, 333

Constructive subversion, 41
Consumerism, ix, 144, 152, 157
Contamination, 114, 119, 155, 236
Contemporary African Literature, iii, v, viii, xii, xviii, 31, 33, 46, 339
Contrapuntal, xvi, 239, 246
Cosmology, 254, 256
Counterpoint, 240, 246
Creative writing, v, vi, 32, 63, 111, 189, 338, 340
Criticisms, v, vi, xviii, 1, 16–17, 28–29, 46, 93, 107–108, 122, 141, 159, 162, 211, 219, 262, 271, 318
Cross River, 239, 325
Cross-breed, 111
Crude oil, vii, 36, 56, 98–99, 113–114, 129, 182, 187, 224–255, 229, 259, 260, 263, 265, 268–269, 277
Culture, vi–viii, 4, 7, 9, 14, 32–33, 75–76, 81–83, 85, 88, 93–94, 98, 110–111, 114, 121–122, 137, 144, 150, 153–155, 157, 164, 169, 172, 176, 179–180, 189, 196, 212, 253, 254, 257, 261, 275–276, 281, 290–291, 298, 300, 322, 326, 334, 339, 341

D

Daglobe Delta, 125, 127–128, 131, 133, 136–137
Daniel Patterson, viii, 45, 46, 93, 257
Dark night, 77, 82
Darkness, 24, 26, 77, 79, 120, 166, 207, 243, 292, 297, 304, 312
Daylight, 77
Defacing, 38
Deforestation, xi, 27, 92, 95, 144, 150, 280, 281, 319
Degradation, iv, vi, xvi, 1, 3, 6, 12–13, 24, 32, 35–36, 45, 49, 51, 56, 64, 66, 69, 95, 98–99, 100, 102, 104, 112, 123–123, 129, 137, 144, 149, 150, 154, 170, 172–173, 175, 183, 199, 215–216, 220–221, 225, 227, 233, 234, 239, 247–248, 251–252, 254, 256–257, 265, 273, 279–280, 282, 288, 292, 295, 299, 309, 319
Deities, 79, 84–86, 89, 249, 254
Deplorable, 43, 68, 115, 170, 252

Desecration, xvi, 23, 63, 111, 161, 164, 277
Despoliation, vi, 31, 44, 50, 57–59, 64, 98, 111, 162, 165, 175, 178, 183, 194, 218, 222, 235, 239, 299
Deteriorating environment, 32
Deterioration in the agro production, 20
Development, iii, xi–xvi, 9–10, 15–16, 18, 26, 28, 31, 35–39, 41, 43, 45, 50, 61, 64, 66, 70, 76, 83, 96, 114, 119–122, 124, 138, 145, 149, 151–155, 158, 160, 164, 184, 193, 198, 224, 227, 231, 240–243, 246, 252–253, 257, 261, 276, 284, 289, 296, 303, 307–308, 339
Development and modernity, 240
Dew in the Morning, xiv, xviii, 2, 6–10, 12–14
Diabolical power, 248
Dictatorship of the centre, 106, 178, 183, 247, 316
Disgust, 111, 114, 118, 135, 294
Disharmony, 15, 111, 113, 164
Dislocation, 48, 113, 325
Displacement, 113, 146, 150, 278, 319
Dogs, 18–19, 24, 87, 276, 290–291, 304, 316
Domestic environment, xvi, 110
Downtrodden, 118
Drama, xiv, 1, 32, 73, 97, 193, 318, 338
Dramatic (*See* Drama)
Dramaturgy, xvii, 94
Dying ecological sphere, 113
Dystopia, iv, 239, 240, 247–248

E

Earth, iii, iv, viii, xii, xvii, 3, 8, 19–20, 24, 31–32, 34, 36, 38, 40, 45, 47, 72, 77, 79–81, 84, 89, 93, 95, 108, 123, 125, 135, 139, 144, 151, 156, 159, 163–168, 172–173, 189, 191, 193–194, 196, 198, 204–213, 220–221, 223–226, 229–230, 236–237, 248, 253, 257, 261, 269, 273, 274, 278, 281, 289, 290, 292–294, 296–301, 313, 315–317
Earth Goddess, 80, 89, 315–317
Ebi Yeibo, 97, 260

INDEX

Eco-Activism, iii, ix, 18, 26, 31, 33–34, 36–37, 41, 43, 47, 50, 55, 57, 58, 61–62, 70, 72, 153
Eco-advocacy, 91
Eco-biological, 111
Ecocentric literature, 111
ecocritical perspective, xvii, 260
Eco-criticism, v, vii, x–xiii, 2, 12, 16–17, 24, 26, 32–33, 90, 141, 162, 193, 197–198, 210, 260, 261, 316
Eco-depleting forces, 23
Eco-hostile, 95
Eco-literacy, iii, xiv, xv, 139, 141–142, 152, 155
Ecological, iii, v, vi, xi–xii, xiv, xvii, 2, 3, 5–8, 13, 16–18, 26–27, 31–34, 40, 42, 46–47, 50–51, 54, 58, 64–66, 76–78, 80–81, 89–93, 95, 108–114, 120–122, 139, 141–142, 144–146, 148–151, 154, 157, 157–158, 161, 166–167, 172, 182, 193, 195–196, 198–199, 201, 210, 215–217, 220–221, 236, 259–260, 262–263, 265–266, 268, 271, 318, 334, 335, 339
Ecological advancement, xiv, 27
Ecological concerns, 18, 210, 260, 262, 263
Ecological damage, 114, 265–266
Ecological dilapidation, 111
Ecological disasters, 111
Ecological function, 78, 149
Ecological interdependence, 26
Ecological issues, xii, xvii, 110, 121, 220, 262
Ecological justice, 111, 129, 340
ecological literacy, v, 32, 76, 96, 91–92
Ecological sensitization, 34
Ecology, v, vii, viii, vxiii, 17, 29, 54, 58, 70, 76, 91, 95–96, 107, 111, 115, 119, 138, 141, 144–145, 149, 159, 162, 174, 194, 197, 198, 211, 213, 236, 263, 264, 271, 273, 276, 279, 285, 319–320, 333
Economic, xvi, 5, 19, 31, 33, 38, 39–40, 41, 43, 59, 63, 66, 97, 109, 121, 124, 138, 144, 152–153, 156, 168, 175, 182, 193, 194, 197, 198, 205, 210, 248, 259, 269, 273, 283, 284, 286, 290, 292, 296, 300, 320
Economy, vii, ix, x, 7, 10, 122, 132, 133, 149–150, 182, 185, 192, 194, 212, 276, 284, 297–298
Eco-poetry, xvi, 193, 197, 198, 210, 236, 263, 270
Ecosystem, 2, 6, 55, 56, 60, 61, 70, 90–92, 109, 113, 121–122, 145, 150–152, 157, 182, 298, 319–320
Ecuador, vi, 34
Eghagha, xvii, 215–216, 218–237
Egwugwu, 82, 88
Ejoor (rtd), Maj. Gen. David, 244–245
Elf, 182, 198, 250, 287–288
Emmanuel Obiechina (*See* Obiechina)
Encroachment, 31, 95, 221
Environment, iii–xvii, 1–5, 11–18, 21, 24, 26–27, 31–40, 42–47, 49–58, 61–62, 64–65, 70–71, 75–78, 80–83, 87–95, 97, 99–100, 102, 106, 109–112, 114, 121–125, 128–129, 134, 136–138, 142–145, 148–150, 152, 154–155, 157–158, 162, 168, 172–173, 175, 179–180, 182–183, 185, 191–198, 200–206, 208, 210–211, 215–218, 221, 223–227, 229–230, 235–236, 241, 247–257, 259, 270, 274, 277–279, 281, 283, 285, 288–289, 291–292, 296–297, 299–301, 303, 309, 312, 314, 317, 319–320, 322–333, 340
Environmental (*See* Environment)
Environmental activism, 22, 33, 59, 63, 71, 106, 151, 155
Environmental advocate, 15
Environmental challenges, 37, 150, 155
Environmental degradation, iv, vi, xvi–xvii, 1, 6, 13, 24, 32, 35, 236, 45, 49, 51, 66, 69, 95, 123–126, 129, 137, 144, 149, 154, 175, 199, 215–216, 220–221, 225, 227, 233–234, 239, 248, 252, 254, 256–257, 273, 279, 282, 288, 292, 309
Environmental despoliation, iv, 31, 59, 179, 218, 222, 235, 239
Environmental elements, 76, 78, 83, 93

Environmental hazards, 16, 182, 267
Environmental injustice, 151, 201,
    216–218, 229, 234, 236
Environmental issues, xii, xv, xvii, 12,
    16, 28, 32, 82, 110, 112, 124, 135,
    157, 266, 269, 271, 303, 304, 311
Environmental laws, 38, 42, 289, 301
Environmental pollution, 31–32, 44, 65,
    222, 250, 267, 278, 287, 297
Environmental preservation, 17
environmental protection, 40, 94, 145,
    153, 185, 253, 277, 286, 289
environmental rights, xiii, 31, 33, 36,
    41, 44, 70, 97, 105, 134, 135, 193,
    217, 257, 278, 289, 300, 301
Environmental Testimonies, 257
Environmentalist, 110, 156, 185, 188,
    209, 217, 278
Epistolary, 50
Ernest Emenyonu, 49, 72
Ethiope water front, 251, 280
ethnic tension, 247
European colonists, 86
Evil, 77, 79, 83, 85, 88–89, 92, 120,
    128–130, 133, 135–136, 166, 184,
    194, 209, 217, 285–286, 291–293,
    296, 301, 315–321
Evil Forest, 79, 83, 88–89, 321
Evil Spirit, 77, 79, 92
Existential, xvi, 110, 112, 177
Existential fulfilment, 112
Expatriates, 112, 115
Exploration, vi, xv, 18, 31, 34–36,
    39–40, 42, 45, 50–55, 64–65, 95–96,
    98–101, 105, 109–114, 120–121,
    144, 149, 195, 198, 204, 218, 222,
    230, 251, 253–254, 259–260, 263–
    264, 267, 269, 273, 286

F
Family, 3–5, 8, 11, 16, 48, 77–78, 80, 82,
    86–88, 101, 126, 132, 136, 144, 167,
    178, 187, 332
Farm, vi, 77, 98–99, 101, 113, 115, 129,
    132, 227, 228–229, 268, 278–279
Farm seedlings, 77
Farmers, 7, 8, 10, 77, 79, 89, 163, 275,
    288, 295, 310

Farming, vi, 7–9, 13, 19–20, 27, 36,
    45, 77, 80–82, 113, 122, 162, 221,
    260, 265, 276, 298, 305, 307,
    310–311
Farming season, 81–82
Fauna, 26, 39, 64, 76, 89–90, 97, 107,
    113–114, 122, 125, 167, 182, 196,
    200, 209, 218, 220, 249, 255, 313
Federal government, 36, 57, 64–65,
    105, 109, 112, 133–134, 136, 177,
    218, 277–283
Feghabo, iii, 47, 338
Female sexuality, 112
Festivals, 15, 84, 285
fig tree, 146–148, 150
film, iv, xiv, xvii, 319, 321–325, 327–334,
    337–341
Fire, 54, 79, 86, 115, 128, 144, 225–228,
    230, 232–234, 244–245, 253, 278,
    288, 308, 333
Firewood, vi, 3, 79, 93, 149, 153, 155,
    320, 324, 331
Flame, iv, vxii, 57, 225, 319, 321–323,
    325–334
Flora, 39, 64, 76, 89–90, 97, 107, 113–
    114, 122, 125, 167, 182, 196, 200,
    209, 218, 220, 249, 255, 313
Folktales, 77, 321
Forest, iv, vi, xvii, 4, 17, 23, 26–27, 29,
    31, 34, 78–79, 83, 86, 88–90, 95,
    114, 150, 153, 167, 169, 182, 186,
    207, 217, 220, 240, 250, 253, 255,
    256, 275, 276–278, 281, 286, 288,
    290, 293, 319, 321–334
Forest environment, 26
Fromm Harold, 271

G
General Sani Abacha (*See* Abacha, Sani)
General Yakubu Gowon, 50
Geography, 76, 78, 145, 322–323, 331
Girl-children, xvi, 110, 111, 117, 121
Global community, vi, 32, 145
Global Green, xviii, 29, 73, 108, 271
Global warming, 31, 149, 225, 281, 293,
    297
Glotfelty, Cheryll, xvii, 174, 211, 271
Goats, 9–11, 19, 23, 88, 249, 304

INDEX

gods, 81, 84–86, 240–241, 253, 255, 296, 315
Gomba, Obari, iv, xvi, 239, 338
Greek, 100, 111, 114, 116–117
Green Belt Movement, 150–151, 155, 159

H
Harmattan, iv, xv, 86, 129, 161, 170–174, 254, 259
Health, vi, 39–40, 89, 92, 102, 109, 113, 123, 128, 148, 177, 193, 236, 254, 268, 283, 292, 297, 307
Heroine, 111, 113, 115, 118
Hills, 23–24, 77, 79, 207, 209, 315
Hit-and-run, 111
Homocentrism, 253
Human right, vii, xiii, 31, 34, 148, 155, 189, 193, 200, 212, 215, 217–218, 230, 236–237, 256, 288, 296

I
Ibiwari Ikiriko, 97, 260
Idjerhe, 243–246
Igbo, xiv, 75–76, 79, 83, 85–86, 88–94, 179–180, 245, 321
Igbo Environment, 76, 92
Igbo worldview, 76
Ijaw Nation, 119
Ijaw youths, 119
Imagination, v, viii, xiii, xviii, 10, 89, 92, 96, 108, 110, 114, 159–160, 184, 192, 200, 212, 257, 259, 269, 274, 278, 284, 294, 315, 318
imperial Europe, 250
Impoverished, 18, 40, 64, 105, 120, 165, 229, 234, 295
Incantations, 274
Inchoate, 110
Indigenes, 40–41, 57–59, 69, 76–78, 96, 99, 109, 113, 218, 222–223, 225, 229, 234–235
Individual, 6, 32, 141, 143–144, 148–149, 155, 157, 159, 176, 182, 229, 325–327
industrial nihilism, 253
Infertile, 2, 12, 113, 123
infrastructural decay, 246

Infrastructure, 68, 119, 218
Infringement, 111
Injustice, 51, 58, 62, 64, 68–69, 71, 97, 113, 151, 185, 199, 201, 216–218, 229, 233–234, 236, 245, 280, 283, 295
Instability, 111, 120, 244, 320
Isidore Okpewho, iii, xiv 47, 50
Islam, vi

J
J. P. Clark, 50, 95, 189, 194, 260, 296
James Tsaaior, iv, xvi, 175
Joyce Ashuntantang, iv, xvii, 303

K
Kaiama Bridge, 254–255
Kainji Dam, 54
Karura Forest, 154
Kenneth Kaunda, 48
Kenya, 28, 34, 137, 144, 146, 147, 150, 151, 152, 153, 155, 174, 335
Kenyan (*See* Kenya)
Kidnapping, 105, 119, 133, 218, 280, 296
Kikuyu, 142144, 147–151
Kuruku, 5, 13
Kwarafa Dam, 54, 56, 60

L
Labyrinths of the Delta, 95, 108, 194, 249, 256, 257
Land, iii, vi, vii, xiv, 1, 20, 22–25, 27, 31, 34–36, 38, 40, 42–45, 64–65, 67, 70, 79–81, 83, 85, 88, 96, 98–102, 105, 109, 112–115, 119, 121–123, 129, 131, 134, 142–144, 146, 149, 151–153, 161, 164, 165, 166–167, 170–172, 184, 186–187, 202, 216, 218, 223–224, 230, 240, 243–244, 246, 249, 250–251, 255–256, 266, 268, 270, 275–278, 280–281, 283, 286, 288, 291–292, 295, 297, 298, 299, 305, 306, 308–311, 313, 315–317, 323, 324
Land cultivation, 19
Landscape, vii, v, xiv, 7, 15, 18, 21, 23–25, 27, 29, 35–37, 40, 96–98, 141

Index

Landscaping, iii, xii, 15–19, 337
Language, 10, 19–20, 107, 135, 159, 181, 213, 219, 220, 232, 237, 245, 294, 323, 332, 337, 339–340
Lasciviousness, 118
Lawrence Buell, xiii, 110
Libation, 84, 247
Livelihood, 33, 36, 38, 40, 54, 96, 99, 112, 114–115, 217, 222, 236, 254, 278
LNG prize, 97
Love my Planet, iii, xv, 72, 123–126, 128, 130, 133–134, 137–138
Lucifer, 3, 5–6

M

Maathai, xv, 34, 137, 142–153, 155, 157, 159
Macaulay Mowarin, iv, xvii, 215
Major Isaac Adaka Boro (*See* Adaka Boro, Isaac)
Maltreatment, 111
mangrove forests, 239
Mankind, ix–xii, xv–xvii, 12, 124, 157, 189, 206
Manyene, 3, 5, 13
Marginalization, 7, 33–34, 36, 41, 51, 55, 66, 69, 99, 154, 195, 197, 244
Marginalized, 2, 36, 40, 113, 179, 181, 187, 203, 206, 243, 244, 324
Marxist framework, 19
Mask, 88, 173, 187, 191, 193, 200, 248, 251, 266, 315, 317
Masquerade, 84, 93, 233, 254
Master, xiii, 83, 220, 275, 282, 285, 337
Maurice Vambe, xiv
Mda, iii, xiv, 31, 33–38, 41–45
Mercantilism, 250
Militancy, 58, 96, 105, 133, 134, 194, 213
Militarization, 246–247, 260
Mineral resources, 35, 178, 216
Minority, iv, xiii, xvi, 33, 50–52, 61–62, 66–67, 175, 178, 179–180, 181, 183, 185–188, 216, 234–236
Minority group, 33, 51, 179, 236
Mixed breed, 117

Mobil, 182, 218, 250
Modernization, 35, 38, 172, 309
Monumental, x, 113, 179, 294
Motif, 51, 154, 170, 239
Mount Kenya, 146, 147
multinational oil companies, vi, vii, 34, 39, 42, 51, 53–55, 57, 60, 64–65, 67–68, 71, 132, 215, 218, 222, 234, 264
Mungoshi, xiv, xviii, 2–6, 12, 14

N

Nation-state, 65, 180, 181, 193, 239
Natural habitat, 34, 149, 223, 254
Natural justice, 88, 283
Natural lines of productivity, 254
Natural resources, ix–xii, xv, 33–35, 39, 41, 44, 52, 86, 125, 142–143, 145, 149, 150, 158, 181, 265
Natural species, 24
Nature writing, 24, 96, 122, 211, 262
nature-centrism, 259
Ndigbo, 89
New Moon, 84, 85
New Yam, 80, 82, 84–85
Ngozi Chuma-Udeh, iii, xv, 109 (*See also* Chuma-Udeh, Ngozi)
Ngugi, iii, xii, 15–29, 48, 63, 144, 167, 174
Niger Coast Protectorate, 239
Niger Delta, iii–vii, xiii–xvii, 16, 33–34, 36, 39, 43, 47, 49–61, 63–72, 95–99, 104–130, 132–134, 138–139, 142, 146, 149, 161–162, 165, 168, 175, 178, 180, 182, 183, 185, 186, 188, 189, 193, 198–199, 202–203, 206, 210, 213, 215–218, 220–228, 229, 230–237, 239–243, 245–254, 256, 259, 260, 262–271, 273, 275, 276278–291, 295–299, 338–340
Niger River, 239
Nigerian federation, 33, 185
Nigerian territory, 109
Nigerian writers, 92, 93, 128, 195
Nixon, Rob, xviii, 29, 72, 160
Nobel, 34, 139, 142, 147, 156, 188, 339
Nonhuman, 261, 262
Norms, 90, 111–112, 117

O

Obari Gomba, iv, xvi, 239
Obichina, Emmanuel, vii, viii, 88, 90, 94, 192, 212
Oeuvre, xvi, 175, 179, 340
Offshore, 36, 52, 113
Ogbowei, iv, xvi, 259–260, 262–271
Ogoni, 50, 61–65, 67, 69–72, 106, 122, 164–165, 185–186, 217–218, 230, 235, 273, 280, 283, 285–286, 296
Oil, 96, 111
Oil boom, 96, 111
Oil companies, vi–vii, xiv, 16, 34, 36, 39–40, 42–43, 44, 49, 51, 53–55, 57–58, 60, 63–65, 67–68, 70–71, 105, 109–112, 115, 119, 129–133, 137, 172, 188, 196, 215, 218, 222, 225, 227, 227, 229, 234, 245, 252, 255, 264, 267, 273, 275, 277–278, 280, 283, 287–289, 295
Oil explorations, vi, 31, 35–36, 39–40, 42, 45, 51, 53–55, 64–65, 95–96, 99–101, 105, 111, 120–121, 149, 198, 204, 222, 251, 230, 251, 259, 263, 267, 269, 286
oil industry, 72, 132, 193, 241, 250, 251, 256, 265
Oil spills, x, 99, 113, 115, 119, 255, 263, 277–279, 287, 289
Oil-rich Niger Delta, 50, 115, 199, 259, 273
Ojaide, Tanure, vii, xvii, 46, 72, 94, 160, 174, 189, 212, 257, 301
Ojaruega, iii, 31, 339
Okolo, Ifeyinwa, iii, xii, xiv, 15, 340, 350
Okuyade, Ogaga, 213, 339
Old Man, 3–4, 6, 13, 120, 313
Olusegun Adekoya, iv, xvi, 273
Onshore, 36
Oracle, 77, 79, 82, 186
Overcrowding, 3, 13, 324
Owhofasa, iii, xv, 123, 340
Ozymandian aspiration, 247

P

Palliative measures, 35
Palm oil, 81, 84, 187, 290, 314
Palm tree, 84, 87, 89, 91, 165, 278, 316–317
Palm wine, iv, 81, 84, 303, 308, 314–318
Paradise, 21, 24, 38, 171, 247–248, 251, 286–287, 290, 314
Pastoral, 8, 17, 22, 24, 96, 123, 144, 273
Paternal, 116
Patriarchal, 102, 112, 322, 324
Persona, 111, 147, 186, 221, 240–242, 246–247, 250–255, 263, 265–269, 280–281, 305, 309
Perspectives, 33, 97, 110, 154, 189, 211, 262
Petroleum Trust Fund, 246
Phenomenon, xi, xx, 82, 95, 112, 124, 140, 146, 228
Philadelphia, 152
Physical landscape, 37, 40
Physical setting, 83, 88
Pipeline, 113, 226, 277, 296
Piriye Dukumo, 50, 51
Plant, 27, 40, 80, 89 153, 260, 280, 287, 299
Planting season, 77–78, 80, 163
Plot, iii, xii, xiv, 8, 15, 18, 26–28, 83, 98, 107, 248, 303, 305, 311, 316, 322
Politics, iii, iv, vii, xiv, xv, xvi, 16, 17, 24, 29, 44, 47, 50–52, 55–56, 61, 62, 66, 68, 71, 93, 105, 109, 124, 142, 144, 145, 155–158, 164, 174–175, 179–181, 184–185, 187, 189, 192–193, 195–196, 199, 211–213, 223, 237, 239, 284, 297, 304, 318, 323, 334, 341
Pollution, 1, 16, 31, 33, 36, 39, 44, 53, 56–57, 65, 96, 102, 122–123, 125, 128, 137, 149, 164, 179, 222, 252, 254–255, 260, 267, 275, 278–280, 287, 291, 293, 296–297, 311
population explosion, 246
postcolonial, 14, 72, 98, 150, 157, 173
Prairie, 20–23, 25
Precolonial, 26, 79, 88, 91, 221
Prejudice, 77, 79
Priest, 81, 84–86, 241, 305, 307–309, 311, 316
Priestess, 77, 79

Pristine, 32–33, 35, 38–39, 95, 98, 153, 206–207, 252
Pristine environment, 33, 35, 38
Privation, 112, 116, 282, 285
Professor Tobore Ede, 42
Profiteering, 242, 245, 247, 266
Proverbs, 315–316
Pseudonyms, 111
Psychological, 4, 6, 71, 110–111, 148, 323
Psychology, 70, 116
Psychological individuality, 110
public sphere, xii, 153, 158, 160
Pumpkin leaves, 84
Python, 85, 90, 184, 283

R
Rachel Carson, iv, xvi, 161
Rainfall, 5, 249, 256, 317
Redness, iii, 31, 33–35, 37–38, 41, 45, 53
Region, vi, xiv, xvii, 7, 18, 32, 34, 36, 39–45, 47, 49–52, 54, 57–58, 60–61, 65, 68, 71, 96, 98, 104–106, 109–114, 120–122, 125–126, 133–134, 137, 148, 177, 180, 182, 193, 195, 198–199, 203, 215–218, 220–225, 227–229, 232–233, 235–237, 239, 241, 242–243, 250, 255, 256, 259–260, 262, 263, 265–266, 271, 273, 279, 280, 282, 284–288, 290, 291, 296, 299, 305, 312, 337, 338
Relationship, v, vi, vii, x, xii, xiii, xiv, xv, xvii, 15, 17, 24–25, 32–34, 39, 49, 52, 65–67, 69, 71, 80, 105, 110–111, 116, 131, 140–142, 144, 146, 147–148, 151, 152, 155, 157, 159, 162, 164, 181, 183, 197, 198–199, 209, 219, 220, 228, 248, 261, 268, 275, 283, 285, 286, 303, 310
Religious doctrine, 85
Religious system, 88
Repulsion, 111
Resistance, 9, 55, 59, 114, 144, 189, 193–194, 197–198, 208, 212, 213, 217, 220, 237, 267, 320, 322
Resources, vii, viiiv ix, x, xi, xii, xiii, xv, xvii, 19–20, 23–24, 32–35, 37, 39, 41, 44–45, 52, 68, 72, 75, 86, 94, 96, 100, 102, 114, 121, 125, 142–143, 149–150, 156–158, 177–182, 185, 198, 204, 216, 218, 239, 241–243, 252, 257, 265, 277, 280–281, 283–285, 290–293, 296, 299, 314, 324, 326, 339
Restiveness of youths, 57, 61, 64, 96, 125, 247, 260
Rethinking Ecoliteracy, iii, 139
Rhetoric, xiv, xv, 193, 198, 200, 210
Rhodesia, 2–3, 6, 9–10, 13–14, 322–323, 330–333
Rhythms of the Last Testament, iv, xvii, 215–216, 219, 221–226, 229–235, 237
Ritual, 78, 81–82, 84, 88, 143, 273, 300, 330
Ritual cleansing, 82
River, 10, 18, 29, 40, 85–86, 91, 99, 101, 102, 120, 127, 131, 239, 245, 248, 249, 254–256, 259, 263–267, 271, 324
Robbery, 69, 125, 133, 201, 202, 246, 285
Robin Palmer, 2
Rochelle Johnson, vii, 45–46, 93, 257
Roselyne Jua, xvi
Rura, xii, 3–4, 7–8, 11–12, 15–17, 19–20, 22, 37, 42, 75–76, 82–84, 87–90, 92, 104, 125, 143, 150–151, 155, 157, 222, 306, 320, 324, 331, 332
Rural communities, 89, 324
Rural pastoral setting, 22
Rural societies, 82
Rural spaces, 16
Rustic environment, 36

S
Sabotage, 119, 244, 278, 296
Sacred, vi, 15, 76, 79, 85, 90, 147–148, 152, 155, 187, 276, 277, 280, 305, 307, 319, 320, 324, 334–335
sacred—mountains, vi
Saro-Wiwa, iii, xiv, 17, 29, 33, 47, 50, 55, 59, 61–73, 97, 105–106, 108, 124, 137, 164–167, 173–174, 185–186, 188, 194, 196, 217–218, 220, 230–232, 237, 273–275, 280, 285–268, 292, 300

Satirical epic, 27
Scholarship, v, vii, viii, 12, 32, 94, 110, 142, 154, 212, 242, 260, 319, 338
Scornful, 111
Scott, Slovic, viii, 45–46, 93, 110, 142, 257
Seashore, 31, 34–35, 37–38, 43
Seashore environment, 35
Seasons, 26, 28, 49, 77, 142, 170, 183, 251, 254, 279, 282
Sentiments, 50, 88
Sexual, 3, 111, 115, 122, 129–131, 324, 327, 329
Sexuality (*See* Sex)
Sexual escapades, 111, 115
Shell, 50, 61–66, 69–70, 164–165, 170, 178, 182, 183, 187, 189, 198, 218, 222, 250, 254, 256, 257, 276, 278–279, 288
Shimmer Chinodya, 18, 13
Silent Spring, iv, xvi, 16, 163, 172–174, 194
Slaymaker, William, xviii, 29, 73, 108, 271
Slow Violence, x, xviii, 55, 72, 160
Slums, 16, 20, 105
Social devastation, 111
Soyinka, Wole, 48, 167, 174, 188, 213, 237, 297–298, 301, 339
Species, xi, 24, 43, 114, 148, 149, 157, 223, 230, 256, 260, 264, 293, 299
Spillage, 52, 56–57, 64, 114, 119, 126, 127, 182, 255, 279, 287
spills and blowouts, vii
Spirits, 62, 77, 79, 81, 86, 92, 165, 172, 154, 255, 277, 281, 297, 321
Stephen Bernard, xv, 271, 340
Stigma, 111
subjected environment, 248, 256
subjection, 239, 248, 256, 324
Subjugation, 68, 109, 119
Subsistence, xv, 8, 34, 111, 122, 143, 145–146, 149, 157, 217, 254
Substantivexvi, 110
Sunny Awhefeada, iii, xiv, 95
Superstitious belief, 90
Survival, iii, iv, xv, xvi, 6, 34, 69, 87, 89–91, 94, 107, 109–110, 114, 149–151, 167, 185, 201, 217, 237, 259–261, 263–266, 269, 280, 309, 312, 313, 317, 320, 331
Sustainability, 15, 114, 124
Symbiotic relationship, xii, xiv, 34, 74, 146, 157, 199, 286, 310
Synergistically, 109, 113

T
Taboo, 81, 90, 92, 204
Task Force on Pollution, 53, 57, 285
Texaco, 218, 250
The Ecocriticism Reader: Landmarks in Literary Ecology, xviii, 138, 174, 198, 211, 271
The Environmental Imagination, xiii, xviii, 257
The Eye of the Earth, 194, 196, 205, 209, 213, 220, 237, 273, 301
The Governor's Lodge and Other Poems, iv, xvii, 215–216, 219, 223, 227, 235, 237
the rape of the land, 1, 280, 299
The Tale of the Harmattan, iv, xvi, 161, 170, 172–174, 254, 257
the wild (*See* wild)
Thunder, 82, 87, 206, 240, 310
Tides, iii, 47, 50, 60–61, 63, 72
Timber, vi, 23, 27, 216, 281
Tourism, 33, 37–38, 45, 287
Tourist, 18–19, 35, 39, 43, 135
Tradition, vii–viii, x, xii, 48, 49, 76, 94, 117, 141, 143, 154, 175, 179, 188, 199, 210, 216, 219, 236, 241, 244, 285–286, 298, 300, 304, 311, 315–317, 326, 335, 341
Traditionally, 24, 96, 118, 148, 198
traditional means of livelihood, 254
Traditional West Africa, vii, 89
transfer of wealth, 246–247
transnational corporations, 242
travesty of national hope, 247
Tropics, 86
Turmoil, xv, 107, 110–111, 113, 192

U
Ughelli, 196, 243–244, 279
Uhuru Park, 152

Unbowed, iii, 139, 142–145, 148–152, 155, 157–159
Underdevelopment, 66, 131, 194, 240, 246, 256–257, 283
Unemployment, 104, 121, 247, 282
United Nations, 43, 146, 160, 185
Urban, 11, 15–16, 18, 22, 124–125, 150, 157, 211
Urban rowdiness, 22
Urban setting, 22
Urbanization, 15, 17, 164, 220
Urhobo, 186, 187, 242, 245, 249, 255, 273, 275, 285, 286, 300
Urther Rwafa, iv, 319
Uzoechi Nwagbaraiv, 33, 191

V

Vandalism, 119, 296
Vandalized, 113, 119
Vegetation, 35, 79, 86, 125, 167, 182, 196, 270, 290, 333
Vicious circle, 118
Victims, iii, xvi, 36–37, 50, 65, 68, 104, 110, 121, 123, 169, 203, 234, 244, 245, 251, 253, 268, 273, 280, 287, 289, 295, 296
Village, xvii, 11, 16, 20–21, 24–26, 35, 37–38, 43, 51–59, 76–78, 80, 82, 84, 87, 93, 98, 103, 106, 113–116, 119, 127–131, 137, 142, 147, 304–305, 307–312, 314, 316, 325–326
Village square, 82, 314
Vincent Egbuson, 124–125
Vulnerable, 34, 104, 112, 123, 132

W

Waiting for the Rain, xiv, xviii, 2–6, 8, 12–14
Warri, 52, 104, 129, 173, 188, 223, 230, 243, 246–247, 288

Waste management, 20
Watervi, 25, 31, 35–36, 38–40, 54, 56, 60, 85–86, 102, 113–114, 119, 123–129, 131–132, 136, 137, 144, 147, 149–150, 155, 172, 216, 218, 222–225, 230, 240, 249, 250, 252–255, 264, 278–279, 288, 290–291, 295, 298, 299, 312–314, 317, 329
Water Bride, 249
Weather, 7, 77, 81, 86, 87, 89
Wild, v, 23, 26, 35, 37, 43, 76, 91–92, 141–142, 146, 198, 255, 273, 304, 325
Wilderness, 21–26, 163, 198
Wildlife, 1, 31, 86, 89–90, 125, 248–249, 288
Wizard of the Crow, iii, xii, xiv, 15–16, 18–19, 28–29
Wizardry, 21, 28
Wole Soyinka (*See* Soyinka, Wole)
Women, iii, xv, xvi, 11–14, 38–40, 43, 67, 70, 79–80, 84, 95, 98–104, 107, 109–112, 114, 116, 118, 121–125, 129–132, 134–138, 143, 150–155, 165, 168, 174, 183, 226–228, 242, 270, 276, 285, 295, 305–311, 322–335, 338
World Wildlife Fund, 248
Worldview, vi, 32, 75–76, 147–148, 150, 197, 254

Y

Yellow-Yellow, iii, xiv, xv, 95, 97–100, 107, 109, 110–113, 120–122, 130, 138

Z

Zimbabwe, iv, xiv, 1, 2, 5–6, 12, 14, 319, 321–335, 340
Zimunya, 4

www.ingramcontent.com/pod-product-compliance
Lightning Source LLC
Chambersburg PA
CBHW012128010526
44113CB00042B/2657